Multilingual Lexicon for Universiade Sports

Multilingual Lexicon for Universiade Sports

Deutsch
Русский

English
Français
Español

R. L. Busch and Hans J. Bergman
General Editors

Kyril T. Holden and Paul Figueroa
Associate Editors

Edited in cooperation with the Sports Supervisors, Sports Division, Universiade '83

The University of Alberta Press

First published by
The University of Alberta Press
450 Athabasca Hall
Edmonton, Alberta
Canada T6G 2E8

This edition copyright © The University of
Alberta Press 1983

ISBN 0-88864-057-9

Canadian Cataloguing in Publication Data

Main entry under title:
Multilingual lexicon for Universiade sports

Terms in English, French, Spanish, German, and Russian.
Includes index.
ISBN 0-88864-057-9

1. Sports – Dictionaries – Polyglot.
2. Dictionaries, Polyglot.
    I. Busch, Robert L. (Robert Louis), 1939–
    II. Bergman, Hans J., 1948–
    III. Universiade (1983: Edmonton, Alta.)

GV567.M84   796'.03   C83-091155-3

Printed by Printing Services of The University of Alberta

Contents

vii Acknowledgements
ix A message from the President
ix Message du Président
x Mensaje del Presidente de la Universidad
x Eine Mitteilung vom Präsidenten
xi Послание Президента университета
xiii Guide to the use of this Lexicon
xiv Mode d'utilisation du lexique
xv Indicaciones para el uso del Léxico
xvi Anweisungen zum Gebrauch dieses Lexikons
xvii Как пользоваться словарем
xix Transliteration key

2 Athletics
  Athlétisme
  Atletismo
  Leichtathletik
  Лёгкая атлетика

26 Basketball
  Basket-ball
  Baloncesto
  Basketball
  Баскетбол

52 Cycling
  Cyclisme
  Ciclismo
  Radrennen
  Велосипедный спорт

74 Diving
  Plongeon
  Saltos ornamentales
  Kopfsprung
  Прыжки в воду

94 Fencing
  Escrime
  Esgrima
  Fechten
  Фехтование

114 Gymnastics
  Gymnastique
  Gimnasia
  Turnen
  Гимнастика

134 Swimming
  Natation
  Natación
  Schwimmen
  Плавание

148 Tennis
  Tennis
  Tenis
  Tennis
  Теннис

166 Volleyball
  Volley-ball
  Voleibol
  Volleyball
  Волейбол

184 Water-polo
  Water-polo
  Polo acuático
  Water-polo
  Водное поло

200   Appendix of important general phrases
      Annexe des principales expressions d'usage
         courant
      Apéndice de frases de uso corriente
      Anhang wichtiger allgemeiner
         Redewendungen
      Приложение : Важные выражения общего
         значения

243   Index en français
261   Indice en español
279   Deutsches Inhaltsverzeichnis
297   Русский указатель

Acknowledgements

Our warmest thanks go to the various institutions, organizations, and experts for their assistance and advice. Special recognition is extended to the following individuals for making the publication of this lexicon possible: M. Horowitz, President, The University of Alberta; E.D. Zemrau, President, Universiade '83; R. Macnab, Vice-President, University Liaison, Universiade '83; G. Redmond, Chairman, The University of Alberta Press Committee.

We would like to acknowledge the excellent work and cooperation of the following individuals involved in the translation and production of this lexicon: Stephanie Piaumier, A.A.T., Senior-Translator, Linguistic Services, Universiade '83, Edmonton Corporation; and Hans Altman, Jean Brechbühl, Boris Briker, Heliodoro Briongos, Roger Burrows, Earl Culham, Ekkehard Goetting, Norma Gutteridge, Doreen Hawryshko, Andrij Hornjatkeyyč, Anna Kaplansky, Stephane Leroy, Brian Mader, Gamila Morcos, Michelle Mousseau, Dale Olchowy, Marc Piaumier, Joanne Poon, Allan Reid, Debbie Reinhart, Robert Riddell, Jorge Caso-Rohlaud, Alexander Smirnov, Polina Smirnov, Alexander Tumanov, Vladimir Tumanov, and Katherine Wensel.

The contributions of the University of Alberta's Computing Services and Printing Services are also gratefully acknowledged.

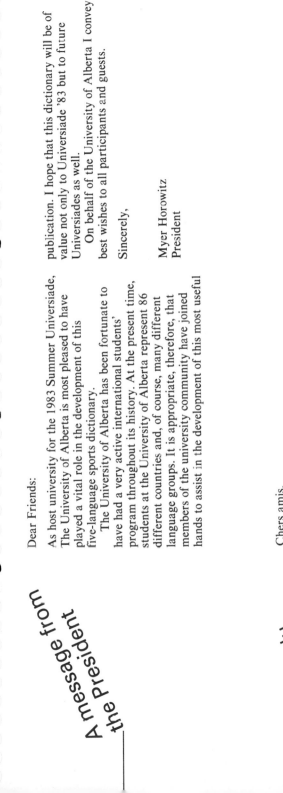

A message from the President

Dear Friends:

As host university for the 1983 Summer Universiade, The University of Alberta is most pleased to have played a vital role in the development of this five-language sports dictionary.

The University of Alberta has been fortunate to have had a very active international students' program throughout its history. At the present time, students at the University of Alberta represent 86 different countries and, of course, many different language groups. It is appropriate, therefore, that members of the university community have joined hands to assist in the development of this most useful publication. I hope that this dictionary will be of value not only to Universiade '83 but to future Universiades as well.

On behalf of the University of Alberta I convey best wishes to all participants and guests.

Sincerely,

Myer Horowitz
President

Message du Président

Chers amis,

L'Université de l'Alberta, en sa qualité d'université hôte des Jeux mondiaux universitaires, est heureuse d'avoir pu apporter une contribution essentielle à l'élaboration de ce dictionnaire des sports en cinq langues.

Depuis sa création, l'Université de l'Alberta offre un programme intensif pour les étudiants de pays étrangers. Actuellement, les étudiants inscrits à l'Université de l'Alberta représentent 86 pays différents et, par conséquent, divers groupes de langues. Il était donc naturel que les membres de la communauté universitaire s'unissent pour collaborer à la réalisation de cet important ouvrage. J'espère que ce dictionnaire sera d'une grande utilité aussi bien pour l'Universiade de 1983 que pour les universiades suivantes.

Au nom de l'Université de l'Alberta, je transmets mes meilleurs souhaits à tous les participants et invités.

Myer Horowitz
Président

Mensaje del Presidente de la Universidad

Estimados amigos:

La Universidad de Alberta, como organizadora de la Universiada de Verano de 1983, siente sumo placer en haber tenido un papel primordial en la compilación en cinco idiomas de este diccionario.

La Universidad de Alberta ha disfrutado a lo largo de su historia de una laboriosa actividad para estudiantes internacionales. En la actualidad, hay en la Universidad estudiantes de 86 países del mundo representando varios grupos lingüísticos. Es justo pues, que miembros de la comunidad universitaria hayan colaborado en la compilación de esta utilísima obra. Abarco la esperanza de que este diccionario sea de valor, no solamente durante la Universiada de 1983, pero también durante las Universiadas venideras.

En nombre de la Universidad de Alberta les transmito mis mejores deseos a todos los participantes y asistentes.

Sinceramente,

Myer Horowitz
Presidente

Eine Mitteilung vom Präsidenten

Liebe Freunde,

Als Gastgeber der Weltuniversitätsspiele 1983 ist die Universität Alberta besonders stolz darauf, bei der Veröffentlichung des vorliegenden fünfsprachigen Wörterbuches eine massgebliche Rolle gespielt zu haben.

Die Universität von Alberta ist in der glücklichen Lage, seit ihrer Gründung traditionell in besonderem Masse internationale Studien- und Studentenprogramme aktiv gefördert zu haben. Zum gegenwärtigen Zeitpunkt repräsentieren die Studenten der Universität von Alberta nicht weniger als 86 Nationalitäten und dementsprechend zahlreiche Sprachgruppen.

Von daher ist es nur angemessen, dass sich Mitglieder der Universitätsgemeinde zu dem gemeinsamen Vorhaben zusammengeschlossen haben, die Veröffentlichung des vorliegenden äusserst hilfreichen Wörterbuches tatkräftig zu unterstützen. Ich bin der festen Überzeugung, dass dieses Wörterbuch nicht nur für die Teilnehmer der Weltuniversitätsspiele '83, sondern darüberhinaus für Veranstalter, Teilnehmer und Besucher künftiger Weltuniversitätsspiele von grossem Nutzen sein wird.

Im Namen der Universität von Alberta wünsche ich allen Teilnehmern und Besuchern guten Erfolg.

Mit besten Grüssen

Myer Horowitz
Präsident

Послание Президента Университета

Дорогие друзья!

Университет Альберты, принимающий в Эдмонтоне летнюю Универсиаду 83, был рад активно участвовать в создании этого пятиязычного спортивного словаря.

Вся история Университета Альберты отмечена существованием важной и благоприятной для Университета активной интернациональной студенческой программы. В настоящее время студенты Университета Альберты представляют 86 разных стран и, конечно, множество разнообразных языковых групп. Поэтому естественно, что представители университета объединили свои усилия, чтобы помочь выпуску этого полезного издания. Я надеюсь, что этот словарь окажется ценным не только для Универсиады 83, но и для будущих всемирных студенческих игр.

От имени Университета Альберты я хочу передать наилучшие пожелания всем участникам Универсиады 83 и ее гостям.

Искренне,

Майер Хоровиц
Президент

Guide to the use of this Lexicon

This lexicon is primarily intended to assist athletes, coaches, and translators in communicating about the ten sports of the World University Games. Both the individual sports and their terminology are ordered alphabetically in English. Consequently, no English index is required, but comprehensive indexes for the remaining languages are included. A user looking for specific terms in a given language should be able to locate them together with their numbers and then turn to the numbers within the lexicon where the corresponding terms in the four other languages will be cross-listed.

The compilers have sought to be reasonably comprehensive in the inclusion of important terms for a given sport and have benefited from the valuable advice of experts from the International University Sports Federation and elsewhere. Nevertheless, no claims to exhaustiveness are being made for any given sport. For reasons of clarity, directness, and economy, the compilers have sought basic adequacy both in the number of terms covered and in the expression of equivalence across the languages. This means that multiple terms for a given English expression have, as a rule, not been included. Some exceptions to this rule for the

exclusion of synonymy have been made, especially for Old World and New World usage in the appendix of general phrases, which is subdivided by categories, e.g. numerals, weather, shopping, meals, etc. Further considerations of homogeneity, directness, and economy have compelled the compilers reluctantly to list only masculine terminological forms, it being hoped that most of the lexicon's principal users will be able to generate changes in gender as required.

The choice of English, French, Spanish, German, and Russian has been motivated by the prominent role of these languages in sports throughout the world, a fact reflected in their official designation as working languages at the CESU/HISPA Conference and Congress held in conjunction with Universiade '83. The addition of Cyrillic orthography for Russian has necessitated a Latin transliteration to approximate pronunciation. The system used is basically a modified version of that approved by the U.S. Board on Geographic Names and frequently employed in popular publications. For the user's convenience, details of this system are provided in the following transliteration key.

Mode d'utilisation du lexique

Ce lexique est destiné avant tout à aider les athlètes, les entraîneurs, et les traducteurs à communiquer entre eux à propos des dix sports des Jeux mondiaux universitaires. Les dix sports aussi bien que la terminologie correspondante sont classés par ordre alphabétique en anglais. Pour chacune des quatre autres langues, un index alphabétique permettra de retrouver aisément les termes et leur traduction. L'utilisateur cherchant des termes spécifiques dans une langue donnée trouvera ceux-ci dans l'index avec leur numéro d'ordre qui renvoie aux termes correspondants dans les autres langues.

Les auteurs ont voulu inclure les termes importants dans chacun des sports de façon à former un ensemble relativement complet. En cela, l'aide qu'ils ont reçue d'experts de la Fédération Internationale du Sport Universitaire a été précieuse. Néanmoins, cet ouvrage ne prétend pas être exhaustif. Dans un but de clarté, d'efficacité, et d'économie, on a cherché à accorder l'étendue du vocabulaire repris et les équivalents donnés. En conséquence, pour chaque expression anglaise, une seule possibilité de traduction a été retenue. Quelques exceptions existent cependant, particulièrement dans l'appendice consacré au

vocabulaire d'usage courant (divisé en catégories: nombres, le temps qu'il fait, repas, dans le magasin, etc.) où on a dû tenir compte des différences entre les habitudes linguistiques de l'Ancien et du Nouveau Monde. Pour les mêmes raisons d'homogénéité, d'efficacité, et d'économie, les auteurs ont été contraints de ne considérer que la forme masculine des mots, en espérant que les principaux utilisateurs de ce lexique seront capables d'effectuer par eux-mêmes le changement de genre approprié.

Le choix de l'anglais, du français, de l'espagnol, de l'allemand, et du russe est motivé par le rôle essentiel que jouent ces langues dans le domaine du sport au niveau international. Leur utilisation comme langues de travail officielles de la conférence de la CESU et du congrès de l'HISPA, qui se tiendront à la même époque que les Jeux, en est une preuve. Pour raisons évidentes, le russe a été l'objet d'une translitération en caractères latins. Le système utilisé est une version modifiée de celui utilisé par le U.S. Board on Geographic Names qui est fréquemment employé dans des ouvrages destinés au grand public. Afin d'aider l'utilisateur, un tableau qui suit donnera le détail des conventions d'écriture.

Indicaciones para el uso del Léxico

Se dedica este léxico multilingüe a todos los atletas, entrenadores y traductores que tendrán que comunicarse con sus colegas sobre las diez disciplinas de los Juegos Universitarios Mundiales. Las mismas han sido clasificadas en orden alfabético en inglés de acuerdo con sus terminologías. Por esa razón, no se ha confeccionado un índice en inglés, pero índices completos para los otros cuatro idiomas están incluídos. El usuario que busca un término específico en uno de estos idiomas encontrará éste al lado de su número de asiento. Para encontrar el término correspondiente en los otros idiomas, se tendrá que buscar ese número de asiento en el texto.

La intención editorial ha sido la de incluir los términos básicos de cada disciplina. Los editores se han beneficiado de la asesoría de peritos de la Federación de los Juegos Universitarios y de otras entidades. Sin embargo, no se pretende haber reunido todos los términos técnicos. Para compilar una obra de uso fácil, se han incluído los términos

técnicos más importantes sin dar, por lo general, sinónimos. Se han hecho excepciones, a veces, en el caso de una diferencia entre el uso europeo y americano, sobre todo en el apéndice de términos generales (que incluye los temas: números, el tiempo, compras, comidas, etc.). Por razones de sencillez y economía, se ha dado la forma masculina, dejando al usuario el trabajo de hacer las transformaciones del género cada vez que lo encuentre necesario.

Han sido incluídos, por su importancia en el mundo deportivo, los idiomas: inglés, francé, español, alemán, y ruso. Los mismos son oficialmente designados como las lenguas de trabajo de la conferencia y congreso de la CESU/HISPA, actos que se celebrarán junto con la Universiada del 83. El idioma ruso está escrito en la ortografía cirílica junto a la transliteración latina en la versión popular aprobada por la U.S. Board on Geographic Names. Se adjunta detalles de este sistema más adelante.

Anweisungen zum Gebrauch dieses Lexikons

Dieses Lexikon ist primär für Sportler, Betreuer, und Übersetzer gedacht, die sich untereinander über die zehn bei den Weltuniversitätsspielen vertretenen Sportarten verständigen wollen. Weil sowohl die einzelnen Sportbereiche wie auch die damit verbundene Terminologie alphabetisch geordnet sind, ist kein englischer Index erforderlich; für die anderen Sprachen stehen jedoch vollständige Verzeichnisse der verwendeten Wörter zur Verfügung. Wer bestimmte Ausdrücke in einer gewissen Sprache sucht, wird sie mit ihren Kodenummern auffinden, und sollte dann in diesem Lexikon zu jenen Kategorien gehen, wo ihre Entsprechungen in den vier anderen Sprachen aufgelistet sind.

Die Herausgeber haben sich bemüht, die wichtigsten Wörter in diesem Verzeichnis anführen zu können, die für eine gewisse Sportart in Frage kommen, und sind zu ihrer Erfassung den Experten der International University Sports Federation und anderen für ihre wertvolle Hilfe sehr dankbar; dennoch kann für keine Sportart Anspruch auf tatsächliche Vollständigkeit erhoben werden. Aus Gründen der Klarheit der Präsentation, der Händlichkeit und Effizienz haben sich die Herausgeber mit einem Grundstock in der Zahl der angeführten Ausdrücke und der Entsprechungen in den anderen Sprachen begnügen müssen. In der Praxis bedeutet dies, dass in der Regel verschiedene Ausdrücke für dieselben englischen Sinninhalte nicht

gegeben werden; Ausnahmen wurden nur im Appendix und in Kategorien wie Zahlwörter, Wetter, Einkauf und Mahlzeiten geordneten allgemeinen Wörter und Wendungen gemacht wo Unterschiede in ihrem Gebrauch zwischen Alter und Neuer Welt bestehen. Aus Platzgründen mussten sich die Zusammensteller dieses Handbuches auch damit zufriedengeben, nur die männlichen Formen der Terminologie anzugeben; dies geschah in der Zuversicht, dass die meisten Benützer in der Lage sein wurden, die notwendigen grammatikalischen Veränderungen zum Ausdruck der Feminina selbst vornehmen zu können.

Die Wahl des Englischen, Französischen, Spanischen, Deutschen, und Russischen für dieses Handbuch erklärt sich daraus, dass diese Sprachen in der Welt des Sportes an vorrangiger Stelle stehen; dies zeigt sich auch in ihrer Verwendung als Konferenzsprachen der CESU/HISPA Konferenz und des Kongresses, die im Zusammenhang mit der Universiade '83 abgehalten werden. Die Verwendung des Kyrillischen für Russisch verlangte eine lateinische Umschrift, welche der tatsächlichen Aussprache nahekommt. Das dafür verwendete System ist im Prinzip eine etwas abgeänderte Version der von der U.S. Board on Geographic Names approbierten, die in gängigen Publikationen häufig anzutreffen ist. Details dieses Systems sind dem beigefügten Aussprachenschlüssel zu entnehmen.

Как пользоваться словарем

Словарь предназначен для помощи в общении спортсменов, тренеров и переводчиков на Всемирных университетских играх и включает десять видов спорта. Отдельные виды спорта и их терминология расположены в алфавитном порядке на английском языке. Поэтому нет указателя для английского языка, но включены указатели для других языков. Чтобы найти нужный термин в каждом данном языке, необходимо определить номер слова и затем по этому номеру установить эквиваленты на остальных четырех языках.

При включении терминов, важных для каждого вида спорта, составители стремились к достаточно широкому охвату терминологии и пользовались ценными советами специалистов из Международной федерации университетского спорта и других организаций. Тем не менее, нельзя говорить об абсолютной полноте словаря по каждому виду спорта. Исходя из соображений ясности, стройности и экономии, составители стремились дать достаточное количество основных терминов и их эквиваленты в разных языках. Этим объясняется то, что, как правило, многочисленные выражения для одного и того же английского термина не включаются в словарь. Некоторые нарушения этого правила, исключающего синонимику, были допущены, в

частности, в случаях разного употребления лексики в Старом и Новом Свете в приложении "Важные выражения общего значения", которое подразделено на отдельные категории (Цифры, Погода, Покупки, Еда и т.п.). Другие соображения, связанные с однородностью, простотой и экономией, заставили составителей включить терминологию только в мужском роде в надежде, что большинство пользующихся словарем может, если нужно, изменить род.

Выбор английского, французского, испанского, немецкого и русского языков объясняется важной ролью, которую эти языки играют в мировом спорте, что нашло отражение в признании их в качестве рабочих языков на конференции и конгрессе КЕСУ/ХИСПА, которые состоятся в связи с Универсиадой 83. Введение кириллицы для русской орфографии привело к необходимости латинской транслитерации для относительно правильного произношения. Принятая система транслитерации это, в основном, модифицированная версия системы, одобренной Советом географических названий Соединенных Штатов, часто используемой в популярных изданиях. Для удобства пользующихся словарем детали этой системы помещены в нижеприведенном ключе.

Transliteration key

Cyrillic	Latin		Cyrillic	Latin
Аа	a		Пп	p
Бб	b		Рр	r
Вв	v		Сс	s
Гг¹	g¹		Тт	t
Дд	d		Уу	u
Ее	ye, e		Фф	f
Ёё	yo		Хх	h
Жж	zh		Цц	ts
Зз	z		Чч	ch
Ии	i		Шш	sh
Йй	y		Щщ	shch
Кк	k		Ъъ	"
Лл	l		Ыы²	i
Мм	m		Ьь²	'
Нн	n		Ээ	e
Оо	o		Юю	yu²
			Яя²	ya²

1. -ого > -ово; -его > -(у)ево
2. -т(ь)ся > -tsa

Athletics

Athlétisme

Atletismo

Leichtathletik

Легкая атлетика

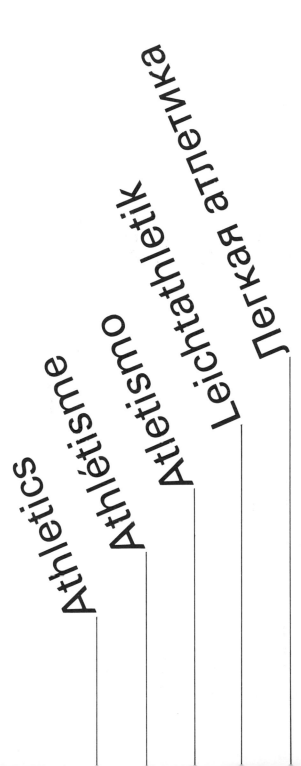

Athletics	Athlétisme	Atletismo	Leichtathletik	Легкая атлетика
1 acceleration zone	zone d'élan	zona de impulso	Anlauffläche	длина разбега (dlina razbega)
2 action in the air	phase aérienne	fase aérea	Flugphase	действие в воздухе (deystviye v vozduhe)
3 additional trial	essai supplémentaire	intento de mejora	wiederholter Versuch	добавочная попытка (dobavochnaya popitka)
4 adjustment of starting blocks	réglage des blocs de départ	regulación de los bloques de salida	Einstellung der Startblöcke	установка стартовых колодок (ustanovka startovih kolodok)
5 angle of approach	angle d'approche	ángulo de acercamiento	Anlaufwinkel	угол приближения (ugol priblizheniya)
6 angle of the takeoff	angle d'appel	ángulo del bote	Absprungwinkel	угол отскока (ugol otskoka)
7 antidoping control	contrôle de dopage	medidas contra el uso de las drogas	Dopingkontrolle	антидопинговый контроль (antidopingoviy kontrol')
8 apparatus	engin	aparato	Gerät	снаряд (snaryad)
9 area	aire	área	Raum	площадь (ploshchad')
10 arena	arène	campo	Arena	арена (arena)
11 armband	brassard	brazalete	Armbinde	нарукавная нашивка (narukavnaya nashivka)
12 assembly line	ligne de rassemblement	línea de agrupamiento	Sammellinie	линия сбора бегунов перед стартовой линией (liniya sbora begunov pered startovoy liniyey)
13 athletes' control center	chambre d'appel	centro de control de atletas	Kontrollzentrum für Athleten	место сбора спортсменов (mesto sbora sportsmenov)
14 attempt	tentative	prueba	Versuch	попытка (popitka)
15 axis	axe	eje	Achse	ось (os')
16 axis of rotation	axe de rotation	eje de rotación	Drehachse	ось вращения (os' vrashcheniya)
17 back straight	ligne droite opposée	recta contraria	Gegengerade	противоположная прямая (protivopolozhnaya pryamaya)
18 bar	latte de saut	listón	Sprunglatte	планка (planka)
19 baton	témoin	testigo	Stab	эстафетная палочка (estafetnaya palochka)

	English	Français	Español	Deutsch	Русский
20	baton passing	transmission du témoin	pase del testigo	Staffelübergabe	передача палочки (peredacha palochki)
21	bend runner	coureur de virage	corredor especialista en curva	Kurvenläufer	виражист (virazhist)
22	bend running	course en virage	carrera en curva	Kurvenlauf	виражный бег (virazhniy beg)
23	box in runner	enfermer un coureur	cerrar a un corredor	einen Läufer einschliessen	втискивать бегуна (vtiskivat' beguna)
24	break away	action de s'échapper	escapada	Ausreissversuch	вырваться вперед (virvatsa vperyod)
25	bunch	peloton	pelotón	Feld	группа (gruppa)
26	cadence	cadence	cadencia	Kadenz	ритм (ritm)
27	calls; call of the competitors	appel des concurrents	llamada a los participantes	Aufruf der Wettkämpfer	вызов участников (vizov uchastnikov)
28	change of leg	changement de pied	cambio de pie	Fusswechsel	перемена ноги (peremena nogi)
29	change of pace	changement de rythme	cambio de ritmo	Wechsel im Schrittrhythmus	перемена ритма (peremena ritma)
30	check marks	marques	marcas	Markierungen	отметки (otmetki)
31	chief timekeeper	chef-chronométreur	cronometrador-jefe	Zeitnehmerobmann	главный судья-секундометрист (glavniy sud'ya-sekundometrist)
32	clear	franchir	franquear	überqueren	преодолеть (preodolet')
33	clear a height of ...	franchir une hauteur de ...	saltar una altura de ...	eine Höhe von ...überspringen	преодолеть высоту.... (preodolet' visotu....)
34	clear the bar	franchir la barre	franquear el listón	die Latte überspringen	преодолеть высоту планки (preodolet' visotu planki)
35	clearance	passage	franqueamiento	Beseitigung	преодоление (preodoleniye)
36	close finish	arrivée serrée	llegada reñida	knapper Einlauf	близкий финиш (blizkiy finish)
37	coach	entraîneur	entrenador	Trainer	тренер (trener)
38	combined event	épreuve combinée	prueba combinada	Mehrkampf	многоборье (mnogobor'ye)
39	commencement of flight	envol	vuelo	Abflug	начало полета (nachalo polyota)
40	competition	compétition	competición	Wettkampf	соревнование (sorevnovaniye)
	English	**Français**	**Español**	**Deutsch**	**Русский**

	Athletics	Athlétisme	Atletismo	Leichtathletik	Лёгкая атлетика
41	competition director	directeur de la compétition	encargado de la competición	Wettkampfleiter	заведующий соревнованием (zaveduyushchiy sorevnovaniyem)
42	competition officials	officiels de la compétition	jurado de la competición	Offizielle	судьи соревнования (sud'yi sorevnovaniya)
43	cord grip of the javelin	corde de prise du javelot	encordadura de la jabalina	Kordelgriff (am Speer)	верёвочная ручка копья (veryovochnaya ruchka kop'ya)
44	corner flag	fanion de virage	banderín de viraje	Kurvenflagge	угловой флажок (uglovoy flazhok)
45	cross step	pas croisé	paso cruzado; tijera	Kreuzschritt	скрестный шаг (skryostniy shag)
46	crouch start	départ accroupi	salida agachada	Tiefstart	низкий старт (nizkiy start)
47	curb	corde	bordillo	innere Bahneinfassung	бровка (brovka)
48	curved starting line	ligne incurvée de départ	línea curva de partida	gekrümmte Startlinie	кривая стартовая линия (krivaya startovaya liniya)
49	cut in	faire entrer	cerrar el paso	sich eindrängen	переменить дорожки (peremenit' dorozhki)
50	decathlete	décathlonien	decatloniano	Zehnkämpfer	десятиборец (desyatiborets)
51	decathlon	décathlon	decatlón	Zehnkampf	десятиборье (desyatibor'ye)
52	delivery of throwing implement	lâcher de l'engin	disparo del instrumento de lanzar	Abwurf; Abstoss	выталкивание снаряда (vitalkivaniye snaryada)
53	direction	direction	sentido	Richtung	направление (napravleniye)
54	discus	disque	disco	Diskus	диск (disk)
55	discus throw	lancer de disque	lanzamiento del disco	Diskuswurf	метание диска (metaniye diska)
56	discus thrower	lanceur de disque	lanzador de disco	Diskuswerfer	дискобол (diskobol)
57	discus throwing	lancement du disque	lanzamiento de disco	Diskuswerfen	метание диска (metaniye diska)
58	discus throwing facility	lançoir	instalación de lanzamientos de disco	Diskuswurfanlage	сектор метания диска (sektor metaniya diska)
59	dislodge the bar	renverser la barre	desalojar el listón	die Latte berühren	сбить планку (sbit' planku)
60	distance	distance	distancia	Entfernung	дистанция (distantsiya)

	English	Français	Español	Deutsch	Русский
61	distance between the hurdles	distance entre les haies	distancia entre las vallas	Abstand zwischen Hürden	дистанция между барьерами (distantsiya mezhdu bar'yerami)
62	distance between the runners	distance entre les coureurs	distancia entre los corredores	Abstand zwischen Läufern	расстояние между бегунами (rasstoyaniye mezhdu begunami)
63	distance indicator board	rampe de signalisation des distances	indicador de distancia	Messlatte bei Weit und Dreisprung	табло с указателем дистанции (tablo s ukazatelem distantsii)
64	distance marker	pyramide de marquage des distances	pirámide de marcaje de las distancias	Pyramide zum Anzeigen der Weiten	указатель дистанции (ukazatel' distantsii)
65	draw back of the arm	armé du bras	acción del brazo para el lanzamiento	Bewegung des Armes beim Abwurf bzw. Abstoss	отвод руки (otvod ruki)
66	drawing for the lanes	tirage au sort des couloirs	sorteo de calles	Bahnverteilung auslosen	жеребьёвка на дорожки (zhereb'yovka na dorozhki)
67	early part of the flight path	attaque	primera fase de la trayectoria	Absprungphase	начало полета (nachalo polyota)
68	end of the curve	sortie de virage	salida de la curva	Ausgang der Kurve	конец виража (konets virazha)
69	end of the takeover zone	limite de la zone de relais	límite de la zona de relevo	Begrenzung des Wechselraums	конец зоны передачи эстафеты (konets zoni peredachi estafeti)
70	end of the turn	sortie de virage	salida de la curva	Ausgang der Kurve	конец поворота (konets povorota)
71	event	épreuve	prueba	Wettkampf	вид соревнования (vid sorevnovaniya)
72	explosiveness	manière explosive	arranque	Sprungkraft	способность отталкиваться (sposobnost' ottalkivatsa)
73	failure	défaut	fallo	Fehlversuch	неудача (neudacha)
74	fall	chute	caída	Landung	падение (padeniye)
75	false start	faux départ	salida falsa	Fehlstart	фальстарт (fal'start)
76	feeding stations	postes de ravitaillement	puestos de alimentos	Verpflegungsstationen	пункты питания (punkti pitaniya)

	Athletics	Athlétisme	Atletismo	Leichtathletik	Легкая атлетика
77	field events	concours	pruebas de pista	Wettbewerbe	соревнования по прыжкам и метанию (sorevnovaniya po prizhkam i metaniyu)
78	field events judge	juge de concours	juez de pista	Kampfrichter für Sprung-, Wurf-und Stosswettbewerbe	судья по видам прыжков и метаний (sud'ya po vidam prizhkov i metaniy)
79	final bend	dernier virage	última vuelta	Zielkurve	последний вираж (posledniy virazh)
80	final sprint	sprint final	sprint final	Endspurt	последний спринт (posledniy sprint)
81	finals	finales	finales	Endspiele	финалы (finali)
82	finish	arrivée	llegada	Einlauf	финиш (finish)
83	finish judge	juge à l'arrivée	juez de llegada	Zielrichter	судья на финише (sud'ya na finishe)
84	finishing line	ligne d'arrivée	línea de llegada	Ziellinie	линия финиша (liniya finisha)
85	finishing posts	poteaux d'arrivée	postes de llegada	Zielpfosten	столбики финиша (stolbiki finisha)
86	finishing straight	ligne droite d'arrivée	recta de llegada	Zielgerade	финишная прямая (finishnaya pryamaya)
87	finishing tape	fil d'arrivée	cinta de llegada	Zielband	финишная ленточка (finishnaya lentochka)
88	first trial	premier essai	primer intento	erster Versuch	первая попытка (pervaya popitka)
89	flag	drapeau; fanion	bandera; banderín	Fahne	флажок (flazhok)
90	foot plant	blocage	taco de salida	Übersetzen	положение ноги перед отталкиванием (polozheniye nogi pered ottalkivaniyem)
91	foot plates (on starting blocks)	plaques pour les pieds (sur les blocs de départ)	zócalos del taco de salida	Fussplatten (an den Startblöcken)	плитки для ног/на стартовых колодках/ (plitki dlya nog/na startovih kolodkah/)
92	form in the air	phase aérienne	fase aérea	Flugphase	стиль в воздухе (stil' v vozduhe)

6

	English	Français	Español	Deutsch	Русский
93	Fosbury flop	saut "Fosbury"	salto "Fosbury"	"Fosbury Flop"	прыжок фосбюри-флоп (prizhok fosbyuri-flop)
94	Fosbury style	style "Fosbury"	estilo "Fosbury"	"Fosbury-Technik"	стиль фосбюри (stil' fosbyuri)
95	foul	faute	falta	Foul	ошибка (oshibka)
96	free leg	jambe libre	pierna de ataque	Schwingbein	свободная нога (svobodnaya noga)
97	go outside	dépasser	pasar por fuera	übertreten	выйти за... (viyti za...)
98	grip	prise	toma	Griff	хват (hvat)
99	group	peloton	pelotón	Feld	группа (gruppa)
100	hammer	marteau	martillo	Hammer	молот (molot)
101	hammer glove	gant du lanceur de marteau	guante del lanzador de martillo	Hammerwurfhandschuh	перчатка для метания молота (perchatka dlya metaniya molota)
102	hammer throw	lancer de marteau	lanzamiento del martillo	Hammerwurf	метание молота (metaniye molota)
103	hammer thrower	lanceur de marteau	lanzador de martillo	Hammerwerfer	метатель молота (metatel' molota)
104	hammer throwing	lancement du marteau	lanzamiento de martillo	Hammerwerfen	метание молота (metaniye molota)
105	hammer-throwing facility	lançoir de marteau	instalación de lanzamientos de martillo	Hammerwurfanlage	сектор для метания молота (sektor dlya metaniye molota)
106	hammer wire	filin du marteau	cable del martillo	Hammerverbindungs-draht	проволока молота (provoloka molota)
107	heats	séries	eliminatorias	Läufe	забеги (zabegi)
108	height of the bar	hauteur de la barre	altura del listón	Lattenhöhe	высота планки (visota planki)
109	heptathlete	heptathlonien	heptatloniano	Heptathlet	семиборец (semiborets)
110	heptathlon	heptathlon	heptatlón	Siebenkampf	семиборье (semibor'ye)
111	high jump	saut en hauteur	salto de altura	Hochsprung	прыжок в высоту (prizhok v visotu)

	Athletics	Athlétisme	Atletismo	Leichtathletik	Легкая атлетика
112	high jumper	sauteur en hauteur	saltador de altura	Hochspringer	прыгун в высоту (prigun v visotu)
113	high point	flèche	vértice	Kulminationspunkt	максимальная высота (maksimal'naya visota)
114	high point of the flight path	flèche de la trajectoire d'un sauteur	vértice de la trayectoria de la tirada	Kulminationspunkt der Flugkurve eines Springers	максимальная высота полета (maksimal'naya visota polyota)
115	high-jump crossbar	barre transversale du saut en hauteur	listón	Hochsprunglatte	планка для прыжков в высоту (planka dlya prizhkov v visotu)
116	high-jump facility	sautoir en hauteur	instalación de salto de altura	Hochsprunganlage	сектор для прыжков в высоту (sektor dlya prizhkov v visotu)
117	high-jump standards	normes du saut en hauteur	normas del salto de altura	Hochsprungsnormen	стандарты прыжков в высоту (standarti prizhkov v visotu)
118	hit the check marks	respecter ses marques	acertar en las marcas	vorschriftsmässig wechseln	попасть в контрольные отметки (popast' v kontrol'niye otmetki)
119	hold of the implement	tenue de l'engin	sujetar el instrumento	Halten des Geräts	способ держания метательного снаряда (sposob derzhaniya metatel'novo snaryada)
120	home bend	dernier virage	último viraje	Zielkurve	последний вираж (posledniy virazh)
121	hop	cloche-pied	brinco	Hop	скачок/в тройном прыжке/ (skachok/v troynom prizhke/)
122	hug the curb	tenir la corde	correr pegado al bordillo	auf der Innenbahn laufen	держаться бровки (derzhatsa brovki)
123	hug the curb in the turn	prendre un virage à la corde	tomar la curva muy cerrada	in der Innenkurve laufen	держаться бровки при повороте (derzhatsa brovki pri povorote)
124	hurdle	haie	valla	Hürde	барьер (bar'yer)
125	hurdle race	course de haies	carrera de vallas	Hürdenlauf	барьерный бег (bar'yerniy beg)
126	hurdler	coureur de haies	corredor de vallas	Hürdenläufer	барьерист (bar'yerist)

	English	Français	Español	Deutsch	Русский
127	impede a runner	gêner un coureur	obstaculizar a un corredor	einen Läufer behindern	препятствовать бегуну (prepyatstvovat' begunu)
128	impression	empreinte	huella	Eindruck; Abdruck	оттиск (ottisk)
129	impulse	impulsion	impulso	Impuls	сила движения (sila dvizheniya)
130	inclination	déclivité	inclinación	Neigung	наклон (naklon)
131	incoming runner	relayé	portador	stababgebender Läufer	бегун, передающий эстафету (begun, peredayushchiy estafetu)
132	increase the lead	augmenter son avance	aumentar la ventaja	den Vorsprung ausbauen	увеличить опережение (uvelichit' operezheniye)
133	increase the stride rate	accélérer la cadence	accelerar el ritmo	die Schrittfolge erhöhen	увеличить ход (uvelichit' hod)
134	initial height	hauteur initiale	altura inicial	Ausgangshöhe	начальная высота (nachal'naya visota)
135	inner border of the track	corde de la piste	bordillo de la pista	Bahneinfassung	внутренняя бровка дорожки (vnutrennyaya brovka dorozhki)
136	inner lane	couloir intérieur	pasillo interior	innere Bahneinfassung	внутренняя дорожка (vnutrennyaya dorozhka)
137	intermediate time	temps intermédiaire	tiempo intermedio	Zwischenzeit	промежуточное время (promezhutochnoye vremya)
138	International Amateur Athletic Federation (I.A.A.F.)	Fédération Internationale d'Athlétisme Amateur (F.I.A.A.)	Federación Internacional de Atletismo Aficionado (F.I.A.A.)	Internationaler Leichtathletikverband (I.A.A.F.)	Международная любительская федерация легкой атлетики ИААФ/ (mezhdunarodnaya lyubitel'skaya federatsiya lyohkoy atletiki/IAAF/)
139	javelin	javelot	jabalina	Speer	копье (kop'yo)
140	javelin throw	lancer de javelot	lanzamiento de la jabalina	Speerwurf	метание копья (metaniye kop'ya)
141	javelin thrower	lanceur de javelot	lanzador de jabalina	Speerwerfer	метатель копья (metatel' kop'ya)
142	javelin throwing	lancement du javelot	lanzamiento de jabalina	Speerwerfen	метание копья (metaniye kop'ya)
	English	**Français**	**Español**	**Deutsch**	**Русский**

	Athletics	Athlétisme	Atletismo	Leichtathletik	Лёгкая атлетика
143	javelin-throwing facility	lançoir de javelot	instalación de lanzamientos de jabalina	Speerwurfanlage	сектор метания копья (sektor metaniya kop'ya)
144	judges	juges	jueces	Kampfrichter	судьи (sud'yi)
145	jump	saut	salto	Sprung	прыжок (prizhok)
146	jump off	barrage	desempate (en saltos)	Stichkampf	перепрыжка (pereprizhka)
147	jumper	sauteur	saltador	Springer	прыгун (prigun)
148	jumping events	épreuves de sauts	pruebas de saltos	Sprungwettbewerbe	виды прыжков (vidi prizhkov)
149	jumping facility	sautoir	saltadero	Sprunganlage	сектор прыжков (sektor prizhkov)
150	jury of appeal	jury d'appel	jurado de apelación	Schiedsgericht	апелляционное жюри (apellyatsionnoye zhyuri)
151	landing	réception au sol	caída al suelo	Landung	приземление (prizemleniye)
152	landing area	aire de chute	área de caída	Wurfsektor; Stosssektor; Sprunggrube	зона приземления (zona prizemleniya)
153	landing cushion	coussin de réception	colchoneta	Sprungmatten	подушка для приземления (podushka dlya prizemleniya)
154	landing mattress	matelas de réception	colchoneta	Sprungmatten	мат для приземления (mat dlya prizemleniya)
155	lane	couloir	calle	Bahn	дорожка (dorozhka)
156	lane marker	pyramide de marquage des couloirs	marcador de calle	Pyramide zur Bahnbezeichnung	колышек для разметки дорожки (kolishek dlya razmetki dorozhki)
157	lane race	course en couloir	carrera por pasillo	Lauf in Bahnen	бег по дорожке (beg po dorozhke)
158	lap scorer	compteur de tours	contador de vueltas	Rundenzähler	судья-счётчик кругов (sud'ya-schyotchik krugov)
159	last lap	dernier tour	última vuelta	letzte Runde	последний круг (posledniy krug)
160	last trial	dernier essai	último intento	letzter Versuch	последняя попытка (poslednyaya popitka)
161	lead	avance	ventaja	Vorsprung	лидирование (lidirovaniye)

	English	Français	Español	Deutsch	Русский
162	lead (to)	mener	ir adelante	führen	лидировать (lidirovat')
163	lead by one lap	avoir un tour d'avance	llevar una vuelta de ventaja	eine Runde Vorsprung haben	лидировать на один круг (lidirovat' na odin krug)
164	lead by x points	avoir x points d'avance	llevar x puntos de ventaja	x Punkte Vorsprung haben	лидировать на...очков (lidirovat' na...ochkov)
165	lead by x seconds	avoir x secondes d'avance	llevar x segundos de ventaja	x Sekunden Vorsprung haben	лидировать на...секунд (lidirovat' na...sekund)
166	lead in points	mener à la marque	puntear	nach Punkten führen	вести в очках (vesti v ochkah)
167	leader	coureur de tête	puntero	führender Läufer	лидер (lider)
168	leading group	groupe de tête	grupo delantero	Führungsgruppe	лидирующая группа (lidiruyushchaya gruppa)
169	leading leg	jambe d'attaque	pierna de ataque de fondo	Schwungbein	маховая нога (mahovaya noga)
170	long distance	fond	fondo	Langstrecken	дальняя дистанция (dal'nyaya distantsiya)
171	long-distance race	course de fond	carrera de fondo	Langstreckenlauf	бег на дальнюю дистанцию (beg na dal'nyuyu distantsiyu)
172	long-distance runner	coureur de fond	corredor de fondo	Langstreckenläufer	бегун на дальней дистанции (begun na dal'niye distantsii)
173	long jump	saut en longueur	salto de longitud	Weitsprung	прыжок в длину (prizhok v dlinu)
174	long-jump facility	sautoir en longueur	saltadero para el salto de longitud	Weitsprunganlage	сектор прыжков в длину (sektor prizhkov v dlinu)
175	long jumper	sauteur en longueur	saltador de longitud	Weitspringer	прыгун в длину (prigun v dlinu)
176	lose contact	détacher, se	despegarse	sich lösen	отделиться от... (otdelitsa ot...)
177	main group	gros du peloton	grueso del pelotón	Hauptfeld	основная группа (osnovnaya gruppa)
178	maintain the lead	conserver son avance	mantener la ventaja	den Vorsprung halten	поддерживать лидирование (podderzhivat' lidirovaniye)
179	maintain the stride rate	maintenir la cadence	mantener la cadencia	die Schrittfolge beibehalten	поддерживать ритм бега (podderzhivat' ritm bega)
	English	**Français**	**Español**	**Deutsch**	**Русский**

	Athletics	Athlétisme	Atletismo	Leichtathletik	Лёгкая атлетика
180	management officials	officiels de direction	encargados de la competición	offiz. Leitung	руководители (rukovoditeli)
181	marathon	marathon	maratón	Marathon	марафон (marafon)
182	marathon runner	coureur de marathon	corredor de maratón	Marathonläufer	марафонец (marafonets)
183	mark	empreinte	huella	Eindruck; Abdruck	след (sled)
184	marker	fiche de marquage	banderín marcador de la tirada	Pflock	отметка (otmetka)
185	marker flag indicating the national (olympic, world) record	fanion indicateur du record national (olympique, mondial)	banderín indicador del récord nacional (olímpico, mundial)	Flagge, die den Landesrekord (Olympischen Rekord, Weltrekord) anzeigt	флажок с обозначением национального/ олимпийского, мирового/ рекорда (flazhok s oboznacheniyem natsional'novo/olimpiyskovo, mirovovo/rekorda)
186	marshall	commissaire du terrain	comisario de pista	Obmann der Platzaufsicht	заведующий сбором спортсменов (zaveduyushchiy sborom sportsmenov)
187	marshalling area	chambre d'appel	cámara de llamadas	Meldestelle	место сбора (mesto sbora)
188	measurement of field events	mesurage des sauts et des lancers	medición de los saltos y de los lanzamientos	Messen bei Sprung, Stoss und Wurf	измерение прыжков и метаний (izmereniye prizhkov i metaniy)
189	measuring rod	toise	vara de medir	Messlatte	рейка для измерения высоты планки (reyka dlya izmereniya visoti planki)
190	measuring tape	ruban de mesure	métrica	Massband	измерительная лента (izmeritel'naya lenta)
191	medal (gold; silver; bronze)	médaille (or; argent; bronze)	medalla (presea de oro; plata; bronce)	Medal (Gold; Silber; Bronze)	медаль/золотая; серебряная; бронзовая/ (medal'/zolotaya; serebryanaya; bronzovaya/)
192	meet	compétition	encuentro	Wettkampf	состязание (sostyazaniye)
193	meet director	directeur de la compétition	director de la competencia	Wettkampfleiter	начальник состязания (nachal'nik sostyazaniya)

English	Français	Español	Deutsch	Русский
194 meet officials	officiels de la compétition	oficiales del encuentro	Offizielle	официальные лица состязания (ofitsial'niye litsa sostyazaniya)
195 men's individual events	épreuves individuelles hommes	pruebas individuales hombres	Einzelwettbewerbe, Männer	личные мужские соревнования (lichniye muzhskiye sorevnovaniya)
196 men's team events	épreuves par équipes hommes	pruebas por equipos hombres	Mannschaftswett-bewerbe, Männer	мужские командные соревнования (muzhskiye komandniye sorevnovaniya)
197 middle-distance race	course de demi-fond	carrera de media distancia	Mittelstreckenlauf	бег на средние дистанции (beg na sredniye distantsii)
198 middle-distance runner	coureur de demi-fond	corredor de medio fondo	Mittelstreckenläufer	бегун на средние дистанции (begun na sredniye distantsii)
199 minimum height	hauteur minimum	altura mínima	Minimalhöhe	минимальная высота (minimal'naya visota)
200 national anthem	hymne national	himno nacional	Nazionalhymne	государственный гимн (gosudarstvenniy gimn)
201 number	dossard	número dorsal	Startnummer	номер участника (nomer uchastnika)
202 officals' stand	échelle	tribuna de los jueces	Zeitnehmertreppe	трибуна для официальных лиц (tribuna dlya ofitsial'nih lits)
203 official surveyor	géomètre officiel	medidor oficial	Vermessungstechniker	судья-измеритель (sud'ya-izmeritel')
204 officially ratified record	record homologué	récord homologado	als Rekord anerkannt	официально утвержденный рекорд (ofitsial'no utverzhdyonniy rekord)
205 officials of the meeting	officiels de la réunion	oficiales de la reunión	Offizielle des Treffens	официальные лица встречи (ofitsial'niye litsa vstrechi)
206 "on your marks!"	"à vos marques!"	"¡a sus puestos!"	"auf die Plätze!"	"на старт!" ("na start!")
207 outdistance	distancer	dejar atrás	den Vorsprung ausbauen	обойти (oboyti)
208 outgoing runner	relayeur	receptor del testigo	stababnehmender Läufer	бегун, принимающий палочку (begun, prinimayushchiy palochku)
English	Français	Español	Deutsch	Русский

13

	Athletics	Athlétisme	Atletismo	Leichtathletik	Легкая атлетика
209	overstep	empiéter	pisar la raya	überqueren	заступить (zastupit')
210	overtake	dépasser	adelantar; rebasar	überholen	догнать (dognat')
211	pass	doubler	pasar	überholen	опередить (operedit')
212	passing zone	zone de passage du témoin d'arrivée	zona de transmisión del batón	Wechselraum	зона передачи палочки (zona peredachi palochki)
213	pentathlon	pentathlon	pentatlón	Fünfkampf	пятиборье (pyatibor'ye)
214	performance indicator board	panneau d'affichage des performances	indicador de las marcas	Anzeigetafel	табло результатов (tablo rezul'tatov)
215	photo finish	photo-d'arrivée	fotografía de llegada	Zielfoto	фотофиниш (fotofinish)
216	photo-finish camera	caméra d'arrivée	cámara para los finales de carrera	Zielkamera	фотофинишный аппарат (fotofinishniy apparat)
217	planting box	boîte d'appel	cajetín	Einstichkasten	ящик для упора шеста (yashchik dlya upora shesta)
218	planting of the pole	piquer de la perche	picar la pértiga	Einstich des Sprungstabes	втыкание шеста (vtikaniye shesta)
219	plasticine	plasticine	plastilina	Plastilin	пластилин (plastilin)
220	plasticine board	planche de plasticine	tablón de plastilina	Plastilinstreifen	пластилиновый валик (plastilinoviy valik)
221	pole	perche	pértiga; garrocha	Sprungstab	шест (shest)
222	pole vault	saut à la perche	salto con pértiga	Stabhochsprung	прыжок с шестом (prizhok s shestom)
223	pole vaulter	sauteur à la perche	saltador de pértiga	Stabhochspringer	прыгун с шестом (prigun s shestom)
224	pole-vault facility	sautoir à la perche	saltadero de pértiga	Stabhochsprunganlage	сектор для прыжков с шестом (sektor dlya prizhkov s shestom)
225	pole-vault standards; uprights	poteaux du saut à la perche	postes de salto de pértiga	Sprungständer für Stabhochsprung	стойки для прыжков с шестом (stoyki dlya prizhkov s shestom)
226	post	poteau de saut	poste de salto	Sprungständer	стойка (stoyka)

	English	Français	Español	Deutsch	Русский
227	powerful extension	extension puissante	esfuerzo dínámico	Sprungkraft	сильное выпрямление при отталкивании (sil'noye vipryamleniye pri ottalkivanii)
228	preliminary discus swings	balancement préparatoire du disque	balanceo preparatorio para el lanzamiento del disco	Anschwung des Diskus	предварительное раскачивание диска (predvaritel'noye raskachivaniye diska)
229	preliminary heats	éliminatoires	eliminatorias; series	Ausscheidungswett-kämpfe	предварительные забеги (predvaritel'niye zabegi)
230	preliminary swings of hammer	moulinet	molinete	Anschwung des Hammers	предварительные махи молотом (predvaritel'niye mahi molotom)
231	protest	réclamation	reclamación	Protest	протест (protest)
232	put	lance–	lanzamiento de peso	stossen	толкать (tolkat')
233	putter	lanceur	lanzador de disco	Kugelstosser	толкатель ядра (tolkatel' yadra)
234	putting	lancement	lanzamiento del peso	Stoss	толкание ядра (tolkaniye yadra)
235	putting facility	lançoir	instalación de lanzamientos	Stossanlage	сектор толкания ядра (sektor tolkaniya yadra)
236	race	course	carrera	Lauf	бег (beg)
237	radius lines of sector	limites du secteur	límites del sector	Sektorgrenzen	боковые границы сектора (bokoviye granitsi sektora)
238	ratify	homologuer	homologar	anerkennen	утвердить (utverdit')
239	reaction time	temps de réaction	tiempo de reacción	Zeitreagierung	время реакции на стартовый сигнал (vremya reaktsii na startoviy signal)
240	recall shot	coup de feu de rappel	disparo de salida nula	Wiederholschuss bei einem Fehlstart	повторный выстрел (povtorniy vistrel)
241	recall starter	starter de rappel	juez de llamada de salida	Rückstarter	стартер, возвращающий бегунов (startyor, vozvrashchayushchiy begunov)
242	recorder	secrétaire du jury	secretario del jurado	Schriftführer	секретарь (sekretar')
243	referee	juge-arbitre	juez árbitro	Schiedsrichter	судья (sud'ya)

	Athletics	Athlétisme	Atletismo	Leichtathletik	Лёгкая атлетика
244	referee for field events	juge-arbitre pour les concours	juez de las pruebas de pista	Schiedsrichter für Sprung-, Wurf-und Stosswettbewerbe	судья по метаниям и прыжкам (sud'ya po metaniyam i prizhkam)
245	referee for track events	juge-arbitre pour les courses	juez árbitro para las carreras	Schiedsrichter für Laufwettbewerbe	судья по бегу (sud'ya po begu)
246	referee for walking events	juge-arbitre pour les épreuves de marche	juez árbitro para las pruebas de marcha	Schiedsrichter für Gehwettbewerbe	судья по спортивной ходьбе (sud'ya po sportivnoy hod'be)
247	refreshment stations	postes de ravitaillement	puestos de refresco	Verpflegungsstationen	питательные пункты (pitatel'niye punkti)
248	relay	relais	relevo	Staffel	эстафета (estafeta)
249	relay baton	témoin	testigo	Staffelstab	эстафетная палочка (estafetnaya palochka)
250	relay race	course de relais	carrera de relevos	Staffellauf	эстафетный бег (estafetniy beg)
251	relay runner	coureur de relais	corredor de relevos	Staffelläufer	бегун в эстафете (begun v estafete)
252	relay team	équipe de relais	equipo de relevos	Staffelmannschaft	эстафетная команда (estafetnaya komanda)
253	relay zone; takeover zone)	zone de relais	zona de relevo	Wechselraum	зона передачи эстафеты (zona peredachi estafeti)
254	release of throwing implement	lâcher de l'engin	disparo del instrumento de lanzar	Abwurf; Abstoss	сбрасывание метательного снаряда (sbrasivaniye metatel'novo snaryada)
255	reporting time	heure d'appel	hora de presentación	Berichtungszeit	время явки на соревнование (vremya yavki na sorevnovaniye)
256	reserve timekeeper	chronométreur suppléant	cronometrado suplente	Ersatzzeitnehmer	запасной хронометрист (zapasnoy hronometrist)
257	road events	épreuves sur route	pruebas en carretera	Wettbewerbe auf der Strasse	соревнования вне стадиона (sorevnovaniya vne stadiona)
258	road walking	marche sur route	marcha en ruta	Strassengehen	спортивная ходьба (sportivnaya hod'ba)

	English	Français	Español	Deutsch	Русский
259	rounds	rondes; tours	series	Runden	предварительные забеги (predvaritel'niye zabegi)
260	run up	course d'élan	carrera de impulso	Anlauf	разбег (razbeg)
261	run up (to)	prendre son élan	tomar impulso	Anlauf nehmen	разбегаться (razbegatsa)
262	run-up area	aire d'élan	zona de impulso	Anlaufbahn	зона разбега (zona razbega)
263	runner	coureur	corredor	Läfer	бегун (begun)
264	running	course	carrera	Rennen	бег (beg)
265	runway	piste d'élan	pista de impulso	Anlaufbahn	дорожка для разбега (dorozhka dlya razbega)
266	sag of the bar	flèche de la barre	arqueamiento del listón	Durchhang der Sprunglatte	провисание планки (provisaniye planki)
267	sand leveller	appareil de nivellement du sable	nivelador de arena	Sandplaniergerät	гладилка (gladilka)
268	schedule of events	calendrier des compétitions	programa	Wettkampfprogramm	расписание соревнований (raspisaniye sorevnovaniy)
269	secretary	secrétaire de la réunion	secretario de la reunión	Schriftführer	секретарь (sekretar')
270	sector	secteur	sector	Sektor	сектор (sektor)
271	sector flag	fanion du secteur	banderín de sector	Sektorenfahne	флажок сектора (flazhok sektora)
272	"set!"	"prêts!"	"¡listos!"	"fertig!"	"внимание!" ("vnimaniye!")
273	shot	poids	peso; bala	Kugel; Schuss	ядро (yadro)
274	shot put	lancer de poids	lanzamiento del peso	Kugelstossen	толкание ядра (tolkaniye yadra)
275	shot putter	lanceur de poids	lanzador de peso	Kugelstosser	толкатель ядра (tolkatel' yadra)
276	shot putting	lancement du poids	lanzamiento de peso	Kugelstoss	толкание ядра (tolkaniye yadra)
277	shot-putting facility	lançoir de poids	instalación de lanzamientos de peso	Kugelstossanlage	сектор толкания ядра (sektor tolkaniya yadra)
278	spiked shoes	chaussures à pointes	zapatillas de tacos	Dornschuhe	шиповки (shipovki)
279	spikes	pointes	tacos	Dornen	шипы (shipi)
280	sprint	course de vitesse	carrera de velocidad	Kurzstreckenlauf	спринт (sprint)
281	sprinter	coureur de vitesse	velocista	Kurzstreckenläufer	спринтер (sprinter)

	Athletics	Athlétisme	Atletismo	Leichtathletik	Легкая атлетика
282	stagger	décalage	compensación de curvas a la salida	Kurvenvorgabe	расстановка бегунов на разные стартовые линии (rasstanovka begunov na razniye startoviye linii)
283	staggered start	départ en décalage	salida con compensación	versetzter Start	старт с разных стартовых линий (start s raznih startovih liniy)
284	standing start	départ debout	salida de pie	Hochstart	высокий старт (visokiy start)
285	start	départ	arranque	Start	старт (start)
286	start list	liste de départ	lista de salida	Startliste	стартовый список (startoviy spisok)
287	start of the curve	entrée du virage	entrada en la curva	Eingang der Kurve	вход в поворот (vhod v povorot)
288	start of the final straight	entrée de la ligne droite	llegada a la recta final	Eingang der Zielgeraden	начало финишной прямой (nachalo finishnoy pryamoy)
289	starter	starter	juez de salida	Starter	стартер (startyor)
290	starter's assistant	aide-starter	auxiliar del juez de salida	Startordner	помощник стартера (pomoshchnik startyora)
291	starter's stand	estrade de starter	estrado del juez de salida	Stand für Starter	возвышение стартера (vozvisheniye startyora)
292	starting block	bloc de départ	taco de salida	Startblock	стартовая колодка (startovaya kolodka)
293	starting line	ligne de départ	línea de salida	Startlinie	стартовая линия (startovaya liniya)
294	starting pistol	pistolet de starter	pistola de salida	Startpistole	стартовый пистолет (startoviy pistolet)
295	starting position	position de départ	posición de salida	Startstellung	стартовая позиция (startovaya pozitsiya)
296	starting signal	signal de départ	señal de salida	Startzeichen	стартовый сигнал (startoviy signal)
297	steeplechase	steeple (course d'obstacles)	carrera de obstáculos	Hindernislauf	стипль-чез (stipl'-chez)

	English	Français	Español	Deutsch	Русский
298	steeplechase barriers	barrières de steeple	obstáculos	Hindernislaufsperren	барьеры для стипль-чеза (bar'yeri dlya stipl'-cheza)
299	steeplechase flags	fanions de steeple	banderines de la carrera de obstáculos	Hindernislaufflaggen	флажки для стипль-чеза (flazhki dlya stipl'-cheza)
300	steeplechase hurdle	haie de steeple	valla de la carrera de obstáculos	Hürde für Hindernislauf	барьер для бега с препятствиями (bar'yer dlya bega s prepyatstviyami)
301	steeplechase track (3000 m)	piste de 3000 m steeple	pista de obstáculos de 3000 m	Hindernislauf auf einer Strecke von 3000 m	три тысячи-метровая дорожка для бега с препятствиями (tri tisyachi-metrovaya dorozhka dlya bega s prepyatstviyami)
302	step	foulée	paso	eine Schrittlänge	шаг (shag)
303	step over	empiètement	sobrepaso	Übertreten	заступ (zastup)
304	step over a hurdle	franchir une haie	franquear una valla	die Hürde überlaufen	перешагнуть барьер (pereshagnut' bar'yer)
305	stewards for competitors, officials and press	délégués aux concurrents, au jury et à la presse	delegados para atender a los participantes, jurado y prensa	Betreuer für Wettkämpfer, Offizielle und Presse	сопровождающие и гиды для спортсменов, официальных лиц и прессы (soprovozhdayushchiye i gidi dlya sportsmenov, ofitsial'nih lits i pressi)
306	stop board	butoir	madera de contención	Stossbalken	сегмент (segment)
307	stop watch	chronomètre	cronómetro	Stoppuhr	секундомер (sekundomer)
308	straight	ligne droite	recta de la pista	Gerade	прямая (pryamaya)
309	stride	foulée	zancada	Schrittlänge	шаг (shag)
310	stride pattern	rythme de foulée	combinaciones de zancadas	Schrittrhythmus	последовательность шагов (posledovatel'nost' shagov)
311	stride rate	cadence de foulée	ritmo de zancada	Schrittfolge	темп шагов (temp shagov)
312	strong finisher	finisseur	velocista en el remate	starker Endspurtläufer	обладающий сильным финишем (obladayushchiy sil'nim finishem)
313	style	style	estilo	Stil	стиль (stil')
	English	**Français**	**Español**	**Deutsch**	**Русский**

	Athletics	Athlétisme	Atletismo	Leichtathletik	Лёгкая атлетика
314	substitute runner	coureur remplaçant	corredor suplente	Ersatzläufer	запасной бегун (zapasnoy begun)
315	successful trial	essai réussi	intento válido	gültiger Versuch	успешная попытка (uspeshnaya popitka)
316	swinging arm	bras libre	brazo libre	Schwungarm	маховая рука (maxovaya ruka)
317	swinging leg	jambe libre	pierna de ataque	Schwungbein	маховая нога (maxovaya noga)
318	takeoff	appel	bote	Absprung	толчок (tolchok)
319	takeoff and early part of the hurdle clearance	attaque de la haie	posición para pasar la valla	Angehen der Hürde	атака барьера (ataka bar'yera)
320	takeoff and early part of the bar clearance	attaque de la barre	toma de impulso y acercamiento al listón	Sprungphase	атака планки (ataka planki)
321	takeoff board	planche d'appel	tabla de impulso	Sprungbalken	брусок для отталкивания (brusok dlya ottalkivaniya)
322	takeoff foot	pied d'appel	pie de impulso	Sprungfuss	толчковая нога (tolchkovaya noga)
323	takeoff leg	jambe d'appel	pierna de impulso	Sprungbein	толчковая нога (tolchkovaya noga)
324	takeoff line	ligne d'appel	raya de salida	Absprunglinie	толчковая линия (tolchkovaya liniya)
325	takeover zone	zone de passage du témoin	zona de transmisión del testigo	Wechselraum	зона передачи эстафетной палочки (zona peredachi estafetnoy palochki)
326	team race	course par équipes	carrera por equipos	Mannschaftslauf	командный бег (komandniy beg)
327	technical director	directeur technique	director técnico	technischer Leiter	заведующий оборудованием (zaveduyushchiy oborudovaniyem)
328	technique	technique	técnica	Technik	техника (tehnika)
329	throw	lancer	lanzar; lanzamiento	Werfen; Stossen	бросок (brosok)
330	thrower	lanceur	lanzador	Werfer; Stosser	метатель (metatel')
331	throwing	lancement	lanzamiento	Wurf; Stoss	метание (metaniye)

	English	Français	Español	Deutsch	Русский
332	throwing arm	bras lanceur	brazo de impulso	Wurfarm; Stossarm	метаюшая рука (metayushchaya ruka)
333	throwing cage	cage de protection	jaula de protección	Schutzgitter	предохранительная сетка (predohranitel'naya setka)
334	throwing circle	cercle de lancer	círculo de lanzamiento	Stosskreis; Wurfkreis	круг для метания (krug dlya metaniya)
335	throwing direction	direction du lancer	dirección del lanzamiento	Wurfrichtung; Stossrichtung	направление метания (napravleniye metaniya)
336	throwing events	épreuves de lancers	pruebas de lanzamientos	Wurf- und Stossdisziplinen	виды метания (vidi metaniya)
337	throwing facility	lançoir	instalación de lanzamientos	Wurfanlage ; Stossanlage	сектор для метания (sektor dlya metaniya)
338	throwing rotation	volte	vuelta de impulso	Drehung	вращение при метании (vrashcheniye pri metanii)
339	throwing sector	secteur de lancement	sector de lanzamiento	Wurfsektor	сектор для метания (sektor dlya metaniya)
340	tie	ex aequo	empate	Gleichstand	равный результат (ravniy rezul'tat)
341	tight finish	arrivée serrée	llegada reñida	knapper Einlauf	близкий финиш (blizkiy finish)
342	timekeeper	chronométreur	cronometrador	Zeitnehmer	судья-секундометрист (sud'ya-sekundometrist)
343	topometer	topomètre	topómetro	Topometer; Entfernungsmesser	топометр (topometr)
344	toppling force of the hurdle	force de résistance de la haie	resistencia de la valla	Hürdenwiederstand	сила, сбивающая барьер (sila, sbivayushchaya bar'yer)
345	track	piste	pista	Piste	дорожка (dorozhka)
346	track and field athlete	athlète	atleta	Leichtathlet	легкоатлет (lyohkoatlet)
347	track events	épreuves sur piste	pruebas en pista	Laufwettbewerbe	соревнования по бегу (sorevnovaniya po begu)
348	track inclination	déclivité de la piste	inclinación de la pista	Bahnneigung	наклон дорожки (naklon dorozhki)
	English	Français	Español	Deutsch	Русский

	Athletics	Athlétisme	Atletismo	Leichtathletik	Лёгкая атлетика
349	track umpire	commissaire de course	juez de carrera	Bahnrichter	судья на дистанции (sud'ya na distantsii)
350	track walking	marche sur piste	marcha en pista	Bahngehen	ходьба по дорожке (hod'ba po dorozhke)
351	trail leg	pied arrière	pie posterior	nachkommendes Bein	вторая нога, проходящая над барьером (vtoraya noga, prohodyashchaya nad bar'yerom)
352	trajectory of an implement	trajectoire d'un engin	trayectoria de un instrumento	Flugkurve des Stoss bzw. Wurfgeräts; Flugbahn des Stoss bzw. Wurfgeräts	траектория снаряда (trayektoriya snaryada)
353	trial	essai	intento	Versuch	попытка (popitka)
354	triple jump	triple saut	triple salto	Dreisprung	тройной прыжок (troynoy prizhok)
355	triple jumper	sauteur de triple saut	saltador de triple salto	Dreispringer	прыгун тройным прыжком (prigun troynim prizhkom)
356	triple-jump facility	sautoir de triple saut	saltadero de triple salto	Dreisprunganlage	сектор для тройных прыжков (sektor dlya troynih prizhkov)
357	two-minute clock	appareil de chronométrage de 2 minutes	marcador de dos minutos	Zwei-Minuten-Uhr	двухминутные часы (dvuhminutniye chasi)
358	unsuccessful trial	essai manqué	intento fallido	Fehlversuch	неудачная попытка (neudachnaya popitka)
359	upright	poteau de saut	poste de salto	Sprungständer	стойка для планки в прыжках в высоту (stoyka dlya planki v prizhkah v visotu)
360	valid trial	essai valable	intento válido	gültiger Versuch	засчитанная попытка (zaschitannaya popitka)
361	verification	vérification	verificación	Überprüfung	проверка (proverka)
362	vest	maillot	camiseta	Trikot	майка (mayka)

	English	French	Spanish	German	Russian
363	victory ceremony	cérémonie de la victoire	ceremonia de palmarés	Siegesprotokoll	церемония награждения (tseremoniya nagrazhdeniya)
364	victory rostrum	podium des vainqueurs	podio de palmarés	Siegerpodest	пьедестал почета (p'yedestal pochyota)
365	walker	marcheur	andarín	Geher	ходок (hodók)
366	walking	marche	marcha	Gehen	спортивная ходьба (sportivnaya hod'ba)
367	walking-events judge	juge de marche	juez de marcha	Gehrichter	судья по видам спортивной ходьбы (sud'ya po vidam sportivnoy hod'bï)
368	warm-up	échauffement	precalentamiento	Aufwärmen	разминка (razminka)
369	warm-up area	aire d'échauffement	área de precalentamiento	Aufwärmraum	площадка для разминки (ploshchadka dlya razminki)
370	warm-up running	course d'échauffement	carrera de precalentamiento	Einlaufen	бег для разминки (beg dlya razminki)
371	water jump	fossé d'eau; rivière	foso de agua	Wassergraben	прыжок через яму с водой (prizhok cherez yamu s vodoy)
372	water-jump barrier	barrière de rivière	valla del foso de agua	Balken des Wassergrabens	яма с водой (yama s vodoy)
373	wind gauge	anémomètre	anemómetro	Windmesser	анемометр (anemometr)
374	wind gauge operator	préposé à l'anémomètre	operador del anemómetro	Bediener des Windmessers	управляющий анемометром (upravlyayushchiy anemometrom)
375	women's individual events	épreuves individuelles femmes	pruebas individuales de mujeres	Einzelwettbewerbe, Frauen	женские одиночные виды соревнований (zhenskiye odinochniye vidi sorevnovaniy)
376	women's team events	épreuves par équipes femmes	pruebas por equipos mujeres	Mannschaftswettbewerbe, Frauen	женские командные виды соревнований (zhenskiye komandniye vidi sorevnovaniy)
377	zone-limit flag	fanion de limite de zone	banderín de limite de zona	Begrenzungsflagge	флажок на границе зоны (flazhok na granitse zoni)

Basketball

Basket-ball

Baloncesto

Basketball

Баскетбол

	Basketball	Basket-ball	Baloncesto	Basketball	Баскетбол
378	act of shooting	action de shooter	en el proceso de tirar	das Werfen	бросание (brosaniye)
379	advance the ball	progression avec le ballon	avanzar con el balón	Fortbewegung mit dem Ball	продвигаться вперед с мячом (prodvigatsa vperyod s myachom)
380	advantage situation	avantage	ventaja	im Vorteil sein	выгодная ситуация (vigodnaya situatsiya)
381	appeal	faire appel	apelar	Einspruch erheben	обжаловать (obzhalovat')
382	arc of the ball	trajectoire du ballon	trayectoria del balón	Bogen des Balles	траектория полета мяча (trayektoriya polyota myacha)
383	assist	aide	ayuda	Hilfe	пасовка на гол (pasovka na gol)
384	assistant coach	aide-entraîneur	entrenador auxiliar	Hilfstrainer	помощник тренера (pomoshchnik trenera)
385	attack	attaque	ataque	Angriff	атака (ataka)
386	back court	zone arrière	zona de defensa	Rückfeld	тыловая зона (tilovaya zona)
387	back court violation	violation en zone arrière	falta en la zona de defensa	Regelverletzung im Rückfeld	нарушение в тыловой зоне (narusheniye v tilovoy zone)
388	backboard	panneau	tablero de meta	Spielbrett	щит (shchit)
389	backboard markings	marquage sur le panneau	marcaje del tablero	Anzeige des Spielbretts	разметки на щите (razmetki na shchite)
390	ball becomes alive	ballon est vivant	balón está vivo	der Ball wird lebend	мяч становится "живым" (myach stanovitsa "zhivim")
391	ball becomes dead	ballon est mort	balón está muerto	der Ball wird tot	мяч выходит из игры (myach vihodit iz igri)
392	ball control	contrôle du ballon	control del balón	Ballkontrolle	владение мячом (vladeniye myachom)
393	ball handling	manipulation du ballon	manejo del balón	Ballbehandlung	владение мячом (vladeniye myachom)
394	ball in play	ballon en jeu	balón en juego	Ball im Spiel	мяч в игре (myach v igre)
395	ball is awarded	ballon est remis à	balón a favor de	der Ball ist zugesprochen	мяч присужден (myach prisuzhdyon)

	English	Français	Español	Deutsch	Русский
396	ball out-of-bounds	ballon hors-jeu	balón fuera de banda	Ausball	мяч за границами площадки (myach za granitsami ploshchadki)
397	ball possession	possession du ballon	posesión de la pelota	Ballbesitz	контролирование мяча (kontrolirovaniye myacha)
398	baseball pass	passe à une main	tiro con una mano	Baseballpass	пас одной рукой (pas odnoy rukoy)
399	baseline	ligne de fond	línea de base	Grundlinie	лицевая линия (litsevaya liniya)
400	basket	panier	cesta	Korb	корзина (korzina)
401	basket interference	intervention au panier	interferencia sobre la cesta	Korbstörung	защита корзины от мяча (zashchita korzini ot myacha)
402	basket rim	anneau du panier	aro	Korbfassung	кольцо корзины (kol'tso korzini)
403	basket support	support des paniers	poste	Korbstützung	конструкция, поддерживающая корзину (konstruktsiya, podderzhivayushchaya korzinu)
404	basketball	ballon de basket-ball	balón de baloncesto	Basketball	баскетбольный мяч (basketbol'niy myach)
405	basketball coach	entraîneur de basket-ball	entrenador de baloncesto	Basketballtrainer	баскетбольный тренер (basketbol'niy trener)
406	basketball game; match	partie de basket-ball; match	partido de baloncesto	Basketballspiel	баскетбольная игра (basketbol'naya igra)
407	basketball player	basketteur	jugador de baloncesto	Basketballspieler	баскетболист (basketbolist)
408	beginning of game	début de la partie	comienzo del partido	Spielbeginn	начало игры (nachalo igri)
409	behind-the-back dribble	dribble par derrière le dos	regate por detrás de la espalda	Dribbling hinter dem Rücken	ведение мяча за спиной (vedeniye myacha za spinoy)
410	behind-the-back pass	passe par derrière le dos	entrega por detrás de la espalda	Pass hinter dem Rücken	передача из-за спины (peredacha iz-za spini)
411	bench	banc	banco	Bank	скамья (skam'ya)
412	bench strength	force des joueurs au banc	valorización de los suplentes	Stärke der Ersatzspieler	количество и качество игроков на скамье (kolichestvo i kachestvo igrokov na skam'ye)
	English	**Français**	**Español**	**Deutsch**	**Русский**

	Basketball	Basket-ball	Baloncesto	Basketball	Баскетбол
413	blind pass	passe aveugle	pase ciego	Blinderpass	передача вслепую (peredacha vslepuyu)
414	block	bloquer	bloquear	blockieren	блокировать (blokirovat')
415	block a shot	bloquer un lancer	bloquear un disparo	einen Wurf blocken	блокировать бросок (blokirovat' brosok)
416	block out	empêcher l'accès au panier	estrategia de bloqueo frente a la cesta	Blockierung	блокировать противника от корзины (blokirovat' protivnika ot korzini)
417	blocking	blocage	bloqueo	Block	накрывание (nakrivaniye)
418	blocking foul	faute d'obstruction	faul de bloqueo	blockendes Foul	фол при блокировке (fol pri blokirovke)
419	bounce pass	passe avec rebond	pase de rebote	Reboundpass	передача отскоком (peredacha otskokom)
420	boundary lines	lignes délimitant le terrain	líneas de demarcación	Seitenlinie	линии, ограничивающие площадку (linii, ogranichivayushchiye ploshchadku)
421	box and one defence	carré et un (placement défensif)	defensa de zona de cuatro y un volante	Loge und eine Verteidigung	зонная защита/квадрат с одним лично опекающим игроком (zonnaya zashchita / kvadrat s odnim lichno opekayushchim igrokom)
422	box out	empêcher l'accès au panier	posición defensiva frente a la cesta	ausdrücken	блокировать противника от корзины (blokirovat' protivnika ot korziny)
423	break away	échapper, s'	hacer un aclarado, una escapada	ausreissen	оторваться от соперника (otorvatsa ot sopernika)
424	bucket	panier	cesta	Eimer	корзина (korzina)
425	captain	capitaine	capitán	Kapitän	капитан команды (kapitan komandi)
426	carry the ball	porter le ballon	llevar la pelota	den Ball tragen	нести мяч (nesti myach)

English	Français	Español	Deutsch	Русский
427 catch the ball	attraper le ballon	coger el balón	den Ball abnehmen	поймать мяч (poymat' myach)
428 center	centre	centro delantero	Center	центровой (tsentrovoy)
429 center circle	cercle central	círculo central	Mittelkreis	центральный круг (tsentral'niy krug)
430 center jump	saut au centre	salto en el círculo	Centersprung	центровой прыжок (tsentrovoy prizhok)
431 center line	ligne médiane	línea central	Mittellinie	центральная линия (tsentral'naya liniya)
432 chalk talk	"briefing"; stratégie	sesión de estrategia	"chalk talk"	указания тренера команде (ukazaniya trenera komande)
433 change baskets	changer de panier	cambio de campo	die Körbe wechseln	менять корзины (menyat' korzini)
434 change of direction	changement de direction	cambio de dirección	Richtungswechsel	перемена направления (peremena napravleniya)
435 change of pace	changement de rythme	cambio de ritmo	Rhythmuswechsel	смена ритма (smena ritma)
436 charge	charge	carga	rempeln	нападение на игрока (napadeniye na igroka)
437 charge an opponent	charger un adversaire	arremeter al adversario	den Gegner rempeln	напасть на игрока (napast' na igroka)
438 charged time-out	temps mort accordé	tiempo muerto cargado	gerechnete Auszeit	выделенное "мертвое" время (videlennoye "myortvoye" vremya)
439 chest pass	passe au niveau de la poitrine	pase al nivel del pecho	Druckpass	передача от груди (peredacha ot grudi)
440 choice of ball	choix du ballon	elección de balón	Ballwahl	выбор мяча (vibor myacha)
441 choice of basket	choix du panier	elección de campo	Korbwahl	выбор корзины (vibor korzini)
442 clearout	libre champ	despeje	den Platz freimachen	освобождение места для броска (osvobozhdeniye mesta dlya broska)
443 close-in shot	lancer de près	tiro de cerca	Nahschuss	близкий бросок (blizkiy brosok)

	Basketball	Basket-ball	Baloncesto	Basketball	Баскетбол
444	clutch shooter	shooteur favori	tirador controlado	Griffwerfer	ключевой игрок (klyuchevoy igrok)
445	coach	entraîneur	entrenador	Trainer	тренер (trener)
446	collision	collision	choque	Zusammenstoss	столкновение (stolknoveniye)
447	combination defence	défense mixte	defensa mixta	gemischte Verteidigung	комбинированная защита (kombinirovannaya zashchita)
448	continuity	continuité	continuación	Kontinuität	непрерывность (neprerivnost')
449	control the ball	exercer le contrôle du ballon	controlar el balón	die Ballkontrolle haben	контролировать мяч (kontrolirovat' myach)
450	controlled offence	attaque maîtrisée	ataque controlado	absichtlicher Angriff	контролированное нападение (kontrolirovannoye napadeniye)
451	court	terrain	pista	Spielfeld	площадка (ploshchadka)
452	court dimensions	dimensions du terrain	medidas del campo	Spielfeldabmessungen	размеры площадки (razmeri ploshchadki)
453	crew chief	chef des officiels de soutien	encargado de oficiales	Mannschaftsführer	руководитель вспомогательного штата (rukovoditel' vspomogatel'novo shtata)
454	cross-court pass	passe à travers le terrain	pase a través de la cancha	der Ball überquert das Feld	передача через игровую площадку (peredacha cherez igrovuyu ploshchadku)
455	cross-over dribble	action de dribbler des deux mains	cambio al rebote	wechselndes Dribbling	ведение мяча со сменой рук (vedeniye myacha so smenoy ruk)
456	cut	couper	cortar	abschneiden	резко изменить направление (rezko izmenit' napravleniye)
457	cylinder	cylindre	cilindro	Zylinder	цилиндр (tsilindr)
458	dead ball	ballon mort	balón muerto	toter Ball	"мёртвый" мяч/мяч вне игры ("myortviy" myach/myach vne igri)
459	defence	défense	defensa	Verteidigung	защита (zashchita)

	English	Français	Español	Deutsch	Русский
460	defender	défenseur	defensor	Verteidiger	защитник (zashchitnik)
461	defensive balance	équilibre de défense	equilibrio de defensa	Verteidigungs-gleichgewicht	равновесие в защите (ravnovesiye v zashchite)
462	defensive rebound	rebond de défense	rebote defensivo	Verteidigungsabpraller	подбор у своего щита (podbor u svoyevo shchita)
463	defensive set	position de défense	posición defensiva	Verteidigungsposition	расположение защиты (raspolozheniye zashchiti)
464	defensive slides (zone)	déplacement de défense (zone)	defensivo deslizante (zona)	Verteidigungsrutsche (Zone)	перемещение защитной зоны (peremeshcheniye zashchitnoy zoni)
465	delay offence	attaque retardée	ataque atrasado	verzögerter Angriff	замедленное нападение (zamedlennoye napadeniye)
466	delay the game	retarder le jeu	demorar el juego	das Spiel verzögern	замедлить игру (zamedlit' igru)
467	direct pass	passe directe	pase directo	Direktpass	прямая передача (pryamaya peredacha)
468	disallowed basket	panier annulé	anotación anulada	ungültiger Korberfolg	незасчитанный мяч (nezaschitanniy myach)
469	disqualification	disqualification	descalificación	Disqualifikation	дисквалификация (diskvalifikatsiya)
470	disqualified player	joueur disqualifié	jugador descalificado	disqualifizierter Spieler	дисквалифицированный игрок (diskvalifitsirovanniy igrok)
471	disqualifying foul	faute disqualifiante	falta descalificante	disqualifizierendes Foul	дисквалифицирующий фол (diskvalifitsiruyushchiy fol)
472	distract the free thrower	distraire le lanceur du lancer franc	distraer al lanzador de tiros libres	den Freiwerfer stören	мешать игроку, пробивающему штрафной бросок (meshat' igroku, probivayushchemu shtrafnoy brosok)
473	double dribble	double dribble	doble dribleo	Doppeldribbling	двойное ведение (dvoynoye vedeniye)
474	double foul	double-faute	falta doble	Doppelfoul	двойной фол (dvoynoy fol)
475	double pivot	double pivot	pivote doble	Doppel-Center	сдвоенный центр (sdvoyenniy tsentr)
	English	**Français**	**Español**	**Deutsch**	**Русский**

	Basketball	Basket-ball	Baloncesto	Basketball	Баскетбол
476	double screen	double écran	pantalla doble	Doppelblock	двойной заслон (dvoynoy zaslon)
477	double team	doubler la défense	doble defensa	Doppelmannschaft	двойная опека (dvoynaya opeka)
478	dribble	dribbler	driblar; regatear	dribbeln	вести мяч (vesti myach)
479	dribble with alternating hands	dribble des deux mains	regate con dos manos	beidhändiges Dribbeln	вести мяч со сменой рук (vesti myach so smenoy ruk)
480	dribbler	dribbleur	driblador	Dribbler	ведущий мяч (vedushchiy myach)
481	dribbling	dribble	regateo	Dribbeln	ведение мяча (vedeniye myacha)
482	drive to the basket	montée au panier	presión hacia la cesta	schnelles Dribbeln zum Korb	атаковать (atakovat')
483	dunk	lancer coulé	enceste forzoso	Stoss nach unten	бросок сверху из-под кольца (brosok sverhu iz-pod kol'tsa)
484	edge of the backboard	bord du panneau	borde del tablero	Rand des Spielbretts	край щита (kray shchita)
485	ejection	expulsion	expulsión	auswerfen	удаление с площадки (udaleniye s ploshchadki)
486	end line	ligne de fond	linea de fondo	Endlinie	лицевая линия (litsevaya liniya)
487	English (spin)	éffet du ballon (anglais)	efecto inglés	Englisch (Dreh)	бросок, крученый по-английски (brosok, kruchyoniy po-angliyski)
488	expiration of playing time	expiration du temps de jeu	expiración del tiempo de juego	Ende der Spielzeit	конец времени игры (konets vremeni igri)
489	expulsion	expulsion	expulsión	Spielausschluss	удаление игрока с поля игры (udaleniye igroka s polya igri)
490	extra period	prolongation	prórroga	Verlängerung	дополнительный период (dopolnitel'niy period)
491	face guarding	agiter les mains pour gêner la vision	molestar la visión del contrario con las manos	mit den Händen die Sicht verwehren	заслон глаз соперника рукой (zaslon glaz sopernika rukoy)
492	fake	feinte	amago	Täuschung	финт (fint)

English	Français	Español	Deutsch	Русский
493	fake a shot	feinte de lancer	amagar un tiro	Wurftäuschung	сделать обманный бросок (sdelat' obmanniy brosok)
494	fans	accompagnateurs	hincha	Mannschaftsanhänger	болельщики (bolel'shchiki)
495	fast break	contre-attaque rapide	contraataque rápido	schneller Gegenangriff	быстрый отрыв (bistriy otriv)
496	feed the ball	passer le ballon	pasar el balón	den Ball zuführen	пасовать (pasovat')
497	feel of the ball	touche de ballon	manejo del balón	Ballberührung	чувство мяча (chuvstvo myacha)
498	feint	feinte	finta	Täuschung	финт (fint)
499	field goal	panier réussi du terrain de jeu	tiro de campo acertado	gültiger Korbwurf	успешный бросок с игры (uspeshniy brosok s igri)
500	field goal attempt	lancer au panier	intento de tiro de campo	Korbwurfversuch	бросок с игры (brosok s igri)
501	field goal percentage	pourcentage panier	porcentaje de tiros de campo	Korbwurfprozentsatz	процент бросков с игры (protsent broskov s igri)
502	fifth foul	cinquième faute	quinta falta	fünftes Foul	пятый фол (pyatiy fol)
503	fill the lanes	remplir les couloirs	ocupar los carriles	die Linien besetzen	продвигаться по линиям нападения (prodvigatsa po liniyam napadeniya)
504	final score	résultat final	resultado final del juego	Endergebnis	окончательный счет (okonchatel'niy schyot)
505	first half	première mi-temps	primer tiempo	erste Halbzeit	первая половина игры (pervaya polovina igri)
506	five-second rule	règle des 5 secondes	regla de los 5 segundos	fünf-Sekunden-Regel	правило пяти секунд (pravilo pyati sekund)
507	flagrant foul	faute flagrante	violación flagrante	eklatantes Foul	очень грубый фол (ochen' grubiy fol)
508	footwork	jeu de jambes	juego de piernas	Beinarbeit	работа ног (rabota nog)
509	forced shot	lancer forcé	tiro forzado	gezwungener Wurf	вынужденный бросок (vinuzhdenniy brosok)
510	forfeit game	partie perdue par forfait	abandono	Verlust der Spielberechtigung	автоматическая потеря игры (avtomaticheskaya poterya igri)
511	forwards	avants	aleros delanteros	Vorderspieler	нападающие (napadayushchiye)
512	foul	faute	falta	Foul	фол (fol)

	Basketball	Basket-ball	Baloncesto	Basketball	Баскетбол
513	foul out	faute de disqualification	faul fuera	fünftes Foul	фол с удалением (fol s udaleniyem)
514	free foot	pied libre	pie libre	Spielbein	свободная нога (svobodnaya noga)
515	free throw	lancer franc	tiro libre	Freiwurf	штрафной бросок (shtrafnoy brosok)
516	free-throw attempt	essai de lancer franc	intento de tiro libre	Freiwurfversuch	попытка сделать штрафной бросок (popitka sdelat' shtrafnoy brosok)
517	free-throw lane	couloir de lancer franc	pasillo de tiro libre	Freiwurfgasse	область штрафного броска (oblast' shtrafnovo broska)
518	free-throw line	ligne des lancers francs	línea de tiro libre	Freiwurflinie	линия штрафного броска (liniya shtrafnovo broska)
519	free throw made	lancer franc réussi	tiro libre acertado	ausgeführter Freiwurf	успешный штрафной бросок (uspeshniy shtrafnoy brosok)
520	free-throw percentage	pourcentage de lancers francs	porcentaje de tiros libres acertados	Freiwurfprozentsatz	процент штрафных бросков (protsent shtrafnih broskov)
521	freeze the ball	garder le ballon	congelar el balón	auf Zeit spielen	задерживать мяч (zaderzhivat' myach)
522	front court	zone avant	zona de ataque	Vorfeld	передовая зона (peredovaya zona)
523	front foot	pied avant	pie adelantado	vorderer Fuss	нога спереди (noga speredi)
524	full-court man-to-man press defence	défense individuelle par harcèlement sur tout le terrain	defensa individual presionante en todo el campo	Manndeckung durch Pressdeckung über das ganze Spielfeld	прессинг по всему полю в личной защите (pressing po vsemu polyu v lichnoy zashchite)
525	full-court zone press	harcèlement en zone sur tout le terrain	defensa zonal de presión en todo el campo	Zonenpressdeckung	зонный прессинг по всему полю (zonniy pressing po vsemu polyu)
526	fumble	perdre le contrôle du ballon	balón perdido	verunsichert sein	уронить мяч (uronit' myach)

	English	Français	Español	Deutsch	Русский
527	fundamentals	éléments de base	conceptos fundamentales	Grundlage	основы (osnovi)
528	game clock	chronomètre du jeu	cronómetro de juego	Spieluhr	табло игры (tablo igri)
529	game schedule	calendrier des parties	calendario de los partidos	Anschreibebogen	расписание игр (raspisaniye igr)
530	get in the open	démarquer, se	desmarcarse	sich freispielen	открыться (otkritsa)
531	give and go	passe et va	pasa y va	abspielen und freilaufen	пас и атаковать (pas i atakovat')
532	goal	panier	cesta; canasta	Korb	попадание (popadaniye)
533	goal tending	intervention sur le ballon	defensa de la cesta	Ballstörung	защита корзины от мяча (zashchita korzini ot myacha)
534	grasp the rim	empoigner le bord du panier	agarrarse del aro	nach der Fassung greifen	ухватиться за кольцо (uhvatitsa za kol'tso)
535	guard from the rear	marquage par derrière	marcar por detrás	von hinten decken	опекать соперника сзади (opekat' sopernika szadi)
536	guarded player	joueur marqué	jugador marcado	gedeckter Spieler	закрытый игрок (zakritiy igrok)
537	guards	arrières	defensas	Hinterspieler	защитники (zashchitniki)
538	half time	mi-temps	descanso	Halbzeit	половина времени игры (polovina vremeni igri)
539	half-court	centre du terrain	lado	Spielfeldhälfte	половина поля (polovina polya)
540	half-court man-to-man press defence	défense individuelle par harcèlement à partir du centre	defensa individual presionante en medio campo	Manndeckung durch Pressdeckung ab Spielfeldmitte	прессинг в личной защите на одной половине поля (pressing v lichnoy zashchite na odnoy polovine polya)
541	half-court zone press	harcèlement en zone à partir du centre	defensa zonal de presón desde el centro del terreno	Zonenpressdeckung ab Spielfeldmitte	зонный прессинг на своей половине поля (zonniy pressing na svoyey polovine polya)
542	handle the ball	manier le ballon	manejar el balón	Ballbehandlung	владеть мячом (vladet' myachom)
543	head fake	feinte de la tête	finta de cabeza	Kopftäuschung	финт головой (fint golovoy)

	Basketball	Basket-ball	Baloncesto	Basketball	Баскетбол
544	headman the ball	passer le ballon au joueur de tête	pasar el balón al jugador más avanzado	den Ball dem leitenden Spieler geben	передать мяч передовому игроку (peredat' myach peredovomu igroku)
545	held ball	ballon tenu	balón retenido	Halteball	удержанный мяч (uderzhanniy myach)
546	high post	pivot haut	pivote alto	hoher Pivot	центровой в области штрафного броска (tsentrovoy v oblasti shtrafnovo broska)
547	hold an opponent	accrocher un adversaire	sujetar al adversario	den Gegner halten	задержать противника (zaderzhat' protivnika)
548	hook pass	passe à bras roulé	pase de gancho	Hakenpass	передача крюком (peredacha kryukom)
549	hook shot	lancer à bras roulé	tiro de gancho	Hakenwurf	бросок крюком (brosok kryukom)
550	hoop	panier	aro	Ring	кольцо (kol'tso)
551	horn	signal	bocina	Hupe	звонок (zvonok)
552	hustle	effort	presión	sich beeilen	быстро действовать (bistro deystvovat')
553	illegal dribble	dribble irrégulier	regate antirreglamentario	regelwidriges Dribbling	неправильное ведение мяча (nepravil'noye vedeniye myacha)
554	illegal screening	écran effectué illégalement	pantalla no reglamentaria	regelwidriges Sperren	неправильный заслон (nepravil'niy zaslon)
555	illegal use of the hands	usage illégal des mains	uso no reglamentario de los brazos	regelwidrige Benutzung der Hände	неправильное использование рук (nepravil'noye ispol'zovaniye ruk)
556	inside edge of the boundary lines	bord intérieur des lignes délimitant le terrain	borde interno de las líneas de demarcación del terreno de juego	innere Seitenlinienbegrenzung	внутренний край ограничительных линий (vnutrenniy kray ogranichitel'nih liniy)
557	inside screen	écran intérieur	pantalla interior	innerer Schirm	внутренний заслон (vnutrenniy zaslon)

English	Français	Español	Deutsch	Русский
558 intentional foul	faute intentionnelle	falta intencionada	absichtliches Foul	умышленный фол (umishlenniy fol)
559 intercept the ball	intercepter le ballon	interceptar el balón	den Ball abfangen	перехватить мяч (perehvatit' myach)
560 interference	intervention	interferencia	Stören	вмешательство (vmeshatel'stvo)
561 intermission	pause	descanso	Spielpause	перерыв (pereriv)
562 International Amateur Basketball Federation (F.I.B.A.)	Fédération Internationale de Basket-ball Amateur (F.I.B.A.)	Federación Internacional de Baloncesto Amateur (F.I.B.A.)	Internationaler Basketballverband (F.I.B.A.)	международная любительская федерация баскетбола ФИБА/ (mezhdunarodnaya lyubitel'skaya federatsiya basketbola/FIBA/)
563 jump ball	entre-deux	lanzamiento al aire	Sprungball	спорный мяч (sporniy myach)
564 jump circle	cercle de mise en jeu	círculo central	Mittelkreis	круг для прыжков (krug dlya prizhkov)
565 jump hook	lancer en suspension à bras roulé	tiro de gancho en suspensión	Sprunghakenwurf	бросок крюком в прыжке (brosok kryukom v prizhke)
566 jump shot	lancer en suspension	tiro en suspensión	Sprungwurf	бросок в прыжке (brosok v prizhke)
567 jumper	sauteur	saltador	Springer	прыгун (prigun)
568 key	bouteille	zona	Birne	область штрафного броска (oblast' shtrafnovo broska)
569 lay up	lancer déposé	tiro en carrera	Korbleger	бросок одной рукой в прыжке (brosok odnoy rukoy v prizhke)
570 lead official	arbitre de terrain avant	árbitro de la línea de fondo	Schiedsrichter im Vorderfeld	судья переднего поля (sud'ya perednevo polya)
571 lead pass	passe au joueur de tête	pase adelantado	führender Pass	передача передовому игроку (peredacha peredovomu igroku)
572 left forward	avant gauche	ala izquierdo	linker Vorderspieler	левый нападающий (leviy napadayushchiy)
573 left guard	arrière gauche	defensa izquierdo	linker Hinterspieler	левый защитник (leviy zashchitnik)

	Basketball	Basket-ball	Baloncesto	Basketball	Баскетбол
574	legal guarding position	position légale de défense	posición de defensa reglamentaria	gesetzliche Deckungsstellung	правильная опекающая позиция (pravil'naya opekayushchaya pozitsiya)
575	live ball	ballon vivant	balón vivo	lebender Ball	"живой" мяч ("zhivoy" myach)
576	lob pass	passe en cloche	pase bombeado	Bogenpass	навесная передача (navesnaya peredacha)
577	loose ball	ballon libre	balón suelto	freier Ball	плохо управляемый мяч (ploho upravlyayemiy myach)
578	lose the ball	perdre le ballon	perder el balón	den Ball verlieren	потерять мяч (poteryat' myach)
579	loss of the ball (penalty)	perte du ballon (sanction)	pérdida de balón (penalty)	Ballverlust (Strafe)	потеря мяча/наказание (poterya myacha/nakazaniye/)
580	low post	pivot bas	pivote bajo	tiefer Pivot	центровой под щитом (tsentrovoy pod shchitom)
581	man-to-man defence	défense individuelle	defensa personal	Manndeckung	защита "игрок в игрока" (zashchita "igrok v igroka")
582	marker (to indicate number of fouls)	plaquette du marqueur	plaqueta del marcador	Schild zum Anzeigen der Anzahl der Fouls	указка фолов (ukazka folov)
583	marshalls	commissaires du terrain	jefes del terreno	Platzwärter	вспомогательный штат (vspomogatel'niy shtat)
584	match-up zone	zone de désignation	correspondencia en la defensa	match-up Zone	зона подбора опеки (zona podbora opeki)
585	match-ups	égaler et désigner	marcaje hombre a hombre	Zusammenpassung	подбор опеки (podbor opeki)
586	minor officials' table	table des officiels mineurs	mesa de los anotadores	Kampfrichtertisch	стол для вспомогательного штата (stol dlya vspomogatel'novo shtata)
587	minutes played	minutes de jeu écoulées	tiempo corrido	Minuten gespielt	прошедшие минуты игры (proshedshiye minuti igri)
588	miss the basket	manquer le panier	fallar al cesto	den Korb verfehlen	промахнуться по корзине (promahnutsa po korzine)

	English	Français	Español	Deutsch	Русский
589	missed free throw	lancer franc manqué	tiro libre fallado	verfehlter Freiwurf	неудавшийся штрафной бросок (neudavshiysya shtrafnoy brosok)
590	missed shot	lancer manqué	tiro fallado	Fehlwurf	промах (promah)
591	moving screen	écran mobile	bloqueo en movimiento	beweglicher Schirm	подвижный заслон (podvizhniy zaslon)
592	multiple foul	faute multiple	falta múltiple	Mehrfachfoul	многократный фол (mnogokratniy fol)
593	multiple free throws	lancers francs multiples	tiros libres múltiples	mehrere Freiwürfe	многократные штрафные броски (mnogokratniye shtrafniye broski)
594	net	filet	red	Netz	сетка корзины (setka korzini)
595	non-pivot foot	pied libre	pie libre	Spielbein	неопорная нога (neopornaya noga)
596	offence	attaque	ataque	Angriff	нападение (napadeniye)
597	offence against man-to-man defence	attaque d'une défense individuelle	ataque contra una defensa personal	Angriff aus der Manndeckung	нападение против личной защиты (napadeniye protiv lichnoy zashchiti)
598	offence against zone defence	attaque d'une défense de zone	ataque contra la zona de defensa	Angriff aus der Zonendeckung	нападение против зонной защиты (napadeniye protiv zonnoy zashchiti)
599	offensive board	panneau d'attaque	tablero ofensivo	Angriffsbrett	щит соперника (shchit sopernika)
600	offensive foul	faute offensive	falta de ataque	Angreiferfoul	фол в нападении (fol v napadenii)
601	offensive pattern	plan d'attaque	plan de juegos de ataque	Angriffsschema	схема нападения (shema napadeniya)
602	offensive player	attaquant	atacante	Angreifer	нападающий (napadayushchiy)
603	offensive rebound	rebond d'attaque	rebote ofensivo	Angriffsabpraller	подбор у щита соперника (podbor u shchita sopernika)

	Basketball	Basket-ball	Baloncesto	Basketball	Баскетбол
604	offensive set	position d'attaque	posición de ataque	Angriffsposition	распределение нападающих (raspredeleniye napadayushchih)
605	official scorer	marqueur officiel	marcador oficial	offizieller Anschreiber	официальный счётчик (ofitsial'niy schyotchik)
606	official scoresheet	feuille de marque officielle	acta de arbitraje	offizieller Spielberichts-bogen	официальный протокол игры (ofitsial'niy protokol igri)
607	officials	officiels	oficiales	Spielrichter	официальные лица (ofitsial'niye litsa)
608	official's signals	signaux d'arbitre	señales del árbitro	Zeichen der Schiedsrichter	жесты судьи (zhesti sud'yi)
609	one-hand pass	passe à une main	pase con una mano	einhändiger Pass	передача одной рукой (peredacha odnoy rukoy)
610	one-hand shot	lancer à une main	tiro con una mano	Einhandwurf	бросок одной рукой (brosok odnoy rukoy)
611	opening jump; opening toss	mise en jeu d'engagement	sorteo	Anspiel	начальный спорный мяч (nachal'niy sporniy myach)
612	opponent's basket	panier adverse	cesta del adversario	Korb des Gegners	корзина противника (korzina protivnika)
613	out-of-bounds	hors du terrain	fuera del terreno de juego	ausserhalb des Spielfeldes	за границами поля/аут (za granitsami polya/aut)
614	out-of-bounds play	jeu de l'extérieur du terrain	jugada del puesto en juego	Einwurfspiel	игра из-за границ (igra iz-za granits)
615	outnumbering situations	situations de surnombre	ventaja numérica	Überzahlverhältnis	ситуации численного превосходства (situatsii chislennovo prevoshodstva)
616	outside screen	écran extérieur	bloqueo exterior	äusserer Schirm	наружный заслон (naruzhniy zaslon)
617	over and back	retour du ballon en arrière	avanzar y retroceder	den Ball rückspielen	выйти из своего поля защиты и в него вернуться (viyti iz svoyevo polya zashchiti i v nevo vernutsa)

	English	Français	Español	Deutsch	Русский
618	over play	marquage par devant	anticipo de pase por la defensa	überspielen	не давать противнику поймать мяч (ne davat' protivniku poymat' myach)
619	overhead pass	passe par-dessus la tête	pase por encima de la cabeza	über dem Kopf passen	передача сверху (peredacha sverhu)
620	overload	surcharge	sobrecarga	Überbelastung	перегрузка (peregruzka)
621	overtime	prolongation	prolongación	Verlängerung	дополнительное время (dopolnitel'noye vremya)
622	own basket	propre panier	cesta propia	eigener Korb	своя корзина (svoya korzina)
623	pass	passe	pase	Pass	пас (pas)
624	pass the ball	passer le ballon	pasar el balón	den Ball passen	пасовать мяч (pasovat' myach)
625	passer	passeur	pasador	Zuspieler	пасующий (pasuyushchiy)
626	path of the player	trajet effectué par un joueur	trayectoria del jugador	Spielerweg	путь игрока (put' igroka)
627	penalty	pénalité	penalty	Strafe	штраф (shtraf)
628	penetrate	percer la défense	penetrar la defensa	die Verteidigung durchbrechen	прорвать защиту (prorvat' zashchitu)
629	period	période de jeu	período de juego	Spielperiode	тайм (taym)
630	personal contact	contact personnel	contacto personal	Körperberührung	персональное столкновение (personal'noye stolknoveniye)
631	personal foul	faute personnelle	falta personal	persönliches Foul	персональный фол (personal'niy fol)
632	pick	écran	pantalla; bloqueo	Schirm	заслон (zaslon)
633	pick and roll	faire écran et rouler	amagar hacia el defensa girando hacia la cesta	sperren und rollen	заслон и поворот (zaslon i povorot)
634	pivot	pivot	pivote	Pivot	поворот (povorot)
635	pivot foot	pied de pivot	pie de apoyo	Pivot-Fuss	опорная нога (opornaya noga)
636	pivot play	jeu de pivot central	juego de pivote central	Center-Pivotspiel	центровая комбинация (tsentrovaya kombinatsiya)
637	player numbers	numérotage des joueurs	numeración de los jugadores	Spielernumerierung	номера игроков (nomera igrokov)
	English	Français	Español	Deutsch	Русский

	Basketball	Basket-ball	Baloncesto	Basketball	Баскетбол
638	player substitution	remplacement de joueur	cambio de jugador	Auswechseln	замена игрока (zamena igroka)
639	playing court	terrain de jeu	superficie de juego	Spielfeld	игровая площадка (igrovaya ploshchadka)
640	playing time	temps de jeu	tiempo de juego	Spielzeit	время игры (vremya igri)
641	playmaker	constructeur de jeu	jugador base	Spielmacher	дирижер (dirizhyor)
642	point average	moyenne des points	promedio de puntos	Punktendurchschnitt	среднее количество очков (sredneye kolichestvo ochkov)
643	points	points	puntos	Punkte	очки (ochki)
644	possession	possession	posesión	Besitz	владение мячом (vladeniye myachom)
645	possession game	jeu de possession	juego de posesión	Besitzspiel	игра с контролированием мяча (igra s kontrolirovaniyem myacha)
646	post	joueur-poste	jugador de pivote	Pivot-Spieler	центровой (tsentrovoy)
647	post play	jeu de pivot central	juego del pivote central	Center-Pivotspiel	комбинация центрового (kombinatsiya tsentrovovo)
648	post split	jeu de pivot séparé	ataque triple de pivote con dos	Korbspielzerteilung	двусторонний обход центрового (dvustoronniy obhod tsentrovovo)
649	power lay up	lancer déposé en force	tiro forzado en carrera	kräftiger Korbleger	силовой бросок одной рукой в прыжке (silovoy brosok odnoy rukoy v prizhke)
650	press	harcèlement	presión	Pressdeckung	прессинг (pressing)
651	pressure an opponent	presser un adversaire	presionar a un contrario	den Gegner decken	вынуждать противника (vynuzhdat' protivnika)
652	progress with the ball	progresser avec le ballon	avanzar con el balón	sich mit dem Ball vorwärts bewegen	продвигаться с мячом (prodvigatsa s myachom)
653	putting the ball into play	mise en jeu	puesta en juego	den Ball ins Spiel bringen	введение мяча в игру (vvedeniye myacha v igru)
654	rebound	rebond	rebote	Zurückprallen	отскок (otskok)
655	rebound (to)	capter le rebond	coger el rebote	zurückprallen	подбирать (podbirat')

	English	Français	Español	Deutsch	Русский
656	recover the ball	récupérer le ballon	recuperar el balón	sich wieder im Ballbesitz bringen	вновь завладеть мячом (vnov' zavladet' myachom)
657	referee	arbitre	árbitro principal	erster Schiedsrichter	судья (sud'ya)
658	referee (to)	arbitrer	arbitrar	Entscheidungen treffen	судить (sudit')
659	request substitution	demander un remplacement	pedir una sustitución	einen Wechsel verlangen	просить замену (prosit' zamenu)
660	reverse dribble	dribble à l'envers	regate de pronación	reverses Dribbling	ведение мяча с поворотом (vedeniye myacha s povorotom)
661	right forward	avant droit	alero derecho	rechter Vorderspieler	правый нападающий (praviy napadayushchiy)
662	right guard	arrière droit	defensa derecho	rechter Hinterspieler	правый защитник (praviy zashchitnik)
663	rim of the basket	bord du panier	aro	Ringrand	обод корзины (obod korzini)
664	roll back to the ball	rouler vers le ballon	amago de alejarse del balón seguido del impulso hacia el balón	zum Ball zurückrollen	возвратиться к мячу (vozvratitsa k myachu)
665	roll to the hoop	rouler vers le panier	girar hacia la cesta	bis zum Ring rollen	повернуться к корзине (povernutsa k korzine)
666	rule violation	infraction aux règles	infracción de las reglas	Regelübertretung	нарушение правила (narusheniye pravila)
667	schedule of games	calendrier des parties	calendario de partidos	Führung des laufenden Ergebnisses	расписание игр (raspisaniye igr)
668	score	marquer un panier	anotar	einen Korb erzielen	забросить мяч (zabrosit' myach)
669	scoreboard	tableau de marque	marcador	Anzeigetafel	табло счета (tablo schyota)
670	scorer	marqueur	anotador	Anschreiber	судья-секретарь (sud'ya-sekretar')
671	scorer's table	table du marqueur	mesa del anotador	Kampfrichtertisch	стол секретаря соревнования (stol sekretarya sorevnovaniya)
672	scoresheet	feuille de marque	acta del partido	Anschreibebogen	протокол игры (protokol igri)

	Basketball	Basket-ball	Baloncesto	Basketball	Баскетбол
673	scouting	observer une autre équipe	observación de otro equipo	Erkundung	наблюдение за командой противника (nablyudeniye za komandoy protivnika)
674	screen	écran	pantalla	Schirm	заслон (zaslon)
675	screen (to)	faire écran	realizar un bloqueo	sperren	заслонить (zaslonit')
676	screen and roll	faire écran et rouler	bloquear y girar hacia la cesta	sperren und rollen	заслон и поворот (zaslon i povorot)
677	screen away from the ball	écran effectué loin du ballon	bloqueo indirecto	Sperren weit vom Ball	сделать заслон далеко от мяча (sdelat' zaslon daleko ot myacha)
678	screen close to the ball	écran près du ballon	pantalla cerca del balón	Sperren in der Nähe des Balls	сделать заслон вблизи от мяча (sdelat' zaslon vblizi ot myacha)
679	scrimmage	jeu d'essai	fogueo	Gedränge	игра для разминки (igra dlya razminki)
680	second half	deuxième mi-temps	segundo tiempo	zweite Spielhälfte	вторая половина игры (vtoraya polovina igri)
681	semi-circle	demi-cercle	semicírculo	Halbkreis	полукруг (polukrug)
682	set-play offence	attaque organisée	ataque planeado	Positionsangriff	позиционное нападение (pozitsionnoye napadeniye)
683	set shot	lancer sur place	lanzamiento en firme	vorbereiteter Korbwurf	подготовленный бросок (podgotovlenniy brosok)
684	shoot the ball	lancer le ballon	tirar el balón	den Ball werfen	бросить мяч по корзине (brosit' myach po korzine)
685	shooter	lanceur	lanzador	Korbwerfer	бросающий игрок (brosayushchiy igrok)
686	shooting angle	angle de lancer	ángulo del tiro	Wurfwinkel	угол броска (ugol broska)
687	shooting form	forme de lancer	forma de lanzamiento	Wurfart	техника броска (tehnika broska)
688	shot	lancer	tiro	Wurf	бросок (brosok)
689	shuffle cut	couper à partir d'un écran	cortar después de una pantalla de pivote alto	Verkehrung nach Pivotschirm	прорвать оборону от заслона (prorvat' oboronu ot zaslona)

English	Français	Español	Deutsch	Русский
690 sideline	ligne de touche	línea de toque	Seitenlinie	боковая линия поля (bokovaya liniya polya)
691 sideline throw-in	remise en jeu de la ligne de touche	saque de banda	Einwurf von der Seitenlinie	введение мяча из-за боковой линии (vvedeniye myacha iz-za bokovoy linii)
692 signalling of player fouling	désignation du joueur fautif	indicación del infractor	Anzeige des Foulspielers	сигнал, обозначающий фол (signal, oboznachayushchiy fol)
693 sink a basket	panier réussi	anotación	einen Korb erzielen	успешный бросок (uspeshniy brosok)
694 slam dunk	lancer coulé violent	enceste muy brusco	Stoss nach unten	сильный бросок в корзину сверху (sil'niy brosok v korzinu sverhu)
695 sloughing defence	défense restreinte	defensa floja	abwerfende Verteidigung	пассивная защита (passivnaya zashchita)
696 spin dribble	dribble en vrille	dribleo con efecto	Drehdribbling	кручёное ведение мяча (kruchyonoye vedeniye myacha)
697 spin on the ball	effet du ballon	efecto al balón	Balldrehung	кручение мяча (krucheniye myacha)
698 start of the game	début de la partie	comienzo del partido	Spielbeginn	начало игры (nachalo igri)
699 starting line-up	formation de départ	formación de salida	Aufstellung bei Spielbeginn	стартовый состав (startoviy sostav)
700 stationary screen	écran fixe	pantalla fija	Sperren im Stand	неподвижный заслон (nepodvizhniy zaslon)
701 statistician	statisticien	estadístico	Statistiker	статистик (statistik)
702 statistics	statistiques	estadística	Statistik	статистика (statistika)
703 steal the ball	subtiliser le ballon	arrebatar el balón	den Ball wegschnappen	отобрать мяч (otobrat' myach)
704 stop	arrêt	parón	Abstoppen	остановка (ostanovka)
705 stop the clock	arrêter le chronomètre	parar el cronómetro	die Uhr stoppen	остановить секундомер (ostanovit' sekundomer)
706 stoppage of play	arrêt du jeu	tiempo muerto	Spielunterbrechung	остановка игры (ostanovka igri)

	Basketball	Basket-ball	Baloncesto	Basketball	Баскетбол
707	streak shooter	shooteur éclair	tirador relámpago	Blitzkorbwerfer	непостоянно попадающий игрок (nepostoyanno popadayushchiy igrok)
708	strong side	côté fort	lado fuerte	starke Seite	сильная сторона (sil'naya storona)
709	stuff shot	lancer coulé	enceste brusco	Steckwurf	бросок сверху (brosok sverhu)
710	substitute player	remplaçant	suplente	Auswechselspieler	запасной игрок (zapasnoy igrok)
711	substitution	remplacement	cambio	Wechsel	замена (zamena)
712	successful basket	panier réussi	canasta anotada	erfolgreicher Korb	попадание (popadaniye)
713	successful free throw	lancer franc réussi	tiro libre convertido	erfolgreicher Freiwurf	успешный штрафной бросок (uspeshniy shtrafnoy brosok)
714	support official	officiel de soutien	oficial auxiliar	Hilfsfunktionär	помощник судей (pomoshchnik sudey)
715	switching	permutation	permutación	Wechsel	перемена опекаемых (peremena opekayemih)
716	takeoff foot	pied d'appel	pierna de impulso	Sprungbein	нога отскока (noga otskoka)
717	talk on defence	communication entre joueurs défensifs	comunicación entre la defensa	Verteidigungsgespräch zwischen den Spielern	разговор на защите (razgovor na zashchite)
718	tap	taper	palmear la pelota	zutippen	направить мяч (napravit' myach)
719	team	équipe	equipo	Mannschaft	команда (komanda)
720	team bench	banc de l'équipe	banco del equipo	Mannschaftsbank	скамья для команды (skam'ya dlya komandi)
721	team captain	capitaine d'équipe	capitán del equipo	Mannschaftsführer	капитан команды (kapitan komandi)
722	team game	jeu d'équipe	juego de equipo	Mannschaftsspiel	командная игра (komandnaya igra)
723	team line-up	disposition des joueurs sur le terrain	colocación de los jugadores en la pista	Spieleraufstellung	расстановка игроков (rasstanovka igrokov)
724	team list	liste des joueurs inscrits	lista de los jugadores inscriptos	Anschreibebogen	список команды (spisok komandi)

English	Français	Español	Deutsch	Русский
725 team roster	composition de l'équipe	composición del equipo	Mannschaftsaufstellung	состав команды (sostav komandi)
726 technical foul	faute technique	falta técnica	technisches Foul	технический фол (tehnicheskiy fol)
727 ten-second line	ligne de centre	línea central	Mittellinie	центральная линия (tsentral'naya liniya)
728 ten-second rule	règle des 10 secondes	regla de los 10 segundos	10-Sekunden-Regel	правило десяти секунд (pravilo desyati sekund)
729 thirty-second clock operator	opérateur de l'appareil des trente secondes	operador del marcador de 30 segundos	30-Sekunden-Zeitnehmer	секундометрист тридцатисекундного времени (sekundometrist tridtsatisekundnovo vremeni)
730 thirty-second rule	règle des 30 secondes	regla de los 30 segundos	30-Sekunden-Regel	правило тридцати секунд (pravilo tridtsati sekund)
731 three-for-two rule	règle de trois pour deux	regla de tres por dos	drei-für-zwei-Regel	правило три на два (pravilo tri na dva)
732 three-point play	jeu de trois points	jugada de tres puntos	drei-Punkten-Spiel	штрафной бросок после успешного броска (shtrafnoy brosok posle uspeshnovo broska)
733 three-second area	zone des trois secondes	zona de los tres segundos	drei-Sekunden-Zone	трехсекундная зона (tryohsekundnaya zona)
734 three-second rule	règle des trois secondes	regla de los tres segundos	drei-Sekunden-Regel	правило трех секунд (pravilo tryoh sekund)
735 throw-in	remise en jeu	puesta en juego	Einwurf	вбрасывание (vbrasivaniye)
736 tie score	égalité des points	tanteo empatado	Gleichstand	равный счет (ravniy schot)
737 tiebreaker for team standings	procédé subsidiaire pour classement d'équipe	desempate de puestos	"Tiebreaker" für Mannschaftsresultate	спорный матч для команд с равным счетом (sporniy match dlya komand s ravnim schyotom)
English	**Français**	**Español**	**Deutsch**	**Русский**

	Basketball	Basket-ball	Baloncesto	Basketball	Баскетбол
738	tight man-to-man	marquage agressif	marcaje hombre a hombre severo	aggressive Manndeckung	плотная защита "игрок в игрока" (plotnaya zashchita "igrok v igroka")
739	time in	reprise du temps de jeu	reanudación del juego	Wiederaufnahme der Spielzeit	возобновление игры (vozobnovleniye igri)
740	time limit for free throw	délai de lancer franc	plazo para el tiro libre	Zeit für Freiwurf	время, выделенное для штрафного броска (vremya, videlennoye dlya shtrafnovo broska)
741	time limit for injury	délai accordé pour blessure	tiempo concedido por lesiones	Zeitzuschuss wegen Verletzung	время, данное на травму (vremya, dannoye na travmu)
742	time limit for substitution	durée du remplacement	plazo para sustitución	Dauer des Spielerwech-sels	время, данное на замену (vremya, dannoye na zamenu)
743	time out	temps mort	tiempo muerto	Auszeit	минутный перерыв (minutniy pereriv)
744	time-out clock	chronomètre des temps morts	cronómetro de los tiempos muertos	Auszeituhr	секундомер минутного перерыва (sekundomer minutnovo pereriva)
745	time-out request	demande de temps mort	solicitud de tiempo muerto	die Auszeit verlangen	просьба о минутном перерыве (pros'ba o minutnom pererive)
746	timekeeper; timer	chronométreur	cronometrador	Zeitnehmer	секундометрист (sekundometrist)
747	tip	taper	palmear	tippen	добить (dobit')
748	tip in (to)	taper le ballon dans le panier	tirar la pelota en la cesta	in den Korb tippen	добить мяч в корзину (dobit' myach v korzinu)
749	tip-in	lancer tapé	acierto	Zutippen	добивание (dobivaniye)
750	toss for baskets (coin toss)	tirage au sort des paniers	sorteo de las cestas	die Korbwahl auslosen	жеребьёвка на корзины (zhereb'yovka na korzini)
751	touch the free-throw line	toucher la ligne de lancer franc	pisar la línea de tiros libres	die Freiwurflinie berühren	касание линии штрафного броска (kasaniye linii shtrafnovo broska)

English	Français	Español	Deutsch	Русский
752 trail official	arbitre de terrain central	árbitro del centro del campo	Schiedsrichter im Mittelfeld	судья центрального поля идущий сзади (sud'ya tsentral'novo polya idushchiy szadi)
753 trailer	à la remorque	zaguero	nachkommender Spieler	игрок, преследующий мяч (igrok, presleduyushchiy myach)
754 trajectory of the ball	trajectoire du ballon	trayectoria del balón	Flugbahn des Balls	траектория полета мяча (trayektoriya polyota myacha)
755 travelling	marcher	marchar	Schrittfehler	пробежка (probezhka)
756 turn-around jump shot	lancer en vrille	tiro a media vuelta con salto	Drehschuss	бросок в прыжке с поворотом (brosok v prizhke s povorotom)
757 turnover	renversement du jeu	cambio de posesión	Wende im Spielverlauf	потеря мяча (poterya myacha)
758 two free throws	deux lancers francs	dos tiros libres	Zwei Freiwürfe	два штрафных броска (dva shtrafnih broska)
759 two-hand bounce pass	passe à deux mains par bond du ballon	pase de rebote con dos manos	beidhändiger Bodenpass	передача двумя руками отскоком (peredacha dvumya rukami otskokom)
760 two-hand overhead shot	lancer à deux mains par-dessus la tête	tiro por encima de la cabeza con dos manos	beidhändiger Überkopfwurf	бросок двумя руками из-за головы (brosok dvumya rukami iz-za golovi)
761 two-hand pass	passe à deux mains	pase con dos manos	beidhändiger Pass	передача двумя руками (peredacha dvumya rukami)
762 two-hand shot	lancer à deux mains	tiro con las dos manos	Beidhandwurf	бросок двумя руками (brosok dvumya rukami)
763 umpire	aide-arbitre	árbitro auxiliar	zweiter Schiedsrichter	судья (sud'ya)
764 underhand shot	lancer par-dessous	tiro por abajo	Wurf von unten	бросок снизу (brosok snizu)
765 unguarded player	joueur démarqué	jugador desmarcado	freistehender Spieler	неопекаемый игрок (neopekayemiy igrok)
766 unsportsmanlike conduct	conduite antisportive	conducta antideportiva	unsportliches Verhalten	неспортивное поведение (nesportivnoye povedeniye)
767 violation	violation	infracción	Regelverletzung	нарушение (narusheniye)

	Basketball	**Basket-ball**	**Baloncesto**	**Basketball**	**Баскетбол**
768	walking violation	marcher	infracción contra la regla de pasos	Schrittfehler	пробежка (probezhka)
769	warm-up drill	exercice d'échauffement	ejercicios de precalentamiento	Aufwärmübung	разминочные упражнения (razminochniye uprazhneniya)
770	weak side	côté faible	lado flojo.	schwache Seite	слабая сторона (slabaya storona)
771	whistle	sifflet	silbato	Pfeifen	свисток (svistok)
772	win by forfeit	gagner par forfait	ganar por ausencia del equipo contrario	das Spiel nach Strafpunkten gewinnen	выиграть из-за неявки противника (viigrat' iz-za neyavki protivnika)
773	wing attack	attaque par l'aile	ataque por el ala	Flügelangriff	атака по краю (ataka po krayu)
774	zone	zone	zona	Zone	зона (zona)
775	zone defence	défense de zone	defensa de zona	Zonenverteidigung	зонная защита (zonnaya zashchita)

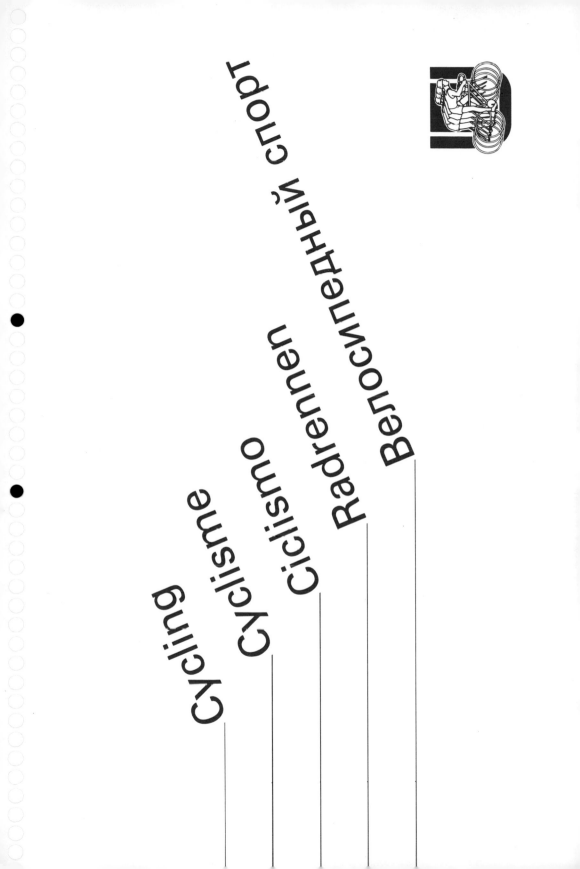

Cycling

Cyclisme

Ciclismo

Radrennen

Велосипедный спорт

	Cycling	Cyclisme	Ciclismo	Radrennen	Велосипедный спорт
776	adjustable wrench	clef à molette	llave inglesa	Radschlüssel	разводной ключ (razvodnoy klyuch)
777	ankle sock	socquette	calcetines	Söckchen	носок (nosok)
778	ankling	jeu de cheville	pedalear	Pedalarbeit	работа педалями (rabota pedalyami)
779	approval of a record	homologation d'un record	homologación de un récord	einen Rekord homologisieren	утверждение рекорда (utverzhdeniye rekorda)
780	armband	brassard	brazalete	Armbinde	нарукавная нашивка (narukavnaya nashivka)
781	assistance between riders	aide entre coureurs	ayuda entre corredores	Hilfe unter den Fahrern	взаимопомощь велосипедистов (vzaimopomoshch' velosipedistov)
782	attack	attaquer	atacar	angreifen	атаковать (atakovat')
783	attack from the front	attaquer en tête	ataque delantero	an der Spitze angreifen	атака из головной группы (ataka iz golovnoy gruppi)
784	attack from the rear	attaque par derrière	ataque desde atrás	Angriff von hinten	атака сзади (ataka szadi)
785	authorized follower	suiveur autorisé	seguidor autorizado	Begleiter	уполномоченный сопровождающий (upolnomochenniy soprovozhdayushchiy)
786	axle	axe	eje	Achse	ось (os')
787	back straight; back stretch	ligne opposée	línea de contrameta	Gegengerade	противоположная прямая (protivopolozhnaya pryamaya)
788	back wheel	roue arrière	rueda trasera	Hinterrad	заднее колесо (zadneye koleso)
789	backing up	marche arrière	marcha atrás	Rückwärtsgang	езда назад (yezda nazad)
790	ball bearing	bille de roulement	bola	Radlager	шарикоподшипник (sharikopodshipnik)
791	banking of the track	inclinaison de la piste	inclinación de la pista	Neigung der Piste	угол наклона трека (ugol naklona treka)
792	be in form	être en forme	estar preparado	in Form sein	быть в форме (bit' v forme)
793	bearing	palier	cojinete de bolas	Kugellager	подшипник (podshipnik)

	English	Français	Español	Deutsch	Русский
794	bell	cloche	campana	Glocke	колокол (kolokol)
795	bell ringer	préposé à la cloche	encargado de la campana	Glöckner	судья у колокола (sud'ya u kolokola)
796	bend	virage	viraje	Wende	вираж (virazh)
797	bend judge	juge au virage	juez de vuelta	Wendepunktrichter	судья на вираже/повороте (sud'ya na virazhe/povorote)
798	bicycle	bicyclette	bicicleta	Rennrad	велосипед (velosiped)
799	bicycle accessories	accessoires de la bicyclette	accesorios de la bicicleta	Radzubehör	инструменты и запчасти велосипеда (instrumenti i zapchasti velosipeda)
800	bicycle track	vélodrome	velódromo	Radrennbahn	велотрек (velotrek)
801	bicyclist	cycliste	ciclista	Rennfahrer	велосипедист (velosipedist)
802	block an opponent	gêner l'adversaire	molestar al adversario	den Gegner behindern	загородить путь соперника (zagorodit' put' sopernika)
803	blocking	tassage	obstrucción	Behinderung	заграждение пути (zagrazhdeniye puti)
804	blow out	éclater	reventar	platzen	спуститься/о шине/ (spustitsa / o shine/)
805	blue line	ligne de mensuration	línea de medición	Abstandlinie	голубая линия (golubaya liniya)
806	board man	ardoisier	anotador	Fahrbeobachter	гонщик на треке (gonshchik na treke)
807	bolt	boulon	perno	Bolzen	болт (bolt)
808	bordure	bordure	bordillo	Pisteneinfassung	эшелон (eshelon)
809	bottom bracket axle	axe de manivelle	eje de la manivela	Achse der Kurbel	ось шатуна (os' shatuna)
810	box in a rider	enfermer un cycliste	cerrar a un corredor	einen Fahrer in die Zange nehmen	зажать велосипедиста (zazhat' velosipedista)
811	box spanner	clef à pipe	llave de pipa	Steckschlüssel	гаечный ключ (gayechniy klyuch)
812	bracket	braquet	sistema de propulsión	Kettenrad	место опоры шатуна (mesto opori shatuna)
813	brake	frein	freno	Bremse	тормоз (tormoz)
	English	**Français**	**Español**	**Deutsch**	**Русский**

	Cycling	Cyclisme	Ciclismo	Radrennen	Велосипедный спорт
814	brake (to)	freiner	frenar	bremsen	затормозить (zatormozit')
815	brake block	patin de frein	zapata de freno	Bremsbelag	тормозная колодка (tormoznaya kolodka)
816	brake hoods	poignée de frein	empuñadura de freno	Bremsgriff	предохраняющие покрышки на тормозных рычагах (predohranyayushchiye pokrishki na tormoznih richagah)
817	braking	freinage	frenaje	Bremsen	торможение (tormozheniye)
818	breach	infraction	infracción	Regelverletzung	нарушение правил (narusheniye pravil)
819	break away	échapper, s'	escaparse	ausreissen	оторваться (otorvatsa)
820	break down	accident mécanique	accidente mecánico	mechanischer Defekt	поломка (polomka)
821	breakaway	échappée	escapada	Ausreissversuch	отрыв (otriv)
822	breakaway rider	coureur échappé	corredor escapado	Ausreisser	оторвавшийся велосипедист (otorvavshiysya velosipedist)
823	broken chain	bris de chaîne	cadena rota	Kettenbruch	сломанная цепь (slomannaya tsep')
824	broken frame	bris du cadre	cuadro roto	Rahmenbruch	сломанная рама (slomannaya rama)
825	bunch	peloton	pelotón	Feld	группа (gruppa)
826	bunch finish	arrivée en peloton	llegada en pelotón	Massenankunft	групповой финиш (gruppovoy finish)
827	burst	éclater	reventar	platzen	проколоться/о шине/ (prokolotsa/o shine/)
828	burst of speed	emballage	sprint	Spurt	разрыв (razriv)
829	call of the riders	appel des coureurs	llamada a los corredores	Startaufruf	сбор велосипедистов (sbor velosipedistov)
830	cap	casquette	gorra	Mütze	велошапочка (veloshapochka)
831	caravan	caravane	caravana	Konvoi	сопровождающие (soprovozhdayushchiye)

English	Français	Español	Deutsch	Русский
832 category of riders	catégorie de coureurs	categoría de corredores	Klasseneinteilung	категория велосипедистов (kategoriya velosipedistov)
833 chain	chaîne	cadena	Kette	цепь (tsep')
834 chainring; chainwheel	plateau	plato	Kettenblatt	передняя шестерня (perednyaya shesternya)
835 chainset	pédalier	sistema de propulsión	Kurbellager	каретка (karetka)
836 change gear	changer de vitesse	cambiar de velocidad	Tempowechsel	переключить передачу (pereklyuchit' peredachu)
837 change of cycle	changement de vélo	cambio de bicicleta	Rennradwechsel	замена велосипеда (zamena velosipeda)
838 change pace	changer de cadence	cambiar de ritmo	Tempowechsel	переменить ритм (peremenit' ritm)
839 chase	chasse	persecución	Jagd	преследование (presledovaniye)
840 chin strap	jugulaire	correa del casco	Riemen der Sturzkappe	ремешок шлема (remeshok shlema)
841 circuit	circuit	circuito	Strecke	кольцо (kol'tso)
842 classification	classement	clasificación	Wertung	классификация (klassifikatsiya)
843 close finish	arrivée serrée	llegada reñida	knapper Zieleinlauf	близкий финиш (blizkiy finish)
844 coach	entraîneur	entrenador	Trainer	тренер (trener)
845 college of commissaries	collège des commissaires	colegio de comisarios	Kampfrichterkollegium	судейская коллегия (sudeyskaya kollegiya)
846 commissaries' car	voiture des commissaires	vehículo de comisarios	Rennleitungswagen	автомобиль судейской коллегии (avtomobil' sudeyskoy kollegii)
847 commissary	commissaire	juez de carrera	Wettkampfrichter	судья (sud'ya)
848 compact bunch	peloton groupé	pelotón compacto	geschlossenes Feld	плотная группа (plotnaya gruppa)
849 competition committee	comité de course	comité de competición	Wettfahrausschuss	комитет соревнования (komitet sorevnovaniya)
850 competitors' compound	quartier des coureurs	alojamiento de los competidores	Fahrerlager	сборный пункт участников (sborniy punkt uchastnikov)
English	**Français**	**Español**	**Deutsch**	**Русский**

	Cycling	Cyclisme	Ciclismo	Radrennen	Велосипедный спорт
851	contest	épreuve	prueba	Wettbewerb	состязание (sostyazaniye)
852	control post; control station	poste de contrôle	puesto de control	Kontrollpfosten	контрольный пункт (kontrol'niy punkt)
853	controllers of the race	direction de la course	dirección de la carrera	Rennleitung	руководители гонки (rukovoditeli gonki)
854	convoy	caravane	caravana	Konvoi	сопровождение (soprovozhdeniye)
855	corner judge	commissaire de virage	juez de curva	Kurvenbeobachter	судья на вираже (sud'ya na virazhe)
856	course	parcours	recorrido	Strecke	маршрут (marshrut)
857	covered track	piste couverte	pista cubierta	überdachte Bahn	закрытый трек (zakritiy trek)
858	crank	manivelle	biela	Kurbel	шатун (shatun)
859	crank axle	axe de pédalier	eje "pedalier"	Pedalachse	ось шатуна (os' shatuna)
860	curve	virage	curva	Kurve	вираж (virazh)
861	cycle stadium	vélodrome	velódromo	Radrennbahn	велодром (velodrom)
862	cycling	cyclisme	ciclismo	Radsport	велосипедный спорт (velosipedniy sport)
863	cycling shoes	chaussures cyclistes	zapatillas de ciclista	Radrennschuhe	велосипедные туфли (velosipedniye tufli)
864	cyclist	cycliste	ciclista	Radfahrer	велосипедист; велогонщик (velosipedist; velogonshchik)
865	dead heat	course nulle	empate	totes Rennen	нулевой заезд (nulevoy zayezd)
866	degree of banking	inclinaison d'un virage	inclinación en el viraje	Kurvenneigung	угол наклона виража (ugol naklona virazha)
867	derailleur	dérailleur	cambio tipo derailleur	Kettenschaltung	переключатель передач (pereklyuchatel' peredach)
868	descent	descente	bajada	Gefälle	спуск (spusk)
869	disqualification of a team	mise hors-course d'une équipe	descalificación de un equipo	Disqualifikation einer Mannschaft	дисквалификация команды (diskvalifikatsiya komandi)

English	Français	Español	Deutsch	Русский
870 disqualified	hors de course	descalificado	aus dem Rennen disqualifiziert	дисквалифицированный (diskvalifitsirovanniy)
871 dope control	contrôle de dopage	control antidoping	Antidopingkontrolle	антидопинговый контроль (antidopingoviy kontrol')
872 doping	dopage	doping	Doping	допинг (doping)
873 draw by lots	tirage au sort	sorteo	Losen	жеребьёвка (zhereb'yovka)
874 drop an opponent	lâcher un adversaire	despegarse de un adversario	einen Gegner abhängen	оставить позади соперника (ostavit' pozadi sopernika)
875 drop behind	décoller	quedarse atrás	sich lösen	отстать (otstat')
876 dropped rider	coureur lâché	pedalista rezagado	Nachzügler	отставший гонщик (otstavshiy gonshchik)
877 echelon	éventail	abanico	gestaffelte Formation	эшелон (eshelon)
878 eliminating heat	épreuve éliminatoire	carrera eliminatoria	Ausscheidungsrennen	предварительный заезд (predvaritel'niy zayezd)
879 entry	engagement	inscripción	Meldung	вход в соревнование (vhod v sorevnovaniye)
880 event	épreuve	prueba	Wettbewerb	вид соревнования (vid sorevnovaniya)
881 executive committee	comité directeur	comité directivo	Wettkampfleitung	руководящий комитет (rukovodyashchiy komitet)
882 fall	chute	caída	Sturz	падение (padeniye)
883 false start	faux départ	salida falsa	Fehlstart	фальстарт (fal'start)
884 feeding	ravitaillement	avituallamiento	Verpflegung	питание (pitaniye)
885 feeding station	poste de ravitaillement	puesto de alimentos	Verpflegungsstelle	пункт питания (punkt pitaniya)
886 feinted attack	feinte de démarrage	simular un arranque	ein Antreten vortäuschen	ложная атака (lozhnaya ataka)
887 final	finale	final	Finale	финал (final)
888 fine	amende	multa	Strafpunkt	штраф (shtraf)
889 finish	arrivée	llegada	Ziel	финиш (finish)
890 finishing control	contrôle des arrivées	control de llegada	Zielkontrolle	контроль финиша (kontrol' finisha)
English	**Français**	**Español**	**Deutsch**	**Русский**

	Cycling	Cyclisme	Ciclismo	Radrennen	Велосипедный спорт
891	finishing judge	juge à l'arrivée	juez de llegada	Zielrichter	судья на финише (sud'ya na finishe)
892	finishing line	ligne d'arrivée	meta	Ziellinie	финишная линия (finishnaya liniya)
893	flat	crevaison	pinchazo	Platzen (Reifen)	спущенная шина (spushchennaya shina)
894	flying start	départ lancé	salida lanzada	fliegender Start	старт с ходу (start s hodu)
895	follow a wheel	coller à la roue	pegarse a la rueda	am Rad kleben	сидеть на колесе у... (sidet' na kolese u...)
896	following car	voiture suiveuse	vehículo acompañante	Begleitfahrzeug	сопровождающая машина (soprovozhdayushchaya mashina)
897	following van	camionnette suiveuse	vehículo seguidor	Begleitfahrzeug	сопровождающий автобус (soprovozhdayushchiy avtobus)
898	fork	fourche	horquilla	Gabel	вилка (vilka)
899	fork crown	tête de fourche	cabeza de horquilla	Gabelkopf	верхний конец вилки (verhniy konets vilki)
900	frame	cadre	cuadro	Rahmen	рама (rama)
901	frame break	bris du cadre	rotura del cuadro	Rahmenbruch	поломка рамы (polomka rami)
902	frame number	plaque de cadre	número de cuadro	Fahrradnummertafel	номер на раме (nomer na rame)
903	freewheel	faire roue libre	hacer rueda libre	rollen lassen	катиться свободно (katitsa svobodno)
904	front wheel	roue avant	rueda delantera	Vorderrad	переднее колесо (peredneye koleso)
905	gear	développement	velocidades	Schaltung	скорость (skorost')
906	gear lever	changeur de vitesse	palanca de cambio	Gangschaltung	рычаг переключения передач (richag pereklyucheniya peredach)
907	give the start	donner le départ	dar la salida	das Startzeichen geben	дать знак на старт (dat' znak na start)

English	Français	Español	Deutsch	Русский
908 green flag	drapeau vert	bandera verde	grüne Fahne	зеленый флажок (zelyoniy flazhok)
909 green pennant	fanion vert	banderín verde	grüne Fahne	зеленый вымпел (zelyoniy vimpel)
910 half-lap	demi-tour	media vuelta	halbe Runde	половина круга (polovina kruga)
911 half-lap timing	chronométrage par demi-tour	cronometraje cada media vuelta	Zwischenzeit nach halber Bahnlänge	измерение времени на половине круга (izmereniye vremeni na polovine kruga)
912 handlebar	guidon	manillar	Lenker	руль (rul')
913 handlebar extension	potence	tija de la horquilla	Vorbau des Rennlenkers	балка, поддерживающая руль (balka, podderzhivayushchaya rul')
914 handlebar grip	poignée du guidon	empuñadura del manillar	Handgriff	ручка руля (ruchka rulya)
915 handlebar tape	guidoline	cinta de manillar	Lenkerband	изоляция на руле (izolyatsiya na rule)
916 head wind	vent de face	viento en contra	Gegenwind	встречный ветер (vstrechniy veter)
917 heat	belle	serie eliminatoria; buena	Entscheidungsrennen	заезд; гит (zayezd; git)
918 heat winner	tête de série	ganador de serie	Gruppenführer	победитель в заезде (pobeditel' v zayezde)
919 helmet	casque	casco protector	Sturzkappe	шлем (shlem)
920 hill	montée	ascenso	Steigung	холм (holm)
921 home straight; home stretch	ligne droite	recta de llegada	Zielgerade	финишная прямая (finishnaya pryamaya)
922 "honk"	pédaler en danseuse	pedalear parado	in Wiegetritt fahren	крутить педали стоя (krutit' pedali stoya)
923 hub	moyeu	cubo de la rueda	Nabe	ступица (stupitsa)
924 individual pursuit	poursuite individuelle	persecución individual	Einzelverfolgungsrennen	индивидуальное преследование (individual'noye presledovaniye)

	Cycling	Cyclisme	Ciclismo	Radrennen	Велосипедный спорт
925	individual race	course individuelle	carrera individual	Einzelfahren	индивидуальная гонка (individual'naya gonka)
926	individual road event	épreuve individuelle sur route	prueba individual sobre carretera	Einzelstrassenfahren	индивидуальное шоссейное соревнование (individual'noye shosseynoye sorevnovaniye)
927	individual road race	course individuelle sur route	prueba individual en carretera	Strasseneinzelfahren	индивидуальная шоссейная гонка (individual'naya shosseynaya gonka)
928	individual start	départ individuel	salida individual	Einzelstart	раздельный старт (razdel'niy start)
929	individual track event	épreuve individuelle sur piste	prueba individual sobre pista	Einzelfahren auf der Bahn	индивидуальное соревнование на треке (individual'noye sorevnovaniye na treke)
930	indoor track	piste couverte	pista cubierta	überdachte Bahn	закрытый трек (zakritiy trek)
931	indoor track cycling	cyclisme sur piste couverte	ciclismo en velódromo cubierto	Bahnrennen auf überdachten Bahnen	езда на велосипеде по закрытому треку (yezda na velosipede po zakritomu treku)
932	information board	tableau	pizarra	Tafel	доска объявлений (doska obyavleniy)
933	infringement	infraction	infracción	Regelverletzung	нарушение (narusheniye)
934	injury	accident corporel	lesión	Verletzung	травма (travma)
935	inner tube	chambre à air	cámara de aire	Schlauch	камера шины (kamera shini)
936	inside edge of the track	corde	borde interior de la pista	innerer Rand der Bahn	внутренняя бровка дорожки (vnutrennyaya brovka dorozhki)
937	International Cycling Union (U.C.I.)	Union Cycliste Internationale (U.C.I.)	Unión Ciclista Internacional (U.C.I.)	Internationale Radfahrer-Union (I.R.U.)	Международная федерация велосипедистов/УСИ/ (mezhdunarodnaya federatsiya velosipedistov/USI/)
938	jersey	maillot	jersey	Trikot	майка (mayka)

English	Français	Español	Deutsch	Русский
939 jersey number	dossard	dorsal (número)	Startnummer	номер на майке (nomer na mayke)
940 jury of appeal	jury d'appel	jurado de apelación	Berufungsgericht	апелляционное жюри (apellyatsionnoye zhyuri)
941 kilometer time trial	kilomètre contre la montre	kilómetro contra reloj	ein-km Zeitfahren	километровый заезд (kilometroviy zayezd)
942 lap	tour	vuelta	Runde	круг (krug)
943 lap counter	compteur de tours	juez de las vueltas	Rundenzähler	счетчик кругов (schyotchik krugov)
944 lap in front	tour d'avance	vuelta de ventaja	Vorgaberunde	круг спереди (krug speredi)
945 lap of the track	tour de piste	vuelta a la pista	Runde	круг трека (krug treka)
946 launching an attack	démarrage	arrancada	antreten	порыв (poriv)
947 lead	mener	llevar	führen	лидировать (lidirovat')
948 leader	leader	puntero	der Führende Fahrer	лидер (lider)
949 leading group	peloton de tête	grupo de fugados	Spitzengruppe	ведущая группа (vedushchaya gruppa)
950 leading rider	coureur de tête	corredor delantero	Fahrer an der Spitze	лидирующий гонщик (lidiruyushchiy gonshchik)
951 leave a gap	faire le trou	dejar un hueco	eine Lücke machen	оставить пробел (ostavit' probel)
952 licence	licence	licencia	Lizenz	лицензия (litsenziya)
953 licence check	vérification des licences	comprobación de licencias	Überprüfung der Lizenzen	проверка лицензии (proverka litsenzii)
954 link of a chain	maillon de chaîne	eslabón de cadena	Kettenglied	звено цепи (zveno tsepi)
955 "locomotive"	"locomotive"	"locomotoras"	"Lokomotive"	"локомотив" ("lokomotiv")
956 machine	machine	máquina	Maschine	велосипед (velosiped)
957 main bunch	gros du peloton	grueso del pelotón	Hauptfeld	главная группа (glavnaya gruppa)
958 make an echelon	faire la bordure	correr en abanico	eine Gestaffelte Formation machen	сформировать эшелон (sformirovat' eshelon)
English	**Français**	**Español**	**Deutsch**	**Русский**

	Cycling	Cyclisme	Ciclismo	Radrennen	Велосипедный спорт
959	mark the course	jalonner le parcours	trazar el recorrido	die Strecke markieren	обозначить трассу (oboznachit' trassu)
960	mass crash	chute collective	caída colectiva	Massensturz	групповое падение (gruppovoye padeniye)
961	mass start	départ en groupe	salida en grupo	Massenstart	групповой старт (gruppovoy start)
962	match	manche	etapa del recorrido	Rennen	заезд (zayezd)
963	measurement of the track	mesure de la piste	medida de la pista	Bahnlänge	размер трека (razmer treka)
964	mechanic	mécanicien	mecánico	Mechaniker	механик (mehanik)
965	mechanical	mécanique	mecánico	mechanisch	механический (mehanicheskiy)
966	meet	rencontre	encuentro	Treffen	встреча (vstrecha)
967	middle of the bunch	milieu de peloton	centro del pelotón	Mitte des Feldes	середина группы (seredina gruppi)
968	middle of the track	milieu de piste	centro de pista	Mittelbahn	середина трека (seredina treka)
969	mid-race	mi-course	carrera a medio terminar	halbes Rennen	половина гонки (polovina gonki)
970	milestone	borne kilométrique	mojón kilométrico	Kilometerstein	километровая отметка (kilometrovaya otmetka)
971	mobile hospital	clinicar	clínica ambulante	Arztwagen	передвижной пункт медицинской помощи (peredvizhnoy punkt meditsinskoy pomoshchi)
972	musette	musette de ravitaillement	bolsa de avituallamiento	Proviantbeutel	сумка с питанием (sumka s pitaniyem)
973	neutral lap	tour de neutralisation	vuelta de neutralización	Neutralisationsrunde	нейтральный круг (neytral'niy krug)
974	notice board	tableau d'affichage	tablero de avisos	Anzeigetafel	доска объявлений (doska obyavleniy)
975	nut	écrou	tuerca	Mutter	гайка (gayka)

	English	Français	Español	Deutsch	Русский
976	official	dirigeant	dirigente	Offizieller	официальное лицо (ofitsial'noye litso)
977	official car	voiture officielle	coche oficial	Wagen der Wettkampfleitung	официальный автомобиль (ofitsial'niy avtomobil')
978	officials' car	voiture des commissaires	vehículo de comisarios	Rennleitungswagen	автомобиль судейской коллегии (avtomobil' sudeyskoy kollegii)
979	open-ended spanner	clef plate	llave fija	Flachschlüssel	плоский ключ (ploskiy klyuch)
980	order of arrival	ordre d'arrivée	orden de llegada	Reihenfolge des Zieleinlaufs	порядок прибытия (poryadok pribitiya)
981	outdoor track	piste de plein air	pista al aire libre	offene Bahn	открытый трек (otkritiy trek)
982	overtake	rattraper; doubler	adelantar	überholen	догнать (dognat')
983	overtake on the inside	rattraper ou dépasser par l'intérieur	alcanzar (o: ir hacia adelante) al lado interior	auf der Innenbahn überholen	догнать изнутри (dognat' iznutri)
984	overtake on the outside	rattraper ou doubler à l'extérieur	alcanzar (o: ir hacia adelante) al lado exterior	auf der Aussenbahn überholen	догнать снаружи (dognat' snaruzhi)
985	pace	vélocité	velocidad	Tempo	темп (temp)
986	pass	doubler	adelantar	Überholen	проехать мимо (proyehat' mimo)
987	peak of the saddle	bec de selle	pico del sillín	Sattelspitze	передняя часть седла (perednyaya chast' sedla)
988	pedal	pédale	pedal	Pedal	педаль (pedal')
989	pedal (to)	pédaler	pedalear	treten	педалировать (pedalirovat')
990	pedal out of the saddle	pédaler en danseuse	pedalear parado	im Wiegetritt fahren	крутить педали стоя (krutit' pedali stoya)
991	penalty	pénalité	penalización	Strafe	штраф (shtraf)
992	permanent commission	commission permanente	comisión permanente	Ständige Kommission	постоянная комиссия (postoyannaya komissiya)
993	photo finish	photo-d'arrivée	fotografía de llegada	Zielfoto	фотофиниш (fotofinish)
	English	**Français**	**Español**	**Deutsch**	**Русский**

	Cycling	Cyclisme	Ciclismo	Radrennen	Велосипедный спорт
994	placing	classement	clasificación	Klassement	место занятое (mesto zanyatoye)
995	protest	réclamation	reclamación	Reklamation	протест (protest)
996	pump	pompe	bomba de aire	Pumpe	насос (nasos)
997	puncture	crevaison	pinchazo	Platzen (Reifen)	прокол (prokol)
998	pursuit	poursuite	persecución	Verfolgung	преследование (presledovaniye)
999	pursuit match	match-poursuite	encuentro de persecución	Verfolgungsrennen	заезд преследования (zayezd presledovaniya)
1000	push the big gear	mettre le grand braquet	poner gran desarrollo	heraufschalten	поставить большую передачу (postavit' bol'shuyu peredachu)
1001	pusher	lanceur	auxiliar de salida	Starthelfer	подталкивающий помощник (podtalkivayushchiy pomoshchnik)
1002	qualification	qualification	calificación	Qualifikation	квалификация (kvalifikatsiya)
1003	qualifying heat	série qualificative	carrera de calificación	Qualifikationsrennen	квалификационный заезд (kvalifikatsionniy zayezd)
1004	quick release	ailette	palomilla	Flügelschraube	рычаг на колесе (richag na kolese)
1005	race	course	carrera	Rennen	гонка (gonka)
1006	race director	directeur de course	director de carrera	Rennleiter	руководитель гонки (rukovoditel' gonki)
1007	race officials	officiels des compétitions	oficiales de competición	Offizielle des Rennens	официальные лица гонки (ofitsial'niye litsa gonki)
1008	racing bicycle	vélo de course	bicicleta de carreras	Rennrad	гоночный велосипед (gonochniy velosiped)
1009	racing shorts	cuissard	pantalón corto	Rennhose	гоночные трусы (gonochniye trusi)
1010	radio car	voiture-radio	vehículo radio	Funkwagen	машина с радиопередатчиком (mashina s radioperedatchikom)

	English	Français	Español	Deutsch	Русский
1011	raincoat	imperméable de cyclisme	impermeable de ciclismo	Regenmantel	плащ (plaśñ ch)
1012	ratification of a record	homologation d'un record	homologación de un récord	einen Rekord homologisieren	утверждение рекорда (utverzhdeniye rekorda)
1013	record	record	récord	Rekord	рекорд (rekord)
1014	red flag	drapeau rouge	bandera roja	rote Fahne	красный флажок (krasniy flazhok)
1015	red pennant	fanion rouge	banderín rojo	rote Fahne	красный вымпел (krasniy vimpel)
1016	regulation	réglementaire	reglamentario	regelgemäss	по правилам (po pravilam)
1017	regulations	règlement	reglamento	Regeln	правила (pravila)
1018	relay	relais	relevo	Staffel	эстафета (estafeta)
1019	relegation	déclassement	relegación	Deklassierung	штрафное передвижение в конец группы (shtrafnoye peredvizheniye v konets gruppi)
1020	repechage	repêchage	repesca	Hoffnungslauf	утешительный заезд (uteshitel'niy zayezd)
1021	re-ride	courir à nouveau	volver a correr	wiederholen	повторить заезд (povtorit' zayezd)
1022	result	résultat	resultado	Resultat	результат (rezul'tat)
1023	retirement	abandon	abandono	Aufgabe	выход из гонки (vihod iz gonki)
1024	ride	courir	correr	fahren	ехать (yehat')
1025	rider	coureur	corredor	Fahrer	гонщик (gonshchik)
1026	riders' quarters; team pits	quartier des coureurs	cuartel de corredores	Fahrerlager	помещение для гонщиков (pomeshcheniye dlya gonshchikov)
1027	rim	jante	llanta	Felge	обод (obod)
1028	road	route	carretera	Strasse	дорога (doroga)
1029	road circuit	circuit routier	circuito de carretera	Rennstrecke	дорожное кольцо (dorozhnoye kol'tso)

	Cycling	Cyclisme	Ciclismo	Radrennen	Велосипедный спорт
1030	road cycle	vélo de route	bicicleta de carretera	Strassenrennrad	шоссейный велосипед (shosseyniy velosiped)
1031	road cycling	cyclisme sur route	ciclismo en ruta	Strassenrennsport	езда по шоссе (yezda po shosse)
1032	road jersey; road vest	maillot de route	camiseta de carretera	Strassentrikot; Strassenweste	дорожная майка (dorozhnaya mayka)
1033	road signpost	indicateur de route	indicador de carretera	Richtungsanzeiger	дорожный разметочный столб (dorozhniy razmetochniy stolb)
1034	road team event	épreuve sur route par équipes	prueba por equipos en carretera	Mannschafts-strassenfahren	командная гонка по шоссе (komandnaya gonka po shosse)
1035	road tire	boyau de route	neumático de carretera	Strassenreifen	дорожная шина (dorozhnaya shina)
1036	road-racing cycle	vélo de route	bicicleta de ruta	Strassenrennrad	шоссейный велосипед (shosseyniy velosiped)
1037	roadman	coureur routier	corredor de carretera	Strassenfahrer	гонщик-шоссейник (gonshchik-shosseynik)
1038	roadside repairs	dépannage	reparaciones en el camino	Reparatur	починка велосипеда у краёв дороги (pochinka velosipeda u krayov dorogi)
1039	roadway	chaussée	calzada	Strasse	шоссе (shosse)
1040	roll off (a tire)	déjanter	quitar el neumático	den Reifen von der Felge nehmen	откатить/шину/ (otkatit'/shinu/)
1041	rolling along	enrouler	rodando	aufrollen	катиться (katitsa)
1042	rules	règles	reglamento	Regeln	правила (pravila)
1043	running repairs	dépannage	arreglos mientras el ciclista anda	Reparatur unterwegs	починка на ходу (pochinka na hodu)
1044	saddle	selle	sillín	Sattel	седло (sedlo)
1045	saddle stem	tige de selle	tallo del sillín	Sattelstange	балка, держащая седло (balka, derzhashchaya sedlo)

English	Français	Español	Deutsch	Русский
1046 sag wagon	voiture-balai	coche escoba	Reinigungsfahrzeug	машина для выбывших из гонки велосипедистов (mashina dlya vibivshih iz gonki velosipedistov)
1047 sample	prélèvement	toma de muestras	Vorgabe	антидопинговая проба (antidopingovaya proba)
1048 sanction	pénalité	sanción	Strafe	штраф (shtraf)
1049 screw	vis	tornillo	Schraube	винт (vint)
1050 secretary	secrétaire	secretario	Sekretär	секретарь (sekretar')
1051 seeded competitor	compétiteur classé	clasificado	plazierter Fahrer	классифицированный участник (klassifitsirovanniy uchastnik)
1052 series	série	serie	Vorrennen	серия (seriya)
1053 service van	voiture de service	vehículo de servicio	Servicefahrzeug	автомобиль с ремонтной мастерской (avtomobil' s remontnoy masterskoy)
1054 shellac	gomme laque	goma laca	Shellack	клей; шеллак (kley; shellak)
1055 shoe cleat	cale-pédale	taco	Schuhplatte	шип (ship)
1056 side wind	vent latéral	viento lateral	Seitenwind	боковой ветер (bokovoy veter)
1057 sit in the bunch	coller au peloton	pegarse al pelotón	im Feld bleiben	находиться в группе (nahoditsa v gruppe)
1058 skid; slip	déraper	despistarse	ausrutschen	занос (zanos)
1059 slipstream	sillage	estela	Windschatten	прикрытие от ветра (prikritiye ot vetra)
1060 small tool kit	petit matériel de réparation	estuche de reparación	kleine Reparaturwerkzeuge	комплект маленьких инструментов (komplekt malen'kih instrumentov)
1061 sock	chaussette	calcetín	Socke	носок (nosok)
1062 soigneur	soigneur	cuidador	Betreuer	массажист (massazhist)
1063 spare wheel	roue de rechange	rueda repuesto	Ersatzrad	запасное колесо (zapasnoye koleso)
1064 speed	vitesse	velocidad	Geschwindigkeit	скорость (skorost')
English	**Français**	**Español**	**Deutsch**	**Русский**

Cycling		Cyclisme	Ciclismo	Radrennen	Велосипедный спорт
1065	spill	chute	caída	Sturz	падение (padeniye)
1066	spin	faire le moulinet	pedalear	schnelles Treten	быстро крутить педали (bistro krutit' pedali)
1067	spindle	axe	eje	Achse	ось (os')
1068	split the bunch	secouer le peloton	romper el pelotón	das Feld sprengen	разделить группу (razdelit' gruppu)
1069	spoke	rayon	radio	Speiche	спица (spitsa)
1070	sports manager	directeur sportif	director deportivo	Sportleiter	спортивный руководитель (sportivniy rukovoditel')
1071	sprint	sprint	sprint	Sprint	спринт (sprint)
1072	sprinters' line	ligne des sprinters	línea de los sprinters	Sprintlinie	линия для спринтеров (liniya dlya sprinterov)
1073	sprocket	pignon	piñón	hinterer Zahnkranz	шестерня (shesternya)
1074	standard bicycle	bicyclette standard	bicicleta standard	Standardrad	стандартный велосипед (standartniy velosiped)
1075	standing committee	commission permanente	comisión permanente	ständige Kommission	постоянный комитет (postoyanniy komitet)
1076	standing start	départ arrêté	salida levantado	stehender Start	старт с места (start s mesta)
1077	standing up on the pedals	danseuse	pedalear de pie	Wiegetritt	танцовщица (tantsovshchitsa)
1078	standstill	sur place	parado	Stillstand	сюрпляс (syurplyas)
1079	standstill attempt	tentative de sur place	tentativa de pararse	Stehversuch	попытка сделать остановку (popitka sdelat' ostanovku)
1080	start	départ	salida	Start	старт (start)
1081	start (to)	prendre le départ	arrancar	Starten	стартовать (startovat')
1082	start of the banking	entrée du virage	entrada en el viraje	Kurveneingang	начало виража (nachalo virazha)
1083	start sheet	feuille de départ	hoja de salida	Startliste	стартовый протокол (startoviy protokol)
1084	starter	starter	juez de salida	Starter	стартёр (startyor)

	English	Français	Español	Deutsch	Русский
1085	starting interval	intervalle de départ	intervalo de salida	Startabstand	стартовый интервал (startoviy interval)
1086	starting line	ligne de départ	línea de salida	Startlinie	стартовая линия (startovaya liniya)
1087	starting order	ordre de départ	orden de salida	Startfolge	порядок старта (poryadok starta)
1088	starting pistol	pistolet de starter	pistola de juez de salida	Startpistole	стартовый пистолет (startoviy pistolet)
1089	stayers' line	ligne des stayers	línea de "stayers"	Steherlinie	линия в гонках за мотоциклами (liniya v gonkah za mototsiklami)
1090	stem	potence	tija del sillín	Vorbau des Rennlenkers	балка для седла или руля (balka dlya sedla ili rulya)
1091	stop a rider	arrêter un coureur	parar a un corredor	einen Fahrer anhalten	остановить гонщика (ostanovit' gonshchika)
1092	stoppage of the race	arrêt de la course	paro de la carrera	Abbruch des Rennens	остановка гонки (ostanovka gonki)
1093	suspend	suspendre	suspender	ausschliessen	удалить (udalit')
1094	suspension	suspension	suspensión	Ausschluss	удаление (udaleniye)
1095	switch	changer de position brusquement	desviar	schnell wechseln	резко перестроиться (rezko perestroitsa)
1096	switching	brusque changement de position	desvío	Schnellwechseln	резкая перестройка (rezkaya perestroyka)
1097	tail wind	vent arrière	viento de espalda	Rückenwind	ветер в спину (veter v spinu)
1098	team	équipe	equipo	Mannschaft	команда (komanda)
1099	team favorite	protégé	favorito	Schützling	любимец команды (lyubimets komandi)
1100	team pursuit	poursuite par équipes	persecución por equipos	Mannschafts-verfolgungsrennen	командная гонка преследования (komandnaya gonka presledovaniya)
1101	team race	course par équipes	carrera por equipos	Mannschaftsfahren	командная гонка (komandnaya gonka)
	English	**Français**	**Español**	**Deutsch**	**Русский**

	Cycling	Cyclisme	Ciclismo	Radrennen	Велосипедный спорт
1102	team road race	course sur route par équipes	prueba en carretera por equipos	Strassenmann- schaftsrennen	командная гонка на шоссе (komandnaya gonka na shosse)
1103	technical commission	commission technique	comisión técnica	technische Kommission	техническая комиссия (tehnicheskaya komissiya)
1104	tighten	serrer	apretar	anziehen	закрепить (zakrepit')
1105	time limit for an appeal	délai d'appel	plazo de reclamación	Zeitvorgabe für Reklamation	ограничение времени апелляции (ogranicheniye vremeni apellyatsii)
1106	time trial	contre la montre	prueba contra reloj	Zeitfahren	гонка на время (gonka na vremya)
1107	time-trial race	course contre la montre	carrera contra el reloj	Zeitfahren	гонка на время (gonka na vremya)
1108	timekeeper	chronométreur	cronometrador	Zeitnehmer	хронометрист (hronometrist)
1109	timekeeping	chronométrage	cronometraje	Zeitnehmen	хронометраж (hronometrazh)
1110	timing	chronométrage	cronometraje	Zeitnehmen	хронометраж (hronometrazh)
1111	title holder	titulaire	titular	Titelverteidiger	спортсмен со званием (sportsmen so zvaniyem)
1112	toe clip	cale-pied	calapié	Zeheplatte	туклипс (tuklips)
1113	toe strap	courroie de cale-pied	correa de calapié	Pedalriemen	ремень туклипса (remen' tuklipsa)
1114	tooth	dent	diente	Zahn	зуб (zub)
1115	track	piste	pista	Bahn	трек (trek)
1116	track border	bord de la piste	borde de la pista	Pistenrand	граница трека (granitsa treka)
1117	track center	intérieur de la piste	interior de la pista	Innenraum	центр трека (tsentr treka)
1118	track code	code de la piste	código de la pista	Pistenordnung	правила езды по треку (pravila yezdi po treku)
1119	track cycle	vélo de piste	bicicleta de pista	Bahnrennrad	трековый велосипед (trekoviy velosiped)
1120	track cycling	cyclisme sur piste	ciclismo en pista	Bahnrennsport	езда по треку (yezda po treku)

	English	Français	Español	Deutsch	Русский
1121	track director	directeur de piste	director de pista	Rennleiter	руководитель трека (rukovoditel' treka)
1122	track jersey	maillot de piste	jersey de pista	Bahntrikot	трековая майка (trekovaya mayka)
1123	track mitt	gant cycliste	guante de ciclista	Bremshandschuh	велоперчатки (veloperchatki)
1124	track race	course sur piste	carrera en pista	Bahnrennen	гонка на треке (gonka na treke)
1125	track racer	pistard	corredor de pista	Bahnfahrer	гонщик-трековик (gonshchik-trekovik)
1126	track racing cycle	vélo de piste	bicicleta de pista	Bahnrennrad	трековый велосипед (trekoviy velosiped)
1127	track rider	coureur sur piste	corredor de pista	Bahnfahrer	гонщик на треке (gonshchik na treke)
1128	track team event	épreuve sur piste par équipes	prueba sobre pista por equipos	Mannschaftsfahren auf der Bahn	командная гонка на треке (komandnaya gonka na treke)
1129	track tire	boyau de piste	neumático de pista	Pistenreifen	трековая однотрубка (trekovaya odnotrubka)
1130	track vest	maillot de piste	maillot de pista	Bahntrikot	велорубашка (velorubashka)
1131	traffic regulations	code de la route	código de carretera	Strassenordnung	правила движения (pravila dvizheniya)
1132	training tire	boyau d'entraînement	neumático de entrenamiento	Trainingsreifen	тренировочная однотрубка (trenirovochnaya odnotrubka)
1133	tube	tube	tubo	Schlauch	камера (kamera)
1134	tubular tire	boyau	tubular	Schlauch	однотрубка (odnotrubka)
1135	tubular tire cement	colle à boyau	pegamento para neumático	Schlauchkleber	клей для однотрубки (kley dlya odnotrubki)
1136	turn judge	juge au virage	juez de vuelta	Wendepunktrichter	судья на повороте (sud'ya na povorote)
1137	twiddle	mouliner	pedalear	treten	быстро крутить педалями (bistro krutit' pedalyami)
1138	two-hundred-meter line	ligne des 200 mètres	línea de 200 metros	zweihundert-m-Linie	двестиметровая линия (dvestimetrovaya liniya)
	English	**Français**	**Español**	**Deutsch**	**Русский**

	Cycling	Cyclisme	Ciclismo	Radrennen	Велосипедный спорт
1139	valve	valve	válvula	Ventil	вентиль (ventil')
1140	wall of tire	chape	chapa	Profil	стенка шины (stenka shini)
1141	warning	avertissement	advertencia	Verwarnung	предупреждение (preduprezhdeniye)
1142	water bottle	bidon	botella de bebida	Trinkflasche	фляга (flyaga)
1143	water bottle cage; water bottle carrier	porte-bidon	portarrecipiente	Flaschenhalter	укрепление для фляги (ukreplyeniye dlya flyagi)
1144	weaken	craquer	reventar	reissen	устать (ustat')
1145	wheel	roue	rueda	Rad	колесо (koleso)
1146	wheel change	changement de roue	cambio de rueda	Radwechsel	замена колеса (zamena kolesa)
1147	wheel cover	housse de roue	funda de rueda	Ersatzdecke	крыло (krilo)
1148	wheel spindle	axe de roue	eje de rueda	Radachse	ось колеса (os' kolesa)
1149	win by a tire's width	gagner d'un boyau	ganar por un neumático	mit einer Reifenbreite gewinnen	выиграть на одну ширину шины (viigrat' na odnu shirinu shini)
1150	win by a wheel's length	gagner d'une roue	ganar por una rueda	mit einer Radlänge gewinnen	выиграть на одну длину колеса (viigrat' na odnu dlinu kolesa)
1151	yellow flag	drapeau jaune	bandera amarilla	gelbe Fahne	желтый флажок (zholtiy flazhok)

Diving

Plongeon

Saltos ornamentales

Kopfsprung

Прыжки в воду

	Diving	Plongeon	Saltos ornamentales	Kopfsprung	Прыжки в воду
1152	adjustable fulcrum	cylindre de pivot réglable	punto de apoyo graduable	verstellbare Gummiwalze	регулируемая точка опоры (reguliruyemaya tochka opori)
1153	adverse weather	temps défavorable	tiempo desfavorable	ungünstiges Wetter	неблагоприятная погода (neblagopriyatnaya pogoda)
1154	announcement of the dive	annonce officielle du plongeon	anuncio oficial del salto	Ankündigung des Sprunges	объявление прыжка (obyavleniye prizhka)
1155	any position	toute position	cualquier posición	"D"-Sprung	любая позиция (lyubaya pozitsiya)
1156	approach	approche	aproximación	Anlauf	подход (podhod)
1157	arch	cambrer	ahuecar la espalda	ein Hohlkreuz machen	дуга (duga)
1158	arched	cambré	ahuecada	Hohlkreuz	изогнутый, выгнутый (izognutiy vignutiy)
1159	arm position	position des bras	posición de los brazos	Armhaltung	положение рук (polozheniye ruk)
1160	armstand	équilibre (appui renversé)	parada de manos; equilibrio	Handstand	стойка на руках (stoyka na rukah)
1161	armstand back fall	équilibre et chute en arrière	equilibrio y caída hacia atrás	Handstand mit Rückwärtsabfallen	спад назад из стойки на руках (spad nazad iz stoyki na rukah)
1162	armstand cut-through reverse dive	équilibre, passage avant et plongeon renversé	parada de manos inverso	Handstand, Durchschub und Auerbachsprung	прыжок/сальто/из передней стойки на руках назад (prizhok/sal'to/iz peredney stoyki na rukah nazad)
1163	armstand dive	plongeon à partir d'un appui renversé	salto en equilibrio	Handstandsprünge	прыжок из стойки на руках (prizhok iz stoyki na rukah)
1164	armstand forward cut-through	équilibre et passage avant	parada de manos al frente	Handstand mit Durchschub	прыжок из стойки на руках вперед (prizhok iz stoyki na rukah vperyod)
1165	armstand somersault; with double somersault	équilibre et saut périlleux; et double saut périlleux	parada de manos con una vuelta; con dos vueltas	Handstand, Salto; mit Doppelsalto	сальто из стойки на руках; двойное сальто... (sal'to iz stoyki na rukah; dvoynoye sal'to...)

	English	Français	Español	Deutsch	Русский
1166	assume the starting position	prende position sur le plongeoir	tomar la posición de salida	Ausgangsstellung einnehmen	принять стартовую позицию (prinyat' startovuyu pozitsiyu)
1167	axis	axe	eje	Achse	ось (os')
1168	back dive	plongeon arrière	salto atrás	Rückwärtssprung	прыжок назад (prizhok nazad)
1169	back dive with 1/2 twist	demi tire-bouchon arrière	salto atrás con medio giro	Rückwärtssprung mit halber Schraube	прыжок с полувинтом назад (prizhok s poluvintom nazad)
1170	back somersault tuck	saut périlleux arrière groupé	salto atrás con bola	Salto rückwärts mit Hocke	сальто назад в группировке (sal'to nazad v gruppirovke)
1171	back somersault with 1/2 twist; with 1 twist; with 1 1/2 twists; with 2 twists; with 2 1/2 twists	saut périlleux arrière avec 1/2 tire-bouchon; avec tire-bouchon; avec 1 1/2 tire-bouchon; avec double tire-bouchon; avec 2 1/2 tire-bouchon	vuelta atrás con medio giro; con un giro; con uno y medio giros; con dos giros; con dos y medio giros	Auerbachsalto mit halber Schraube; mit 1 Schraube; mit 1 1/2 Schraube; mit 2 Schrauben; mit 2 1/2 Schrauben	сальто назад с полувинтом; с винтом; с полутора винтами; с двумя винтами; с двумя с половиной винтами (sal'to nazad s poluvintom; s vintom; s polutora vintami; s dvumya vintami; s dvumya s polovinoy vintami)
1172	back takeoff	appel en arrière	salida hacia atrás	Absprung rückwärts	толчок назад (tolchok nazad)
1173	back 1 1/2 somersaults; 2 somersaults; 2 1/2 somersaults	saut périlleux et demi arrière; 2 sauts périlleux arrière; 2 1/2 sauts périlleux arrière	una y media vueltas atrás; dos vueltas atrás; dos y media vueltas atrás	anderthalb Auerbachsalto; 2 Auerbachsalto; 2 1/2 Auerbachsalto	сальто назад в полтора; в два; в два с половиной оборота (sal'to nazad v poltora; v dva; v dva s polovinoy oborota)
1174	backward dive	plongeon en arrière	salto hacia atrás	Rückwärtssprung	прыжок назад (prizhok nazad)
1175	balk	cassé	romper el impulso	abknicken	незавершенное движение (nezavershonnoye dvizheniye)
1176	balk referee	juge-arbitre des plongeons cassés	árbitro de rompimiento de impulso	Schiedsrichter (Abknicken)	судья по незавершенным движениям (sud'ya po nezavershonnim dvizheniyam)
1177	bathing suit (men's)	maillot de bain (pour hommes)	traje de baño (hombres)	Badehose (Herren)	плавки (plavki)
1178	bathing suit (women's)	maillot de bain (pour dames)	traje de baño (mujeres)	Badeanzug (Damen)	купальный костюм (kupal'niy kostyum)

	Diving	Plongeon	Saltos ornamentales	Kopfsprung	Пръжки в воду
1179	board	planche	trampolín	Brett	доска (doska)
1180	bottom of pool	fond du bassin	fondo de la piscina	Beckenboden	дно бассейна (dno basseyna)
1181	bubalator	machine à bouillonner	máquina burbujadora	Sprudelmaschine	производитель пузырьков (proizvoditel' puzir'kov)
1182	bubble entry	plongeon avec bulles	entrada salpicada	Eintauchen mit Sprudeln	вход с пузырьками (vhod s puzir'kami)
1183	calculator (mechanical; cardboard)	machine à calculer (mécanique; à fiches)	calculadora (mécanica; de cartolina)	Rechner (mechanisch; Pappe)	вычислитель/механический; картонный/ (vichislitel'/ mehanicheskiy; kartonniy/)
1184	cast (left; right)	entrée (vers la gauche; vers la droite)	entrar desplomado (hacia la izquierda; hacia la derecha)	eintauchen (nach links; nach rechts)	снос/налево; направо/ (snos/ nalevo; napravo/)
1185	catapult end of the springboard	bord antérieur du tremplin	borde anterior del trampolín	vorderes Ende des Sprungbretts	катапультирующий конец трамплина (katapul'tiruyushchiy konets tramplina)
1186	center line	axe longitudinal	eje longitudinal	Längsachse	продольная ось (prodol'naya os')
1187	cheese board ("maxiflex B")	"cheese board" ("maxiflex B")	"cheese board" (trampolín "Maxiflex B")	"Cheese Board" ("Maxiflex B")	доска "максифлекс B" (doska "maksifleks B")
1188	clean entry	entrée sans éclaboussure	entrada sin salpicar	spritzloses Eintauchen	чистый вход (chistiy vhod)
1189	closed pike	carpé fermé	carpa cerrada	enge Hechte	положение согнувшись (polozheniye sognuvshis')
1190	club	club	club	Verein	клуб (klub)
1191	combined positions	toutes positions	posiciones combinadas	kombinierte Sprünge	комбинированные положения (kombinirovanniye polozheniya)
1192	come out	ouverture	extensión	Streckung	выпрямиться (vipryamitsa)
1193	come out of the pike	décarper	desencarpar	sich aus der Hechtlage strecken	выпрямиться из прыжка согнувшись (vipryamitsa iz prizhka sognuvshis')

English	Français	Español	Deutsch	Русский
1194 come out of the tuck	tendre après la position groupée, se	enderezarse después de la posición agrupada	sich aus der Hocke strecken	выпрямиться из прыжка в группировке (vipryamitsa iz prizhka v gruppirovke)
1195 come out point	point d'ouverture	punto de extensión	Moment der Streckung	момент выпрямления (moment vipryamleniya)
1196 competitive events	programme de la compétition	programa de la competición	Wettkampfprogramm	виды соревнований (vidi sorevnovaniy)
1197 compulsory dives; compulsories	plongeons imposés; imposés	saltos obligatorios; obligatorios	Pflichtsprünge	обязательные прыжки (obyazatel'niye prizhki)
1198 computer	ordinateur	computadora	Computer	компютор, ЭВМ (kompyutor, EVM)
1199 crest (insignia)	écusson (insignes)	insignia	Wappen; Insignien	нашивка (nashivka)
1200 cross line	axe transversal	eje transversal	Querachse	поперечная ось (poperechnaya os')
1201 cross position	position en croix	posición en cruz	kreuzweise Stellung	поперечное положение (poperechnoye polozheniye)
1202 crow hopping	départ répété	segundo impulso	zweifaches Wippen	удвоение (udvoyeniye)
1203 cutaway	couper	salto adentro	"Cutaway"; Delphinkopfsprung	из задней стойки вперед (iz zadney stoyki vperyod)
1204 cutting action	action parasite	salida brusca	abrupte Bewegung	сгибание при отталкивании (sgibaniye pri ottalkivanii)
1205 degree of difficulty	coéfficient de difficulté	coeficiente de dificultad	Schwierigkeitsgrad	степень трудности (stepen' trudnosti)
1206 depth of the water	profondeur de l'eau	profundidad del agua	Wassertiefe	глубина воды (glubina vodi)
1207 dive	plongeon	clavado; salto	Kopfsprung	прыжок (prizhok)
1208 dive (to)	plonger	saltar	springen	прыгать (prigat')
1209 dive indicator board	tableau des plongeons	marcador de clavados	Anzeigetafel der Sprünge	табло прыжков (tablo prizhkov)
1210 dive number	numéro de plongeon	número del salto	Sprungnummer	номер прыжка (nomer prizhka)
1211 diver	plongeur	saltador	Springer	прыгун в воду (prigun v vodu)

	Diving	Plongeon	Saltos ornamentales	Kopfsprung	Прыжки в воду
1212	diving club	club de plongeon	club de saltos ornamentales	Sprungverein	клуб прыжков в воду (klub prizhkov v vodu)
1213	diving competition	compétition de plongeon	competición de saltos	Wettbewerbe im Kopfsprung	соревнование по прыжкам в воду (sorevnovaniye po prizhkam v vodu)
1214	diving groups	groupes de plongeons	grupos de saltos	Sprunggruppen	классы прыжков в воду (klassi prizhkov v vodu)
1215	diving installations	plongeoir	instalaciones para saltos	Sprunganlage	сооружения для прыжков в воду (sooruzheniya dlya prizhkov v vodu)
1216	diving judges	juges de plongeons	jueces de saltos	Wertungsrichter	судьи по прыжкам в воду (sud'yi po prizhkam v vodu)
1217	diving jury	jury	jurado de saltos	Kampfgericht	жюри по прыжкам в воду (zhyuri po prizhkam v vodu)
1218	diving list	liste des plongeons choisis	lista de saltos escogidos	Sprungliste	список прыжков в воду (spisok prizhkov v vodu)
1219	diving secretaries	secrétaires	secretarios	Protokollführer	секретари по прыжкам в воду (sekretari po prizhkam v vodu)
1220	diving tables	répertoire des plongeons	repertorio de los saltos	Sprungtabelle	таблицы прыжков в воду (tablitsi prizhkov v vodu)
1221	diving technique	technique de plongeon	técnica de salto	Sprungtechnik	техника прыжков в воду (tehnika prizhkov v vodu)
1222	diving well	bassin de plongeon	piscina para saltos	Sprungbecken	бассейн для прыжков в воду (basseyn dlya prizhkov v vodu)
1223	double bounce	double appel	doble salida	doppeltes Abspringen	двойной отскок (dvoynoy otskok)
1224	drawing by lot	tirage au sort	sorteo de participantes	Losentscheid	жеребьёвка (zhereb'yovka)
1225	drive off the board	temps de jarret	presión al salir del trampolín	Impuls vom Brett	отталкивание от доски (ottalkivanie ot doski)
1226	drop	ouverture	caída	Öffnung	падение (padeniye)

	English	Français	Español	Deutsch	Русский
1227	dry bounce	saut d'essai	rebote seco	Wippen auf dem Brett	подпрыгивание перед прыжком в воду (podprigivaniye pered prizhkom v vodu)
1228	"duraflex" board	tremplin "duraflex"	trampolín "duraflex"	Brett aus Duraflex	трамплин "дюрафлекс" (tramplin "dyurafleks")
1229	entry	entrée	entrada	Eintauchen	вход (vhod)
1230	event referee	juge-arbitre pour les épreuves	árbitro de pruebas	Schiedsrichter	судья по видам соревнований (sud'ya po vidam sorevnovaniy)
1231	events of the competition	programme de la compétition	programa de la competencia	Wettkampfprogramm	виды соревнований (vidi sorevnovaniy)
1232	execute a dive	exécuter un plongeon	ejecutar un salto	einen Sprung ausführen	выполнить прыжок (vipolnit' prizhok)
1233	execution of a dive	exécution de plongeon	ejecución del salto	Ausführung des Sprunges	выполнение прыжка (vipolneniye prizhka)
1234	exit from dive	tendre après le plongeon, se	enderezarse después de saltar	sich aus dem Sprung strecken	выпрямление из прыжка (vipryamleniye iz prizhka)
1235	exit from pike or tuck	décarper	desencarpar	sich aus der Hechtlage strecken	выпрямиться из прыжка согнувшись или в группировке (vipryamitsa iz prizhka sognuvshis' ili v gruppirovke)
1236	exit from the water	quitter l'eau	salir del agua	das Wasser verlassen	выход из воды (vihod iz vodi)
1237	facing the platform	face à la plate-forme	cara (de frente) a la plataforma	rücklings	лицом к вышке (litsom k vishke)
1238	facing the springboard	face au tremplin	cara (de frente) al trampolín	Gesicht zum Brett	задняя стойка (zadnyaya stoyka)
1239	facing the water	face à l'eau	cara (de frente) al agua	vorlings	передняя стойка (perednyaya stoyka)
1240	fade	arriver dans un fondu	desplomarse	abblenden (den Impuls des Sprunges verlieren)	терять мах прыжка (teryat' mah prizhka)
	English	Français	Español	Deutsch	Русский

	Diving	Plongeon	Saltos ornamentales	Kopfsprung	Прыжки в воду
1241	fading	fondu	desacierto con el rebote del trampolín	Abblende (den Impuls des Sprunges verlieren)	неточное следование действию доски (netochnoye sledovaniye deystviyu doski)
1242	failed dive	plongeon manqué	salto fracasado	missglückter Sprung	неудавшийся прыжок (neudavshiysya prizhok)
1243	falling in the water by accident	chute accidentelle dans l'eau	caída accidental al agua	unbeabsichtigter Fall in das Wasser	случайное падение в воду (sluchaynoye padeniye v vodu)
1244	fast board	planche rapide	trampolín rápido	schnelles Brett	подвижная доска (podvizhnaya doska)
1245	feet-first entry	entrée par les pieds	entrada de pie	mit den Füssen eintauchen	вход в воду ногами вниз (vhod v vodu nogami vniz)
1246	fiberglass board	tremplin en fibre de verre	tabla de fibra de cristal	Plastikbrett	доска из стекловолокна (doska iz steklovolokna)
1247	final dives	finale des plongeons	últimas series de clavados	Endsprünge	финальные прыжки (final'niye prizhki)
1248	final result	résultat final	resultado final	Endstand	окончательный результат (okonchatel'niy rezul'tat)
1249	final results of the competition	classement général	clasificación general	Gesamtergebnis	окончательные результаты состязания (okonchatel'niye rezul'tati sostyazaniya)
1250	finals	finale	finales	Finale	финалы (finali)
1251	first secretary	premier secrétaire	primer secretario	Protokollführer	первый секретарь (perviy sekretar')
1252	flat landing	plat	entrada plana	flaches Eintauchen	плоский вход в воду (ploskiy vhod v vodu)
1253	flying somersault	périlleux au vol	salto mortal al vuelo	fliegender Salto	сальто в воздухе (sal'to v vozduhe)
1254	form in the air	figure	figura	Figur	очертание в воздухе (ochertaniye v vozduhe)
1255	forward approach	approche avant	marcha	Anlauf	разбег (razbeg)

English	Français	Español	Deutsch	Русский
1256 free position	position libre	posición libre	Freistellung	свободное положение (svobodnoye polozheniye)
1257 front dive; with 1/2 twist; with 1 twist	plongeon avant; avec demi tire-bouchon; avec tire-bouchon	salto al frente con medio giro; con un giro	Vorwärtssprung: mit halber Schraube; mit Schraube	прыжок вперед; с полувинтом; с винтом (prizhok vperyod; s poluvintom; s vintom)
1258 front somersault with 1/2 twist; with 1 twist; with 2 twists	saut périlleux avant avec demi tire-bouchon; avec tire-bouchon; avec 2 tire-bouchons	vuelta al frente con medio giro; con un giro; con dos giros	Salto vorwärts mit halber Schraube; 1 Schraube; 2 Schrauben	сальто вперед с полувинтом; с двумя винтами (sal'to vperyod s poluvintom; s vintom; s dvumya vintami)
1259 front somersault; 1 1/2 somersaults; 2 somersaults; 2 1/2 somersaults...	saut périlleux avant; un et demi avant; double saut périlleux avant; double et demi avant...	vuelta al frente; una vuelta al frente; una y media, dos, dos y media vueltas al frente	Salto vorwärts; 1 1/2 Salto vorwärts; 2; 2 1/2...	сальто вперед; в полтора оборота; в два оборота; в два с половиной оборота... (sal'to vperyod; v poltora oborota; v dva oborota; v dva s polovinoy oborota...)
1260 front takeoff	appel en avant	salida hacia adelante	Absprung vorwärts	толчок в прыжке вперед (tolchok v prizhke vperyod)
1261 fulcrum	cylindre de pivot	fulcro	Stellwalze	точка опоры (tochka opori)
1262 Gainer	'Gainer' (saut périlleux renversé)	"Gainer" (salto inverso con los pies por delante)	"Gainer" (Auerbachsalto)	сальто из передней стойки назад (sal'to iz peredney stoyki nazad)
1263 grace of the dive	grâce du plongeon	gracia en el salto	Anmut des Sprunges	грациозность прыжка (gratsioznost' prizhka)
1264 grant a repetition of a dive	accorder une répétition de plongeon	autorizar una repetición del salto	eine Absprung-wiederholung zugestehen	разрешить повторный прыжок (razreshit' povtorniy prizhok)
1265 hand spotting assistance	assistance au plongeur (entraînement)	apoyo (asistencia de entrenamiento)	Hilfestellung	оказание помощи прыгуну (okazaniye pomoshchi prigunu)
1266 hand stand	appui renversé (équilibre)	pino vertical; parada de manos	Handstand	стойка на руках (stoyka na rukah)
1267 head-first entry	entrée par la tête	entrada de cabeza	mit dem Kopf eintauchen	вход в воду головой вниз (vhod v vodu golovoy vniz)

	Diving	Plongeon	Saltos ornamentales	Kopfsprung	Прыжки в воду
1268	height of the dive	hauteur du plongeon	altura del salto	Sprunghöhe	высота прыжка (visota prizhka)
1269	high board (platform-10 m)	plate-forme (plate-forme de 10 m)	plataforma alta (de 10 metros)	Sprungturm (10 m-Turm)	десятиметровая вышка (desyatimetrovaya vishka)
1270	highest mark awarded	note la plus haute	marca más alta concedida	höchste Wertung	самая высокая оценка (samaya visokaya otsenka)
1271	hit the springboard	toucher le tremplin	tocar el trampolín	das Brett berühren	ударить по трамплину (udarit' po tramplinu)
1272	horizontal plane	plan horizontal	plano horizontal	waagerechte Ebene	горизонтальная плоскость (gorizontal'naya ploskost')
1273	hurdle leg	jambe libre	pierna libre	Schwungbein	свободная нога при наскоке (svobodnaya noga pri naskoke)
1274	hurdle step	saut d'appel	paso de impulso	Aufsatzsprung	наскок (naskok)
1275	indicator board	tableau	marcador de clavados	Wertungstafeln	табло (tablo)
1276	initial presentation	présentation	presentación	die Ausgangsstellung aufnehmen	первоначальное представление (pervonachal'noye predstavleniye)
1277	initiation of the takeoff	pré-appel	comienzo de la salida	Schwungholen	начало толчка (nachalo tolchka)
1278	International Diving Committee (F.I.N.A.)	Comité international de plongeon (F.I.N.A.)	Comité Internacional de Saltos Ornamentales (F.I.N.A.)	Internationales Komitee für Wasserspringen (F.I.N.A.)	Интернациональный комитет по прыжкам в воду (internatsional'niy komitet po prizhkam v vodu)
1279	inward dive	plongeon retourné	salto adentro	Delphinkopfsprung	прыжок из задней стойки вперед (prizhok iz zadney stoyki vperyod)
1280	inward dive with 1/2 twist or 1 twist	plongeon retourné avec demi ou 1 tire-bouchon	salto adentro con medio o con un giro	Delphinkopfsprung mit halber oder 1 Schraube	прыжок из задней стойки вперед с полувинтом или винтом (prizhok iz zadney stoyki vperyod s poluvintom ili vintom)

	English	Français	Español	Deutsch	Русский
1281	inward somersault; 1 1/2 somersaults; 2 somersaults; 2 1/2 somersaults...	plongeon retourné périlleux; 1 et demi sauts périlleux; 2 sauts périlleux; 2 et demi sauts périlleux...	vuelta adentro; una y media, dos, dos y media vueltas adentro	Delphinsalto; 1 1/2 Delphinsalto; 2; 2 1/2...	сальто из задней стойки вперед; в полтора оборота; в два оборота; в два с половиной оборота... (sal'to iz zadney stoyki vperyod; v poltora oborota; v dva oborota; v dva s polovinoy oborota...)
1282	inward 1 1/2 somersault with twist; with 2 twists	plongeon retourné périlleux et demi avec tire-bouchon; avec double tire-bouchon	una y media vueltas adentro con un giro; con dos giros	anderthalb Delphinsalto mit Schraube; mit 2 Schrauben	сальто из задней стойки вперед в полтора оборота с винтом; с двумя винтами (sal'to iz zadney stoyki vperyod v poltora oborota s vintom; s dvumya vintami)
1283	judges' awards	notation	puntuación	Bewertung	оценки (otsenki)
1284	judging panel	comité de jugement	comité de evaluación	Wertungsrichter	судейский комитет (sudeyskiy komitet)
1285	judging points	critères de jugement	criterios de juicio	Wertungsfaktoren	судейские критерии (sudeyskiye kriterii)
1286	jump	saut	salto	Sprung	прыжок (prizhok)
1287	jump up	sauter sur ses pieds	saltar empinado	hochspringen	подпрыгнуть (pddprignut')
1288	jury of appeal	jury d'appel	jurado de apelación	Schiedsgericht	жюри по рассмотру протестов (zhyuri po rassmotru protestov)
1289	knee save	sauver des genoux fléchis	saltar con las rodillas dobladas	ein Kniebeuge ausgleichen	подгибание коленей к животу во время входа в воду (podgibaniye koleney k zhivotu vo vremya vhoda v vodu)
1290	lay out	droit	derecho; en la posición extendida	gestreckt	вытянутый (vityanutiy)
1291	leg position	position des jambes	posición de las piernas	Beinhaltung	положение ног (polozheniye nog)
1292	lift	envol	vuelo	Anschweben	подъем (podyom)

	Diving	Plongeon	Saltos ornamentales	Kopfsprung	Прыжки в воду
1293	lining up for the entry	alignement de corps pour l'entrée dans l'eau	alineamiento del cuerpo para la entrada en el agua	den Körper strecken zum Eintauchen in das Wasser	выпрямление тела у входа в воду (vipryamleniye tela u vhoda v vodu)
1294	list of dives	liste des plongeons choisis	lista de saltos escogidos	Sprungliste	список прыжков (spisok prizhkov)
1295	long lineup	entrée longue	entrada pasada	langes Eintauchen	переворот (perevorot)
1296	longitudinal axis	axe longitudinal	eje longitudinal	Längsachse	продольная ось (prodol'naya os')
1297	lowest mark awarded	note la plus basse	puntuación más baja dada	niedrigste Wertung	самая низкая оценка (samaya nizkaya otsenka)
1298	make a flat landing	faire un plat	caer de plano	unsauber eintauchen	плоско войти в воду (plosko voyti v vodu)
1299	make a pike	effectuer un carpé	hacer una carpa	einen Sprung gehechtet ausführen	выполнить прыжок согнувшись (vipolnit' prizhok sognuvshis')
1300	make a tuck	effectuer un groupé	hacer un agrupado	einen Sprung gehockt ausführen	выполнить прыжок в группировке (vipolnit' prizhok v gruppirovke)
1301	mark awarded	note	anotación	Punktwert	присуждённая оценка (prisuzhdyonnaya otsenka)
1302	marking	notation	tanteo	Bewertung	система оценок (sistema otsenok)
1303	marking table	bases de notation	reglas de puntuación	Bewertungsgrundlagen	таблица оценок (tablitsa otsenok)
1304	marks dropped	notes barrées	puntos eliminados	gestrichene Wertungen	потерянные очки (poteryanniye ochki)
1305	marks maintained	notes retenues	puntos válidos	verbleibende Wertungen	количество набранных очков (kolichestvo nabrannih ochkov)
1306	"maxiflex B" board	tremplin "maxiflex-B"	trampolín "maxiflex B"	Maxiflex-B-Brett	трамплин "максифлекс-B" (tramplin "maksifleks-B")
1307	"maxiflex" board	tremplin "maxiflex"	trampolín "maxiflex"	Maxiflexbrett	трамплин "максифлекс" (tramplin "maksifleks")

	English	Français	Español	Deutsch	Русский
1308	mechanical agitation of the water surface	agitation mécanique de la surface de l'eau	agitación mecánica de la superficie del agua	mechanisches Aufwühlen der Oberfläche des Wassers	механическое колебание водной поверхности (mehanicheskoye kolebaniye vodnoy poverhnosti)
1309	meet manager	directeur de la compétition	encargado de la competición	Wettbewerbsleiter	начальник соревнования (nachal'nik sorevnovaniya)
1310	men's platform competition	épreuves hommes haut-vol	prueba de plataforma—hombres	Turmspringen (Herren)	мужские соревнование по прыжкам с вышки (muzhskiye sorevnovaniye po prizhkam s vishki)
1311	men's springboard competition	épreuves hommes au tremplin	prueba masculina de trampolín	Kunstspring-wettbewerbe, Herren	мужское соревнование по прыжкам с трамплина (muzhskoye sorevnovaniye po prizhkam s tramplina)
1312	name of dive	nom du plongeon	nombre del salto	Sprungbezeichnung	название прыжка (nazvaniye prizhka)
1313	non-skid surface of the platform	revêtement anti-dérapant de la plate-forme	esterilla antideslizante de la plataforma	nicht-rutschender Belag der Plattform	нескользящая поверхность вышки (neskol'zyashchaya poverhnost' vishki)
1314	official announcer	annonceur officiel	anunciador oficial	Ansager	диктор соревнований (diktor sorevnovaniy)
1315	official results of the competition	procès-verbal général	resultados oficiales de la competición	Wettkampfprotokoll	официальные результаты соревнования (ofitsial'niye rezul'tati sorevnovaniya)
1316	open	ouvrir	estirarse	sich öffnen	выпрямиться (vipryamitsa)
1317	open pike	carpé ouvert	carpa abierta	offene Hechte	открытый прыжок согнувшись (otkritiy prizhok sognuvshis')
1318	opening	ouverture	extensión	Öffnung	выпрямление (vipryamleniye)
1319	optional dives; optionals	plongeons au choix; libres	saltos optativos; optativos	Kürsprünge	произвольные прыжки (proizvol'niye prizhki)
1320	overthrow	entrée longue	entrada pasada	mehr als gestrecktes Eintauchen	затяжной прыжок; переворот (zatyazhnoy prizhok; perevorot)

	Diving	Plongeon	Saltos ornamentales	Kopfsprung	Прыжки в воду
1321	pay	surnoter	sobreestimar	überwerten	завысить очки (zavisit' ochki)
1322	pike	carpé	carpa; en escuadra	Hechte	согнувшись (sognuvshis')
1323	pike (to)	carper	hacer una carpa	hechten	согнуться (sognutsa)
1324	plane	plan	plano	Ebene	плоскость (ploskost')
1325	platform	plate-forme	plataforma	Plattform	вышка (vishka)
1326	platform competition	concours de haut-vol	competición de saltos de plataforma	Turmspringen	соревнование по прыжкам с вышки (sovernovaniye po prizhkam s vishki)
1327	platform diver	plongeur de haut-vol	saltador de palanca	Turmspringer	прыгун в воду с вышки (prigun v vodu s vishki)
1328	platform diving	plongeon de haut-vol	salto de palanca	Turmspringen	прыжки с вышки (prizhki s vishki)
1329	pointed toes	pieds pointés en extension	pies en punta	Zehen gestreckt	вытянутые пальцы ног (vityanutiye pal'tsi nog)
1330	position	position	posición	Stellung	положение (polozheniye)
1331	power leg	jambe d'appel	pierna de apoyo	Sprungbein	нога отскока (noga otskoka)
1332	power point	point d'impulsion	punto de impulso	Absprungmoment	точка отскока (tochka otskoka)
1333	practice bounces	sauts d'essai	saltos de ensayo	Wippen auf dem Brett	пробные отскоки (probniye otskoki)
1334	preliminaries	éliminatoires	eliminatorias	Vorkämpfe	предварительные соревнования (predvaritel'niye sorevnovaniya)
1335	preliminary dives	plongeons préliminaires	clavados preliminares	Vorkämpfe	предварительные прыжки (predvaritel'niye prizhki)
1336	preliminary results	résultats préliminaires	resultados preliminares	Vorkampfergebnisse	предварительные результаты (predvaritel'niye rezul'tati)
1337	press the board	"écraser" la planche	hundir la tabla	das Sprungbrett niederdrücken	нажать на доску (nazhat' na dosku)
1338	protest	réclamation	reclamación	Einspruch	возражение (vozrazheniye)
1339	push off	impulsion	impulso	Impuls	отталкивание (ottalkivaniye)
1340	recorder	marqueur	apuntador	Berichterstatter	секретарь (sekretar')

English	Français	Español	Deutsch	Русский
1341 recording secretary	secrétaire pour aider les marqueurs	secretario del marcador	Berichtssekretär	секретарь (sekretar')
1342 referee	juge-arbitre	juez árbitro	Schiedsrichter	судья (sud'ya)
1343 refuse the execution of a dive	refuser d'exécuter un plongeon	rehusar saltar	einen Sprung verweigern	отказаться от выполнения прыжка (otkazatsa ot vipolneniya prizhka)
1344 register	inscrire, s'	inscribirse	sich anmelden	зарегистрироваться (zaregistrirovatsa)
1345 registration	inscription	inscripción	Anmeldung	регистрация (registratsiya)
1346 registration fee	droits d' inscription	derechos de inscripción	Anmeldungskosten	стоимость регистрации (stoimost' registratsii)
1347 results sheet	feuille de résultats	hoja de resultados	Ergebnislisten	лист с результатами (list s rezul'tatami)
1348 reverse dive	plongeon renversé	salto inverso	Auerbachsprung	прыжок из передней стойки назад (prizhok iz peredney stoyki nazad)
1349 reverse dive with 1/2 twist; with twist	plongeon renversé avec demi tire-bouchon; avec tire-bouchon	salto inverso con medio giro; con un giro	Auerbachsprung mit halber Schraube; mit Schraube	прыжок из передней стойки назад с полувинтом; с винтом (prizhok iz peredney stoyki nazad s poluvintom; s vintom)
1350 reverse somersault with 1/2 twist; with twist; with 1 1/2 twists; with 2 1/2 twists	plongeon renversé périlleux avec demi tire-bouchon; avec tire-bouchon; avec 1 1/2 tire-bouchon; avec 2 1/2 tire-bouchons	vuelta inversa con medio giro; con un giro; con una y medio giros; con dos y medio giros	Auerbachsalto mit halber Schraube; mit Schraube; mit 1 1/2 Schraube; mit 2 1/2 Schrauben	сальто из передней стойки назад с полувинтом; с винтом; с полутора винтами; с двумя с половиной винтами (sal'to iz peredney stoyki nazad s poluvintom; s vintom; s polutora vintami; s dvumya s polovinoy vintami)

	Diving	Plongeon	Saltos ornamentales	Kopfsprung	Прыжки в воду
1351	reverse somersault; 1 1/2 somersaults; 2 somersaults; 2 1/2 somersaults...	plongeon renversé périlleux; et demi; 2 sauts renversés périlleux; double et demi...	vuelta inversa; una y media, dos, dos y media vueltas inversas	Auerbachsalto; 1 1/2 Salto; 2 doppelter Salto; 2 1/2 Salto	сальто /в полтора оборота; в два оборота; в два с половиной оборота.../ из передней стойки назад (sal'to /v poltora oborota; v dva oborota; v dva s polovinoy oborota.../ iz peredney stoyki nazad)
1352	reverse takeoff	départ renversé	salida inversa	Auerbachabsprung	толчок из передней стойки назад (tolchok iz peredney stoyki nazad)
1353	ride the board	rester accroché au tremplin	impulsarse al rebotar el trampolín	den Brettimpuls total ausnützen	ехать на доске (yehat' na doske)
1354	rip entry	entrée sans bulles	entrada nítida	spritzloses Eintauchen	вход без всплеска (vhod bez vspleska)
1355	running dive	plongeon avec élan	salto con impulso	Sprung mit Anlauf	прыжок с разбега (prizhok s razbega)
1356	running takeoff	appel avec élan	salida con impulso	Absprung aus dem Anlauf	толчок с разбега (tolchok s razbega)
1357	save a dive; scoop	sauver un plongeon	salvar un salto	einen Kopfsprung gutmachen	исправить неправильный прыжок (ispravit' nepravil'niy prizhok)
1358	scoop save	sauver un plongeon jambes pliées, aux genoux	salvar un clavado con las piernas recogidas y los pies arqueados	einen "scoop" gutmachen	исправление прыжка согнув ноги при входе (ispravleniye prizhka sognuv nogi pri vhode)
1359	score	compte des points	puntuación	Sprungergebnis	счет очков (schyot ochkov)
1360	scoreboard	tableau des résultats	tanteador	Resultatstafel	табло счета (tablo schyota)
1361	scoresheet	feuille de notes	hoja de puntuación	Resultatsblatt	судейский протокол соревнования (sudeyskiy protokol sorevnovaniya)
1362	scoring-table personnel	personnel de la table de marque	oficiales de la mesa de puntuación	Kampfrichtertisch-belegschaft	судьи-секретари (sud'yi-sekretari)

	English	Français	Español	Deutsch	Русский
1363	second secretary	second secrétaire	segundo secretario	zweiter Protokollführer	второй секретарь (vtoroy sekretar')
1364	short entry; short lineup	entrée courte	entrada corta	kurze Schlange	вращение, не доходящее до девяноста градусов (vrashcheniye, ne dohodyashcheye do devyanosta gradusov)
1365	slow board	planche lente	trampolín lento	weiches Brett	упругая доска (uprugaya doska)
1366	soft entry	entrée douce	entrada poca salpicada	glattes Eintauchen	мягкий вход в воду (myahkiy vhod v vodu)
1367	somersault	saut périlleux	salto mortal; vuelta	Salto	сальто (sal'to)
1368	somersault save	sauver un saut périlleux	acertar el salto mortal	einen Salto gutmachen	исправление сальто (ispravleniye sal'to)
1369	spin	rotation	giro	Drehung	вращение (vrashcheniye)
1370	splash	éclaboussure	salpicadura	Spritzen	всплеск (vsplesk)
1371	springboard	tremplin	trampolín	Sprungbrett	трамплин (tramplin)
1372	springboard diver	plongeur au tremplin	saltador de trampolín	Brettspringer	прыгун в воду с трамплина (prigun v vodu s tramplina)
1373	springboard diving	plongeon au tremplin	salto de trampolín	Brettspringen	прыжки в воду с трамплина (prizhki v vodu s tramplina)
1374	springiness of the board	élasticité de la planche	elasticidad del trampolín	Elastizität des Brettes	эластичность доски (elastichnost' doski)
1375	stand up	sur place	parado	Stand	стоять неподвижно (stoyat' nepodvizhno)
1376	standing takeoff	appel sur place	salida sin impulso	Sprung aus dem Stand	толчок с места (tolchok s mesta)
1377	start	départ	salida	Abgang	старт (start)
1378	starting order	ordre de départ des concurrents	orden de salida de los participantes	Reihenfolge der Teilnehmer	порядок старта (poryadok starta)
1379	starting position	position de départ	posición de salida	Ausgangsstellung	стартовая позиция (startovaya pozitsiya)

	Diving	Plongeon	Saltos ornamentales	Kopfsprung	Прыжки в воду
1380	steps of the platform	escalier de plateforme	escalera de la torre	Treppen des Sprungturms	ступеньки вышки (stupen'ki vishki)
1381	stiff board	planche dure	trampolín duro	hartes Brett	тугая, неэластичная доска (tugaya, neelastichnaya doska)
1382	straight	droit	derecho	gestreckt	прямо (pryamo)
1383	surface of the water	surface de l'eau	superficie del agua	Wasseroberfläche	поверхность воды (poverhnost' vodi)
1384	takeoff	départ	salida	Absprung	толчок (tolchok)
1385	takeoff angle	angle de départ	ángulo de salida	Absprungwinkel	угол толчка (ugol tolchka)
1386	team	équipe	equipo	Mannschaft	команда (komanda)
1387	thrust	réaction de la planche	reacción del trampolín	Brettwiederstand	отдача доски (otdacha doski)
1388	tie	ex aequo	empate	Gleichstand	ничья (nich'ya)
1389	toe press	poussée de la pointe des pieds	empujón de empeines	Zehedruck	нажим пальцами ног (nazhim pal'tsami nog)
1390	touch the bottom of the pool	toucher le fond du bassin	tocar el fondo del foso de saltos	den Beckenboden berühren	коснуться дна бассейна (kosnutsa dna basseyna)
1391	tower	tour	torre (de saltos)	Turm (Plattform)	вышка (vishka)
1392	tower diving	plongeon de haut-vol	salto de la plataforma	Turmspringen	прыжки с вышки (prizhki s vishki)
1393	trajectory	trajectoire	trayectoria	Flugkurve	траектория (trayektoriya)
1394	tuck	groupé	agrupado; en bola	Hocke	группировка (gruppirovka)
1395	tuck (to)	grouper	agrupar	hocken	группироваться (gruppirovatsa)
1396	twist	tire-bouchon	tirabuzón; giro	Schraube	винт (vint)
1397	twisting dives	plongeons avec tire-bouchons	saltos con tirabuzones; con giros	Schraubensprünge	прыжки с винтом (prizhki s vintom)
1398	vertical entry; vertical lineup	entrée verticale	entrada vertical	vertikales Eintauchen	вертикальный вход (vertikal'niy vhod)
1399	vertical plane	plan vertical	plano vertical	senkrechte Eben	вертикальная плоскость (vertikal'naya ploskost')

	English	French	Spanish	German	Russian
1400	voluntary dives with limit	plongeons au choix avec limite	saltos libres con límite	Kürsprünge mit Limit	произвольные прыжки с ограничением (proizvol'niye prizhki s ogranicheniyem)
1401	voluntary dives without limit	plongeons au choix sans limite	saltos libres sin límite	Kürsprünge ohne Limit	произвольные прыжки без ограничения (proizvol'niye prizhki bez ogranicheniya)
1402	walk (to the end of the board)	marche d'élan	camino hacia el extremo de la plataforma	Anlauf	шаг (shag)
1403	warm-up dive	plongeon d'échauffement	salto de precalentamiento	Probesprung	разминочный прыжок (razminochniy prizhok)
1404	washing over	entrée longue	entrada pasada	Eintauchen von mehr als 90°	переворот (perevorot)
1405	water level	niveau de l'eau	nivel del agua	Wasseroberfläche	уровень воды (uroven' vodi)
1406	water temperature	température de l'eau	temperatura del agua	Wassertemperatur	температура воды (temperatura vodi)
1407	women's platform competition	épreuves femmes haut-vol	prueba de plataforma—mujeres	Turmspringen (Damen)	женское соревнование по прыжкам с вышки (zhenskoye sorevnovaniye po prizhkam s vishki)
1408	women's springboard competition	épreuves femmes au tremplin	prueba femenina de trampolín	Kunstspringwettbewerbe (Damen)	женскэе соревнование по прыжкам с трамплина (zhenskoye sorevnovaniye po prizhkam s tramplina)

Fencing

Escrime

Esgrima

Fechten

Фехтование

	Fencing	Escrime	Esgrima	Fechten	Фехтование
1409	abstention	abstention	abstención	Enthaltung	воздерживание (vozderzhivaniye)
1410	advance	marche	avance	Vorwärtsbewegung	движение вперед (dvizheniye vperyod)
1411	annulment of the hit	annulation de la touche	anulación del toque	den Treffer für ungültig erklären	аннулирование укола (annulirovaniye ukola)
1412	apparatus for testing weapons	appareil de vérification des armes	aparato de comprobación de las armas	Waffenprüfgerät	устройство для проверки оружия (ustroystvo dlya proverki oruzhiya)
1413	"are you ready?"	"êtes-vous prêts?"	"¿listos?"	"fertig?"	"Готовы?" ("gotovi?")
1414	attack	attaque	ataque	Angriff	атака (ataka)
1415	attack by opposition	attaque par opposition	ataque por oposición	Sperrstoss	атака с оппозицией (ataka s oppozitsiyey)
1416	attack on the blade	attaque au fer	ataque al hierro	Klingenangriff	атака на оружие (ataka na oruzhiye)
1417	attacks on the preparation	attaques sur préparation	ataques sobre la preparación	Angriff gegen Angriffsvorbereitung	атака на подготовку (ataka na podgotovku)
1418	backward jump	bond en arrière	salto atrás	Sprung rückwärts	скачок назад (skachok nazad)
1419	balestra	balestra	balestra	Balestra	скачок вперед (skachok vperyod)
1420	barrage	barrage	desempate	Stichkampf	перебой (pereboy)
1421	basic position	position fondamentale	posición fundamental	Grundstellung	стойка (stoyka)
1422	beat	battement	batimiento	Klingenschlag; Battuta	батман (batman)
1423	beat of the foot	appel du pied	impulso del pie	Aufsetzen des Fusses	батман ногой (batman nogoy)
1424	bib	bavette	peto	Maskenlatz	нагрудник (nagrudnik)
1425	bind	liement	ligamento	Bindung mit Transport	завязывание (zavyazivaniye)
1426	blade	lame	hoja	Klinge	клинок (klinok)
1427	blocking parry	parade d'opposition	parada de oposición	Gegendruckparade	отбив с оппозицией (otbiv s oppozitsiyey)
1428	body contact	corps à corps	cuerpo a cuerpo	Körper an Körper	положение "кор-а-кор" (polozheniye "kor-a-kor")

	English	Français	Español	Deutsch	Русский
1429	body wire	fil de corps	pasante	Körperkabel	нательная электропроводящая проволока (natel'naya, elektroprovodyashchaya provoloka)
1430	bout	match	combate	Gefecht; Trainings-gefecht	бой (boy)
1431	broken blade	lame cassée	hoja rota	Klingenbruch	сломанный клинок (slomanniy klinok)
1432	broken-time riposte	riposte à temps perdu	respuesta a tiempo perdido	Riposte mit Zeitfinte	рипост, отнимающий больше одного отрезка фехтовального времени (ripost, otnimayushchiy bol'she odnovo otrezka fehtoval'novo vremeni)
1433	button	bouton	botón	Knopf	пуговка (pugovka)
1434	cadence	cadence	cadencia	Rhythmus	каденс (kadens)
1435	call of the competitors	appel des tireurs	llamada a los tiradores	Aufruf der Fechter	вызов соревнующихся (vyzov sorevnuyushchihsya)
1436	ceding parry	parade en cédant	parada de cesión	Nachgebeparade	уступающая защита (ustupayushchaya zashchita)
1437	change-beat	changez-battez	contra-batimiento	Wechselklingenschlag	изменение батмана (izmeneniye batmana)
1438	change of ends	changement de côté	cambio de lado	Platzwechsel	перемена сторон (peremena storon)
1439	change of engagement	changement d'engagement	cambio de ligamento	Wechsel der Bindung	перемена соединения (peremena soyedineniya)
1440	circular parry	contre	contra	Kreisdeckung	круговая защита (krugovaya zashchita)
1441	classification of competitors	classement des tireurs	clasificación de los tiradores	Klasseneinteilung	классификация соревнующихся (klassifikatsiya sorevnuyushchihsya)
1442	coach	entraîneur	entrenador	Trainer	тренер (trener)

	Fencing	Escrime	Esgrima	Fechten	Фехтование
1443	composed attack	attaque composée	ataque compuesto	zusammengesetzter Angriff	сложная атака (slozhnaya ataka)
1444	composed parry	parade composée	parada compuesta	zusammengesetzte Parade	сложная защита (slozhnaya zashchita)
1445	composed riposte	riposte composée	respuesta compuesta	zusammengesetzte Riposte	сложный рипост (slozhniy ripost)
1446	connecting wire	câble de branchement	cable de conexión	Anschlusskabel	соединительная электропроводящая проволока (soyedinitel'naya elektroprovodyashchaya provoloka)
1447	continuation of attack	continuation d'attaque	continuación del ataque	Fortsetzung des Angriffs	продолжение атаки (prodolzheniye ataki)
1448	conventions	conventions du combat	convenciones	Konventionen	условия (usloviya)
1449	coulé	coulé	filo	Gleitstoss	скользящий укол (skol'zyashchiy ukol)
1450	counter	contre	contra	Kreisdeckung	круговая защита (krugovaya zashchita)
1451	counterattack	contre-attaque	contraataque	Gegenangriff	контратака (kontrataka)
1452	countercutover	contre-coupé	contra-coupé	Anhebestoss ins Tempo	контрперенос; контрпереход (kontrperenos; kontrperehod)
1453	counterdisengage	contre-dégagement	contrapase	Kavation nach Kreisbindung oder Wechselbindung	уколоть с удвоенным переводом (ukolot' s udvoyennim perevodom)
1454	counterfour	contre de quarte	contra de cuarta	Contra-Quart	контрчетыре (kontrchetire)
1455	counteroffensive	contre-offensive	contra ofensiva	Gegenangriff	контрнападение (kontrnapadeniye)
1456	counterparry	contre-parade	contra parada	Kontraparade	круговая защита (krugovaya zashchita)
1457	counterriposte	contre-riposte	contra-respuesta	Contrariposte	контррипост (kontrripost)
1458	countersix	contre de sixte	contra de sexta	Contra-Sixt	контршесть (kontrshest')

English	Français	Español	Deutsch	Русский
1459 countertime	contre-temps	contra-tiempo	Contratempo	контртемп (kontrtemp)
1460 coupé	coupé	coupé	Coupé	перенос (perenos)
1461 cover oneself	couvrir, se	cubrirse	sich decken	закрыться (zakritsa)
1462 croisé	croisé	cruzada	Croisé	укол нажимом (ukol nazhimom)
1463 curvature of the blade	flèche de la lame	curvatura de la hoja	Klingenbiegung	изгиб клинка (izgib klinka)
1464 cut with the cutting edge	coup de taille	golpe de filo	Hieb mit der Vorderschneide	ударить лезвием (udarit' lezviyem)
1465 cutover	coupé	volante	Anhebestoss	переход (perehod)
1466 cutting edge of the blade	tranchant de la lame	filo de la hoja	Klingenschneide	лезвие (lezviye)
1467 deceive a parry	tromper une parade	equivocar una parada	eine Parade umgehen	обвести защиту (obvesti zashchitu)
1468 defensive	défensive	defensiva	Defensive	защитный (zashchitniy)
1469 dérobement	dérobement	libramiento; acción de librar la hoja	Ausweichstoss	перевод в темп (perevod v temp)
1470 diagonal parry	parade diagonale	parada diagonal	Diagonalparade	диагональная защита (diagonal'naya zashchita)
1471 direct parry	parade directe	parada directa	direkte Parade	прямой отбив; прямая защита (pryamoy otbiv; pryamaya zashchita)
1472 direct thrust	coup droit	golpe derecho	gerader Stoss	прямой укол (pryamoy ukol)
1473 directoire technique	directoire technique	directorio técnico	technische Leitung	технический директорат (tehnicheskiy direktorat)
1474 director of the competition	directeur de la compétition	director de la competición	Kampfleiter	руководитель соревнования (rukovoditel' sorevnovaniya)
1475 disarming	désarmement	desarme	Entwaffnung	обезоруживание (obezoruzhivaniye)
1476 disengagement	dégagement	pase	Umgehung	перевод (perevod)
1477 displace the body	caver le corps	angular el cuerpo	einen Winkelstoss durchführen	уклониться (uklonitsa)
1478 displacement	déplacement	desplazamiento	Platzwechsel	уклонение (ukloneniye)

97

	Fencing	Escrime	Esgrima	Fechten	Фехтование
1479	distance	mesure	distancia	Mensur; Abstand	дистанция (distantsiya)
1480	double engagement	double engagement	doble ligamiento	Koppelbindung	двойное соединение (dvoynoye soyedineniye)
1481	double hit	coup double	golpe doble	Doppeltreffer	двойной укол (dvoynoy ukol)
1482	duck	esquive	esquiva	Ausweichen	уклонение от удара (ukloneniye ot udara)
1483	duration of a bout	durée de l'assaut	duración del asalto	Dauer des Assaut	продолжительность боя (prodolzhitel'nost' boya)
1484	electrical épée	épée électrique	espada eléctrica	elektrischer Degen	электрофиксирующая шпага (elektrofiksiruyushchaya shpaga)
1485	electrical equipment	équipement électrique	equipo eléctrico	elektrische Ausrüstung	электрофиксирующее оборудование (elektrofiksiruyushcheye oborudovaniye)
1486	electrical pointe d'arrêt	pointe d'arrêt électrique	punta eléctrica de arresto	elektrische Spitzenkrone	электрофиксирующий наконечник (elektrofiksiruyushchiy nakonechnik)
1487	electrical scoring apparatus	appareil électrique de signalisation des touches	aparato eléctrico de señalización	elektrische Trefferanzeigetafel	электрофиксирующая аппаратура (elektrofiksiruyushchaya apparatura)
1488	elimination round	tour éliminatoire	vuelta eliminatoria	Ausscheidungsrunde	круговая система с выбыванием (krugovaya sistema s vibivaniyem)
1489	engage	prendre l'engagement	ligar	binden	соединить (soyedinit')
1490	engagement	engagement	ligamento	Bindung	соединение (soyedineniye)
1491	envelopment	enveloppement	envolvimiento	doppelte Übertragung	круговое завязывание (krugovoye zavyazivaniye)
1492	épée	épée	espada	Degen	шпага (shpaga)

	English	Français	Español	Deutsch	Русский
1493	épée blade	lame d'épée	hoja de espada	Degenklinge	клинок шпаги (klinok shpagi)
1494	épée event	épreuve d'épée	prueba de espada	Degenwettbewerb	соревнование на шпагах (sorevnovaniye na shpagah)
1495	épée fencer	épéiste	espadista	Degenfechter	шпажист (shpazhist)
1496	épée fencing	escrime à l'épée	esgrima de espada	Degenfechten	фехтование на шпагах (fehtovaniye na shpagah)
1497	épée guard	coquille d'épée	cazoleta de espada	Degenglocke	гарда шпаги (garda shpagi)
1498	evade a parry	tromper une parade	esquivar una parada	eine Parade umgehen	уклониться от отбива (uklonitsa ot otbiva)
1499	evasion	esquive	esquiva	Ausweichen	уклонение (ukloneniye)
1500	event	épreuve	prueba	Gefecht	вид соревнования (vid sorevnovaniya)
1501	failure of the electrical equipment	défaillance du matériel électrique	fallo del equipo eléctrico	Fehler im E-Material	неисправность электрофиксирующего оборудования (neispravnost' elektrofiksiruyushchevo oborudovaniya)
1502	false attack	fausse attaque	falso ataque	falscher Angriff	ложная атака (lozhnaya ataka)
1503	faulty weapon	arme défectueuse	arma defectuosa	defekte Waffe	дефектное оружие (defektnoye oruzhiye)
1504	feint	feinte	finta	Finte	финт; обман (fint; obman)
1505	feint of the attack	feinte d'attaque	finta de ataque	Fintangriff	обман атаки (obman ataki)
1506	feint of the parry	feinte de parade	finta de parada	Fintparade	обманный отбив (obmanniy otbiv)
1507	"fence!"	"allez!"	"¡adelante!"	"los!"	"Але!" "Начинайте!" ("ale!" "nachinayte!")
1508	fence (to)	tirer	tirar	fechten	фехтовать (fehtovat')
1509	fence a barrage	tirer en barrage	desempatar	einen Stichkampf austragen	вести перебой (vesti pereboy)
1510	fencer	escrimeur	esgrimidor	Fechter	фехтовальщик (fehtoval'shchik)
	English	**Français**	**Español**	**Deutsch**	**Русский**

	Fencing	Escrime	Esgrima	Fechten	Фехтование
1511	fencing at close quarters	combat rapproché	combate cuerpo a cuerpo	Nahkampf	фехтование на близком расстоянии (fehtovaniye na blizkom rasstoyanii)
1512	fencing breeches; fencing pants	culotte d'escrime	pantalón de esgrima	Fechthose	фехтовальные брюки (fehtoval'niye bryuki)
1513	fencing competitor	tireur	tirador	Fechter	участник соревнования по фехтованию (uchastnik sorevnovaniya po fehtovaniyu)
1514	fencing distance	distance	distancia	Fechtabstand	фехтовальная дистанция (fehtoval'naya distantsiya)
1515	fencing dress	costume d'escrime	traje de esgrima	Fechtanzug	фехтовальная одежда (fehtoval'naya odezhda)
1516	fencing glove	gant d'escrime	guante de esgrima	Fechthandschuh	фехтовальная перчатка (fehtoval'naya perchatka)
1517	fencing hall	salle d'armes	sala de esgrima	Fechtsaal	фехтовальный зал (fehtoval'niy zal)
1518	fencing jacket	veste d'escrime	chaquetilla de esgrima	Fechtjacke	электропроводящая куртка (elektroprovodyashchaya kurtka)
1519	fencing mask	masque d'escrime	careta de esgrima	Fechtmaske	фехтовальная маска (fehtoval'naya maska)
1520	fencing master	maître d'armes	maestro de armas	Fechtmeister	мастер по фехтованию (master po fehtovaniyu)
1521	fencing measure	distance	distancia	Fechtabstand	фехтовальная дистанция (fehtoval'naya distantsiya)
1522	fencing phrase	phrase d'armes	frase de esgrima	Fechtgang	серия фехтовальных движений (seriya fehtoval'nih dvizheniy)
1523	fencing position	position d'escrime	posición de esgrima	Fechtstellung	фехтовальная позиция (fehtoval'naya pozitsiya)
1524	fencing shoes	chaussures d'escrime	zapatillas de esgrima	Fechtschuhe	фехтовальные туфли (fehtoval'niye tufli)

	English	Français	Español	Deutsch	Русский
1525	fencing socks	bas d'escrime	medias de esgrima	Fechstrümpfe	фехтовальные чулки (fehtoval'niye chulki)
1526	fencing strip	piste d'escrime	pista de esgrima	Fechtbahn	фехтовальная дорожка (fehtoval'naya dorozhka)
1527	fencing time	temps d'escrime	tiempo (de esgrima)	Fechttempo	время фехтовального движения (vremya fehtoval'novo dvizheniya)
1528	fencing uniform	costume d'escrime	traje de esgrima	Fechtanzug	фехтовальная форма (fehtoval'naya forma)
1529	fencing weapon	arme d'escrime	arma de esgrima	Fechtwaffe	фехтовальное оружие (fehtoval'noye oruzhiye)
1530	final pool	poule finale	grupo final de tiradores	Endrunde	финальная пулька (final'naya pul'ka)
1531	finger play	doigté	dedeo	Klingenführung mit den Fingern	ведение клинка пальцами (vedeniye klinka pal'tsami)
1532	first intention	première intention	primera intención	erste Absicht	первое намерение (pervoye namereniye)
1533	flanconnade	croisé au flanc	flanconada	Flanconnade	скользящий укол в бок (skol'zyashchiy ukol v bok)
1534	flèche	flèche	flecha	Pfeilangriff	атака стрелой (ataka streloy)
1535	floor judge	juge de terre	juez de toques al suelo	Bodenrichter	судья, фиксирующий удары в пол (sud'ya, fiksiruyushchiy udari v pol)
1536	foible of the blade	faible de la lame	parte débil de la hoja	Klingenschwäche	слабая часть клинка (slabaya chast' klinka)
1537	foil	fleuret	florete	Florett	рапира (rapira)
1538	foil blade	lame de fleuret	hoja de florete	Florettklinge	клинок рапиры (klinok rapiri)
1539	foil event	épreuve de fleuret	prueba al florete	Florettwettbewerb	соревнование на рапирах (sorevnovaniye na rapirah)
1540	foil fencer	fleurettista	floretista	Florettfechter	рапирист (rapirist)
1541	foil fencing	escrime au fleuret	esgrima de florete	Florettfechten	фехтование на рапирах (fehtovaniye na rapirah)
	English	**Français**	**Español**	**Deutsch**	**Русский**

Fencing	Escrime	Esgrima	Fechten	Фехтование
1542 foil guard	coquille du fleuret	cazoleta de florete	Florettglocke	гарда рапиры (garda rapiri)
1543 foil tip	mouche du fleuret	botón del florete	Florettknopf	кончик рапиры (konchik rapiri)
1544 footwork	jeu de jambes	juego de piernas	Beinbewegung	работа ног (rabota nog)
1545 forte of the blade	fort de la lame	fuerte de la hoja	Klingenstärke	сильная часть клинка (sil'naya chast' klinka)
1546 forward jump	bond en avant	salto hacia adelante	Sprung vorwärts	скачок вперед (skachok vperyod)
1547 forward step	marche	paso hacia adelante	Vorwärtsbewegung	шаг вперед (shag vperyod)
1548 French grip	poignée française	empuñadura francesa	Französischer Griff	французская рукоятка (frantsuzskaya rukoyatka)
1549 froissement	froissement	resbalamiento	Gleitbindung	легко коснуться (lehko kosnutsa)
1550 fundamental position	position fondamentale	posición fundamental	Grundstellung	позиция в стойке (pozitsiya v stoyke)
1551 glide; graze	coulé	filo	Gleitstoss	скользящий укол (skol'zyashchiy ukol)
1552 green light	lumière verte	luz verde	grüne Anzeigelampe	зеленый свет (zelyoniy svet)
1553 grip	poignée	empuñadura	Griff	хват (hvat)
1554 guard	coquille	cazoleta	Glocke	гарда (garda)
1555 guard position	garde	posición de guardia	Fechtstellung	защитное положение (zashchitnoye polozheniye)
1556 guide of the weapon	tenue de l'arme	forma de empuñar el arma	Waffenhaltung	способ держать оружие (sposob derzhat' oruzhiye)
1557 half feint	demi-feinte	semifinta	halbe Finte	полуфинт (polufint)
1558 half turn	demi-volte	semivuelta	halbe Volte	полуоборот (poluoborot)
1559 "halt!"	"halte!"	"¡alto!"	"halt!"	"стойте!" ("stoyte!")
1560 hand position	position de la main	posición de la mano	Faustlage	положение руки (polozheniye ruki)
1561 handle	poignée	puño	Griff	рукоятка (rukoyatka)
1562 hit	touche	tocado	Treffer	укол (ukol)
1563 hit (to)	toucher	tocar	treffen	уколоть (ukolot')

	English	Français	Español	Deutsch	Русский
1564	"hit against the left"	"à gauche, touché!"	"¡tocado a la izquierda!"	"links, getroffen!"	"укол налево" ("ukol nalevo")
1565	"hit against the right!"	"à droite, touché!"	"¡tocado a la derecha!"	"rechts, getroffen!"	"укол направо" ("ukol napravo")
1566	hit awarded	touche donnée	tocado concedido	gegebener Treffer	укол засчитывается (ukol zaschitivayetsa)
1567	hit not valid	touche non valable	tocado no válido	ungültiger Treffer	укол не засчитывается (ukol ne zaschitivayetsa)
1568	hit received	touche reçue	tocado recibido	erhaltener Treffer	полученный укол (poluchenniy ukol)
1569	hit with the cutting edge	coup de taille	golpe de filo	Hieb mit der Vorderschneide	укол лезвием клинка (ukol lezviyem k:inka)
1570	hit with the point	coup d'estoc	estocada	Stoss	укол наконечником (ukol nakonechnikom)
1571	individual competition	compétition indivicuelle	competición individual	Einzelkampf	личное соревнование (lichnoye sorevnovariye)
1572	in-fighting	combat rapproché	combate cuerpo a cuerpo	Nahkampf	ближний бой (blizhniy boy)
1573	inquartata	inquartata	incuartata	Inquartata	перевод в четвёртую позицию (perevod v chetvyortuyu pozitsiyu)
1574	International Fencing Federation (F.I.E.)	Fédération Internationale d'Escrime (F.I.E.)	Federación Internacional de Esgrima (F.I.E.)	Internationaler Fechtverband (F.I.E.)	Международная федерация фехтования/ФИЭ/ (mezhdunarodnaya federatsiya fehtovaniya/FIE/)
1575	invalid hit	touche non valable	tocado no válido	ungültiger Treffer	недействительный укол (nedeystvitel'niy ukol)
1576	invalid target	surface non valable	superficie no válida	ungültige Trefffläche	неадэкватная поражаемая поверхность (neadekvatnaya porazhayemaya poverhnost')
1577	invitation	invite	invitación	Einladung	вызов (vizov)
1578	Italian grip	poignée italienne	empuñadura italiana	Italienischer Griff	итальянская рукоятка (ital'yanskaya rukoyatka)

	Fencing	Escrime	Esgrima	Fechten	Фехтование
1579	judge	juge	juez	Kampfrichter	судья (sud'ya)
1580	judging error	erreur de jugement	error de juicio	Fehler in der Entscheidung	судейская ошибка (sudeyskaya oshibka)
1581	jump	bond	salto	Sprung	скачок (skachok)
1582	jury	jury de compétition	jurado de la competición	Wettkampfgericht	жюри (zhyuri)
1583	jury of appeal	jury d'appel	jurado de apelación	Berufungsstelle	апелляционное жюри (apellyatsiomnoye zhuri)
1584	leading foot	pied avant	pie adelante	vorderes Bein	передняя нога (perednyaya noga)
1585	length of the blade	longueur de la lame	longitud de la hoja	Klingenlänge	длина клинка (dlina klinka)
1586	length of the piste	longueur de la piste	longitud de la pista	Bahnlänge	длина дорожки (dlina dorozhki)
1587	liement	liement	ligamento	Bindung	завязывание (zavyazivaniye)
1588	lines	lignes	líneas	Linien	линии (linii)
1589	loose play	assaut	asalto	Freigefecht	тренировочный бой (trenirovochniy boy)
1590	loss of ground	perte de terrain	pérdida de terreno	Bodenverlust	потеря дорожки (poterya dorozhki)
1591	lunge	développement	estocada (acción)	Ausfall	выпад (vipad)
1592	lunge (to)	développer, se	tirarse a fondo	einen Ausfall machen	сделать выпад (sdelat' vipad)
1593	martingale	martingale	martingala	Schlingband	петля (petlya)
1594	materiality of the hit	matérialité de la touche	materialidad del tocado	Aufkommen eines Treffers	ощутимость укола (oshchutimost' ukola)
1595	measure	mesure	distancia	Fechtabstand	фехтовальная дистанция (fehtoval'naya distantsiya)
1596	meet	rencontre	encuentro	Begegnung	встреча (vstrecha)
1597	metallic piste	piste métallique	pista metálica	Metallmatte	электропроводящая дорожка (elektroprovodyashchaya dorozhka)
1598	metallic vest	plastron métallique	chaquetilla metálica	Metallweste	электропроводящий жилет (elektroprovodyashchiy zhilet)

English	Français	Español	Deutsch	Русский
1599 "no hit!"	"pas de touche!"	"¡no hay tocado!"	"nicht getroffen!"	"не был!" ("ne bil!")
1600 non-valid hit	touche non valable	tocado no válido	ungültiger Treffer	недействительный укол (nedeystvitel'niy ukol)
1601 octave	octave	octava	Oktav	восьмая позиция (vos'maya pozitsiya)
1602 off-target hit	touche non valable	tocado no válido	ungültiger Treffer	укол не по цели (ukol ne po tseli)
1603 off the strip	franchissement des limites	fuera de la pista	Überschreiten der Bahnbegrenzung	пересечение границ (peresecheniye granits)
1604 offensive	offensive	ofensiva	Offensive	атака (ataka)
1605 on guard line	ligne de mise en garde	raya de posición de guardia	Startlinie	положение в линии (polozheniye v linii)
1606 on guard position	position de garde	posición de guardia	Fechtstellung	положение к бою (polozheniye k boyu)
1607 "on guard"	"en garde!"	"¡en guardia!"	"Stellung!"	"к бою!" ("k boyu!")
1608 "on the ground!"	"par terre!"	"¡al suelo!"	"Bodentreffer!"	"в пол!" ("v pol!")
1609 "one meter!"	"un mètre!"	"¡un metro!"	"ein Meter!"	"один метр!" ("odin metr!")
1610 one-two	une-deux	un-dos	Einfachfinte	один два (odin dva)
1611 one-two-three	une-deux-trois	un-dos-tres	Doppelfinte	один два три (odin dva tri)
1612 opening	ouverture	abertura	Eröffnung	открытое место (otkritoye mesto)
1613 opposition	opposition	oposición	Opposition	оппозиция (oppozitsiya)
1614 opposition parry	parade d'opposition	parada de oposición	Gegendruckparade	отбив с оппозицией (otbiv s oppozitsiyey)
1615 orthopedic grip	poignée orthopédique	empuñadura ortopédica	orthopädischer Griff	ортопедическая рукоятка (ortopedicheskaya rukoyatka)
1616 outside the piste	hors-piste	fuera de la pista	ausserhalb der Bahn	вне дорожки (vne dorozhki)
1617 "parried!"	"paré!"	"¡parado!"	"pariert!"	"укол отбит!" ("ukol otbit!")
1618 parry	parade	parada	Parade	отбив (otbiv)
1619 passata di sotto	passata di sotto	passata di sotto	Passata di sotto	укол вниз (ukol vniz)
1620 passing	dépassement	adelantamiento	Überschreiten	проход мимо (prohod mimo)

	Fencing	Escrime	Esgrima	Fechten	Фехтование
1621	penalty hit	touche de pénalisation	tocado de penalización	Straftreffer	штрафной укол (shtrafnoy ukol)
1622	piste	piste d'escrime	pista de esgrima	Fechtbahn	дорожка (dorozhka)
1623	"play!"	"allez!"	"¡adelante!"	"los!"	"начинайте!" ("nachinayte!")
1624	point of the blade	pointe de la lame	punta de la hoja	Klingenspitze	наконечник клинка (nakonechnik klinka)
1625	pommel	pommeau	pomo	Knauf	головка эфеса (golovka efesa)
1626	pool	poule	grupo de tiradores	Runde	пулька (pul'ka)
1627	pool sheet	feuille de poule	hoja de poule	Rundentabelle	протокол пульки (protokol pul'ki)
1628	predetermined defence	défense de parti-pris	defensa preparada	vorherbestimmte Verteidigung	преднамеренная защита (prednamerennaya zashchita)
1629	preparation of an attack	préparation d'attaque	preparación de ataque	Angriffsvorbereitung	подготовка атаки (podgotovka ataki)
1630	president of a bout	président d'un match	presidente de un match	Kampfleiter	старший судья (starshiy sud'ya)
1631	president of the jury	président du jury	presidente del jurado	Obmann des Wettkampfgerichts	старший судья (starshiy sud'ya)
1632	pressure	pression	presión	Anlehnung	давление (davleniye)
1633	prime	prime	primera	Prim	первая позиция (pervaya pozitsiya)
1634	priority	priorité	prioridad	Treffvorrecht	преимущество (preimushchestvo)
1635	prise de fer	prise de fer	toma de hierro	Bindung	атака с захватом; захват (ataka s zahvatom; zahvat)
1636	pronation	pronation	pronación	Faustlage mit Handrücken oben	пронация (pronatsiya)
1637	protect oneself	couvrir, se	cubrirse	sich decken	защититься (zashchititsa)
1638	putting on guard	mise en garde	puesta en guardia	Antreten in Fechtstellung	защитная позиция (zashchitnaya pozitsiya)
1639	quarte	quarte	cuarta	Quart	четвёртая позиция (chetvyortaya pozitsiya)

English	Français	Español	Deutsch	Русский
1640 quinte	quinte	quinta	Quint	пятая позиция (pyataya pozitsiya)
1641 rassemblement	rassemblement	retirada de pie	Wiederaufnahme der Grundstellung	уклонение ноги (ukloneniye nogi)
1642 rear limit	ligne de fin de piste	línea de final de pista	Endlinie	задняя граница дорожки (zadnyaya granitsa dorozhki)
1643 red light	lumière rouge	luz roja	rote Anzeigelampe	красный свет (krasniy svet)
1644 redoublement; renewal	redoublement	redoble	Angriffswiederholung	возобновление (vozobnovleniye)
1645 reel; spool	enrouleur	carrete	Kabelrolle	катушка (katushka)
1646 remise	remise	insistencia	Rimesse	повторный укол (povtorniy ukol)
1647 reprise	reprise	reanudación	Reprise	повторная атака (povtornaya ataka)
1648 reprise of the attack	reprise d'attaque	repetición del ataque	Angriffswiederholung	повторение атаки (povtorenie ataki)
1649 retire	rompre	romper	einen Schritt rückwärts machen	отступить (otstupit')
1650 retreat	retraite	retirada de cuerpo	zurückweichen	отступление (otstupleniye)
1651 rhythm	cadence	cadencia	Rhythmus	ритм (ritm)
1652 right-of-way	priorité	prioridad	Treffvorrecht	преимущество (preimushchestvo)
1653 riposte	riposte	respuesta	Riposte	ответный удар; рипост (otvetniy udar; ripost)
1654 running attack	attaque en flèche	ataque en flecha	Pfeilangriff	атака бегом (ataka begom)
1655 sabre	sabre	sable	Säbel	сабля (sablya)
1656 sabre blade	lame de sabre	hoja de sable	Säbelklinge	клинок сабли (klinok sabli)
1657 sabre event	épreuve de sabre	prueba de sable	Säbelwettbewerb	соревнование на саблях (sorevnovaniye na sablyah)
1658 sabre fencing	escrime au sabre	esgrima de sable	Säbelfechten	фехтование на саблях (fehtovaniye na sablyah)
1659 sabre guard	coquille du sabre	cazoleta de sable	Säbelglocke	гарда сабли (garda sabli)
English	**Français**	**Español**	**Deutsch**	**Русский**

Fencing	Escrime	Esgrima	Fechten	Фехтование
1660	sabreur	sabreur	sablista	Säbelfechter	саблист (sablist)
1661	salute	salut	saludo	Fechtergruss	приветствие (privetstviye)
1662	scoreboard	tableau des résultats	tablero de resultados	Anzeigetafel	табло (tablo)
1663	scorer	marqueur	marcador	Schreiber	судья-секретарь (sud'ya-sekretar')
1664	scoring light	lampe-témoin	lámpara testigo	Anzeigelampe	лампочка (lampochka)
1665	second intention	seconde intention	segunda intención	zweite Absicht	второе намерение (vtoroye namereniye)
1666	second intention tactic	tactique de deuxième intention	táctica de segunda intención	Taktik des Angriffs in zweiter Absicht	тактика второго намерения (taktika vtorovo namereniya)
1667	seconde	seconde	segunda	Sekond	вторая позиция (vtoraya pozitsiya)
1668	seeded competitor	concurrent classé	clasificado	plazierter Fechter	классифицированный участник соревнования (klassifitsirovanniy uchastnik sorevnovaniya)
1669	semi-circular parry	parade semi-circulaire	parada semicircular	Halbkreisparade	полукруговая защита (polukrugovaya zashchita)
1670	septime	septime	séptima	Septime	седьмая позиция (sed'maya pozitsiya)
1671	simple attack	attaque simple	ataque simple	einfacher Angriff	простая атака (prostaya ataka)
1672	simple parry	parade simple	parada simple	Parade	простая защита (prostaya zashchita)
1673	simple riposte	riposte simple	respuesta simple	einfache Riposte	ответный удар; рипост (otvetniy udar; ripost)
1674	simultaneous action	action simultanée	acción simultánea	gleichzeitige Aktion	одновременное действие (odnovremennoye deystviye)
1675	simultaneous attacks	attaques simultanées	ataques simultáneos	gleichzeitige Angriffe	одновременные атаки (odnovremenniye ataki)
1676	sixte	sixte	sexta	Sixt	шестая позиция (shestaya pozitsiya)

English	Français	Español	Deutsch	Русский
1677 sleeve	manchette	manga	Stulpe	рукав (rukav)
1678 slide	glissement	deslizamiento	Abrutschen	скольжение (skol'zheniye)
1679 step and lunge	marche et fente (développement)	marcha con fondo	Schritt vorwärts und Ausfall	шаг-выпад (shag-vipad)
1680 step back	retraite	retirado de cuerpo	Schritt rückwärts	шаг назад (shag nazad)
1681 stop	arrêt	arresto	Unterbrechung	остановка (ostanovka)
1682 stop cut to the glove	arrêt à la manchette	golpe de arresto al guante	Armvorhieb	контратака по перчатке (kontrataka po perchatke)
1683 stop hit	coup d'arrêt	golpe de arresto	Aufhaltstoss	контратака (kontrataka)
1684 stop hit with opposition	coup d'arrêt avec opposition	golpe de arresto con oposición	Aufhaltstoss mit Opposition	контратака с оппозицией (kontrataka s oppozitsiyey)
1685 stop thrust	coup d'arrêt	golpe de arresto	Aufhaltstoss	останавливающий укол (ostanavlivayushchiy ukol)
1686 stop thrust with opposition	coup d'arrêt avec opposition	golpe de arresto con oposición	Zwischenstoss mit Opposition	останавливающий укол с оппозицией (ostanavlivayushchiy ukol s oppozitsiyey)
1687 straight thrust	coup droit	golpe recto	gerader Stoss	прямой укол (pryamoy ukol)
1688 strike	toucher	tocar	treffen	ударить (udarit')
1689 superintendent of the electrical apparatus	préposé à l'appareil électrique	encargado del aparato eléctrico	Verantwortlicher für die E-Anlage	ответственный за электрофиксирующее устройство (otvetstvenniy za elektrofiksiruyushcheye ustroystvo)
1690 supination	supination	supinación	Faustlage mit Handrücken unten	супинация (supinatsiya)
1691 taking of blade	prise de fer	toma de hierro	Klingenbindung	завязывание (zavyazivaniye)
1692 team	équipe	equipo	Mannschaft	команда (komanda)
1693 team captain	capitaine d'équipe	capitán del equipo	Mannschaftsführer	капитан команды (kapitan komandi)
English	**Français**	**Español**	**Deutsch**	**Русский**

	Fencing	Escrime	Esgrima	Fechten	Фехтование
1694	team competition	compétition par équipe	competición por equipos	Mannschaftskampf	командное соревнование (komandnoye sorevnovaniye)
1695	test weight	poids de contrôle	peso de control	Kontrollgewicht	вес, проверяющий гибкость клинка (ves, proveryayushchiy gibkost' klinka)
1696	testing the electrical point	contrôle de la pointe électrique	control de la punta eléctrica	Kontrolle der elektrischen Spitze	проверка электрофиксирующего наконечника (proverka elektrofiksiruyushchevo nakonechnika)
1697	thrust with the point	coup d'estoc	estocada (acción)	Stoss	укол наконечником (ukol nakonechnikom)
1698	tierce	tierce	tercera	Terz	третья позиция (tret'ya pozitsiya)
1699	time hit	coup de temps	golpe de tiempo	Kontraktion	останавливающий удар (ostanavlivayushchiy udar)
1700	timekeeper	chronométreur	cronometrador	Zeitnehmer	хронометрист (hronometrist)
1701	tip	bouton	punta	Knopf	кончик (konchik)
1702	touch	touche	tocado	Treffer	укол (ukol)
1703	touch (to)	toucher	tocar	treffen	уколоть (ukolot')
1704	tournament	rencontre	encuentro	Begegnung	турнир (turnir)
1705	trailing arm	bras non armé	brazo desarmado	freier Arm	невооруженная рука (nevooruzhonnaya ruka)
1706	trailing foot	pied arrière	pie atrás	hinteres Bein	задняя нога (zadnyaya noga)
1707	turn	volte	vuelta	Volte	поворот (povorot)
1708	"two meters!"	"deux mètres!"	"¡dos metros!"	"zwei Meter!"	"два метра!" ("dva metra!")
1709	unarmed arm	bras non armé	brazo no armado	unbewaffneter Arm	невооруженная рука (nevooruzhonnaya ruka)
1710	valid hit	touche valable	tocado válido	gültiger Treffer	действительный укол (deystvitel'niy ukol)

	English	French	Spanish	German	Russian
1711	valid target	surface valable	superficie no válida	gültige Trefffläche	поражаемая поверхность (porazhayemaya poverhnost')
1712	wall target	coussin d'exercice	maniquí	Stosskissen	мишень для уколов (mishen' dlya ukolov)
1713	warning	avertissement	advertencia	Verwarnung	предупреждение (preduprezhdeniye)
1714	warning line	ligne d'avertissement	línea de advertencia	Warnlinie	линия предупреждения (liniya preduprezhdeniya)
1715	weapon arm; leading arm	bras armé	brazo armado	waffenführender Arm	вооруженная рука (vooruzhonnaya ruka)
1716	weapon control	vérification des armes	comprobación de las armas	Waffenkontrolle	осмотр оружия (osmotr oruzhiya)
1717	white light	lumière blanche	luz blanca	weisse Anzeigelampe	белый свет (beliy svet)
1718	width of the blade	largeur de la lame	anchura de la hoja	Breite der Klinge	ширина клинка (shirina klinka)
1719	width of the piste	largeur de la piste	anchura de la pista	Breite der Fechtbahn	ширина дорожки (shirina dorozhki)
1720	wire mesh of the mask	grillage de masque	rejilla de la careta	Maskengitter	сетка маски (setka maski)
1721	yellow light	lumière jaune	luz amarilla	gelbe Lampe	желтый свет (zholtiy svet)

Gymnastics

Gymnastique

Gimnasia

Turnen

Гимнастика

	Gymnastics	Gymnastique	Gimnasia	Turnen	Гимнастика
1722	A part	partie A	parte A	A-Teil	элемент группы А (element gruppi A)
1723	acrobatic element	élément acrobatique	elemento acrobático	akrobatisches Element	акробатический элемент (akrobaticheskiy element)
1724	acrobatic flight element	élément de vol acrobatique	elemento de vuelo acrobático	akrobatisches Flug-element	элемент акробатического полета (element akrobaticheskovo polyota)
1725	acrobatic series	série acrobatique	series acrobáticas	akrobatische Serie	ряд акробатических движений (ryad akrobaticheskih dvizheniy)
1726	acrobatic strength element	élément de force acrobatique	elemento de fuerza acrobática	akrobatisches Kraftelement	акробатический силовой элемент (akrobaticheskiy silovoy element)
1727	additional C	partie C exécutée en plus	parte C adicional	zusätzlicher C	дополнительный элемент группы С (dopolnitel'niy element gruppi C)
1728	adjusting the apparatus	réglage de l'engin	regulación del aparato	Einstellen des Geräts	установка снаряда (ustanovka snaryada)
1729	all-around competition	finale concours multiples	final de concursos múltiples	Mehrkampf	абсолютное первенство (absolyutnoye pervenstvo)
1730	alternate gymnast	gymnaste suppléant	gimnasta suplente	Ersatzturner	запасной гимнаст (zapasnoy gimnast)
1731	amplitude	amplitude	amplitud	Amplitude	амплитуда (amplituda)
1732	amplitude of the movements	amplitude des mouvements	amplitud de los movimientos	Bewegungsamplitude	амплитуда движений (amplituda dvizheniy)
1733	announcing the vault	indication du saut	indicación de salto	Anzeigen des Sprunges	объявление прыжка (obyavleniye prizhka)
1734	approach	élan	impulso	Anlauf	подход; разбег (podhod; razbeg)
1735	arch	cambrer	arquearse	sich ins Hohlkreuz strecken	прогибаться (progibatsa)

	English	Français	Español	Deutsch	Русский
1736	artistic gymnastics	gymnastique artistique	gimnasia artística	Kunstturnen	художественная гимнастика (hudozhestvennaya gimnastika)
1737	assistance	aide	ayuda	Unterstützung	страховка (strahovka)
1738	assistant	assistant	asistente	Helfer	страхующий (strahuyushchiy)
1739	average of the two middle scores	moyenne des deux notes intermédiaires	promedio entre dos notas intermedias	Mittelwert der beiden mittleren Noten	усреднённая из двух средних оценок (usrednyonnaya iz dvuh srednih otsenok)
1740	B part	partie B	parte B	B-Teil	элемент или соединение группы B (element ili soyedineniye gruppi B)
1741	balance beam	poutre d'équilibre	barra de equilibrio	Schwebebalken	бревно (brevno)
1742	balance element	élément d'équilibre	elemento de equilibrio	Gleichgewichtsteil	элемент на равновесие (element na ravnovesiye)
1743	bar change	changement de barre	cambio de barra	Barrenwechsel	замена брусьев (zamena brus'yev)
1744	base score	note de départ	anotación de base	Basisnote	исходная оценка (ishodnaya otsenka)
1745	basic position	position fondamentale	posición fundamental	Grundstellung	основная стойка (osnovnaya stoyka)
1746	beam	poutre	barra	Schwebebalken	бревно (brevno)
1747	beam exercise	exercice à la poutre	ejercicio en la barra	Übung am Schwebebalken	упражнение на бревне (uprazhneniye na brevne)
1748	beatboard	tremplin	plancha de muelles	Sprungbrett	гимнастический мостик (gimnasticheskiy mostik)
1749	beginning of the exercise	début de l'exercice	comienzo del ejercicio	Beginn der Übung	начало упражнения (nachalo uprazhneniya)
1750	bend	fléchir	doblar	beugen	наклониться (naklonitsa)
1751	bonus points	bonification	bonificación	Gutpunkte	прибавка (pribavka)
1752	brevet	brevet	patente	Brevet	свидетельство интернациональной известности (svidetel'stvo internatsional'noy izvestnosti)

	Gymnastics	Gymnastique	Gimnasia	Turnen	Гимнастика
1753	C part	partie C	parte C	C-Teil	группа С (gruppa C)
1754	cassette recorder	magnétophone à cassette	magnetófono para cassette	Kassettenrecorder	магнитофон (magnitofon)
1755	cassette tape	ruban-cassette	cinta magnética	Tonband	кассета (kasseta)
1756	chalk	carbonate de magnésium	carbonato de magnesio	Magnesium	магнезия (magneziya)
1757	change of hand position during the inverted support	marcher pendant l'appui renversé	marchar durante el equilibrio (apoyo invertido)	"Gehen" im Handstand	перемена положения руки во время упора прогнувшись (peremena polozheniya ruki vo vremya upora prognuvshis')
1758	chassée	pas chassé	paso chassé	Chassée (Seitschritt)	шаги шассе (shagi shasse)
1759	code of points	code de pointage	código de puntuación	Wertungsvorschriften	таблица трудности (tablitsa trudnosti)
1760	combinations	combinaisons	combinaciones	Kombinationen	комбинации (kombinatsii)
1761	combined results	classement combiné	clasificación combinada	kombinierte Wertung	комбинированные результаты (kombinirovanniye rezul'tati)
1762	competition director	directeur du concours	director de la competición	Wettkampfleiter	организатор соревнования (organizator sorevnovaniya)
1763	competition IA; IB; II; III	concours IA; IB; II; III	competición IA; IB; II; III	Wettkampf IA; IB; II; III	соревнование IA; IБ; II; III (sorevnovaniye IA; IB; II; III)
1764	competitive order	ordre de passage	orden de actuación	Reihenfolge der Turner	порядок выступления гимнастов (poryadok vistupleniya gimnastov)
1765	compilation center	bureau des calculs	oficina de cálculos	Berechnungsstelle	центр вычисления результатов (tsentr vichisleniya rezul'tatov)
1766	compilation sheet	feuille de compilation	hoja de compilación	Berechnungskarte	список гимнастов и видов соревнований (spisok gimnastov i vidov sorevnovaniy)
1767	composition deduction	déduction de composition	deducción de composición	Abzug in der Bewertung der Kombination	сбавка за композицию (sbavka za kompozitsiyu)
1768	composition of the exercise	composition de l'exercice	composición del ejercicio	Übungszusammen-stellung	композиция упражнения (kompozitsiya uprazhneniya)

	English	Français	Español	Deutsch	Русский
1769	conclusion of an exercise	fin d'un exercice	fin de un ejercicio	Ende einer Übung	конец упражнения (konets uprazhneniya)
1770	connecting movement	élément de liaison	elemento de conexión	Verbindungsteil	движение соединения (dvizheniye soyedineniya)
1771	connecting part	liaison	enlace	Verbindung von Übungselementen	элемент связки (element svyazki)
1772	connection	liaison	enlace	Verbindung	связка (svyazka)
1773	content of the exercise	contenu de l'exercice	contenido del ejercicio	Inhalt der Übung	содержание упражнения (soderzhaniye uprazhneniya)
1774	correct body position	bonne tenue	porte correcto	gute Haltung	правильное положение тела (pravil'noye polozheniye tela)
1775	counter swings	contre mouvement	balanceo al revés	Rückschwünge	обратные махи (obratniye mahi)
1776	crossed step	pas croisé	paso cruzado	Kreuzschritt	скрестный шаг (skryostniy shag)
1777	crouch	accroupir, s'	ponerse en cuclillas	hocken	присесть (prisest')
1778	croup	croupe	grupa	Kreuz	круп (krup)
1779	deduction for execution; combination; composition; difficulty	déduction pour faute d'exécution; combinaison; composition; difficulté	deducción por ejecución; combinación; composición; dificultad	Abzug in der Bewertung der Ausführung; Kombination; Komposition; Schwierigkeit	сбавка за ошибки в исполнении; комбинации; композиции; трудности (sbavka za oshibki v ispolnenii; kombinatsii; kompozitsii; trudnosti)
1780	deduction 1.0 point; 0.1; 0.5; etc.	déduction de point entier; 0.1; 0.5; etc.	deducción de 1.0 punto; 0.1; 0.5; etc.	Abzug eines ganzen Punktes; 1.0; 0.1; 0.5; etc.	сбавка на 1.0 балл; 0.1; 0.5; и т.д. (sbavka na 1.0 ball; 0.1; 0.5 i t.d.)
1781	definite stop	arrêt prononcé	parada pronunciada	ausgeprägter Halt	несомненная остановка (nesomnennaya ostanovka)
1782	degree of difficulty	coefficient de difficulté	coeficiente de dificultad	Schwierigkeitskoeffizient	коэффициент трудности (koeffitsient trudnosti)
1783	delegation head	chef de mission	jefe de delegación	Mannschaftsführer	глава делегации (glava delegatsii)
1784	difficulty	difficulté	dificultad	Schwierigkeit	трудность (trudnost')

	Gymnastics	Gymnastique	Gimnasia	Turnen	Гимнастика
1785	direct change	changement direct	cambio directo	direkter Wechsel	прямое изменение (pryamoye izmeneniye)
1786	direct connection	liaison directe	enlace directo	direkte Verbindung	прямая связка (pryamaya svyazka)
1787	dismount	sortie	llegada al suelo	Abgang	соскок (soskok)
1788	dismount (to)	sortir	bajarse	vom Gerät gehen	соскочить (soskochit')
1789	draw for finals	tirage au sort pour finale	sorteo de finales	die Endspiele entscheiden	жеребьёвка на финал (zhereb'yovka na final)
1790	draw for judges	tirage au sort pour répartition des juges	sorteo de jueces	die Kampfrichter entscheiden	жеребьёвка на распределение судей (zhereb'yovka na raspredeleniye sudey)
1791	draw for rotations	tirage au sort pour les rotations	sorteo de rotaciones	die Reihenfolge der Turner entscheiden	жеребьёвка на порядок выступления (zhereb'yovka na poryadok vistupleniya)
1792	duration of the exercise	durée de l'exercice	duración del ejercicio	Dauer der Übung	продолжительность упражнения (prodolzhitel'nost' uprazhneniya)
1793	duration of the positions	durée des parties de maintien	duración de las posturas	Dauer der Halteteile	продолжительность положения (prodolzhitel'nost' polozheniya)
1794	electronic scoreboard	système électronique d'affichage	marcador electrónico	elektronische Anzeigetafel	электронное табло (elektronnoye tablo)
1795	electronic signals	signaux électroniques	señales electrónicas	elektronische Zeichen	электронные сигналы (elektronniye signali)
1796	electronic timing (beam; floor exercise)	chronométrage électronique (poutre; exercices au sol)	control electrónico (barra de equilibrio; gimnasia a manos libres)	elektronische Zeitnahme (Schwebebalken; Bodenübung)	электронное вычисление времени/бревно; вольные упражнения/ (elektronnoye vichisleniye vremeni/brevno; vol'niye uprazhneniya/)
1797	element groups	groupes d'éléments	grupos de elementos	Elementgruppen	группы элементов (gruppi elementov)
1798	elements	éléments	elementos	Elemente	элементы (elementi)

	English	Français	Español	Deutsch	Русский
1799	elements from swing to handstand	éléments à partir de l'élan à l'appui renversé	elementos de impulso a pino vertical	Elemente vom Schwung bis zum Handstand	элементы от маха до стойки на руках (elementi ot maha do stoyki na rukah)
1800	emery paper; sand paper	papier d'émeri	papel de lija	Schmirgelpapier	наждачная бумага (nazhdachnaya bumaga)
1801	end of an exercise	fin d'un exercice	fin de un ejercicio	Ende einer Übung	конец упражнения (konets uprazhneniya)
1802	evaluating system	système d'évaluation	sistema de evaluación	Übungsbewertung	система оценок (sistema otsenok)
1803	evaluation in the finals	taxation pour les finales	evaluación para los finales	Finalbewertung	оценки в финалах (otsenki v finalah)
1804	evaluation of the execution; combination; composition; difficulty	appréciation de l'exécution; combinaison; composition; difficulté	apreciación de la ejecución; com-binación; composición; dificultad	Bewertung der Ausführung; Kombination; Komposition; Schwierigkeit	оценка исполнения; комбинации; композиции; трудности упражнения (otsenka ispolneniya; kombinatsii; kompozitsii; trudnosti uprazhneniya)
1805	event finals	finale aux engins	finales en los aparatos	Endspiele	соревнования для финалистов (sorevnovaniya dlya finalistov)
1806	evident stop	arrêt marqué	parada limpia	angedeuteter Halt	явная остановка (yavnaya ostanovka)
1807	excellent execution	exécution avec virtuosité	atuación magnífica	hervorragende Ausführung	отличное выполнение (otlichnoye vipolneniye)
1808	execution	exécution	ejecución	Ausführung	выполнение (vipolneniye)
1809	execution fault	faute d'exécution	falta de ejecución	Fehler in der Ausführung	ошибка при выполнении (oshibka pri vipolnenii)
1810	execution of an exercise	exécution d'un exercice	ejecución de un ejercicio	Ausführung einer Übung	выполнение упражнения (vipolneniye uprazhneniya)
1811	exercise on the pommel horse	exercice au cheval-arçons	ejercicio con el caballo de arzón	Übung am Seitpferd	упражнение на коне для махов (uprazhneniye na kone dlya mahov)

119

	Gymnastics	Gymnastique	Gimnasia	Turnen	Гимнастика
1812	exercise on the uneven bars	exercice aux barres asymétriques	ejercicio de barras asimétricas	Übung am Stufenbarren	упражнение на брусьях разной высоты (uprazhneniye na brus'yah raznoy visoti)
1813	extra swing	balancer intermédiaire	balanceo intermedio	zusätzlicher Anschwung	дополнительный мах (dopolnitel'niy mah)
1814	fall	chute	caída	Sturz	падение (padeniye)
1815	far end	cou (partie éloignée)	extremo final	das andere Ende	дальняя часть (dal'nyaya chast')
1816	fault	faute	falta	Fehler	ошибка (oshibka)
1817	fault in body position	faute de tenue	falta en la posición del cuerpo	Fehler in der Haltung	ошибка в положении тела (oshibka v polozhenii tela)
1818	fault in the interpretation	faute d'interprétation	falta de interpretación	Fehler in der Interpretation	ошибка в интерпретации (oshibka v interpretatsii)
1819	final score	pointage final	tanteo final	Endergebnis	финальная оценка (final'naya otsenka)
1820	finalist	finaliste	finalista	Finalist	финалист (finalist)
1821	finals	finale	final	Endkämpfe	финалы (finali)
1822	flashed vault	indication du saut	indicación de salto	Anzeigen des Sprunges	прыжок, номер которого уже показан (prizhok, nomer kotorovo uzhe pokazan)
1823	flex	fléchir	doblar	Beugen	согнуться (sognutsa)
1824	flexibility	souplesse	agilidad	Geschmeidigkeit	гибкость (gibkost')
1825	flight	vol	vuelo	Flug	полет (polyot)
1826	flight elements	éléments de vol	elementos de vuelo	Flugelemente	элементы полета (elementi polyota)
1827	floor	sol	suelo	Boden	пол (pol)
1828	floor exercise	exercice au sol	ejercicio a manos libres	Bodenübung	вольное упражнение (vol'noye uprazhneniye)
1829	floor exercise mat	tapis pour exercices au sol	tarima para ejercicios a manos libres	Matte	мат для вольных упражнений (mat dlya vol'nih uprazhneniy)
1830	front split	grand écart facial	gran spagat facial	Querspagat	шпагат вперед (shpagat vperyod)

English	Français	Español	Deutsch	Русский
1831 green signal	lumiére verte	luz verde	grüne Lampe	зеленый сигнал (zelyoniy signal)
1832 grip	prise	presa	Griff	хват (hvat)
1833 grip change	changement de prise	cambio de puño	Griffwechsel	перемена хвата (peremena hvata)
1834 gym shoes	chaussures de gymnastique	zapatillas de gimnasia	Gymnastikschuhe	гимнастические туфли (gimnasticheskiye tufli)
1835 gymnast	gymnaste	gimnasta	Turner	гимнаст (gimnast)
1836 gymnastic apparatus	agrès	aparato de gimnasia	Turngeräte	гимнастический снаряд (gimnasticheskiy snaryad)
1837 gymnastics chairperson	président du comité de gymnastique	presidente del comité de gimnasia	Turnvorsitzende	руководитель соревнований по гимнастике (rukovoditel' sorevnovaniy po gimnastike)
1838 gymnastics organizing committee	comité d'organisation de gymnastique	comité organizador de gimnasia	Turnorganisations-komitee	гимнастический организационнный комитет (gimnasticheskiy organizatsionniy komitet)
1839 gymnastics series	série de gymnastique	series de gimnasia	Turnserie	ряд гимнастических движений (ryad gimnasticheskih dvizheniy)
1840 gymnastics supervisor	responsable de la gymnastique	supervisor de gimnasia	Turnleiter	инспектор соревнований по гимнастике (inspektor sorevnovaniy po gimnastike)
1841 half-inverted position	position mi-renversée	posición seminvertida	Oberarmkipplage	положение согнувшись (polozheniye sognuvshis')
1842 hand placement	pose des mains	colocación de las manos	Aufsetzen der Hände	положение рук (polozheniye ruk)
1843 hand placement fault	faute de pose des mains	fallo en la colocación de las manos	Fehler im Handaufsatzes	ошибка в положении рук (oshibka v polozhenii ruk)
1844 hand placement on the croup	pose des mains sur la croupe	colocación de las manos sobre la grupa	Aufsetzen der Hände am Kreuz	положение рук на крупе (polozheniye ruk na krupe)
1845 hand placement on the neck	pose des mains sur le cou	colocación de las manos sobre el cuello	Aufsetzen der Hände am Hals	положение рук на шее (polozheniye ruk na shee)

	Gymnastics	Gymnastique	Gimnasia	Turnen	Гимнастика
1846	handgrasp	prise	presa	Griff	хват (hvat)
1847	handguards	protège-mains	guantes	Handleder	перчатки, предохраняющие руки (perchatki, predohranyaushiye ruki)
1848	handspring elements	éléments de renversement	elementos de salto de paloma	Überschlagelemente	элементы переворота (elementi perevorota)
1849	handstand	appui renversé	pino vertical; parada de manos	Handstand	стойка на руках (stoyka na rukah)
1850	head judge	juge-arbitre	juez árbitro	Kampfrichterobmann	главный судья (glavniy sud'ya)
1851	head of the delegation	chef de mission	jefe de delegación	Mannschaftsführer	руководитель делегации (rukovoditel' delegatsii)
1852	head scorer	marqueur principal	puntero (a)	Hauptanschreiber	главный секретарь (glavniy sekretar')
1853	head-judge deductions	déductions du juge-arbitre	deducciones del juez árbitro	Abzüge des Oberkampfrichters	снижение оценок главным судьей (snizheniye otsenok glavnim sud'yoy)
1854	hecht elements	éléments de hecht	elementos de hecht	Hechtelemente	элементы полета (elementi polyota)
1855	height of the apparatus	hauteur de l'engin	altura del aparato	Höhe des Geräts	высота снаряда (visota snaryada)
1856	held position	maintien	posición mantenida	Halte	выдержка (viderzhka)
1857	high bar	barre haute	barra fija	hoher Holm	верхняя жердь (verhnyaya zherd')
1858	horizontal axis	axe de largeur	eje de anchura	Breitenachse	горизонтальная ось (gorizontal'naya os')
1859	horizontal bar	barre fixe	barra fija	Reck	перекладина (perekladina)
1860	horizontal-bar exercise	exercice à la barre fixe	ejercicio en la barra fija	Barrenübung	упражнения на перекладине (uprazhneniya na perekladine)
1861	incorrect body position	mauvaise tenue du corps	posición incorrecta del cuerpo	inkorrekte Körperhaltung	неправильное положение тела (nepravil'noye polozheniye tela)

English	Français	Español	Deutsch	Русский
1862 individual competition	compétition individuelle	competición individual	Einzelkampf	личные соревнования (lichniye sorevnovaniya)
1863 individual results	classement individuel	clasificación individual	Einzelwertung	личные результаты (lichniye rezul'tati)
1864 inspection of the apparatus	vérification des engins	verificación de los aparatos	Überprüfung der Geräte	осмотр снаряда (osmotr snaryada)
1865 intermediate swing	balancement intermédiaire	balanceo intermedio	zusätzlicher Anschwung	промежуточный мах (promezhutochniy mah)
1866 International Gymnastics Federation; F.I.G.	Fédération Internationale de Gymnastique (F.I.G.)	Federación Internacional de Gimnasia (F.I.G.)	Internationaler Turnverband (F.I.G.)	Международная федерация гимнастики/ФИЖ/ (mezhdunarodnaya federatsiya gimnastiki/FIZH)
1867 international meet	rencontre internationale	encuentro internacional	internationaler Turnwettkampf	международная встреча (mezhdunarodnaya vstrecha)
1868 interrupted series	séries interrompues	series interrumpidas	unterbrochene Serie	прерванный ряд движений (prervanniy ryad dvizheniy)
1869 join	joindre	juntar (las piernas)	schliessen (Beine)	приставить ноги (pristavit' nogi)
1870 joint technical committee	comité technique conjoint	comité técnico conjunto	gemeinsame technische Kommission	объединённая техническая комиссия (obyedinyonnaya tehnicheskaya komissiya)
1871 judge	juge	juez	Kampfrichter	судья (sud'ya)
1872 judge for difficulties	juge des difficultés	evaluar dificultades	Kampfrichter (Schwierigkeit)	судья по трудностям (sud'ya po trudnostyam)
1873 judges' ballot	bulletin des juges	votación de los jueces	Abstimmung der Kampfrichter	судейский список оценки (sudeyskiy spisok otsenki)
1874 judges' conference	conférence des juges	conferencia de jueces	Kampfrichterkonferenz	совещание судей (soveshchaniye sudey)
1875 judges' consultation	consultation des juges	consulta de jueces	Befragung der Kampfrichter	консультация судей (konsul'tatsiya sudey)

	Gymnastics	Gymnastique	Gimnasia	Turnen	Гимнастика
1876	judges' courses	cours de juges	cursos de jueces	Kampfrichterlehrgänge	отбор общих критерий судьями (otbor obshchih kriteriy sud'yami)
1877	judging	taxation	evaluación	Taxation	судейство (sudeystvo)
1878	judging assignment	assignation des juges	labor de actuar como juez	Taxationsübertragung	распределение судей (raspredeleniye sudey)
1879	judging system	système de taxation	sistema de evaluación	Taxationssystem	судейская система (sudeyskaya sistema)
1880	jump	sauter	saltar	springen	прыгнуть (prignut')
1881	jury of appeal	jury d'appel	jurado de apelación	Berufungsgericht	апелляционное жюри (apellyatsionnoye zhyuri)
1882	kip	basculer	bascular	kippen	подняться силой (podnyatsa siloy)
1883	kips	bascules	básculas	Schwünge	подъемы силой (podyomi siloy)
1884	lack of amplitude; continuity; harmony; rhythm	manque d'amplitude; continuité; harmonie; rythme	falta de amplitud; continuación; armonia; ritmo	fehlende Amplitude; Bewegungsablauf; Harmonie; Rhytmus	отсутствие амплитуды; слитности; гармоничности; ритмичности (otsustviye amplitudi; slitnosti; garmonichnosti; ritmichnosti)
1885	landing	réception	llegada al suelo	Landung	приземление (prizemleniye)
1886	landing mat	tapis de chute	colchoneta de salida	Weichboden	мат для приземления (mat dlya prizemleniya)
1887	large faults	fautes graves	faltas graves	grosser Fehler	грубые ошибки (grubiye oshibki)
1888	lateral split	grand écart transversal	spagat transversal	seitlicher Spagat	горизонтальный шпагат (gorizontal'niy shpagat)
1889	leotard	justaucorps	leotardo	Leotard	трико (triko)
1890	lift up	lever, se	elevarse	heben	поднять/ся/ (podnyat'/sa/)
1891	line fault	faute de zone	falta de línea	Zonenfehler	ошибка на линии (oshibka na linii)
1892	line judge	juge de limites (lignes)	juez de límites	Zonenrichter	судья на линии (sud'ya na linii)

English	Français	Español	Deutsch	Русский
1893 long axis	axe de longueur	eje longitudinal	Längsachse	продольная ось (prodol'naya os')
1894 long horse (men)	cheval-sautoir en longueur (épreuves masculines)	caballo para saltos (hombres)	Langpferd (Männer)	конь для мужских опорных прыжков (kon' dlya muzhskih opornih prizhkov)
1895 longitudinal axis	axe longitudinal	eje longitudinal	Längsachse	продольная ось (prodol'naya os')
1896 low bar	barre basse	barra baja	niedriger Holm	нижняя жердь (nizhnyaya zherd')
1897 magnesium chalk	carbonate de magnésium	carbonato de magnesio	Magnesium	магнезия (magnesiya)
1898 manual signals	signaux manuels	señales manuales	Handzeichen	ручные сигналы (ruchniye signali)
1899 mat	tapis	colchoneta	Bodenturnfläche	мат (mat)
1900 maximum deduction	déduction maximum	deducción máximo	Punkthöchstabzug	максимальная сбавка (maksimal'naya sbavka)
1901 medium faults	fautes moyennes	faltas medianas	allgemeiner Fehler	средние ошибки (sredniye oshibki)
1902 men's technical committee	comité technique masculin	comité técnico masculino	technische Kommission für Männerwettbewerbe	мужская техническая комиссия (muzhskaya tehnicheskaya komissiya)
1903 minor assistance	aide légère	ayuda menor	leichte Hilfe	небольшая страховка (nebol'shaya strahovka)
1904 monotony in presentation	composition monotone	actuación monótona	eintönige Darstellung	однообразие в выступлении (odnoobraziye v vistuplenii)
1905 mount	entrée	entrada a	Aufgang	наскок (naskok)
1906 mount (to)	entrer	entrar a	die Übung beginnen	наскочить (naskochit')
1907 musical accompaniment	accompagnement musical	acompañamiento musical	Musikbegleitung	музыкальное сопровождение (muzikal'noye soprovozhdeniye)
1908 near end	croupe	extremo de abordaje	das nähere Ende	ближняя часть (blizhnyaya chast')
1909 neck of the pommel horse	cou du cheval-arçons	cuello del caballo de arcos	Hals	дальняя часть коня с ручками (dal'nyaya chast' konya s ruchkami)
English	Français	Español	Deutsch	Русский

	Gymnastics	Gymnastique	Gimnasia	Turnen	Гимнастика
1910	neck of the vaulting horse	cou du cheval-sautoir	cuello del caballo de saltos	Hals	дальная часть коня для прыжков (dal'nyaya chast' konya dlya prizhkov)
1911	neutral deductions	déductions neutres	deducciones neutrales	neutrale Abzüge	общие сбавки (obshchiye sbavki)
1912	open scoring	pointage ouvert	puntuación abierta	offene Wertung	открытое присуждение оценок (otkritoye prisuzhdeniye otsenok)
1913	optional exercises	exercices à volonté	ejercicios facultativos	Kürübungen	произвольные упражнения (proizvol'niye uprazhneniya)
1914	orchestrated music	musique orchestrée	música instrumental	orchestrierte Musik	оркестрованная музыка (orkestrovannaya muzika)
1915	order of passage	ordre de passage	orden de paso a la ejecución	Verlaufsfolge	порядок выступления гимнастов (poryadok vistupleniya gimnastov)
1916	original value	valeur d'originalité	mérito de originalidad	Originalitätswert	оценка оригинальности (otsenka original'nosti)
1917	originality of the exercise	originalité de l'exercice	originalidad del ejercicio	Originalität der Übung	оригинальность упражнения (original'nost' uprazhneniya)
1918	out-of-bounds	hors limites	fuera de juego	im Aus	за границами (za granitsami)
1919	panel	jury	jurado	Kampfgericht	группа судей (gruppa sudey)
1920	panel judge	juge	juez colegial	Juror	главный судья (glavniy sud'ya)
1921	parallel bars	barres parallèles	paralelas	Barren	брусья (brus'ya)
1922	part of the exercise	partie de l'exercice	parte del ejercicio	Übungsteil	часть упражнения (chast' uprazhneniya)
1923	perfect performance	exécution parfaite	ejecución perfecta	tadellose Ausführung	безупречное выполнение (bezuprechnoye vipolneniye)
1924	perform a full turn	pivoter	girar	eine Schraube ausführen	сделать полный оборот (sdelat' polniy oborot)
1925	pianist	pianiste	pianista	Klavierspieler	пианист (pianist)
1926	piano	piano	piano	Klavier	фортепьяно (fortep'yano)
1927	pirouette	pirouetter	hacer piruetas	eine Schraube ausführen	сделать пируэт (sdelat' piruet)

	English	Français	Español	Deutsch	Русский
1928	planche (hanging scale)	planche (suspension horizontale)	plancha (suspensión horizontal)	Stützwaage	горизонтальный упор (gorizontal'niy upor)
1929	platform; podium	podium	podio	Podium	помост (pomost)
1930	pommel horse	cheval-arçons	potro con arzón	Pauschenpferd	конь с ручками (kon's ruchkami)
1931	pommels	arçons	arcos	pauschen	ручки коня (ruchki konya)
1932	president of the jury	président du jury	presidente del jurado	Präsident der Wettkampfleitung	председатель жюри (predsedatel' zhyuri)
1933	protest	réclamation	reclamación	Einspruch	протест (protest)
1934	range between two middle scores	écart entre deux notes intermédiaires	diferencia entre dos marcas medianas	Entfernung zwischen zwei Durchschnitts-spielständen	расстояние между двумя средними оценками (rasstoyaniye mezhdu dvumya srednimi otsenkami)
1935	rare value	valeur exceptionnelle	mérito excepcional	Seltenheitswert	редкая оценка (redkaya otsenka)
1936	reach a position	établir, s'	establecerse	in die Streckung gehen	принять положение (prinyat' polozheniye)
1937	red signal	lumière rouge	luz roja	rote Lampe	красный сигнал (krasniy signal)
1938	regulations	règlements	reglamentos	Satzung	правила (pravila)
1939	removal of a judge	révocation d'un juge	destitución de un juez	Absetzung eines Kampfrichters	удаление судьи (udaleniye sud'yi)
1940	repetition of an element	répétition d'un élément	repetición de un elemento	Wiederholung eines Elementes	повторение элемента (povtoreniye elementa)
1941	repetition of the exercise	reprise de l'exercice	repetición del ejercicio	Wiederholung einer Übung	повторение упражнения (povtoreniye uprazhneniya)
1942	requirements of the exercise	exigences de l'exercice	exigencias del ejercicio	Erfordernisse der Übung	требования упражнения (trebovaniya uprazhneniya)
1943	reverse	inverser	invertir	eine Übung gegengleich ausführen	сделать обратное движение (sdelat' obratnoye dvizheniye)
1944	rhythm	rythme	ritmo	Rythmus	ритмичность (ritmichnost')
1945	ring exercise	exercice aux anneaux	ejercicio de anillas	Übung an den Ringen	упражнение на кольцах (uprazhneniye na kol'tsah)

	Gymnastics	Gymnastique	Gimnasia	Turnen	Гимнастика
1946	rings	anneaux	anillas	Ringe	кольца (kol'tsa)
1947	rise	élever,s'	elevarse	sich aufrichten	подняться (podnyatsa)
1948	risk	risque	riesgo	Risiko	риск (risk)
1949	rosin	arcanson	resina	Harz	канифоль (kanifol')
1950	rotation of exercises	rotation des épreuves	rotación de pruebas	Wechsel der Geräte	порядок упражнений (poryadok uprazhneniy)
1951	rotation of teams	rotation des équipes	rotación de equipos	Wechsel der Mannschaften	порядок выступления команд (poryadok vistupleniya komand)
1952	rules	règles	estatutos	Regeln	правила (pravila)
1953	run	course d'élan	carrera de impulso	Anlauf	разбег (razbeg)
1954	running	élan	impulso	Anlauf	бег (beg)
1955	saddle	selle	silla	Sattel	седло (sedlo)
1956	salto	salto	salto	Salto	сальто (sal'to)
1957	scientific technical collaborator	collaborateur technique-scientifique	colaborador técnico-científico	technischer Mitarbeiter	научный технический сотрудник (nauchniy tehnicheskiy sotrudnik)
1958	score	pointage	puntuación	Stand	оценка (otsenka)
1959	score sheet	feuille de pointage	hoja de puntuación	Resultatsblatt	протокол (protokol)
1960	scoring	taxation	evaluación	Taxation	присуждение оценок (prisuzhdeniye otsenok)
1961	scoring system	système de pointage	sistema de puntuación	Wertungsvorschrift	оценочная система (otsenochnaya sistema)
1962	secretariat coordinator	chef compilateur	jefe compilador	Koordinator des Berechnungsausschusses	заведующий вычислением результатов (zaveduyushchiy vichisleniyem rezul'tatov)
1963	session	séance	sesión	Sitzung	сессия (sessiya)
1964	side horse (women)	cheval-sautoir en largeur (épreuves féminines)	caballo de través (mujeres)	Seitpferd (Frauen)	конь для женских опорных прыжков (kon' dlya zhenskih opornih prizhkov)

English	Français	Español	Deutsch	Русский
1965 side split	grand écart latéral	spagat lateral	Seitenspagat	шпагат продольно (shpagat prodol'no)
1966 small faults	petites fautes	faltas menores	kleine Fehler	маленькие ошибки (malen'kiye oshibki)
1967 special requirements of the apparatus	exigences spéciales pour les engins	requisitos especiales del aparato	besondere Erfondernisse der Geräte	специальные требования для работы на снаряде (spetsial'niye trebovaniya dlya raboti na snaryade)
1968 split	grand écart	spagat	Spagat	шпагат (shpagat)
1969 spring	faire une impulsion	hacer un bote	springen	давать толчок (davat' tolchok)
1970 squat position	position accroupie	posición en cuclillas	gehockt	присед (prised)
1971 stability	stabilité	estabilidad	Stabilität	устойчивость (ustoychivost')
1972 stability on landing	stabilité à la réception	estabilidad en la llegada	Stabilität in der Landung	устойчивость при приземлении (ustoychivost' pri prizemlenii)
1973 stand	station	posición en firmes	Stand	стойка (stoyka)
1974 starting position	position de départ	posición de salida	Ausgangsstellung	стартовая позиция (startovaya pozitsiya)
1975 steps; side steps	pas chassé	pasos; pasos laterales	Schritte; Seitschritte	шаги; шаги шассе (shagi; shagi shasse)
1976 stop	arrêt	parada	Unterbrechung	остановка (ostanovka)
1977 stopwatch	chronomètre individuel	cronómetro individual	Stoppuhr	секундомер (sekundomer)
1978 strength part	partie de force	parte de fuerza	Kraftteil	силовая часть (silovaya chast')
1979 stretch	étendre	extenderse	strecken	вытягивать (vityagivat')
1980 substitute gymnast	gymnaste suppléant	gimnasta suplente	Ersatzturner	запасной гимнаст (zapasnoy gimnast)
1981 superior judge	juge-arbitre	juez árbitro	Schiedsrichter	старший судья (starshiy sud'ya)
1982 supplementary deduction	déduction supplémentaire	deducción suplementaria	zusätzlicher Abzug	добавочная сбавка (dobavochnaya sbavka)
1983 support	appui	apoyo	Stütz	упор (upor)
1984 support officials	officiels de soutien	oficiales auxiliares	Hilfsschiedsrichter	помощники судей (pomoshchniki sudey)
English	**Français**	**Español**	**Deutsch**	**Русский**

	Gymnastics	Gymnastique	Gimnasia	Turnen	Гимнастика
1985	swing	balancé	balanceo	Anschwung	мах (mah)
1986	swing part	partie d'élan	parte de balanceo	Schwungteil	маховая часть (mahovaya chast')
1987	table of bonus points (R.O.V.)	tableau R.O.V.	cuadro R.O.V.	Gutpunktfaktor (R.O.V.)	таблица прибавок за POB (tablitsa pribavok za ROV)
1988	table of difficulties	tableau de difficultés	cuadro de dificultades	Schwierigkeits-gradtabelle	таблица трудности (tablitsa trudnosti)
1989	table of faults	tableau des fautes	tabla de faltas	Fehlertabelle	таблица ошибок (tablitsa oshibok)
1990	takeoff	appel	bote	Aufruf	отталкивание (ottalkivaniye)
1991	tape recorder	appareil enregistreur	magnetofón	Tonband	магнитофон (magnitofon)
1992	team	équipe	equipo	Mannschaft	команда komanda)
1993	team leader	chef d'équipe	director de equipo	Mannschaftsführer	руководитель команды (rukovoditel' komandi)
1994	team results	classement par équipe	calificación por equipos	Mannschaftsresultaten	командные результаты (komandniye rezul'tati)
1995	technical execution	exécution technique	realización técnica	technische Ausführung	техническое выполнение (tehnicheskoye vypolneniye)
1996	technical officials	officiels techniques	oficiales técnicos	technische Schiedsrichter	технические официальные лица (tehnicheskiye ofitsial'niye litsa)
1997	technical regulation	règlement technique	reglamento técnico	technisches Reglement	технический регламент (tehnicheskiy reglament)
1998	thirty-second warm-up	échauffement de 30 secondes	precalentamiento de los 30 segundos	dreissig-Sekunden Aufwärmen	тридцатисекундная разминка (tritsatisekundnaya razminka)
1999	time fault	faute de durée	falta de tiempo	Zeitfehler	ошибка во времени (oshibka vo vremeni)
2000	time signal	signal sonore (durée)	señal acústica	Tonzeichen	сигнал времени (signal vremeni)
2001	timer	chronométreur	cronometrador	Zeitnehmer	хронометрист (hronometrist)
2002	touch the apparatus	toucher l'engin	tocar el aparato	das Gerät berühren	коснуться снаряда (kosnutsa snaryada)

English	Français	Español	Deutsch	Русский
2003 training site	salle d'entraînement	local de entrenamiento	Trainingslager	место тренировки (mesto trenirovki)
2004 travel	transport latéral	desplazamiento lateral	Wanderkreisen	переход (perehod)
2005 turn	tourner	dar la vuelta	drehen	поворачиваться (povorachivatsa)
2006 two-foot takeoff	appel des deux pieds	despegue a dos pies	Abdruck der Füsse	толчок двумя ногами (tolchok dvumya nogami)
2007 uncharacteristic elements	éléments non caractéristiques	elementos no característicos	untypische Elemente	нетипичные элементи (netiphniye elementi)
2008 uneven bars	barres asymétriques	paralelas asimétricas	Stufenbarren	брусья разной высоты (brus'ya raznoy visoti)
2009 upward swings	établissements	elevaciones	Aufwärtsschwünge	махи вверх (mahi vverh)
2010 value parts	parties de valeur	partes de valor	Wertteile	оценочные элементы (otsenochniye elementi)
2011 value raising	augmentation de la valeur	incremento al valor de la ejecución	Erhöhung des Werts	повышение ценности (povisheniye tsennosti)
2012 vault families (men)	familles des sauts (hommes)	series de saltos (hombres)	Sprungfamilien (Herren)	типы прыжков/мужчины/ (tipi prizhkov/muzhchini/)
2013 vault groups (women)	groupes des sauts (femmes)	series de saltos (mujeres)	Sprunggruppen (Damen)	группы прыжков/женчины/ (gruppi prizhkov/zhenshchini)
2014 vault values	valeur des sauts	valor de los saltos	Schwierigkeitsgrad der Sprünge	ценность прыжков (tsennost' prizhkov)
2015 vaulting horse	cheval; cheval-sautoir	potro	Sprungpferd	конь для прыжков (kon' dlya prizhkov)
2016 vertical axis	axe de longueur	eje longitudinal	Längsachse	вертикальная ось (vertikal'naya os')
2017 virtuosity	virtuosité	virtuosidad	Virtuosität	виртуозность (virtyoznost')
2018 warm-up area	aire d'échauffement	área de precalentamiento	Aufwärmhalle	место для разминки (mesto dlya razminki)
2019 warm-up exercises	exercices d'échauffement	ejercicios de precalentamiento	Übungen zum Aufwärme	разминочные упражнения (razminochniye uprazhneniya)

	Gymnastics	Gymnastique	Gimnasia	Turnen	Гимнастика
2020	warm-up suit	tenue d'échauffement	vestuario de precalentamiento	Aufwärmsanzug	костюм для разминки (kostyum dlya razminki)
2021	withdraw from the competition	retirer du concours,se	retirarse de la competición	nicht am Wettkampf teilnehmen	отказаться от участия в соревновании (otkazatsa ot uchastiya v sorevnovanii)
2022	women's technical committee	comité technique féminin	comité técnico femenino	technische Kommission für Frauewettbe-werbe	женская техническая комиссия (zhenskaya tehnicheskaya komissiya)

Swimming

Natation

Natación

Schwimmen

Плавание

	Swimming	Natation	Natación	Schwimmen	Плавание
2023	additional official	officiel supplémentaire	oficial auxiliar	Mitarbeiter des Kampfgerichts	дополнительный судья (dopolnitel'niy sud'ya)
2024	anchor man (relay)	dernier partant (relais)	relevista de cierre	Schlussschwimmer	последний пловец/эстафета/ (posledniy plovets/estafeta/)
2025	announcer	annonceur	locutor	Ansager	диктор (diktor)
2026	arm action	action des bras	braceo	Armarbeit	действие рук (deystviye ruk)
2027	arm recovery	retour du bras	recobro del brazo	Rückholphase der arme	вынос руки (vinos ruki)
2028	arms	bras	brazos	ärme	руки (ruki)
2029	attack	attaquer	atacar	attakieren	атаковать (atakovat')
2030	automatic time and place judging system	appareil automatique de chronométrage et de classement	marcador electrónico de cronometraje y clasificación	automatische Zeitmessanlage und Resultatanzeige	автоматическое устройство для определения времени и места (avtomaticheskoye ustroystvo dlya opredeleniya vremeni i mesta)
2031	backstroke	nage sur le dos	braza de espalda	Rückenschwimmen	плавание на спине (plavaniye na spine)
2032	backstroke flags	fanions de repère- nage de dos	banderines indicadores de las vueltas para estilo espalda	Rückenfahnen	флажки для заплыва на спине (flazhki dlya zapliva na spine)
2033	backstroke start	départ de dos	salida de espalda	Rückenstart	старт на спине (start na spine)
2034	backstroke swimmer	nageur de dos	espaldista	Rückenschwimmer	пловец на спине (plovets na spine)
2035	backstroke turn	virage de dos	viraje de espalda	Rückenwende	поворот в плавании на спине (povorot v plavanii na spine)
2036	backstroke, 100 m; 200 m	dos 100 m; 200 m	espalda, 100 m; 200 m	Rückenschwimmen, 100-m; 200-m	на спине, 100 м.; 200 м. (на спине, 100 m.; 200 m.)
2037	be stationary (starting position)	tenir immobile, se (position de départ)	mantenerse inmóvil (posición de salida)	in Startstellung verharren	неподвижность/стартовая позиция/ (nepodvizhnost'/ startovaya pozitsiya/)
2038	bilateral breathing	respiration bilatérale	respiración bilateral	Dreierzugatmung	двустороннее дыхание (dvustoronneye dihaniye)

	English	Français	Español	Deutsch	Русский
2039	bottom of the pool	fond de la piscine	fondo de la piscina	Boden des Schwimm-beckens	дно бассейна (dno basseyna)
2040	breaststroke	brasse	braza de pecho	Brustschwimmen	брасс (brass)
2041	breaststroke kick	coup de pied de brasse	patada de braza	Beinarbeit beim Brustschwimmen	движение ног при плавании брассом (dvizheniye nog pri plavanii brassom)
2042	breaststroke swimmer	brasseur	pechista	Brustschwimmer	брассист (brassist)
2043	breaststroke turn	virage de brasse	viraje de braza	Brustwende	поворот в плавании брассом (povorot v plavanii brassom)
2044	breaststroke, 100 m; 200 m	brasse 100 m; 200 m	pecho, 100 m; 200 m	Brustschwimmen; ein 100-m; 200-m	брасс, 100 м.; 200 м. (brass, 100 m.; 200 m.)
2045	breathing in	inspiration	inspiración	Einatmung	вдыхание (vdihaniye)
2046	breathing out	expiration	espiración	Ausatmung	выдыхание (vidihaniye)
2047	breathing rhythm	rythme respiratoire	ritmo de respiración	Atemrhythmus	ритм дыхания (ritm dihaniya)
2048	breathing technique	technique de respiration	técnica de respiración	Atemtechnik	техника дыхания (tehnika dihaniya)
2049	broken tempo	cadence irrégulière	ritmo irregular	unregelmässiger Beinschlag	прерванный темп (prervanniy temp)
2050	buoyancy	flottabilité	flotabilidad	Schwimmfähigkeit	плавучесть (plavuchest')
2051	butterfly	papillon	mariposa	Schmetterlingsschwim-men	баттерфляй (batterflyay)
2052	butterfly kick	coup de pied de papillon	patada de mariposa	Delphinbeinschlag	работа ног в баттерфляе (rabota nog v batterflyaye)
2053	butterfly stroke	nage papillon	braza de mariposa	Schmetterlingsschwim-men	гребок в баттерфляе (grebok v batterflyaye)
2054	butterfly swimmer	nageur de papillon	mariposista	Schmetterlingsschwim-mer	пловец баттерфляем (plovets batterflyayem)
2055	butterfly, 100 m; 200 m	papillon 100 m; 200 m	mariposa, 100 m; 200 m	Schmetterlingsschwim-men, 100-m; 200-m	стилем баттерфляй, 100 м.; 200 м. (stilem batterflyay, 100 m.; 200 m.)

135

	Swimming	Natation	Schwimmen	Natación	Плавание
2056	Canadian Amateur Swimming Association (C.A.S.A.)	Association Canadienne de Natation Amateur (A.C.N.A.)	Kanadischer Amateurschwimm-verband (C.A.S.A.)	Asociación Canadiense de Natación Amateur (A.C.N.A.)	Канадская любительская ассоциация плавания КАСА/ (kanadskaya lyubitel'skaya assotsiatsiya plavaniya/KASA/)
2057	chief judge (electronic)	juge en chef (électronique)	Schiedsrichterobmann (elektronisch)	juez en jefe por cronometraje eléctrico	главный судья (glavniy sud'ya)
2058	chief timer	chef-chronométreur	Zeitnehmerobmann	cronometrador jefe	главный секундометрист (glavniy sekundometrist)
2059	chlorinated water	eau chlorée	gechlortes Wasser	agua con cloro	хлорированная вода (hlorirovannaya voda)
2060	clerk of the course	commissaire de course	Mitarbeiter in der Auswertung	comisario del encuentro	контролер соревнования (kontrolyor sorevnovaniya)
2061	close finish	arrivée serrée	Massenankunft	llegada cerrada	близкий финиш (blizkiy finish)
2062	coach	entraîneur	Trainer	entrenador	тренер (trener)
2063	competition pool	bassin de compétition	Wettkampfbecken	piscina de competición	бассейн для соревнования (basseyn dlya sorevnovaniya)
2064	competitive swimmer	nageur de compétition	Wettkampfschwimmer	nadador de competición	соревнующийся пловец (sorevnuyushchiysya plovets)
2065	competitive swimming	nage de compétition	Wettkampfschwimmen	natación de competición	соревнование по плаванию (sorevnovaniye po plavaniyu)
2066	complete the distance	couvrir la distance	eine Strecke zurücklegen	recorrer la distancia	закончить дистанцию (zakonchit' distantsiyu)
2067	crawl	crawl	Kraul	crawl	кроль (krol')
2068	crawl swimmer	nageur de crawl	Kraulschwimmer	crolista	пловец стилем кроль (plovets stilem krol')
2069	deck	pont	Deck	cubierta	борт бассейна (bort basseyna)
2070	digital pace-clocks	horloges digitales pour rythme d'entraînement	Digitalstoppuhren für Rhytmus beim Training	relojes digitales para controlar el ritmo del paso	цифровое табло для измерения темпа (tsifrovoye tablo dlya izmereniya tempa)

English	Français	Español	Deutsch	Русский
2071 disqualification	disqualification	descalificación	Disqualifikation	дисквалификация (diskvalifikatsiya)
2072 dolphin	dauphin	delfín	Delphin	дельфин (del'fin)
2073 dolphin kick	battement de dauphin	movimiento de piernas estilo delfín	Beinarbeit beim Delphin	работа ног в дельфине (rabota nog v del'fine)
2074 double-stroke breathing	respiration à deux temps	respiración a doble brazada	Doppelzugatmung	вдыхание в двухкратном такте (vdihaniye v dvuhkratnom takte)
2075 dryland training	entraînement hors piscine	entrenamiento en seco	auf festem Boden trainieren	тренировка на суше (trenirovka na sushe)
2076 electronic time	temps automatique	tiempo electrónico	automatische Zeitnahme	электронное время (elektronnoye vremya)
2077 electronic timing equipment	équipement de chronométrage électronique	equipo de cronometraje eléctronico	elektronische Zeitnehmerausrüstung	оборудование для электронного хронометража (oborudovaniye dlya elektronnovo hronometrazha)
2078 emerge	émerger	salir del agua	auftauchen	всплыть (vsplit')
2079 end wall	mur d'extrémité	lado opuesto	Stirnwände	конечная стенка (konechnaya stenka)
2080 entry	attaque du bras	entrada al agua	Eintauchen ins Wasser	захват (zahvat)
2081 exhalation	expiration	espiración	Ausatmung	выдыхание (vidihaniye)
2082 false start	faux départ	salida falsa	Fehlstart	фальстарт (fal'start)
2083 false-start posts	supports-signalisation de faux départs	señales de salida falsa	Fehlstartpfosten	столбики фальстарта (stolbiki fal'starta)
2084 false-start rope	corde de signalisation de faux départ	cuerda de salida falsa	Fehlstartleine	верёвка фальстарта (veryovka fal'starta)
2085 fast pool	piscine rapide	piscina para carreras	Kurzstreckbecken	"быстрый" бассейн ("bistriy" basseyn)
English	**Français**	**Español**	**Deutsch**	**Русский**

	Swimming	Natation	Natación	Schwimmen	Плавание
2086	Federation Internationale de Natation Amateur (F.I.N.A.)	Fédération Internationale de Natation Amateur (F.I.N.A.)	Federación Internacional de Natación Amateur (F.I.N.A.)	Internationaler Schwimmverband (F.I.N.A.)	Интернациональная федерация любительского плавания ФИНА/ (internatsional'naya federatsiya lyubitel'skovo plavaniya/FINA/)
2087	finish	arrivée	llegada	Ziel	финиш (finish)
2088	finish wall	mur des arrivées	pared de llegadas	Zielanschlag	стенка финиша (stenka finisha)
2089	finishing judge	juge d'arrivée	juez de llegada	Zielrichter	судья на финише (sud'ya na finishe)
2090	floats	flotteurs	flotadores	Schwimmkörper	поплавки (poplavki)
2091	"fly"	papillon	mariposa	Schmetterling	баттерфляй (batterflyay)
2092	four x 100 m freestyle relay; 200 m	relais nage libre 4 x 100 m; 4 x 200 m	relevo libre, 400 m; 800 m	vier x 100-m Freistil-schwimmen; vier x 200-m	эстафета вольным стилем, 4 x 100 м; 4 x 200 м. (estafeta vol'nim stilem, 4 x 100 m.; 4 x 200 m.)
2093	four x 100 m medley relay	relais quatre nages 4 x 100 m	relevo combinado, 400 m	vier x 100 m Lagen-schwimmen	четыре на 100 м. комбинированная эстафета (chetirenastometrovaya kombinirovannaya estafeta)
2094	four-stroke breathing	respiration à quatre temps	respiración cada cuatro brazadas	Viererzugatmung	вдыхание в четырехкратном такте (vdihaniye v chetiryohkratnom takte)
2095	freestyle	nage libre	libre; libres	Freistilschwimmen	вольный стиль (vol'niy stil')
2096	freestyle relay	relais de nage libre	relevo libre	Freistilstaffel	эстафета вольным стилем (estafeta vol'nim stilem)
2097	freestyle swimmer	nageur de style libre	nadador de estilo libre	Freistilschwimmer	пловец вольным стилем (plovets vol'nim stilem)
2098	freestyle, 100 m; 200 m; 400 m; 800 m; 1500 m	nage libre 100 m; 200 m; 400 m; 800 m; 1500 m	libres, 100 m; 200 m; 400 m; 800 m; 1500 m	100-m-Freistil-schwimmen; 200-m; 400-m; 800-m; 1500-m	вольный стиль, 100 м.; 200 м.; 400 м.; 800 м.; 1500 м. (vol'niy stil', 100 m.; 200 m.; 400 m.; 800 m.; 1500 m.)
2099	glide	coulée	corriente	Gleitphase	скольжение (skol'zheniye)

English	Français	Español	Deutsch	Русский
2100 goggles	lunettes de nage	gafas de natación	Schwimmbrille	защитные очки (zashchitniye ochki)
2101 grab start	départ agrippé	salida de agarre	Grab-Start	старт схватившись (start shvativshis')
2102 gun start	coup de feu	disparo	Startschuss	старт со стартовым пистолетом (start so startovim pistoletom)
2103 gutters	goulottes	rebosaderos	Überlaufrinne	сточные канавки (stochniye kanavki)
2104 hand time	chronomètre à main	cronometrador manual	Handzeitnahme	время по ручному секундомеру (vremya po ruchnomu sekundomeru)
2105 handbells	sonnerie	campanillas	Schellen	предупредительные звонки (predupreditel'niye zvonki)
2106 head set	écouteurs	auriculares	Kopfhörer	наушники для связи (naushniki dlya svyazi)
2107 heat sheet	feuille de série	acta de series	Laufberichtsbogen	список предварительных заплывов (spisok predvaritel'nih zaplivov)
2108 heats	séries	series	Läufe	предварительные заплывы (predvaritel'nih zaplivi)
2109 individual medley turn	virage en quatre nages individuel	viraje en estilos individual	Wenden beim Lagenschwimmen	поворот при комплексном плавании (povorot pri kompleksnom plavanii)
2110 individual medley, 200 m; 400 m	quatre nages 200 m; 400 m	combinado (estilos), 200 m, 400 m	200-m Lagen-schwimmen; 400-m	комплексное плавание, 200 м. 400 м. (kompleksnoye plavaniye, 200 m.; 400 m.)
2111 indoor pool	piscine intérieure	piscina cubierta	Hallenbad	закрытый бассейн (zakritiy basseyn)
2112 inhalation	inspiration	inspiración	Einatmung	вдыхание (vdihaniye)
2113 inspector of the turns	inspecteur des virages	juez de virajes	Wenderichter	судья на повороте (sud'ya na povorote)
English	**Français**	**Español**	**Deutsch**	**Русский**

	Swimming	Natation	Natación	Schwimmen	Плавание
2114	judges' card	carte des juges	libreta de los árbitros	Karten des Kampfgerichts	судейская карта (sudeyskaya karta)
2115	kick	coup de pied	patada	Beinschlag	движение ног (dvizheniye nog)
2116	kick board	planche d'entraînement	flotador	Beinschlagbrett	пенопластовая доска (penoplastovaya doska)
2117	kick practice	battement de jambes	batido de piernas	Beinarbeit	практика движения ног (praktika dvizheniya nog)
2118	lane	couloir	calle	Bahn	дорожка (dorozhka)
2119	lane assignments	attribution des couloirs	asignación de calles	Bahnverteilung	распределение дорожек (raspredeleniye dorozhek)
2120	lane boxes	vestiaire de couloir	casetas para la ropa del nadador	Bahnblöcke	тумбочки для вещей пловцов (tumbochki dlya veshchey plovtsov)
2121	lane number	numéro du couloir	número de la calle	Bahnnummer	номер дорожки (nomer dorozhki)
2122	lane rope	corde de couloir	cuerda de la calle	Bahnleine	разделительная веревка (razdelitel'naya veryovka)
2123	lap	longueur	vuelta	Bahnlänge	отрезок дистанции (otrezok distantsii)
2124	lap counter	compteur de longueurs	contador de vueltas	Wenderichter	счетчик отрезков дистанции (schyotchik otrezkov distantsii)
2125	lap time	temps de passage	duración de cada vuelta	Zwischenzeit	время на отрезке дистанции (vremya na otrezke distantsii)
2126	leadoff swimmer	premier partant du relais	primer relevista	Startschwimmer	пловец начинающий первым (plovets nachinayushchiy pervim)
2127	leg action	action des jambes	acción de las piernas	Beinarbeit	работа ног (rabota nog)
2128	legal start	départ réussi	salida correcta	gültiger Start	удавшийся старт (udavshiysya start)
2129	length	longueur	largo	Bahnlänge	длина (dlina)

English	Français	Español	Deutsch	Русский
2130 long-distance swimmer	nageur de grand fond	nadador de larga distancia	Langstreckenschwimmer	пловец на дальние дистанции (plovets na dal'niye distantsii)
2131 long-distance swimming	nage de fond	natación de larga distancia	Langstrecken- schwimmen	плавание на дальние дистанции (plavaniye na dal'niye distantsii)
2132 manual timing	chronométrage manuel	cronometraje manual	Handzeitnahme	ручной хронометраж (ruchnoy hronometrazh)
2133 marshalling area	zone de rassemblement	área de agrupamiento	Wendepunktbe- obachtungszone	место сбора перед соревнованием (mesto sbora pered sorevnovaniyem)
2134 medley relay	relais quatre nages	relevo de estilos individual; relevo combinado	Lagenstaffel	комбинированная эстафета (kombinirovannaya estafeta)
2135 medley swimmer	nageur de quatre nages	nadador de estilos	Lagenschwimmer	пловец в комбинированном плавании (plovets v kombinirovannom plavanii)
2136 medley swimming	quatre nages	natación de estilos	Lagenschwimmen	комбинированное плавание (kombinirovannoye plavaniye)
2137 men's individual events	épreuves individuelles hommes	pruebas individuales hombres	Einzelwettbewerbe, Männer	одиночные виды плавания для мужчин (odinochniye vidi plavaniya dlya muzhchin)
2138 men's team events	épreuves par équipes hommes	pruebas por equipos masculinos	Staffelbewerbe, Männer	мужские командные виды соревнований (muzhskiye vidi sorevnovaniy)
2139 middle-distance swimmer	nageur de demi-fond	nadador de media distancia	Mittelstrecken- schwimmer	пловец на среднюю дистанцию (plovets na srednyuyu distantsiyu)
2140 middle-distance swimming	nage de demi-fond	natación de media distancia	Mittelstrecken- schwimmen	плавание на среднюю дистанцию (plavaniye na srednyuyu distantsiyu)
2141 offical time	temps officiel	tiempo oficial	offizielle Zeit	официальное время (ofitsial'noye vremya)

	Swimming	Natation	Natación	Schwimmen	Плавание
2142	officials	officiels	autoridades	Offizielle	судейская коллегия (sudeyskaya kollegiya)
2143	outdoor pool	piscine extérieure	piscina al aire libre	Freibad	открытый бассейн (otkritiy basseyn)
2144	place judge	juge d'arrivée	jueces de lugares	Schwimmrichter	судья, определяющий финиш (sud'ya, opredelyayushchiy finish)
2145	pool	piscine	piscina	Schwimmbad	бассейн (basseyn)
2146	pool ladder	échelle de bassin	escalera de la piscina	Leiter (am Beckenrand)	лестница бассейна (lestnitsa basseyna)
2147	pool staff	personnel de la piscine	responsables de la piscina	Beckenpersonal	служащие бассейна (sluzhashchie basseyna)
2148	protest	réclamation	reclamación	Einspruch	протест (protest)
2149	pull	traction du bras	tracción del brazo	Zugphase	тяга руками (tyaga rukami)
2150	pull buoy	bouée de jambes	tabla flotadora para los pies	Pull-buoys	буёк для поддержки ног (buyok dlya podderzhki nog)
2151	push	poussée du bras	empuje del brazo	Druckphase der Armarbeit	толчок (tolchok)
2152	push off	coulée	salida con impulso	Abstossphase	отталкивание (ottalkivaniye)
2153	qualifying	qualification	clasificación	qualifizierend	квалифицирование (kvalifitsirovaniye)
2154	qualifying time	temps de qualification	tiempo de clasificación	Qualifikationszeit	квалифицирующее время (kvalifitsiruyushcheye vremya)
2155	rate of respiration	rythme respiratoire	ritmo de respiración	Atmungrhythmus	дыхательный ритм (dihatel'niy ritm)
2156	recorder	enregistreur	registrador	Protokollführer	ведущий запись (vedushchiy zapis')
2157	referee	juge-arbitre	juez	Schiedsrichter	судья (sud'ya)
2158	relay	relais	relevos	Staffel	эстафета (estafeta)
2159	relay swimmer	nageur de relais	nadador de relevos	Staffelschwimmer	пловец эстафеты (plovets estafeti)

	English	Français	Español	Deutsch	Русский
2160	relay takeoff judging	contrôle des prises de relais	control de las tomas de relevos	Überwachung der Staffelablösung	судейство отталкивания на эстафете (sudeystvo ottalkivaniya na estafete)
2161	relay team member	équipier de relais	integrante del equipo de relevo	Staffelschwimmer	участник командной эстафеты (uchastnik komandnoy estafeti)
2162	results	résultats	resultados	Resultaten	результаты (rezul'tati)
2163	scoreboard	tableau de marques	marcador	Anzeigetafel	табло очков (tablo ochkov)
2164	scorer	marqueur	anotador	Schreiber	судья-секретарь (sud'ya-sekretar')
2165	scratch	forfait	eliminar una prueba	streichen	исключить из соревнования (isklyuchit' iz sorevnovaniya)
2166	seeding	classement	clasificación por tiempo	Setzen	рассеивание (rasseivaniye)
2167	sensitivity of the touch pad	sensibilité du panneau de touche	sensibilidad de la placa de toque	Empfindlichkeitsgrad der Anschlagmatte	чувствительность панели (chustvitel'nost' paneli)
2168	side wall	mur latéral	pared lateral	Längsseite	боковая стенка (bokovaya stenka)
2169	slope of the starting platform	angle d'inclinaisor de la plate-forme de départ	ángulo de inclinación del partidero	Neigung der Standfläche des Startblocks	наклон стартовой площадки (naklon startovoy ploshchadki)
2170	spin turn	virage-culbute	viraje de voltereta	Überschlagwende	поворот полусальто (povorot polusal'to)
2171	split time	temps de passage	tiempos parciales	Zwischenzeit	время на отрезке дистанции (vremya na otrezke distantsii)
2172	sprint swimmer	nageur de vitesse	nadador de velocidad	Kurzstreckenschwimmer	спринтер (sprinter)
2173	sprint swimming	nage de vitesse	natación de velocidad	Kurzstreckenschwimmen	спринт (sprint)
2174	start	départ	salida	Start	старт (start)
2175	starter	starter	juez de salida	Starter	стартёр (startyor)
2176	starting block	bloc de départ	plataforma de salida	Startblock	стартовая тумба (startovaya tumba)
2177	starting dive	plongeon de départ	salto de salida	Startsprung	стартовый прыжок (startoviy prizhok)

	Swimming	Natation	Schwimmen	Плавание
2178	starting grip	poignée de départ	Haltegriff	стартовый захват (startoviy zahvat)
2179	starting gun	pistolet de départ	Startpistole	стартовый пистолет (startoviy pistolet)
2180	starting podium	podium de départ	Startpodium	стартовая площадка (startovaya ploshchadka)
2181	starting position	position de départ	Startstellung	стартовая позиция (startovaya pozitsiya)
2182	starting technique	technique de départ	Starttechnik	стартовая техника (startovaya tehnika)
2183	stop watch	chronomètre manuel	Stoppuhr	секундомер (sekundomer)
2184	streamlined	hydrodynamique	Hydrodynamik	обтекаемый (obtekayemiy)
2185	stroke judge	juge de nage	Schwimmrichter	судья по гребкам (sud'ya po grebkam)
2186	style	style	Stil	стиль (stil')
2187	style of swimming	mode de nage	Schwimmstil	стиль плавания (stil' plavaniya)
2188	surface	émerger	auftauchen	выйти на поверхность (viyti na poverhnost')
2189	swim	nager	schwimmen	плавать (plavat')
2190	swim suit	costume de natation	Badeanzug	плавки (plavki)
2191	swimmer	nageur	Schwimmer	пловец (plovets)
2192	swimming cap	bonnet de bain	Bademütze	купальная шапочка (kupal'naya shapochka)
2193	swimming competition	concours de natation	Schwimmwettkampf	состязание по плаванию (sostyazaniye po plavaniyu)
2194	swimming event	épreuve de natation	Schwimmwettbewerb	вид плавания (vid plavaniya)
2195	swimming pool	piscine	Schwimmbad	бассейн (basseyn)
2196	swimming technique	technique de nage	Schwimmtechnik	техника плавания (tehnika plavaniya)

English	Français	Español	Deutsch	Русский
2197 T.V. track	rail de T.V.	pasillo para la cámara de televisión	Fernsehkamerabahn	рельсы для телекамеры (rel'si dlya telekameri)
2198 "take your marks!"	"à vos marques!"	"¡a sus puestos!"	"Auf die Plätze!"	"на старт!" ("na start!")
2199 take-up reels	bobines réceptrices	carretes receptores	Aufwickelspulen	катушки (katushki)
2200 temperature of the water	température de l'eau	temperatura del agua	Wassertemperatur	температура воды (temperatura vodi)
2201 timekeeper	chronométreur	cronometrador	Zeitnehmer	судья-секундометрист (sud'ya-sekundometrist)
2202 touch	touche	toque	Berührung	касание (kasaniye)
2203 touch pad	panneau de touche	placas de toque	Anschlagmatte	панель для прикосновения (panel' dlya prikosnoveniya)
2204 training pool	bassin d'entraînement	piscina de entrenamiento	Trainingbecken	тренировочный бассейн (trenirovochnij basseyn)
2205 training schedule	horaire d'entraînement	programa de entrenamiento	Trainingsprogramm	расписание тренировок (raspisaniye trenirovok)
2206 turn	virage	viraje	Wende	поворот (povorot)
2207 turn judge	juge de virage	juez de virajes	Wenderichter	судья на повороте (sud'ya na povorote)
2208 turning technique	mode de virage	técnica de viraje	Wendetechnik	техника поворотов (tehnika povorotov)
2209 unilateral breathing	respiration unilatérale	respiración unilateral	einseitige Zugatmung	одностороннее дыхание (odnostoronneye dihaniye)
2210 video back-up timing	chronométrage auxiliaire video	equipo automático de control secundario de tipo video-tape	Videobandzeitnahme	запасное измерение времени при помощи телекамеры (zapasnoye izmereniye vremeni pri pomoshchi telekameri)
2211 viscosity	viscosité	viscosidad	Viskosität	вязкость (vyazkost')
2212 wall	mur	pared	Wand	стенка (stenka)
2213 water level	niveau de l'eau	nivel del agua	Wasserhöhe	уровень воды (uroven' vodi)
2214 water resistance	résistance de l'eau	resistencia del agua	Wasserwiderstand	сопротивление воды (soprotivleniye vodi)

Swimming	Natation	Natación	Schwimmen	Плавание
2215 water surface	surface de l'eau	superficie del agua	Wasseroberfläche	поверхность воды (poverhnost' vodi)
2216 whip kick	coup de pied rapide	impulso hacia afuera con los pies	schneller Beinschlag	работа ног в брассе (rabota nog v brasse)
2217 win by a body length	gagner d'une longueur	ganar por un largo	mit einer Länge gewinnen	победить на одну длину тела (pobedit' na odnu dlinu tela)
2218 women's individual events	épreuves individuelles femmes	pruebas individuales mujeres	Einzelwettbewerbe, Frauen	одиночные виды плавания для женщин (odinochniye vidi plavaniya dlya zhenshchin)
2219 women's team events	épreuves par équipes femmes	pruebas por equipos femeninos	Staffelwettbewerbe, Frauen	женские командные виды соревнований (zhenskiye komandniye vidi sorevnovaniy)

Tennis

Tennis

Tenis

Tennis

Теннис

	Tennis	Tennis	Tenis	Tennis	Теннис
2220	ace	as	as	As	смертельная подача (smertel'naya podacha)
2221	ad in	avantage service	ventaja al saque	Vorteil Aufschläger	больше у подающего (bol'she u podayushchevo)
2222	ad out	avantage relanceur	ventaja al receptor	Vorteil Rückschläger	меньше у подающего (men'she u podayushchevo)
2223	advantage	avantage	ventaja	Vorteil	преимущество (preimushchestvo)
2224	against the net	contre le filet	contra la red	gegen das Netz	в сетку (v setku)
2225	all	partout	iguales	beide	ровно (rovno)
2226	alley	couloir	banda	Korridor	коридор (koridor)
2227	alternate courts	courts alternés	canchas alternativas	alternierende Plätze	диагональные поля подачи (diagonal'niye polya podachi)
2228	angle volley	volée en angle	volea angulada	gewinkelter Flugball	косой удар с лета (kosoy udar s lyota)
2229	angled shot	coup en angle	tiro angulado	gewinkelter Schlag	косой удар (kosoy udar)
2230	approach shot	coup d'approche	golpe de ataque	Schlag im Vorlaufen	подготовительный удар (podgotovitel'niy udar)
2231	backboard	mur d'entraînement	tablero posterior	Trainingswand	стенка для практики (stenka dlya praktiki)
2232	backcourt	fond de court	cancha del fondo	Grundlinienspiel	задняя часть корта (zadnyaya chast' korta)
2233	backcourt player	joueur de fond de court	jugador de fondo	Grundlinienspieler	игрок на задней части площадки (igrok na zadney chasti ploshchadki)
2234	backhand	revers	devolución del revés	Rückhand	удар слева (udar sleva)
2235	backhand dropshot	amorti de revers	dejada de revés	Rückhandstoppball	тормозженный удар слева (tormozhenniy udar sleva)
2236	backhand grip	prise de revers	agarro al revés	Rückhandgriff	захват ракетки для удара слева (zahvat raketki dlya udara sleva)

	English	Français	Español	Deutsch	Русский
2237	backhand groundstroke	coup au sol en revers	revés al rebote	Grundlinien Rückhand	удар слева с отскока (udar sleva s otskoka)
2238	backhand lob	lob en revers	globo de revés	Rückhandlob	свеча слева (svecha sleva)
2239	backhand side	côté du revers	lado del revés	Rückhandseite	левая сторона (levaya storona)
2240	backhand volley	volée de revers	volea de revés	Rückhandflugball	удар с лета слева (udar s lyota sleva)
2241	backspin	effet vers l'arrière	efecto hacia atrás	Rückwärtsdrall	крученый удар назад (kruchyoniy udar nazad)
2242	backswing	élan arrière	revés	Ausholschwung	замах назад (zamah nazad)
2243	ball	balle	pelota	Ball	мяч (myach)
2244	ball boy	ramasseur de balles	recogepelotas	Balljunge	приносящий мячи (prinosyashchiy myachi)
2245	ball change	changement de balles	cambio de pelotas	Ballwechsel	перемена мячей (peremena myachey)
2246	baseline	ligne de fond	línea de fondo	Grundlinie	задняя линия (zadnyaya liniya)
2247	baseline game	jeu de fond	juego de fondo	Grundlinienspiel	игра у задней линии (igra u zadney linii)
2248	bounce	rebond	bote	Aufprall	отскок (otskok)
2249	bounce (to)	rebondir	botar	aufspringen	отскочить (otskochit')
2250	bounds	limites	límites	Grenzen	линии, ограничивающие площадку (linii, ogranichivayushchiye ploshchadku)
2251	break	prendre le service adverse	romper	Aufschlagsdurchbruch	выиграть с подачи соперника (viigrat' s podachi sopernika)
2252	break-point	balle de break	punto de rompimiento	"break"-Punkt	счет меньше на подачу соперника (schyot men'she na podachu sopernika)
2253	bye	exemption	exención	Freilos	быть свободным от игры (bit' svobodnim ot igri)
2254	called off	interrompu	aplazado	unterbrochen	отменено (otmeneno)
	English	**Français**	**Español**	**Deutsch**	**Русский**

	Tennis	**Tennis**	**Tenis**	**Tennis**	**Теннис**
2255	cannonball serve	service-canon	servicio fuerte	Kanonenball-Aufschlag	пушечная подача (pushechnaya podacha)
2256	center court	court central	cancha central	"center court"	центральная площадка (tsentral'naya ploshchadka)
2257	center line	ligne médiane	línea mediana	Mittellinie	центральная линия (tsentral'naya liniya)
2258	center service line	ligne médiane de service	línea de división de servicio	Aufschlagsmittellinie	центральная линия подачи (tsentral'naya liniya podachi)
2259	chair umpire	arbitre de chaise	juez de silla	Stuhlrichter	судья на вышке (sud'ya na vishke)
2260	chip shot	coup chopé	rechazo	Chopschlag	подрезка (podrezka)
2261	close game	jeu serré	partido reñido	hart umkämpftes Spiel	близкая игра (blizkaya igra)
2262	coach	entraîneur	entrenador	Trainer	тренер (trener)
2263	coach (to)	entraîner	entrenar	trainieren	тренировать (trenirovat')
2264	competition	compétition	competición	Wettkampf	соревнование (sorevnovaniye)
2265	competitors	concurrents	competidores	Wettkämpfer	соревнующиеся (sorevnuyushchiyesya)
2266	consolation match	match de consolation	partido de consolación	Trostspiel	утешительный матч (uteshitel'niy match)
2267	continental grip	prise continentale	agarro continental	"Kontinental-Griff"; Einheitsgriff	континентальный захват ракетки (kontinental'niy zahvat raketki)
2268	court	court	cancha	Platz	корт (kort)
2269	cross-court backhand	revers croisé	revés cruzado	Rückhand-Cross	косой удар слева (kosoy otboy sleva)
2270	cross-court return	renvoi croisé	devolución cruzada	Rückschlag-Cross	косой отбой (kosoy otboy)
2271	cross-court shot	coup en diagonale	tiro cruzado	"Cross-Schlag"	косой удар (kosoy udar)
2272	cross-court volley	volée croisée	volea cruzada	"Cross"-Flugball	косой удар с лета (kosoy udar s lyota)
2273	decision	décision	decisión	Entscheid	решение (resheniye)

	English	Français	Español	Deutsch	Русский
2274	deep return	renvoi profond	devolución al fondo	langer Rückschlag	глубокий ответный удар (glubokiy otvetniy udar)
2275	deep shot	coup profond	tiro al fondo	langer Schlag	глубокий удар (glubokiy udar)
2276	default	forfait	abandono	Aufgabe	неявка (neyavka)
2277	default (to)	abandonner	abandonar	aufgeben	выйти из соревнования (vyiti iz sorevnovaniya)
2278	defeat	défait	derrota	Niederlage	поражение (porazheniye)
2279	defeat (to)	battre	derrotar	schlagen	победить (pobedit')
2280	defensive	défensif	defensivo	verteidigend	защитный (zashchitniy)
2281	defensive lob	lob de défense	globo defensivo	Verteidigungslob	защитная свеча (zashchitnaya svecha)
2282	delay	différer	demorar	verzögern	затягивать (zatyagivat')
2283	deuce	égalité	iguales	"Deuce"; Einstand	ровно (rovno)
2284	disqualify	disqualifier	descalificar	disqualifizieren	дисквалифицировать (diskvalifitsirovat')
2285	double fault	double-faute	doble falta	Doppelfehler	вторая неправильная подача (vtoraya nepravil'naya podacha)
2286	doubles	double	dobles	Doppel	парный разряд (parniy razryad)
2287	doubles finals	finale de double	final de dobles	Doppelfinal	финалы парного разряда (finali parnovo razryada)
2288	doubles line	ligne pour le double	línea de dobles	Doppellinie	линия для парного разряда (liniya dlya parnovo razryada)
2289	doubles match	match de double	partido de dobles	Doppelwettkampf	матч парного разряда (match parnovo razryada)
2290	doubles player	joueur de double	doblista	Doppelspieler	игрок парного разряда (igrok parnovo razryada)
2291	doubles sidelines	lignes du double	líneas laterales para dobles	Doppellinien	боковые линии для парного разряда (bokoviye linii dlya parnovo razryada)
2292	down the line	coup le long de la ligne	paralela a la línea	längs der Linie	удар по линии (udar po linii)

	Tennis	Tennis	Tenis	Tennis	Теннис
2293	downswing	élan descendant	impulsado hacia abajo con la raqueta	Schwung nach unten	замах вниз (zamah vniz)
2294	draw by lot	tirer au sort	sortear	auslosen	тянуть жребий (tyanut' zhrebiy)
2295	drawing by lot	tirage au sort	sorteo	Auslosung	жеребьевка (zhereb'yovka)
2296	drive	coup "drive"	drive	Drive; Schlag	сильный удар (sil'niy udar)
2297	drop volley	volée-amortie	dejada de volea	Flugstoppball	торможенный удар с лета (tormozhenniy udar s lyota)
2298	dropshot	amorti	dejada	Stoppball	укороченный удар (ukorochenniy udar)
2299	eastern grip	prise eastern	agarro oriental	"Eastern-Griff"	восточный захват ракетки (vostochniy zahvat raketki)
2300	eliminate	éliminer	eliminar	ausscheiden	выбывать из состязания (vibivat' iz sostyazaniya)
2301	even the score	égaliser	empatar	ausgleichen	сравнять счет (sravnyat' schyot)
2302	fault	faute	falta	Fehler	неправильно поданный мяч (nepravil'no podanniy myach)
2303	firm grip	prise solide	agarro firme	fester Griff	крепкий захват ракетки (krepkiy zahvat raketki)
2304	first round	série initiale	ronda inicial	erste Serie	первый круг (perviy krug)
2305	first service	première balle de service	primer servicio	erster Aufschlag	первая подача (pervaya podacha)
2306	flat drive	coup à plat	drive plano	flacher Schlag	сильный удар без вращения (sil'niy udar bez vrashcheniya)
2307	flat service	service à plat	servicio plano	flacher Aufschlag	плоская подача (ploskaya podacha)
2308	foot fault	faute de pied	falta de pie	Fussfehler	зашаг (zashag)
2309	foot-fault judge	juge de faute de pied	juez de faltas de pie	Fussfehlerrichter	судья по зашагам (sud'ya po zashagam)
2310	forced error	erreur forcée	error forzado	erzwungener Fehler	вынужденная ошибка (vinuzhdennaya oshibka)

	English	Français	Español	Deutsch	Русский
2311	forcing shot	coup de débordement	golpe que obliga	Überrumpelungsschlag	форсирующий удар (forsiruyushchiy udar)
2312	forehand	coup droit	directo	Vorhand	удар справа (udar sprava)
2313	forehand dropshot	amorti en coup droit	dejada de derecho	Vorhandstoppball	тормозенный удар справа (tormozhenniy udar sprava)
2314	forehand grip	prise du coup droit	agarro derecho	Vorhandgriff	захват ракетки для удара справа (zahvat raketki dlya udara sprava)
2315	forehand lob	lob en coup droit	globo directo	Vorhandlob	свеча справа (svecha sprava)
2316	forehand volley	volée du coup droit	volea directa	Vorhandflugball	удар с лета справа (udar s lyota sprava)
2317	forfeit	abandonner	abandonar	aufgeben	проиграть ввиду неявки (proigrat' vvidu neyavki)
2318	forward swing	élan avant	vuelo hacia adelante	Vorwärtsschwung	замах вперед (zamah vperyod)
2319	game	jeu	partido	Spiel	игра (igra)
2320	grip	prise	agarro	Griff	захват ракетки (zahvat raketki)
2321	groundstroke	coup au sol	golpe al rebote	Grundschlag	удар с отскока (udar s otskoka)
2322	gut stringing	corde de boyau	cordaje de tripas	Natursaiten	струны из сухожилий (struni iz suhozhiliy)
2323	half volley	demi-volée	media volea	Halbflugball	удар с полулета (udar s polulyota)
2324	hard-fought match	match chèrement disputé	partido reñido	hart umkämpfter Match	матч с напряженной борьбой (match s napryazhonnoy bor'boy)
2325	high lob	lob élevé	globo elevado	hoher Lob	высокая свеча (visokaya svecha)
2326	hit	coup	golpe	Schlag	удар (udar)
2327	hit (to)	frapper	golpear	schlagen	ударить (udarit')
2328	in play	en jeu	en juego	im Spiel	в игре (v igre)
2329	indoor court	court couvert	cancha interior	Hallenplatz	закрытый корт (zakritiy kort)
2330	inside	dedans	devolución buena	innerhalb	внутри (vnutri)
2331	judge	juge	juez	Richter	судья (sud'ya)
	English	**Français**	**Español**	**Deutsch**	**Русский**

153

	Tennis	Tennis	Tenis	Tennis	Теннис
2332	lead	avantage	ventaja	Vorteil	преимущество (preimushchestvo)
2333	lead (to)	mener	aventajar a	führen	вести игру (vesti igru)
2334	leader	joueur qui mène	líder	der Führende	ведущий игру (vedushchiy igru)
2335	left service court	carré de service gauche	cuadro izquierda de saque	linkes Aufschlagsfeld	левое поле подачи (levoye pole podachi)
2336	left-hander	gaucher	zurdo	Linkshänder	левша (levsha)
2337	let	"let"	saque repetido	Netzball	"сетка" ("setka")
2338	line	ligne	línea	Linie	линия (liniya)
2339	linesman	juge de ligne	juez de línea	Linienrichter	судья на линии (sud'ya na linii)
2340	lob	lob	globo	"Lob"	свеча (svecha)
2341	lob (to)	lober	levantar globos	"loben"	подать свечу (podat' svechu)
2342	lose	perdre	perder	verlieren	проиграть (proigrat')
2343	loser	perdant	perdedor	Verlierer	проигравший (proigravshiy)
2344	loss	défaite	derrota	Niederlage	проигрыш (proigrish)
2345	love	zéro	cero	Null	ноль (nol')
2346	love game	jeu blanc	juego nulo	Nullspiel	сухая игра (suhaya igra)
2347	low shot	coup bas	golpe bajo	niedriger Schlag	низкий удар (nizkiy udar)
2348	low volley	volée basse	volea baja	niedriger Flugball	низкий удар с лета (nizkiy udar s lyota)
2349	main court	court principal	cancha central	Hauptplatz	главный корт (glavniy kort)
2350	make the shot	réussir le coup	acertar el tiro	den Schlag gewinnen	сделать удачный удар (sdelat' udachniy udar)
2351	match	match	partido	Spiel	матч (match)
2352	match point	balle de match	match point	Matchball	матчбол (matchbol)
2353	match up	opposer	emparejar	opponieren	подбирать противника (podbirat' protivnika)
2354	meet	rencontre	encuentro	Treffen	встреча (vstrecha)
2355	meet (to)	rencontrer	enfrentarse con	treffen	встретиться (vstretitsa)

	English	Français	Español	Deutsch	Русский
2356	men's doubles	double messieurs	dobles masculino	Herrendoppel	парный мужской разряд (parniy muzhskoy razryad)
2357	men's singles	simple messieurs	individuales masculino	Herreneinzel	одиночный мужской разряд (odinochniy muzhskoy razryad)
2358	miss	rater	fallar	verfehlen	промахнуться (promahnutsa)
2359	mixed doubles	double mixte	dobles mixtos	gemischtes Doppel	смешанный разряд (smeshanniy razryad)
2360	net	filet	red	Netz	сетка (setka)
2361	net game	jeu de filet	juego en la red	Netzspiel	игра у сетки (igra u setki)
2362	net judge	juge de filet	juez de red	Netzrichter	судья у сетки (sud'ya u setki)
2363	net player	joueur de filet	jugador de red	Netzspieler	игрок у сетки (igrok u setki)
2364	net post	poteau de filet	poste de la red	Netzpfosten	столб сетки (stolb setki)
2365	no man's land	zone neutre	tierra de nadie	neutrale Zone	нейтральная зона (neytral'naya zona)
2366	odd-numbered games	jeux impairs	juegos impares	ungerade Spiele	нечетные игры (nechyotniye igri)
2367	offensive game	jeu offensif	juego ofensivo	Offensivspiel	атакующая игра (atakuyushchaya igra)
2368	offensive lob	lob d'attaque	globo ofensivo	offensiver Lob	свеча при нападении (svecha pri napadenii)
2369	on the line	sur la ligne	sobre la línea	auf der Linie	на линии (na linii)
2370	open tournament	tournoi "open"	torneo abierto	offenes Turnier	открытый турнир (otkritiy turnir)
2371	opening match	match initial	partido inicial	Eröffnungsmatch	начальный матч (nachal'niy match)
2372	opponent	adversaire	adversario	Gegner	соперник (sopernik)
2373	oppose	affronter	enfrentar	begegnen	соперничать (sopernichat')
2374	opposing team	équipe adverse	pareja adversaria	gegnerische Mannschaft	команда противника (komanda protivnika)
2375	out!	hors jeu	fuera	aus; "out"	за! (za)
2376	outdoor court	court extérieur	cancha exterior	Aussenplatz	открытый корт (otkritiy kort)
	English	**Français**	**Español**	**Deutsch**	**Русский**

	Tennis	Tennis	Tenis	Tennis	Теннис
2377	out-of-bounds	hors limites	fuera de los límites	ausserhalb der Grenzen	за пределами площадки (za predelami ploshchadki)
2378	out-of-play	hors jeu	fuera de juego	ausser Spiel	вне игры (vne igri)
2379	outside the line	hors de la ligne	fuera de la línea	ausserhalb der Linie	за линией (za liniyey)
2380	over the net	au-dessus du filet	sobre la red	über das Netz	через сетку (cherez setku)
2381	partner	partenaire	compañero	Partner	партнер (partnyor)
2382	passing shot	passing-shot	passing-shot	Passierschlag	обводящий удар (obvodyashchiy udar)
2383	penalty	pénalité	penalización	Strafe	пенальти (penal'ti)
2384	place (the ball)	placer la balle	colocar la pelota	den Ball plazieren	играть на свободное место (igrat' na svobodnoye mesto)
2385	play	jeu	jugada	Spiel	игра (igra)
2386	play tennis	jouer au tennis	jugar al tenis	Tennis spielen	играть в теннис (igrat' v tennis)
2387	player	joueur	jugador	Spieler	игрок (igrok)
2388	poach	"marauder"	invadir	"wildern"	сыграть по мячу на половине корта партнера (sigrat' po myachu na polovine korta partnyora)
2389	point	point	punto	Punkt	очко (ochko)
2390	point of contact	point de contact	punto de contacto	Treffpunkt	точка соприкосновения (tochka soprikosnoveniya)
2391	position	position	posición	Stellung	позиция (pozitsiya)
2392	postponed	remis	suspendido	verschoben	отменено (otmeneno)
2393	powerful shot	coup puissant	tiro violento	kraftvoller Schlag	мощный удар (moshchniy udar)
2394	practice	entraînement	práctica	Training	тренировка (trenirovka)
2395	practise (to)	pratiquer	practicar	trainieren	тренироваться (trenirovatsa)
2396	protest	protester	protestar	protestieren	заявить протест (zayavit' protest)
2397	qualify	qualifier, se	calificar	sich qualifizieren	добиться участия (dobitsa uchastiya)

English	Français	Español	Deutsch	Русский
2398 quarterfinalist	quart de finaliste	finalista de cuartos	Viertelfinalist	четверть финалист (chetvert' finalist)
2399 quarterfinals	quarts de finale	cuartos de finales	Viertelfinale	четверть финал (chetvert' final)
2400 racquet	raquette	raqueta	Schläger	ракетка (raketka)
2401 racquet face	panier de la raquette	cara de la raqueta	Schlägerfläche	струнная часть ракетки (strunnaya chast' raketki)
2402 racquet frame	cadre de la raquette	marco de la raqueta	Schlägerrahmen	обод ракетки (obod raketki)
2403 racquet handle	manche de la raquette	mango de la raqueta	Schlägergriff	ручка ракетки (ruchka raketki)
2404 racquet head	tête de la raquette	cabeza de la raqueta	Schlägerkopf	голова ракетки (golova raketki)
2405 racquet stringing	cordage de la raquette	cordaje de la raqueta	Schlägerbespannung	струны ракетки (struni raketki)
2406 rally	échange	intercambio	Ballwechsel	обмен ударами (obmen udarami)
2407 rank	classer, se	clasificar	sich klassieren	рассеивать (rasseivat')
2408 ranking	classement	clasificación	Klassierung	рассеивание (rasseivaniye)
2409 ready position	position d'attente	posición de espera	Bereitschaftsstellung	позиция готовности (pozitsiya gotovnosti)
2410 receiver	relanceur	receptor	Rückschläger	принимающий (prinimayushchiy)
2411 receiving order	ordre pour recevoir	orden de recibir	Rückschlagsreihenfolge	порядок приема (poryadok priyoma)
2412 receiving position	position de retour	posición de recepción	Rückschlagstellung	позиция для принятия (pozitsiya dlya prinyatiya)
2413 retire	abandonner	retirarse de	aufgeben	выбывать (vibivat')
2414 return	renvoyer	devolver	zurückschlagen	удар двумя руками слева (udar dvumya rukami sleva)
2415 right service court	carré de service droit	cuadro derecho de saque	rechtes Aufschlagsfeld	правое поле подачи (pravoye pole podachi)
2416 runner-up	finaliste	subcampeón	Finalist	занявший второе место (zanyavshiy vtoroye mesto)
2417 rush the net	précipiter vers le filet, se	abalanzarse hacia la red	zum Netz stürzen	ринуться к сетке (rinutsa k setke)

	Tennis	Tennis	Tenis	Tennis	Теннис
2418	schedule	Spielplan	programa	horaire	расписание (raspisaniye)
2419	scheduled	im Spielplan vorgesehen	programado	prévu	назначенный на... (naznachenniy na...)
2420	score	Spielstand	puntuación	score	счет (schyot)
2421	score (to)	Punkte erzielen	marcar	marquer	забить очко (zabit' ochko)
2422	scoreboard	Anzeigetafel	cuadro de resultados	tableau indicateur des résultats	табло очков (tablo ochkov)
2423	scoresheet	Schiedsrichterblatt	ficha de tanteo	fiche d'arbitrage	судейский протокол (sudeyskiy protokol)
2424	seeded	gesetzt	clasificado	classé	отобранные участники (otobranniye uchastniki)
2425	seeding	das Setzen	clasificación	classement	отбор (otbor)
2426	semifinalist	Halbfinalist	semifinalista	demi-finaliste	полуфиналист (polufinalist)
2427	semifinals	Halbfinale	semifinales	demi-finale	полуфиналы (polufinali)
2428	serve	Aufschlag	saque	service	подача (podacha)
2429	serve (to)	aufschlagen	sacar	servir	подать мяч (podat' myach)
2430	server	Aufschläger	servidor	serveur	подающий (podayushchiy)
2431	service	Aufschlag	servicio	service	подача (podacha)
2432	service and volley	Aufschlag - Flugball	servicio y volea	service-volée	подача и удар с лета (podacha i udar s lyota)
2433	service area	Aufschlagsfeld	área de servicio	carré de service	поле подачи (pole podachi)
2434	service break	Aufschlagdurchbruch	cambio de servicio	"break"	выигрыш принимающего (viigrish prinimayushchevo)
2435	service fault	Aufschlagsfehler	falta de saque	faute de service	неправильная подача (nepravil'naya podacha)
2436	service line	Aufschlaglinie	línea de saque	ligne de service	линия подачи (liniya podachi)
2437	service order	Aufschlagsreihenfolge	orden de saque	ordre de servir	очередность подачи (ocheryodnost' podachi)
2438	service return	Rückschlag	devolución de servicio	retour de service	возвращение подачи (vozvrashcheniye podachi)

English	Français	Español	Deutsch	Русский
2439 service stroke	coup de service	golpe de servicio	Aufschlagsbewegungsablauf	удар при подаче (udar pri podache)
2440 set	set	set	Satz	партия (partiya)
2441 set point	balle de set	set-point	Satzpunkt	решающее очко партии (reshayushcheye ochko partii)
2442 shot	coup	tiro	Schlag	удар (udar)
2443 sidespin	effet latéral	efecto lateral	Seitendrall	боковое кручение (bokovoye krucheniye)
2444 singles	simple	sencillos	Einzel	одиночный разряд (odinochniy razryad)
2445 singles final	finale du simple	final de individuales	Einzelfinal	финал одиночного разряда (final odinochnovo razryada)
2446 singles finalist	finaliste du simple	finalista de individuales	Einzelfinalist	финалист одиночного разряда (finalist odinochnovo razryada)
2447 singles match	match du simple	partido de individuales	Einzelmatch	матч одиночного разряда (match odinochnovo razryada)
2448 singles player	joueur de simple	jugador de individuales	Einzelspieler	игрок одиночного разряда (igrok odinochnovo razryada)
2449 singles sidelines	lignes du simple	líneas laterales para sencillos	Einzellinien	боковые линии для одиночного разряда (bokoviye linii dlya odinochnovo razryada)
2450 slice	balle slicée	efecto lateral	geschnittener Ball	резаный удар (rezaniy udar)
2451 slice (to)	couper la balle	dar efecto lateral	schneiden	срезать (srezat')
2452 slice service	service à effet coupé	servicio cortado	geschnittener Aufschlag	резаная подача (rezanaya podacha)
2453 slow ball	balle lente	pelota lenta	langsamer Ball	медленно летящий мяч (medlenno letyashchiy myach)
2454 smash	smash	remate	Schmetterball	смэш (smesh)
2455 smash (to)	smasher	rematar	Schmettern	гасить (gasit')
2456 speed	vitesse	velocidad	Geschwindigkeit	скорость (skorost')
2457 spin	effet	efecto	Drall	кручение (krucheniye)

	Tennis	Tennis	Tenis	Tennis	Теннис
2458	start	commencement	comienzo	Anfang	начало (nachalo)
2459	start (to)	commencer	iniciar	beginnen	начать (nachat')
2460	straight sets	sets consécutifs	sets consecutivos	aufeinanderfolgende Sätze	все партии, выигранные подряд (vse partii, viigrannie podryad)
2461	string	corder	encordar	bespannen	натягивать струны (natyagivat' struni)
2462	stringing	cordage	cuerdas	Saiten-Bespannung	струны ракетки (struni raketki)
2463	stroke	coup	golpe	Schlag	удар (udar)
2464	surface	surface	superficie	Fläche	поверхность (poverhnost')
2465	suspended	suspendu	suspendido	aufgehoben	отложен (otlozhen)
2466	sweetspot (of the racquet)	coeur du cordage	corazón de la raqueta	Bespannungszentrum	центр струн ракетки (tsentr strun raketki)
2467	swing	élan	voleo	Schwung	замах (zamah)
2468	synthetic stringing	cordage synthétique	cordaje sintético	synthetische Saiten	синтетические струны (sinteticheskiye struni)
2469	synthetic surface	surface synthétique	superficie sintética	synthetische Fläche	синтетическая поверхность (sinteticheskaya poverhnost')
2470	team	équipe	equipo	Mannschaft	команда (komanda)
2471	team captain	capitaine d'équipe	capitán del equipo	Mannschaftskapitän	капитан команды (kapitan komandi)
2472	teammate	coéquipier	compañero	Partner	член той же команды (chlen toy zhe komandi)
2473	tennis elbow	tennis-elbow	codo de tenis	Tennisellbogen	локоть теннисиста (lokot' tennisista)
2474	tension of the strings	tension du cordage	tensión del cordaje	Bespannungshärte	напряжение струн (napryazheniye strun)
2475	tie-breaking set	set décisif	set decisivo	Entscheidungssatz	решающая партия (reshayushchaya partiya)
2476	tie score	égalité	empate	Einstand	равный счет (ravniy schyot)

English	Français	Español	Deutsch	Русский
2477 tie-score match	match nul	partido empatado	Matchausgleich	матч с равным счетом (match s ravnim schyotom)
2478 tie the score	égaliser	empatar la puntuación	ausgleichen	сравнять счет (sravnyat' schyot)
2479 tiebreaker	tie-break	tie-breaker	"Tiebreak"; Entscheidung	решающая игра (reshayushchaya igra)
2480 time out	arrêt du jeu	descanso	Spielunterbruch	перерыв (pereriv)
2481 top seed	classé tête de la compétition	primer clasificado	als Erster gesetzt	отобранный первым (otobranniy pervim)
2482 topspin	effet vers l'avant	liftado	Vorwärtsdrall	топспин (topspin)
2483 topspin service	service à effet toppé	servicio liftado	gelifteter Aufschlag	сверх крученая подача (sverh kruchyonaya podacha)
2484 touch the net	toucher le filet	tocar la red	das Netz berühren	коснуться сетки (kosnutsa setki)
2485 two-fisted forehand	coup droit à deux mains	directo a dos manos	Zweihandvorhand	удар двумя руками справа (udar dvumya rukami sprava)
2486 two-handed backhand	revers à deux mains	revés a dos manos	zweihändige Rückhand	удар двумя руками слева (udar dvumya rukami sleva)
2487 two-handed strokes	coups à deux mains	golpe a dos manos	Zweihandschläge	удары двумя руками (udari dvumya rukami)
2488 two out of three sets	au meilleur de trois sets	dos de tres sets	über zwei Gewinnsätze	две из трех партий (dve iz tryoh partiy)
2489 umpire	arbitre	árbitro	Schiedsrichter	судья (sud'ya)
2490 umpire's chair	chaise de l'arbitre	silla del árbitro	Schiedsrichterstuhl	вышка судьи (vishka sud'yi)
2491 umpire's decision	décision de l'arbitre	decisión del árbitro	Schiedsrichterentscheid	решение судьи (resheniye sud'yi)
2492 underspin	balle coupée	cortado	"Slice"	подрезанный удар (podrezanniy udar)
2493 unforced error	erreur non-forcée	error no forzado	nicht erzwungener Fehler	неоправданная ошибка (neopravdannaya oshibka)
2494 unreturnable shot	coup sans riposte	tiro imparable	Gewinnschlag	невозвращаемый удар (nevozvrashchayemiy udar)
2495 unseeded	non-classé	sin clasificar	nicht gesetzt	не отобранный (ne otobranniy)

	Tennis	Tennis	Tenis	Tennis	Теннис
2496	upset	renversement	victoria inesperada	Sensation	неожиданная победа (neozhidannaya pobeda)
2497	upset (to)	renverser	vencer inesperadamente	umstellen	неожиданно выиграть (neozhidanno viigrat')
2498	upswing	élan ascendant	impulsado hacia arriba con la raqueta	Aufwärtsschwung	взмах вверх (vzmah vverh)
2499	victory	victoire	victoria	Sieg	победа (pobeda)
2500	volley	volée	volea	Flugball	удар с лёта (udar s lyota)
2501	volley (to)	volleyer	volear	Flugball spielen	ударить с лёта (udarit' s lyota)
2502	volleying position	position pour la volée	posición para la volea	Flugschlagstellung	положение для удара с лёта (polozheniye dlya udara s lyota)
2503	warm-up exercises	exercices d'échauffement	ejercicios para entrar en forma	Aufwärmübungen	разминка (razminka)
2504	warning	avertissement	advertencia	Mahnung	предупреждение (preduprezhdeniye)
2505	weak shot	coup faible	tiro débil	schwacher Schlag	слабый удар (slabiy udar)
2506	western grip	prise western	agarro occidental	"Westerngriff"	западный захват ракетки (zapadniy zahvat raketki)
2507	wide shot	coup trop long	tiro fuera	zu langer Schlag	мяч в сторону (myach v storonu)
2508	win	victoire	triunfo	Sieg	выигрыш (viigrish)
2509	win (to)	gagner	ganar	gewinnen	выиграть (viigrat')
2510	winner	gagnant	vencedor	Sieger	победитель (pobeditel')
2511	winning point	point décisif	punto decisivo	Siegespunkt	решающее очко (reshayushcheye ochko)
2512	winning team	équipe victorieuse	pareja vencedora	siegreiche Mannschaft	команда-победительница (komanda-pobeditel'nitsa)
2513	withdrawal	retrait	abandono	Rückzug	выход из состязания (vihod iz sostyazaniya)

2514	women's doubles	double dames	dobles femenino	Damen-Doppel	женский парный разряд (zhenskiy parniy razryad)
2515	women's singles	simple dames	individuales femenino	Damen-Einzel	женский одиночный разряд (zhenskiy odinochniy razryad)
2516	wrong call	faute d'arbitrage	llamada errónea	falscher Ausruf	неправильное решение судьи (nepravil'noye resheniye sud'yi)
2517	zero	zéro	cero	Null	ноль (nol')

Volleyball

Volley-ball

Voleibol

Volleyball

Волейбол

	Volleyball	Volley-ball	Voleibol	Volleyball	Волейбол
2518	ace	as	as	As	смертельная подача (smertel'naya podacha)
2519	antennas	antennes	antenas	Antennen	антенны (antenni)
2520	attack	attaque	ataque	Angriff	атака (ataka)
2521	attack coverage	soutien d'attaque	apoyo en el ataque	Angriffsdeckung	страховка нападающих (strahovka napadayushchih)
2522	attack line	ligne d'attaque	línea de ataque	Angriffslinie	линия нападения (liniya napadeniya)
2523	attack reception	récupération du ballon	recuperación del balón	den Ball unter Kontrolle bringen	прием удара (priyom udara)
2524	attack specialist	spécialiste de l'attaque	especialista de ataque	Angriffsspezialist	специалист по атаке (spetsialist po atake)
2525	attack zone	zone d'attaque	zona de ataque	Angriffszone	зона нападения (zona napadeniya)
2526	attacker	attaquant	atacador	Angriffspieler	атакующий (atakuyushchiy)
2527	backcourt	zone arrière	zona de defensa	Verteidigungszone	зона защиты (zona zashchiti)
2528	backcourt defence	défense arrière	defensa de atrás	Abwehr im Hinterfeld	защита задней линии (zashchita zadney linii)
2529	backcourt players	arrières	jugadores de fondo	Grundspieler	игроки задней линии (igroki zadney linii)
2530	back-row attack	attaque de ligne arrière	ataque de fondo	Grundangriff	атака с задней линии (ataka s zadney linii)
2531	back-row player	joueur de ligne arrière	jugador de la línea trasera	Grundspieler	игрок задней линии (igrok zadney linii)
2532	back-row setter	pénétrant	penetrador	Läufer	пасующий игрок задней линии (pasuyushchiy igrok zadney linii)
2533	backward pass	passe arrière	pase hacia atrás	Rückpass	передача назад (peredacha nazad)
2534	ball	ballon	balón	Ball	мяч (myach)

	English	Français	Español	Deutsch	Русский
2535	ball handling	prendre le ballon en mains	manejo del balón	Berührung des Balls	владение мячом (vladeniye myachom)
2536	ball in play	ballon en jeu	balón en juego	Ball im Spiel	мяч в игре (myach v igre)
2537	ball in the court	ballon bon	balón bueno	der Ball ist gut	мяч в пределах площадки (myach v predelah ploshchadki)
2538	ball in the net	ballon dans le filet	balón sobre la red	Netzball	мяч в сетку (myach v setku)
2539	ball out-of-bounds	ballon dehors	balón fuera	Ausball	мяч за пределами площадки (myach za predelami ploshchadki)
2540	ball out of play	ballon mort	balón muerto	toter Ball	мяч вне игры (myach vne igri)
2541	ball retriever	ramasseur de ballons	recogepelotas	Balljunge	приносящий мяч (prinosyashchiy myach)
2542	ball touching the net	ballon touchant le filet	balón que toca la red	der Ball berührt das Netz	мяч коснувшийся сетки (myach kosnuvshiysya setki)
2543	block	bloc	bloqueo	Block	блок (blok)
2544	block (to)	bloquer	bloquear	blocken	блокировать (blokirovat')
2545	block specialist	spécialiste du contre	especialista del bloqueo	Blockspezialist	специалист по блокированию (spetsialist po blokirovaniyu)
2546	blocked spike	smash contré	remate bloqueado	abgeblockter Schmetterball	блокированный удар (blokirovanniy udar)
2547	blocker	contreur	bloqueador	Blockspieler	блокирующий (blokiruyushchiy)
2548	blocking tactic	tactique de contre	táctica de bloqueo	Blocktaktik	тактика блокирования (taktika blokirovaniya)
2549	boundary lines	lignes de jeu	líneas de juego	Begrenzungslinien	ограничительные линии (ogranichitel'niye linii)
2550	bump	manchette	golpe de puños	unteres Zuspiel	прием снизу (priyom snizu)
2551	bump pass	passe en manchette	pase de puños	unteres Zuspiel	низкая передача (nizkaya peredacha)
2552	bump reception	réception en manchette	devolución de puños	Ballannahme in Baggerstellung	прием снизу (priyom snizu)
2553	captain	capitaine	capitán	Kapitän	капитан (kapitan)

	Volleyball	**Volley-ball**	**Voleibol**	**Volleyball**	**Волейбол**
2554	carry the ball	porter le ballon	llevar el balón	den Ball führen	нести мяч (nesti myach)
2555	catch the ball	saisir le ballon	captura del balón	den Ball fangen	поймать мяч (poymat' myach)
2556	center line	ligne centrale	línea central	Mittellinie	средняя линия (srednyaya liniya)
2557	change of service	changement de service	cambio de saque	Aufgabenwechsel	переход подачи (perehod podachi)
2558	change sides	changement de camp	cambio de campo	Seitenwechsel	сменить стороны (smenit' storoni)
2559	choice of service	choix du service	sorteo del saque	Wahl der Aufgabe	выбор подачи (vibor podachi)
2560	clear space	zone libre	hueco	Abwehrbereich; Freiraum	свободное место (svobodnoye mesto)
2561	clockwise rotation	rotation dans le sens des aiguilles d'une montre	rotación hacia la derecha	Rotation im Uhrzeigersinn	переход по часовой стрелке (perehod po chasovoy strelke)
2562	coach	entraîneur	entrenador	Trainer	тренер (trener)
2563	coin toss	tirage au sort	sorteo	Auslosen	жеребьёвка (zhereb'yovka)
2564	contacting the ball	touche de ballon	toque de balón	Ballberührung	касание мяча (kasaniye myacha)
2565	court	terrain	cancha	Spielfeld	площадка (ploshchadka)
2566	court coverage	couverture du terrain	cobertura del terreno	Positionen; Zonen	расстановка игроков на площадке (rasstanovka igrokov na ploshchadke)
2567	covering the receiver	soutien de réception	apoyo de la recepción	annehmende Unterstützung	страховка принимающего (strahovka prinimayushchevo)
2568	crossing the center line	passage de la ligne centrale	invasión	Überschreiten der Mittellinie	переход средней линии (perehod sredney linii)
2569	crossing the net line	passage du plan du filet	paso del plano vertical de la red	Überschreiten der Mittellinie	переход линии сетки (perehod linii setki)
2570	dead ball	ballon mort	balón muerto	toter Ball	мяч вне игры (myach vne igri)
2571	deciding set	set décisif	set decisivo	Entscheidungssatz	решающая партия (reshayushchaya partiya)
2572	defence	défense	defensa	Verteidigung	защита (zashchita)

	English	Français	Español	Deutsch	Русский
2573	defensive block	contre défensif	bloqueo defensivo	Abwehrblock	защитный блок (zashchitniy blok)
2574	defensive player	défenseur	defensor	Abwehrspieler	защитник (zashchitnik)
2575	defensive position	position de défense	posición de defensa	Abwehrstellung	защитная расстановка (zashchitnaya rasstanovka)
2576	defensive specialist	spécialiste de la défense	especialista de defensa	Abwehrspezialist	специалист по защите (spetsialist po zashchite)
2577	defensive system	système de défense	sistema de defensa	Verteidigungssystem	система защиты (sistema zashchiti)
2578	defensive tactic	tactique défensive	táctica defensiva	Defensivtaktik	защитная тактика (zashchitnaya taktika)
2579	delay the game	retarder intention- nellement le jeu	retardar intenciona- damente el juego	Spielverzögerung	задерживать игру (zaderzhivat' igru)
2580	difficult dig	récupération difficile	recuperación difícil	schwierige Abwehr	доставание трудного низкого мяча (dostavaniye trudnovo nizkovo myacha)
2581	digger	spécialiste de la défense	recuperador	Abwehrspezialist	специалист по низким мячам (spetsialist po nizkim myacham)
2582	digging	récupération du ballon	recuperación del balón; salvar	den Ball unter Kontrolle bringen	прием низкого мяча (priyom nizkovo myacha)
2583	dink the ball	placer le ballon	colocar el balón con la yema de los dedos	den Ball lobben	направить мяч (napravit' myach)
2584	direct attack	attaque en première main	ataque al primer pase	Angriff über den ersten Pass	атака с первой передачи (ataka s pervoy peredachi)
2585	disqualification	exclusion	expulsión	Feldverweis	дисквалификация (diskvalifikatsiya)
2586	dive	plongeon	plancha	Hechtbagger	падение игрока за мячом (padeniye igroka za myachom)
2587	double hit	doublé	doble	Doppelschlag	двойной удар (dvoynoy udar)
2588	down ball	ballon faible	balón no bloquedo a propósito	kraftloser Ball	слабый мяч (slabiy myach)
	English	**Français**	**Español**	**Deutsch**	**Русский**

	Volleyball	Volley-ball	Voleibol	Volleyball	Волейбол
2589	drop	amorti	"drop"	Drop	опустить мяч (opustit' myach)
2590	dump the ball	placer le ballon	enviar el balón después del primer toque	unerwartete Rückkehr nach dem ersten Pass	передать мяч через сетку (peredat' myach cherez setku)
2591	earn a side out	récupérer le service	recuperar el saque	eine Aufgabe gewinnen	выиграть подачу (viigrat' podachu)
2592	end blocker	contreur d'aile	bloqueador del ala	äusserer Spieler bei Dreierblock	крайний блокирующий (krayniy blokiruyushchiy)
2593	end line	ligne de fond	línea de fondo	Grundlinie	лицевая линия (litsevaya liniya)
2594	end of set	fin de set	final del set	Satzende	конец партии (konets partii)
2595	enter the game	entrer en jeu	entrar en juego	in das Spiel eintreten	войти в игру (voyti v igru)
2596	expiration of time out	fin de temps mort	final de tiempo muerto	Ende der Auszeit	окончание перерыва (okonchaniye pereriva)
2597	expulsion	expulsion	expulsión	Feldverweis	удаление (udaleniye)
2598	fake	feinte	finta	täuschen	обманное движение (obmannoye dvizheniye)
2599	fault	faute	falta	Fehler	ошибка (oshibka)
2600	feint	feinte	finta	Täuschung	финт (fint)
2601	feint attack	feinte de smash	finta de remate	Angriffsschlag	обманная атака (obmannaya ataka)
2602	fire pass	passe tendue	pase veloz	schnellgezogener Pass	прострельная передача (prostrel'naya peredacha)
2603	first referee	premier arbitre	primer árbitro	erster Schiedsrichter	первый судья (perviy sud'ya)
2604	flag	fanion	banderín	Flagge	флажок (flazhok)
2605	floating serve	service flottant	saque flotante	Flatteraufgabe	планирующая подача (planiruyushchaya podacha)
2606	follow the ball	accompagner le ballon	seguir el balón	dem Ball folgen	следить за мячом (sledit' za myachom)
2607	foot fault	faute de pied	falta de pie	Fussfehler	зашаг (zashag)
2608	forfeit	forfait	no presentado	Verlust des Spiels	неявка (neyavka)
2609	form the block	former le bloc	formar el bloqueo	einen Block bilden	составить блок (sostavit' blok)

	English	Français	Español	Deutsch	Русский
2610	formation	formation	formación	Aufstellung	расстановка (rasstanovka)
2611	forming a block	fixer le contre	formar un bloqueo	einen Block bilden	расстановка для блока (rasstanovka dlya bloka)
2612	forward pass	passe avant	pase adelante	Pass nach vorn	передача вперед (peredacha vperyod)
2613	foul	faute	falta	Fehler	ошибка (oshibka)
2614	"free ball"	"balle facile"	balón fácil	"leichter Ball"	слабый мяч (slabiy myach)
2615	front dive	plongeon en avant	plancha hacia adelante	Hechtbagger nach vorn	падение вперед (padeniye vperyod)
2616	frontcourt players	avants	delanteros	Netzspieler	игроки передней линии (igroki peredney linii)
2617	front-row player	joueur de ligne avant	jugador de la línea delantera	Netzspieler	игрок линии нападения (igrok linii napadeniya)
2618	game	manche	juego	Satz	игра (igra)
2619	game lost	set perdu	juego perdido	verlorener Satz	проигранная игра (proigrannaya igra)
2620	game won	set gagné	juego ganado	gewonnener Satz	выигранная игра (viigrannaya igra)
2621	half roll	demi-boulé	medio balanceo	halb abrollen	падение полуперекатом (padeniye poluperekatom)
2622	halfway in the deciding set	milieu du set décisif	mitad del juego decisivo	Seitenwechsel während des Entscheidungssatzes	половина решающей партии (polovina reshayushchey partii)
2623	held ball	ballon tenu	balón detenido	Ball gehalten	задержанный мяч (zaderzhanniy myach)
2624	high pass	passe haute	pase alto	hoher Pass	высокая передача (visokaya peredacha)
2625	hook serve	service coupé	saque gancho	Hakenaufgabe	подача крюком (podacha kryukom)

	Volleyball	Volley-ball	Voleibol	Volleyball	Волейбол
2626	International Volleyball Federation (I.V.B.F.)	Fédération Internationale de Volley-Ball (F.I.V.B.)	Federación Internacional de Balonvolea (F.I.V.B.)	Internationaler Volley-ballverband (I.V.V.)	Международная федерация волейбола/ИВБФ/ (mezhdunarodnaya federatsiya voleybola/IVBF/)
2627	interrupted play	jeu interrompu	juego interrumpido	Unterbrechung einer Begegnung	остановленная игра (ostanovlennaya igra)
2628	interruption of play	interruption de jeu	interrupción del juego	Spielunterbrechung	остановка игры (ostanovka igri)
2629	jump pass	passe en suspension	pase en suspensión	Passen im Flug	передача в прыжке (peredacha v prizhke)
2630	kill	achever	rematar	toten	гасить (gasit')
2631	kneepad	genouillère	rodillera	Knieschützer	наколенник (nakolennik)
2632	leave the court	sortir du terrain	salir del terreno	das Spielfeld verlassen	покинуть площадку (pokinut' ploshchadku)
2633	left back	arrière gauche	zaguero izquierdo	hinten links	левый игрок задней линии (leviy igrok zadney linii)
2634	left front	avant gauche	delantero izquierdo	vorne links	левый игрок передней линии (leviy igrok peredney linii)
2635	legal serve	service correct	saque reglamentario	gültige Aufgabe	правильная подача (pravil'naya podacha)
2636	lift the ball	soulever le ballon	levantar el balón	den Ball heben	поднять мяч (podnyat' myach)
2637	line fault	faute de pied	falta de pie	Überschreiten der Linie	ошибка на линии (oshibka na linii)
2638	linesman	juge de ligne	juez de línea	Linienrichter	судья на линии (sud'ya na linii)
2639	lose the rally	perdre l'échange	perder el cambio	einen Ballwechsel verlieren	проиграть обмен (proigrat' obmen)
2640	loss of service	perte du service	pérdida del saque	Aufgabeverlust	потеря подачи (poterya podachi)
2641	make a drop	faire un amorti	amortiguar	Drop spielen	опустить мяч (opustit' myach)
2642	match	rencontre	partido	Wettkampf	матч (match)
2643	match officials	collège des arbitres	colegio de árbitros	Kampfgericht	официальные лица матча (ofitsial'niye litsa matcha)

	English	Français	Español	Deutsch	Русский
2644	match point	ballon de match	último punto del juego	Matchball	решающее очко матча (reshayushcheye ochko matcha)
2645	measuring stick	toise	vara de medir	Messgerät	измерительная планка (izmeritel'naya planka)
2646	middle attacker	attaquant du centre	ataque central	mittlerer Angriffsspieler	средний нападающий (sredniy napadayushchiy)
2647	middle back	arrière centre	defensa central	mittlerer Grundspieler	средний игрок задней линии (sredniy igrok zadney linii)
2648	middle blocker	contreur central	bloqueador central	mittlerer Blocker	средний блокирующий игрок (sredniy blokiruyushchiy igrok)
2649	middle front	avant centre	delantero centro	vorne Mitte	средний игрок передней линии (sredniy igrok peredney linii)
2650	miss the ball	manquer le ballon	fallar al balón	den Ball verfehlen	промахнуться по мячу (promahnutsa po myachu)
2651	moving	déplacement	desplazamiento	Bewegung	движение (dvizheniye)
2652	moving backward	déplacement arrière	desplazamiento hacia atrás	Rückwärtsbewegung	движение назад (dvizheniye nazad)
2653	moving defence	défense mobile	defensa móvil	dynamische Abwehr	подвижная защита (podvizhnaya zashchita)
2654	moving forward	déplacement avant	desplazamiento hacia adelante	Vorwärtsbewegung	движение вперед (dvizheniye vperyod)
2655	moving sideways	déplacement latéral	desplazamiento lateral	Seitwärtsbewegung	движение в сторону (dvizheniye v storonu)
2656	moving to the ball	déplacement vers le ballon	desplazamiento hacia el balón	sich zum Ball stellen	движение к мячу (dvizheniye k myachu)
2657	moving under the ball	déplacement sous le ballon	desplazamiento debajo del balón	sich unter den Ball stellen	движение под мяч (dvizheniye pod myach)
2658	net	filet	red	Netz	сетка (setka)
2659	net cable	câble de filet	cable de la red	Stahlseil zum Spannen des Netzes	канат (kanat)
2660	net fault	faute de filet	falta de red	Netzfehler	касание сетки (kasaniye setki)
	English	**Français**	**Español**	**Deutsch**	**Русский**

	Volleyball	Volley-ball	Voleibol	Volleyball	Волейбол
2661	net height	hauteur du filet	altura de la red	Netzhöhe	высота сетки (visota setki)
2662	net length	longueur du filet	longitud de la red	Länge des Netzes	длина сетки (dlina setki)
2663	net meshes	mailles du filet	mallas de la red	Maschen	петли сетки (petli setki)
2664	net posts	poteaux de filet	poste de la red	Netzpfosten	стойки сетки (stoyki setki)
2665	net serve	service de filet	saque a la red	Netzaufgabe	подача в сетку (podacha v setku)
2666	net width	largeur du filet	anchura de la red	Breite des Netzes	ширина сетки (shirina setki)
2667	net winch	treuil du filet	torno de mano de la red	Netzspanner	лебедка для сетки (lebyodka dlya setki)
2668	offence	attaque	ataque	Angriff	нападение (napadeniye)
2669	offensive block	contre offensif	bloqueo ofensivo	Angriffsblock	нападающий блок (napadayushchiy blok)
2670	offensive system	système d'attaque	sistema de ataque	Angriffssystem	система нападения (sistema napadeniya)
2671	offensive tactic	tactique offensive	táctica ofensiva	Angriffstaktik	тактика нападения (taktika napadeniya)
2672	one-hand bump	manchette à une main	golpe por debajo	einhändig baggern	прием мяча одной рукой (priyom myacha odnoy rukoy)
2673	one-hand dig	récupération à une main	devolución con una mano	mit einer Hand abwehren	прием одной рукой снизу (priyom odnoy rukoy snizu)
2674	one-hand pass	passe à une main	pase de una mano	Pass mit einer Hand	передача одной рукой (peredacha odnoy rukoy)
2675	one-man block	contre individuel	bloqueo individual	Einerblock	одиночный блок (odinochniy blok)
2676	opponent's court	camp adverse	campo contrario	gegnerische Spielfeldhälfte	поле противника (pole protivnika)
2677	out-of-bounds	hors limites	fuera	im Aus	за границами (za granitsami)
2678	out of order	faute de position	fuera del orden	ausser Bewegung sein das Spielfeld	не по порядку (ne po poryadku)
2679	outgoing player	joueur sortant	jugador saliente	verlassender Spieler	выходящий игрок (vihodyashchiy igrok)

	English	Français	Español	Deutsch	Русский
2680	outside attacker	attaquant d'aile	ala	äusserer Angriffspieler	крайний атакующий (krayniy atakuyushchiy)
2681	overhand serve	service au-dessus de l'épaule	saque de espaldas	Tennisaufgabe	верхняя подача (verhnyaya podacha)
2682	overlap	faute de position	falta de secuencia en la rotación	ausser Bewegung sein	не по порядку (ne po poryadku)
2683	overspin	brosser	dar efecto liftado	Topspin	верхнее вращение (verhneye vrashcheniye)
2684	pass	passe	pase	Pass	передача (peredacha)
2685	pass (to)	passer	pasar	passen	пасовать (pasovat')
2686	passing one's hand over the net	passage de la main au-dessus du filet	paso de la mano por encima de la red	über das Netz reichen	перенос руки через сетку (perenos ruki cherez setku)
2687	pause	pause	descanso	Pause	перерыв (pereriv)
2688	penetration	pénétration	penetración	Eindringen	выход с задней линии (vihod s zadney linii)
2689	place for coaches	emplacement des entraîneurs	sitio para entrenadores	Trainerbank	скамейка тренеров (skameyka trenerov)
2690	place for substitutes	emplacement des remplaçants	sitio de los suplentes	Bank für die Auswechselspieler	скамейка запасных (skameyka zapasnih)
2691	player	joueur	jugador	Spieler	игрок (igrok)
2692	players' bench	banc des joueurs	banco de los jugadores	Spielerbank	скамейка игроков (skameyka igrokov)
2693	playing area	surface du jeu	superficie de juego	Spielfeld	игровая площадка (igrovaya ploshchadka)
2694	playing the ball	frappe du ballon	golpear el balón	Ballberührung	удар по мячу (udar po myachu)
2695	position fault	faute de position	falta de posición	Aufstellungsfehler	ошибка в расстановке (oshibka v rasstanovke)
2696	power attack	attaque en force	ataque en fuerza	Angriff aus der ersten Ballberührung	силовая атака (silovaya ataka)
2697	power hit	frappe en puissance	golpear con potencia	Schmettern	силовой удар (silovoy udar)

	Volleyball	Volley-ball	Voleibol	Volleyball	Волейбол
2698	power serve	service puissant	saque en potencia	Scharf geschlagene Aufgabe	силовая подача (silovaya podacha)
2699	rally	échange	cambio de balón	Ballwechsel	обмен ударами (obmen udarami)
2700	receiving formation	formation de réception	formación para recibir el saque	Aufstellung bei der Ballannahme	расстановка при приеме (rasstanovka pri priyome)
2701	receiving team	équipe de réception	equipo receptor	annehmende Mannschaft	принимающая команда (prinimayushchaya komanda)
2702	reception	réception	recibo	Annahme	прием (priyom)
2703	red card	carte rouge	tarjeta roja	rote Karte	красная карточка (krasnaya kartochka)
2704	referee's cards	cartes d'arbitrage	tarjetas del árbitro	Schiedsrichterkarten	карточки судьи (kartochki sud'yi)
2705	referee's stand	chaise d'arbitrage	silla del árbitro	Schiedsrichterstuhl	судейская вышка (sudeyskaya vishka)
2706	replacement	remplacement de joueur	cambio de jugador	Spielerwechsel	замена (zamena)
2707	replacement request	demande de remplacement de joueur	solicitud de cambio de jugadores	Antrag auf Spielerwechsel	просьба о замене (pros'ba o zamene)
2708	rest period	repos	descanso	Pause	отдых (otdih)
2709	right back	arrière droit	zaguero derecho	Rechter hinten rechts	правый игрок задней линии (praviy igrok zadney linii)
2710	right front	avant droit	delantero derecho	Rechter vorne rechts	правый игрок передней линии (praviy igrok peredney linii)
2711	roll	boulé	balanceo	Abrollen	падение перекатом (padeniye perekatom)
2712	rotation	rotation	rotación	Rotation	переход игроков (perehod igrokov)
2713	rotation fault	faute de rotation	falta de rotación	Aufstellungsfehler	ошибка при переходе (oshibka pri perehode)

	English	Français	Español	Deutsch	Русский
2714	rotation order	ordre de rotation des joueurs	posición de los jugadores	Aufstellung der Spieler	порядок перехода (poryadok perehoda)
2715	roundhouse serve	service balancier	saque rotativo	seitliche Aufgabe	верхняя боковая подача (verhnyaya bokovaya podacha)
2716	roundhouse spike	smash balancier	remate rotativo	Hakenschlag	верхний боковой удар (verhniy bokovoy udar)
2717	score	score (pointage)	puntuación	Punktstand	счет (schyot)
2718	score sheet	feuille de match	hoja de anotación	Spielberichtsbogen	протокол игры (protokol igri)
2719	scoreboard	tableau indicateur	tablero indicador	Anzeigetafel	табло счета (tablo schyota)
2720	scorer	marqueur	anotador	Anschreiber	секретарь (sekretar')
2721	scorer's table	table de marque	mesa de marcador	Tisch des Anschreibers	стол судьи-секретаря (stol sud'yi-sekretarya)
2722	screen	écran	pantalla	Sichtblock	заслон (zaslon)
2723	second referee; umpire	second arbitre	segundo árbitro	zweiter Schiedsrichter	второй судья (vtoroy sud'ya)
2724	serve (to)	servir	sacar	aufgeben	подать (podat')
2725	serve; service	service	saque	Aufgabe	подача (podacha)
2726	server	serveur	sacador	Aufgeber	подающий (podayushchiy)
2727	service area	surface de service	zona de saque	Aufgaberaum	поле подачи (pole podachi)
2728	service block	bloc de service	bloqueo al saque	Aufgabeblock	блок подачи (blok podachi)
2729	service error	rater le service	fallar el saque	Aufgabefehler	ошибка при подаче (oshibka pri podache)
2730	service formation	formation au service	formación para el saque	Aufstellung im Augenblick der Aufgabe	расстановка игроков при подаче (rasstanovka igrokov pri podache)
2731	service specialist	spécialiste du service	especialista del saque	Aufgabespezialist	специалист по подачам (spetsialist po podacham)
2732	serving tactic	tactique de service	táctica de saque	Aufgabetaktik	тактика подачи (taktika podachi)
2733	set	set	juego; pase	Satz	пас на удар (pas na udar)
2734	set (to)	passer	preparar la jugada	stellen	дать пас на удар (dat' pas na udar)
	English	**Français**	**Español**	**Deutsch**	**Русский**

	Volleyball	Volley-ball	Voleibol	Volleyball	Волейбол
2735	set point	ballon de set	último punto decisivo del juego	Satzball	решающее очко партии (reshayushcheye ochko partii)
2736	setter	passeur	pasador	Stellspieler	передающий игрок (peredayushchiy igrok)
2737	setup	passe d'attaque	pase de ataque	Stellspiel	передача на удар (peredacha na udar)
2738	short pass	passe courte	pase corto	kurzer Pass	короткая передача (korotkaya peredacha)
2739	side dive	plongeon latéral	plancha lateral	Hechtbagger nach vorn	нырок игрока в сторону (nirok igroka v storonu)
2740	side net markers	marques verticales de côté du filet	bandas laterales de la red	Seitenstreifen des Netzes	ограничительные ленты сетки (ogranichitel'niye lenti setki)
2741	side roll	boulé latéral	balanceo lateral	seitlich abrollen	падение перекатом на бедро (padeniye perekatom na bedro)
2742	sidearm serve	service bas latéral	saque lateral	seitliche Aufgabe	боковая подача (bokovaya podacha)
2743	sideline	ligne de côté	línea lateral	Seitenlinie	боковая линия (bokovaya liniya)
2744	slice serve	service coupé	saque cortado	Hakenaufgabe	резаная подача (rezanaya podacha)
2745	soft block	bloc en douceur	bloqueo suave	weicher Block	блок с отведенными назад кистями (blok s otvedyonnimi nazad kistyami)
2746	specialist	spécialiste	especialista	Spezialist	специалист (spetsialist)
2747	spike	smash	martillo	Schmetterball	атакующий удар (atakuyushchiy udar)
2748	spike (to)	smasher	rematar	schmettern	бить по мячу (bit' po myachu)
2749	spike off the block	smasher dans le contre pour faire sortir le ballon	remate contra el bloqueo para sacar el balón	in den Block schmettern	бить по блоку (bit' po bloku)
2750	spiker	smasheur	rematador	Hauptangriffsspieler	бьющий игрок (b'yushchiy igrok)

English	Français	Español	Deutsch	Русский
2751 start of set	début du set	comienzo del juego	Satzbeginn	начало партии (nachalo partii)
2752 starting player	joueur de départ	jugador que saca	Stammspieler	игрок стартового состава (igrok startovovo sostava)
2753 starting position	position de départ	posición inicial	Aufstellung der Spieler	стартовая расстановка (startovaya rasstanovka)
2754 stuff	donner de la force au ballon	bloqueo fuerte hacia abajo que anota	entscheidender Block	блок, забивающий очко (blok, zabivayushchiy ochko)
2755 substitute	remplaçant	sustituir	Auswechselspieler	заменяющий игрок (zamenyayushchiy igrok)
2756 substitute player	joueur remplaçant	jugador sustituto	Auswechselspieler	запасной игрок (zapasnoy igrok)
2757 switch	permutation	permutación	Switch	перемещение (peremeshcheniye)
2758 system	système	sistema	System	система (sistema)
2759 system for reception	organisation de réception	organización de la recepción	Ballannahme	система приема (sistema priyoma)
2760 tactic	tactique	táctica	Taktik	тактика (taktika)
2761 tactical	tactique	táctico	taktisch	тактический (takticheskiy)
2762 tactical combination	combinaison tactique	combinación táctica	taktische Kombination	тактическая комбинация (takticheskaya kombinatsiya)
2763 tactical movement of players	circulation tactique	circulación táctica	taktisches Aufstellen	тактика перемещения (taktika peremeshcheniya)
2764 tactical plan	schème tactique	esquema táctica	taktisches Schema	тактический план (takticheskiy plan)
2765 tape	bande horizontale du filet	banda horizontal de la red	Netzoberkante	верхний край сетки (verhniy kray setki)
2766 team formation	formation du jeu	formación de juego	Spielaufstellung	расстановка команды (rasstanovka komandi)
2767 team offence	construction d'attaque	construcción del ataque	Angriffstaktik	система игры в нападении (sistema igri v napadenii)
2768 teammate	coéquipier	compañero	Mitspieler	партнер (partnyor)
2769 technique player	joueur universel	jugador universal	Universalspieler	универсальный игрок (universal'niy igrok)
English	Français	Español	Deutsch	Русский

	Volleyball	**Volley-ball**	**Voleibol**	**Volleyball**	**Волейбол**
2770	tennis serve	service tennis	saque de tenis	Tennisaufgabe	верхняя прямая подача (verhnyaya pryamaya podacha)
2771	three-man block	contre à trois	bloqueo de tres	Dreierblock	тройной блок (troynoy blok)
2772	time between sets	pause entre sets	intervalos entre sets	Pause zwischen Sätze	интервал между партиями (interval mezhdu partiyami)
2773	time out	temps mort	tiempo muerto	Auszeit	перерыв (pereriv)
2774	time-out request	demande de temps mort	solicitud de tiempo muerto	Antrag auf Auszeit	просьба о перерыве (pros'ba o pererive)
2775	tip	placement du bout des doigts	golpecito	Lob	направление (napravleniye)
2776	tip the ball	placer le ballon	golpear el balón con los dedos	den Ball lobben	направить мяч (napravit' myach)
2777	tip the ball behind the block	placer le ballon derrière le contre	enviar el balón detrás del bloqueo	den Block überlobben	направить мяч за блок (napravit' myach za blok)
2778	tip the ball in the weak area	placer le ballon dans le trou	meter el balón en el hueco	in die Lücke lobben	направить мяч в незащищённую зону (napravit' myach v nezashchishchyonnuyu zonu)
2779	topspin	brosser	dar efecto liftado	Topspin	топспин (topspin)
2780	touching the opponent's court	contact avec le terrain adverse	contacto con el terreno adversario	Überschreiten der Mittellinie	касание поля игры противника (kasaniye polya igri protivnika)
2781	two-hand bump	manchette à deux mains	golpear con dos manos	beidhändig baggern	прием мяча двумя руками (priyom myacha dvumya rukami)
2782	two-hand dig	récupération à deux mains	recuperación con dos manos	mit zwei Händen abwehren	прием удара двумя руками снизу (priyom udara dvumya rukami snizu)
2783	two-hand pass	passe à deux mains	pase de dos manos	Pass mit beiden Händen	передача двумя руками (peredacha dvumya rukami)
2784	two-man block	contre à deux	bloqueo a dos	Zweierblock	двойной блок (dvoynoy blok)

	English	French	Spanish	German	Russian
2785	underhand serve	service par en dessous	saque de abajo	Aufgabe von unten	нижняя подача (nizhnyaya podacha)
2786	uniform	tenue du joueur	uniforme	Spielerkleidung	форма игроков (forma igrokov)
2787	volleyball ball	ballon de volley-ball	balón de voleibol	Volleyball	волейбольный мяч (voleybol'niy myach)
2788	volleyball player	joueur de volley-ball	jugador de voleibol	Volleyballspieler	волейболист (voleybolist)
2789	volleyball team	équipe de volley-ball	equipo de voleibol	Volleyballmannschaft	волейбольная команда (voleybol'naya komanda)
2790	W formation	formation en W	formación en W	W-Formation	расстановка игроков уступами (rasstanovka igrokov ustupami)
2791	warm-up	échauffement	precalentamiento	Aufwärmen	разминка (razminka)
2792	warning	avertissement	amonestación	Verweis	предупреждение (preduprezhdeniye)
2793	weak area	trou	hueco	Lücke	незащищенное место (nezashchishchyonnoe mesto)
2794	weak area of the court	ouverture	apertura	Lücke	свободное место (svobodnoe mesto)
2795	win a side out	récupérer le service	recuperar el saque	eine Aufgabe gewinnen	выиграть подачу (viigrat' podachu)
2796	win the rally	gagner l'échange	ganar el cambio	einen Ballwechsel gewinnen	выиграть обмен (viigrat' obmen)
2797	winning a point	gain du point	ganancia del punto	einen Punkt erzielen	выигрыш очка (viigrish ochka)
2798	winning of the service	gain du service	ganancia del saque	eine Aufgabe erhalten	выигрыш подачи (viigrish podachi)
2799	wipe off	bloc gagnant	remate contra el bloqueo para hacer salir el balón	nach Ball ins Aus schmettern	выиграть обмен от блока (viigrat' obmen ot bloka)
2800	yellow card	carte jaune	tarjeta amarilla	gelbe Karte	желтая карточка (zholtaya kartochka)

Waterpolo

Water-polo

Polo acuático

Water-polo

Водное поло

	Waterpolo	Water-polo	Polo acuático	Water-polo	Водное поло
2801	actual playing time	temps de jeu effectif	tiempo de juego efectivo	effektive Spielzeit	чистое время игры (chistoye vremya igri)
2802	advantage rule	règle de l'avantage	regla de ventaja	Vorteilregel	правило преимущества (pravilo preimushchestva)
2803	alter a decision	modifier une décision	modificar una decisión	eine Entscheidung ändern	изменить решение (izmenit' resheniye)
2804	announce a goal	annoncer un but	anunciar un gol	ein Tor anzeigen	объявить гол (obyavit' gol)
2805	assistant secretary	assistant du secrétaire	ayudante del secretario	Sekretär des Schiedsrichters	помощник секретаря (pomoshchnik sekretarya)
2806	assistant timer	assistant du chronométreur	ayudante del cronometrador	Zeitnehmerassistent	помощник секундометриста (pomoshchnik sekundometrista)
2807	attacking player	joueur attaquant	delantero	Angreifer	атакующий игрок (atakuyushchiy igrok)
2808	back player	arrière	defensa	Verteidiger	защитник (zashchitnik)
2809	backhand shot	lancer de revers	tiro de revés	Rückhandwurf	бросок назад (brosok nazad)
2810	bad conduct	mauvaise conduite	mala conducta	unsportliches Verhalten	плохое поведение (plohoye povedeniye)
2811	ball crossing over the goal line	passage du ballon derrière la ligne de but	pasar el balón sobre la línea de meta	der Ball geht hinter der Torlinie	мяч за линию ворот (myach za liniyu vorot)
2812	ball out of play	ballon hors-jeu	balón fuera de juego	Ball im Aus	мяч вне игры (myach vne igri)
2813	ball passes completely over the goal line	ballon franchit entièrement la ligne de but	balón que franqueó por completo la línea del gol	der Ball hat mit dem gesamten Umfang die Torlinie überschritten	мяч совсем переходит линию ворот (myach sovsem perehodit liniyu vorot)
2814	ball ricocheting off the water	ballon ricochant sur l'eau	balón rebotando sobre el agua	auf dem Wasser aufsetzen	мяч, отскакивающий от воды (myach, otskakivayushchiy ot vodi)
2815	ball shot into the water	ballon lancé dans l'eau	balón lanzado al agua	den Ball ins Wasser werfen	мяч, брошенный в воду (myach, broshenniy v vodu)
2816	ball shot on the water	ballon lancé sur l'eau	balón lanzado al ras del agua	den Ball auf das Wasser werfen	мяч, брошенный по воде (myach, broshenniy po vode)

	English	Français	Español	Deutsch	Русский
2817	ball-handling technique	maniement du ballon	técnica del manejo del balón	Ballbehandlung	техника владения мячом (tehnika vladeniya myachom)
2818	ball-holding equipment	panier de support	soporte para el balón	Ballkorb	корзина для мячей (korzina dlya myachey)
2819	bathing trunks	caleçon de bain	traje de baño	Schwimmhose	плавки (plavki)
2820	be in possession of the ball	être en possession du ballon	estar en posesión del balón	in Ballbesitz sein	владеть мячом (vladet' myachyom)
2821	blue cap	bonnet bleu	gorro azul	blaue Kappe	голубая шапочка (golubaya shapochka)
2822	blue flag	fanion bleu	banderín azul	blaue Flagge	голубой флажок (goluboy flazhok)
2823	bottom of the pool	fond du bassin	fondo de la piscina	Beckenboden	дно бассейна (dno basseyna)
2824	boundary of the field of play	délimitation du champ de jeu	delimitación del campo de juego	Spielfeldgrenze	граница поля игры (granitsa polya igri)
2825	boundary of the pool	extrémité du bassin	límite de la piscina	Beckenbegrenzung	граница бассейна (granitsa basseyna)
2826	cap untied	bonnet détaché	gorro desabrochado	unbefestigte Kappe	шапочка, не завязанная под подбородком (shapochka, ne zavyazannaya pod podborodkom)
2827	captain	capitaine	capitán	Kapitän	капитан (kapitan)
2828	carry the ball	emporter le ballon	llevar el balón	den Ball führen	нести мяч (nesti myach)
2829	center forward	centre-avant	centro delantero	Mittelstürmer	центральный нападающий (tsentral'niy napadayushchiy)
2830	center line	ligne du milieu	línea de medio campo	Mittellinie	центральная линия (tsentral'naya liniya)
2831	change a decision	modifier une décision	modificar una decisión	eine Entscheidung ändern	переменить решение (peremenit' resheniye)
2832	change ends	changement de camp	cambio de campo	Wechsel der Spielfeldseiten	поменяться сторонами (pomenyatsa storonami)
2833	check an opponent	marquer l'adversaire	marcar al adversario	den Gegner decken	опекать противника (opekat' protivnika)

	Waterpolo	Water-polo	Polo acuático	Water-polo	Водное поло
2834	choice of caps	choix des bonnets	elección del gorro	Farbwahl der Kappen	выбор шапочек (vibor shapochek)
2835	choice of ends	choix du camp	elección de campo	Seitenwahl	выбор сторон (vibor storon)
2836	clear the ball	dégager le ballon	despejar el balón	den Ball freispielen	отбить мяч (otbit' myach)
2837	colors	couleurs	colores	Farben	цвета (tsveta)
2838	competition cap	bonnet de compétition	gorro de baño	Wettbewerbmütze	шапочка (shapochka)
2839	corner throw	coup de coin	saque de esquina	Eckwurf	угловой бросок (uglovoy brosok)
2840	court floats	corde de limite	corchera de demarcación	Korkleine	плавающие линии поля (plavayushchiye linii polya)
2841	crossbar (of the goal)	barre transversale du but	travesaño	Torlatte	поперечная перекладина ворот (poperechnaya perekladina vorot)
2842	deep end	partie profonde du bassin	parte honda de la piscina	tiefer Beckenteil	глубокая сторона (glubokaya storona)
2843	defenceman	joueur de défense	defensa	Verteidiger	защитник (zashchitnik)
2844	defender	défenseur	defensor	Verteidiger	игрок защиты (igrok zashchiti)
2845	draw lots	tirage au sort	sorteo	Auslosen	тянуть жребий (tyanut' zhrebiy)
2846	dribbling the ball	dribbler le ballon	avanzar con el balón	den Ball dribbeln	дриблинг (dribling)
2847	dribbling the ball right up to the goal	dribbler le ballon jusqu'au but	driblar con el balón hasta la portería	den Ball bis ins Tor dribbeln	привести мяч прямо к воротам (privesti myach pryamo k vorotam)
2848	drop the ball	lâcher le ballon	soltar el balón	den Ball verlieren	уронить мяч (uronit' myach)
2849	edge of the pool	bord du bassin	rebosadero de la piscina	Beckenrand	борт бассейна (bort basseyna)
2850	excluded player	joueur expulsé	jugador expulsado	herausgestellter Spieler	удаленный игрок (udalyonniy igrok)
2851	field player	joueur de champ	jugador de campo	Feldspieler	полевой игрок (polevoy igrok)
2852	first half	première mi-temps	primer tiempo	erster Spielabschnitt	первый тайм (perviy taym)
2853	flag	fanion	banderín	Flagge	флажок (flazhok)
2854	forward	avant	delantero	Stürmer	нападающий (napadayushchiy)

	English	Français	Español	Deutsch	Русский
2855	fouled player	joueur victime d'une faute	jugador víctima de una falta	Spieler, an dem ein Foul begangen wurde	игрок, пострадавший от нарушения правил (igrok, postradavshiy ot narusheniya pravil)
2856	four-meter area	zone des 4 mètres	área de los 4 metros	vier-m-Raum	четырехметровая зона (chetiryohmetrovaya zona)
2857	four-meter line	ligne des 4 mètres	línea de los 4 metros	vier-m-Linie	четырехметровая линия (chetiryohmetrovaya liniya)
2858	free throw	coup franc	tiro libre	Freiwurf	свободный бросок (svobodniy brosok)
2859	free throw awarded	coup franc accordé	golpe franco concedido	einen Freiwurf zuerkennen	свободный бросок назначен (svobodniy brosok naznachen)
2860	full strength	équipe complète	equipo completo	vollzählige Mannschaft	полная команда (polnaya komanda)
2861	game clock	chronomètre de _eu	cronómetro del juego	Spieluhr	хронометр игры (hronometr igri)
2862	get away from the check	démarquer, se	desmarcarse	sich anbieten	уйти от соперника (uyiti ot sopernika)
2863	goal	but	tanto; portería	Tor	гол (gol)
2864	goal allowed	but accordé	gol concedido	anerkanntes Tor	мяч засчитан (myach zaschitan)
2865	goal judge	juge de but	juez de gol	Torlinienrichter	судья у линии ворот (sud'ya u linii vorot)
2866	goal judge's flag	fanion du juge de but	banderín del juez de gol	Flagge des Torlinien-richters	флажок судьи у ворот (flazhok sud'yi u vorot)
2867	goal line	ligne de but	línea de gol	Torlinie	линия ворот (liniya vorot)
2868	goal net	filet de but	red	Netz	сетка ворот (setka vorot)
2869	goal post	poteau de but	poste de portería	Torpfosten	стойка ворот (stoyka vorot)
2870	goal scored	but marqué	gol anotado	Tor erzielt	гол забит (gol zabit)
2871	goal throw	remise en jeu par le gardien de but	saque del portero	Torabwurf	бросок от ворот (brosok ot vorot)
2872	goalkeeper	gardien de but	guardameta	Torwart	вратарь (vratar')

	Waterpolo	Water-polo	Polo acuático	Water-polo	Водное поло
2873	goalkeeper's cap	bonnet de gardien de but	gorro del portero	Torhüterkappe	шапочка вратаря (shapochka vratarya)
2874	grease one's body	enduire son corps de graisse	engrasar el cuerpo	sich den Körper mit Fett einschmieren	намазать свое тело (namazat' svoyo telo)
2875	half of the field	camp	campo	Hälfte des Spielfelds	половина поля (polovina polya)
2876	half-way line	ligne du milieu	línea central	Mittellinie	центральная линия (tsentral'naya liniya)
2877	heading the ball	lancer de la tête	tiro con la cabeza; cabecear	den Ball mit dem Kopf spielen	ударить мяч головой (udarit' myach golovoy)
2878	height of the crossbar	hauteur de la barre transversale	altura del travesaño	Höhe der Torlatte	высота поперечной перекладины (visota poperechnoy perekladini)
2879	hinder an opponent	gêner un adversaire	entorpecer a un contrario	einen Gegner behindern	препятствовать противнику (prepyatstvovat' protivniku)
2880	hit an opponent	frapper un adversaire	golpear a un contrario	einen Gegner schlagen	ударить противника (udarit' protivnika)
2881	hit the ball with a closed first	frapper le ballon avec le poing fermé	golpear el balón con el puño	den Ball mit der geballten Faust schlagen	ударить мяч сжатым кулаком (udarit' myach szhatim kulakom)
2882	hold back an opponent	retenir un adversaire	retener al contrario	einen Gegner festhalten	удерживать противника (uderzhivat' protivnika)
2883	hold the ball under water	tenir le ballon sous l'eau	hundir el balón	den Ball untertauchen	топить мяч (topit' myach)
2884	hold the ball with the palm up	prise du ballon par en dessous	sostener el balón con la palma de la mano	Schöpfgriff	подхватывать мяч (podhvativat' myach)
2885	inflated ball	ballon gonflé	balón inflado	aufgepumpter Ball	надутый мяч (nadutiy myach)
2886	injured player	joueur blessé	jugador lesionado	verletzter Spieler	травмированный игрок (travmirovanniy igrok)
2887	interval between quarters	repos entre les périodes	descanso	Viertelpause	интервал между периодами (interval mezhdu periodami)

	English	Français	Español	Deutsch	Русский
2888	kick	donner des coups de pied	dar patadas	mit den Füssen treten	ударить ногой (udarit' nogoy)
2889	kick off from opponent	élancer par coup de pied à l'adversaire, s'	impulsarse sobre el contrario	sich mit dem Fuss vom Gegner abstossen	оттолкнуться от противника ногами (ottolknutsa ot protivnika nogami)
2890	kill time	perdre volontairement du temps	perder tiempo adrede	verzögern	нарочно тратить время (narochno tratit' vremya)
2891	leave the water	quitter l'eau	salir del agua	das Wasser verlassen	выйти из воды (viyti iz vodi)
2892	left back	arrière gauche	defensa izquierdo	linker Verteidiger	левый защитник (leviy zashchitnik)
2893	left forward	avant gauche	delantero izquierdo	linker Vorderspieler	левый нападающий (leviy napadayushchiy)
2894	length of actual time	durée du jeu effectif	duración del juego efectivo	Dauer der effektiven Spielzeit	продолжительность чистого времени (prodolzhitel'nost' chistovo vremeni)
2895	lift the ball	soulever le ballon	levantar el balón	den Ball heben	поднять мяч (podnyat' myach)
2896	line with floats	corde de liège	corchera	Korkleine	линия с буйками (liniya s buykami)
2897	lines of the field of play	délimitation du champ de jeu	delimitación del campo de juego	Spielfeldgrenze	линии, ограничивающие поле игры (linii, ogranichivayushchiye pole igri)
2898	lob	lob	pase bombeado	Lob	свеча (svecha)
2899	lob shot	lancer en lob	levantar globos	Bogenwurf	навесной бросок (navesnoy brosok)
2900	major foul	faute grave	falta grave	schwerer Fehler	грубая ошибка (grubaya oshibka)
2901	man advantage	supériorité numérique	superioridad numérica	zahlenmässige Überlegenheit	команда в большинстве (komanda v bol'shinstve)
2902	man disadvantage	infériorité numérique	inferioridad numérica	zahlenmässige Unterlegenheit	команда в меньшинстве (komanda v men'shinstve)
2903	man-to-man checking	marquage individuel	marcaje individual	Manndeckung	опека один на один (opeka odin na odin)
	English	**Français**	**Español**	**Deutsch**	**Русский**

	Waterpolo	Water-polo	Polo acuático	Water-polo	Водное поло
2904	mark one's opponent	marquer l'adversaire	marcar al contrario	den Gegner decken	опекать своего противника (opekat' svoyevo protivnika)
2905	measuring the goal	mesurage des buts	medición de las porterías	Torausmasse	измерение ворот (izmereniye vorot)
2906	minimum depth of water	profondeur minimum de l'eau	profundidad mínima del agua	Mindestwassertiefe	минимальная глубина воды (minimal'naya glubina vodi)
2907	minor foul	faute mineure	falta menor	kleiner Fehler	простая ошибка (prostaya oshibka)
2908	misconduct	mauvaise conduite	mala conducta	unsportliches Verhalten	плохое поведение (plohoye povedeniye)
2909	moving play	jeu mobile	juego movido	schnelles Spiel	подвижная игра (podvizhnaya igra)
2910	non-regulation ball	ballon non réglementaire	balón antirreglamentario	der Ball entspricht nicht den Regeln	мяч, не отвечающий правилам (myach, ne otvechayushchiy pravilam)
2911	non-regulation field of play	camp de jeu non réglementaire	campo de juego antirreglamentario	nicht den Regeln entsprechendes Spielfeld	поле игры, не отвечающее правилам (pole igri, ne otvechayushcheye pravilam)
2912	numbered cap	bonnet numéroté	gorro numerado	mit einer Nummer versehene Kappe	шапочка с номером (shapochka s nomerom)
2913	offending player	joueur fautif	jugador en falta	Spieler, der einen Fehler begeht	провинившийся игрок (provinivshiysya igrok)
2914	offside	hors-jeu	fuera de juego	im Abseits	офсайд/вне игры (ofsayd/vne igri)
2915	one-hand shot	lancer à une main	tiro con una mano	mit einer Hand werfen	бросок одной рукой (brosok odnoy rukoy)
2916	opponent's goal	but de l'équipe adverse	gol del equipo contrario	gegnerisches Tor	ворота противника (vorota protivnika)
2917	opposite half	camp adverse	campo opuesto	gegnerische Hälfte	сторона противника (storona protivnika)

	English	Français	Español	Deutsch	Русский
2918	order a player to leave the water	ordonner á un jouer de sortir de l'eau	expulsar del agua	einen Spieler herausstellen	приказать игроку выйти из воды (prikazat' igroku viyti iz vodi)
2919	order out of the game	exclure du jeu	exclusión de un jugador	vom Spiel ausschliessen	приказать выйти из игры (prikazat' viyti iz igri)
2920	overtime	prolongation du jeu	prórroga	Spielverlängerung	дополнительное время (dopolnitel'noye vremya)
2921	own goal line	propre ligne de but	línea de meta de la defensa	eigene Torlinie	своя линия ворот (svoya liniya vorot)
2922	palm of the hand	paume de la main	palma de la mano	Handfläche	ладонь руки (ladon' ruki)
2923	pass	passe	pase	Pass	пас (pas)
2924	pass the ball	passer le ballon	pasar el balón	den Ball zuspielen	передать мяч (peredat' myach)
2925	penalty	pénalité	penal	Strafe	пенальти (penal'ti)
2926	penalty clock	cronomètre de pénalité	reloj de exclusión	Strafuhr	штрафной секундомер (shtrafnoy sekundomer)
2927	penalty shot	lancer de pénalité	tiro de penal	Strafwurf	штрафной бросок (shtrafnoy brosok)
2928	period	période	tiempo	Viertel	период (period)
2929	period of exclusion	durée de l'exclusion	plazo de la exclusión	Dauer der Herausstellung	период удаления (period udaleniya)
2930	personal foul	faute personnelle	falta personal	persönlicher Fehler	персональная ошибка (personal'naya oshibka)
2931	play waterpolo	jouer au water-polo	jugar al polo acuático	Wasserball spielen	играть в водное поло (igrat' v vodnoye polo)
2932	player designated for the restart of play	joueur désigné pour la remise en jeu	jugador designado para la reanudación	Hinweis für den Herausgestellten	игрок, назначенный для возобновления игры (igrok, naznachenniy dlya vozobnovleniya igri)
2933	playing field	champ de jeu	campo de juego	Spielfeld	поле игры (pole igri)
2934	playing rule	règle du jeu	regla del juego	Spielregel	правило игры (pravilo igri)
	English	**Français**	**Español**	**Deutsch**	**Русский**

	Waterpolo	Water-polo	Polo acuático	Water-polo	Водное поло
2935	pop shot	lancer en raquette	"sueco"	Selbstdoppler	толчок с подбрасыванием (tolchok s podbrasivaniyem)
2936	pull back one's opponent	tirer à soi son adversaire	retener al adversario	den Gegner an sich ziehen	подтягивание противника (podtyagivaniye protivnika)
2937	punching	lancer avec le poing	arremeter con el puño	den Ball mit der Faust schlagen	ударить кулаком (udarit' kulakom)
2938	push off	poussée	empujón	Abstoss	отталкивание (ottalkivaniye)
2939	push off from an opponent	repousser de l'adversaire, se	separarse de un adversario por empujón	sich vom Gegner abstossen	оттолкнуться от противника (ottolknutsa ot protivnika)
2940	push off from wall of pool	repousser du mur du bassin, se	lanzar apoyándose en la pared de la piscina	sich vom Beckenrand abstossen	оттолкнуться от бортика (ottolknutsa ot bortika)
2941	push shot	lancer en piston	tiro de presión	Druckwurf	толчок мяча (tolchok myacha)
2942	push the opponent under	couler un adversaire	hundir al adversario	einen Gegner untertauchen	топить противника (topit' protivnika)
2943	pushing off the bottom	élancer du fond du bassin, s'	apoyarse en el fondo de la piscina	vom Beckengrund hochspringen	отталкивания от дна (ottalkivaniya ot dna)
2944	put into play by the referee	mise en jeu par l'arbitre	neutral	Schiedsrichtereinwurf	введенный в игру судьей (vvedyoniy v igru sud'yoy)
2945	put the ball into play	remettre le ballon en jeu	poner el balón en juego	den Ball wieder ins Spiel bringen	ввести мяч в игру (vvesti myach v igru)
2946	rebound	rebondir	rebotar	abprallen	отскочить (otskochit')
2947	rebound from the goal post	rebondir sur le poteau	rebotar en el poste	am Pfosten abprallen	отскочить от стойки ворот (otskochit' ot stoyki vorot)
2948	receiving the ball	réception de ballon	recepción del balón	Ballannahme	получить мяч (poluchit' myach)
2949	red cap	bonnet rouge	gorro rojo	rote Kappe	красная шапочка (krasnaya shapochka)
2950	red flag	fanion rouge	banderín rojo	rote Flagge	красный флажок (krasniy flazhok)
2951	red marker	marque rouge	marcador rojo	rote Markierung	красная разметка (krasnaya razmetka)

	English	Français	Español	Deutsch	Русский
2952	referee's flag	fanion de l'arbitre	banderín del árbitro	Schiedsrichterflagge	флажок судьи (flazhok sud'yi)
2953	referee's platform	tribune d'arbitre	tribuna del árbitro	Schiedsrichterplatz	вышка судьи (vishka sud'yi)
2954	restart of play after a goal	remise en jeu après un but	reanudación del partido después de un gol	Anwurf nach Torerfolg	возобновление игры после гола (vozobnovleniye igri posle gola)
2955	restart of play by the referee	remise en jeu par l'arbitre	reanudación del juego por el árbitro	Schiedsrichterball	возобновление игры судьей (vozobnovleniye igri sud'yoy)
2956	retake the play	reprendre le jeu	reanudarse el juego	das Spiel wiederaufnehmen	переиграть игру (pereigrat' igru)
2957	return to the game	revenir au jeu	volver al juego	wieder ins Spiel gehen	вернуться к игре (vernutsya k igre)
2958	right back	arrière droit	defensa izquierdo	rechter Verteidiger	правый защитник (praviy zashchitnik)
2959	right forward	avant droit	delantero derecho	rechter Vorderspieler	правый нападающий (praviy napadayushchiy)
2960	rough play	jeu dur	juego sucio	hartes Spiel	грубая игра (grubaya igra)
2961	rover	demi-centre	medio centro	Verbinder	полузащитник (poluzashchitnik)
2962	score	marquer un but	marcar un gol	ein Tor erzielen	забить гол (zabit' gol)
2963	second half	deuxième mi-temps	segundo tiempo	zweite Spielzeit	второй тайм (vtoroy taym)
2964	secretary	secrétaire	secretario	Sekretär	секретарь (sekretar')
2965	seven-minute quarter	période de sept minutes	período de 7 minutos	Spielzeit von 7 Minuten	семиминутный период (semiminutniy period)
2966	shallow end	partie peu profonde (du bassin)	parte llana	flacher Beckenteil	мелкая сторона (melkaya storona)
2967	shoot	lancer	lanzar	werfen	бросить мяч (brosit' myach)
2968	shooting at the goal	lancer au but	lanzar a la portería	aufs Tor werfen	бросить мяч по воротам (brosit' myach po vorotam)
2969	shooting from a pass	lancer à la volée	tiro de volea	doppeln	бросить с паса (brosit' s pasa)
2970	shooting without delay	lancer ininterrompu	lanzamiento seguido	ohne Verzögerung werfen	бросить без промедления (brosit' bez promedleniya)
	English	Français	Español	Deutsch	Русский

	Waterpolo	Water-polo	Polo acuático	Water-polo	Водное поло
2971	shot clock	chronomètre de 35 secondes	cronómetro de los 35 minutos	fünfunddreissig-Sekundenuhr	тридцатипятисекундный секундомер (tridtsatipyatisekundniy sekundomer)
2972	side line	ligne de côté	línea lateral	Seitenlinie	боковая линия (bokovaya liniya)
2973	sidestroke	nage sur le côté	estilo marinero	Seitschwimmen	плавание на боку (plavaniye na boku)
2974	signal the start of play	donner le signal de la mise en jeu	señalar el comienzo del juego	das Spiel anpfeifen	дать сигнал начала игры (dat' signal nachala igri)
2975	signal to stop the play	signal d'arrêt de jeu	señal para parar el juego	das Spiel abpfeifen	сигнал остановить игру (signal ostanovit' igru)
2976	signal with the flag	signaler avec le fanion	señalar con el banderín	mit der Fahne anzeigen	давать сигнал флажком (davat' signal flazhkom)
2977	sink one's opponent	couler son adversaire	hundir al adversario	den Gegner unter dem Wasser festhalten	топить своего противника (topit' svoyevo protivnika)
2978	slow play	jeu lent	juego estático	langsames Spiel	медленная игра (medlennaya igra)
2979	splash	asperger	salpicar el agua	spritzen	плескаться (pleskatsa)
2980	stand on the bottom	prendre pied sur le fond du bassin	apoyarse en el fondo de la piscina	auf dem Beckengrund stehen	стоять на дне бассейна (stoyat' na dne basseyna)
2981	start of play	début de jeu	comienzo del juego	Spielbeginn	начало игры (nachalo igri)
2982	starting position	placement de départ	posición inicial	Spielerstellung beim Anspiel und Wiederbeginn	стартовая позиция (startovaya pozitsiya)
2983	starting signal	signal de départ	señal de partida	Startsignal	сигнал старта (signal starta)
2984	static play	jeu statique	juego poco movido	wenig bewegendes Spiel	неподвижная игра (nepodvizhnaya igra)
2985	stop a shot	arrêter un tir	parar un tiro	einen Schuss halten	остановить удар (ostanovit' udar)
2986	stop the clock	arrêter le chronomètre	parar el cronómetro	die Uhr anhalten	остановить секундомер (ostanovit' sekundomer)

	English	Français	Español	Deutsch	Русский
2987	stop the game	arrêter le jeu	parar el juego	das Spiel unterbrechen	остановить игру (ostanovit' igru)
2988	straight shot	lancer droit	tiro derecho	Direktwurf	прямой бросок (pryamoy brosok)
2989	strike an opponent	frapper un adversaire	golpear a un contrario	einen Gegner schlagen	ударить противника (udarit' protivnika)
2990	striking the ball with a closed fist	frapper le ballon avec le poing fermé	golpear el balón con el puño	den Ball mit der geballten Faust schlagen	ударить по мячу сжатым кулаком (udarit' po myachu szhatim kulakom)
2991	submerge an opponent	couler un adversaire	hundir al adversario	einen Gegner untertauchen	топить противника (topit' protivnika)
2992	substitute player	joueur remplaçant	jugador suplente	Ersatzspieler	запасной игрок (zapasnoy igrok)
2993	swim off from the goal line	départ de la ligne de but	salida desde la línea de gol	Spielanfang von der Torlinie	отплыть от линии ворот (otplit' ot linii vorot)
2994	swimming with the ball	dribbler le ballon	avanzar con el balón	den Ball dribbeln	плыть с мячом (plit' s myachom)
2995	swimming with the ball right up to the goal	dribbler le ballon jusqu'au but	driblar con el balón hasta la meta	den Ball ins Tor dribbeln	подплыть с мячом прямо к воротам (podplit' s myachom pryamo k vorotam)
2996	take a free throw	exécuter un coup franc	lanzar un tiro franco	einen Freiwurf ausführen	сделать свободный бросок (sdelat' svobodniy brosok)
2997	take the ball under water	enfoncer le ballon sous l'eau	hundir el balón	den Ball untertauchen	взять мяч под воду (vzyat' myach pod vodu)
2998	throw	lancer	lanzar	werfen	бросить (brosit')
2999	timekeeper	chronométreur	cronometrador	Zeitnehmer	секундометрист (sekundometrist)
3000	tip shot	lancer du bout des doigts	"sueco" (con los dedos)	Wurf mit Fingerspitzen	толчок с подбрасыванием (tolchok s podbrasivaniyem)
3001	touch the ball	toucher le ballon	tocar el balón	den Ball berühren	дотронуться до мяча (dotronutsa do myacha)

195

	Waterpolo	Water-polo	Polo acuático	Water-polo	Водное поло
3002	touch the ball with both hands at the same time	toucher le ballon des deux mains en même temps	tocar el balón con las dos manos al mismo tiempo	den Ball mit beiden Händen gleichzeitig berühren	дотронуться до мяча двумя руками одновременно (dotronutsa do myacha dvumya rukami odnovremenno)
3003	treading water	nager debout	mantenerse a flote	das Wasser treten	ходьба в воде (hod'ba v vode)
3004	two-meter area	zone des 2 mètres	zona de 2 metros	zwei-m-Raum	двухметровая зона (dvuhmetrovaya zona)
3005	two-meter line	ligne des 2 mètres	línea de 2 metros	zwei-m-Linie	двухметровая линия (dvuhmetrovaya liniya)
3006	under-water work	travail sous l'eau	trabajo bajo el agua	Unterwasserarbeit	работа под водой (rabota pod vodoy)
3007	validity of a goal	validité d'un but	validez de un gol	Anerkennung eines Tores	действительность гола (deystvitel'nost' gola)
3008	violent play	jeu violent	juego rudo	rauhes Spiel	грубая игра (grubaya igra)
3009	wait for the referee's signal	attendre le signal de l'arbitre	esperar la señal del árbitro	das Schiedsrichter-zeichen abwarten	ждать сигнала судьи (zhdat' signala sud'yi)
3010	waste time	perdre volontairement du temps	perder tiempo adrede	verzögern	затягивать время (zatyagivat' vremya)
3011	waterpolo ball	ballon de water-polo	balón de polo acuático	Wasserball	мяч для водного поло (myach dlya vodnovo polo)
3012	waterpolo player	joueur de water-polo	jugador de polo acuático	Wasserballspieler	игрок водного поло (igrok vodnovo polo)
3013	waterpolo referee	arbitre de water-polo	árbitro de polo acuático	Wasserballschiedsrichter	судья в водном поло (sud'ya v vodnom polo)
3014	waterpolo rule	règlement de water-polo	reglamento de polo acuático	Wasserballregel	правило водного поло (pravilo vodnovo polo)
3015	waterpolo team	équipe de water-polo	equipo de polo acuático	Wasserballmannschaft	команда водного поло (komanda vodnovo polo)
3016	weight of the ball	poids du ballon	peso del balón	Ballgewicht	вес мяча (ves myacha)
3017	whistle	sifflet	pito	Pfiff	свисток (svistok)

3018	white cap	bonnet blanc	gorro blanco	weisse Kappe	белая шапочка (belaya shapochka)
3019	white flag	fanion blanc	banderín	weisse Flagge	белый флажок (beliy flazhok)
3020	white marker	marque blanche	marca blanca	weisse Markierung	белая разметка (belaya razmetka)
3021	width of the pool	largeur du bassin	ancho de la piscina	Beckenbreite	ширина бассейна (shirina basseyna)
3022	yellow marker	marque jaune	marca amarilla	gelbe Markierung	желтая разметка (zholtaya razmetka)

Appendix of important
general phrases

Annexe des principales courant
expressions de frases

Apéndice de frases
de uso corriente

Anhang wichtiger Redewendungen
allgemeiner

Приложение: Важные выражения
общего значения

Important Phrases	L'Essentiel en peu de mots	Lo más importante en pocas palabras	Das Wichtigste in Kürze	Важные фразы, выражения
Mr ...	Monsieur ...	Señor ...	Herr ...	господин (gospodin)
Mrs ...	Madame ...	Señora ...	Frau ...	госпожа (gospozha)
Miss ...	Mademoiselle ...	Señorita ...	Fräulein ...	девушка (devushka)
Good morning	Bonjour	Buenos días	Guten Morgen	Доброе утро (dobroye utro)
Good afternoon	Bonjour	Buenas tardes	Guten Tag	Добрый день (dobriy den')
Good evening	Bonsoir	Buenas tardes	Guten Abend	Добрый вечер (dobriy vecher)
Good night	Bonne nuit	Buenas noches	Gute Nacht	Спокойной ночи (spokoynoy nochi)
Hello; Hi	Salut!	¡Hola!	Guten Tag	Привет! (privet!)
How are you?	Comment ça va?	¿Cómo está (Vd.)?	Wie geht es Ihnen (Dir)?	Как дела? (kak dela?)
Fine, thank you	Très bien, merci	Bien, gracias	Danke, gut	Спасибо, хорошо (spasibo, horosho)
What's your name?	Comment vous appelez-vous?	¿Cómo se Llama Vd.?	Was ist Ihr Name?	Как вас зовут? (kak vas zovut?)
Good-bye	Au revoir	Hasta la vista	Auf Wiedersehen	До свидания (do svidaniya)
Where's (are) ...?	Où est (sont) ...?	¿Dónde está (está) ...?	Wo ist (sind) ...?	Где? (gde?)
Where can I get ...?	Où puis-je trouver ...?	¿Dónde puedo adquirir ...?	Wo bekomme ich ...?	Где я могу получить...? (gde ya mogu poluchit'...?)
Please bring (give, tell, show) me ...	Apportez- (donnez-, dites-, montrez-) moi, s'il vous plaît ...	Por favor, tráigame (déme, dígame, enséñeme) ...	Bringen (geben, sagen, zeigen) Sie mir bitte ...	Пожалуйста, принесите/дайте, скажите, покажите/мне... (pozhalusta, prinesite/dayte, skazhite, pokazhite/mne...)
I need (would like) ...	J'ai besoin de (Je voudrais) ...	Necesito (Quisiera) ...	Ich brauche (möchte) ...	Мне нужно/Я бы хотел/... (mne nuzhno/ya bi hotel...)
Have you ...?	Avez-vous ...?	¿Tiene usted ...?	Haben Sie ...?	У вас есть...? (u vas yest'...?)
How much is ...?	Combien coûte ...?	¿Cuánto cuesta ...?	Wieviel kostet ...?	Сколько стоит...? (skol'ko stoit...?)

English	French	Spanish	German	Russian
I don't speak German (English, French, Spanish, Russian)	Je ne parle pas allemand (anglais, français, espagnol, russe)	No hablo alemán (inglés, francés, español, ruso)	Ich spreche nicht Deutsch (English, Französisch, Spanisch, Russisch)	Я не говорю по-немецки, по-английски, по-французский, по-испанский, по-русски (ya ne govoru po-nemetski, po-angliyski, po-frantsuzski, po-ispanski, po-russki)
I don't understand you	Je ne vous comprends pas	No le comprendo	Ich verstehe Sie nicht	Я вас не понимаю (ya vas ne ponimayu)
Pardon?	Comment?	¿Cómo?	Wie bitte?	Простите (prostite)
Please speak more slowly	Parlez un peu plus lentement, s'il vous plaît!	Hable usted un poco más despacio, por favor	Sprechen Sie bitte etwas langsamer!	Пожалуйста, говорите медленнее (pozhalusta, govorite medlenneye)
Please write it down	Voudriez-vous l'écrire?	¡Escriba usted esto!	Schreiben Sie es bitte auf!	Пожалуйста, запишите (pozhalusta, zapishite)
Yes	Oui	Si	Ja	Да (da)
No	Non	No	Nein	Нет (net)
Thank you	Merci	Muchas gracias	Danke	Спасибо (spasibo)
You're welcome	Je vous en prie	De nada	Bitte	Пожалуйста (pozhalusta)
Sorry!	Pardon!	¡Perdón!	Verzeihung!	Извините! (izvinite!)

Weather	Le temps qu'il fait	El tiempo	Wetter	Погода
What's the weather like?	Quel temps fait-il?	¿Qué tiempo hace?	Wie ist das Wetter?	Какая сейчас погода? (kakaya seychas pogoda?)
There's going to be a change in the weather	Le temps va changer	Va a cambiar el tiempo	Das Wetter wird sich ändern	Погода изменится (pogoda izmenitsa)
The sun is shinning	Le soleil brille	Hace sol	Die Sonne scheint	Солнце светит (sontse svetit)
It's cloudy	Le ciel est couvert	El cielo está cubierto	Es ist bewölkt	Сейчас облачно (seychas oblachno)

It's windy	Il fait du vent	Hace viento	Es ist windig	Сейчас ветрено (seychas vetreno)
There's a thunderstorm brewing	Il y aura un orage	Habrá tormenta	Es gibt ein Gewitter	Будет гроза (budet groza)
It's raining	Il pleut	Está lloviendo	Es regnet	Идет дождь (idyot dozhd')
The weather is clearing up	Le ciel s'éclaircit	El tiempo se aclara	Es klärt sich auf	Погода проясняется (pogoda proyasnyayetsa)
The wind has dropped (shifted)	Le vent est tombé (a tourné)	El viento se ha apaciguado (ha cambiado)	Der Wind hat sich gelegt (gedreht)	Ветер утих/переменился/ (veter utih/peremenilsa/)
It's cold (hot, oppressively hot)	Il fait frais (très chaud, lourd)	Hace fresco (calor, un calor insoportable)	Es ist kühl (heiss, schwül)	Холодно/жарко, душно/ (holodno/zharko, dushno)

Numerals	Nombres	Números	Zahlen	Цифры
1 one	un	uno	eins	один (odin)
2 two	deux	dos	zwei	два (dva)
3 three	trois	tres	drei	три (tri)
4 four	quatre	cuatro	vier	четыре (chetire)
5 five	cinq	cinco	fünf	пять (pyat')
6 six	six	seis	sechs	шесть (shest')
7 seven	sept	siete	sieben	семь (sem')
8 eight	huit	ocho	acht	восемь (vosem')
9 nine	neuf	nueve	neun	девять (devyat')
10 ten	dix	diez	zehn	десять (desyat')
11 eleven	onze	once	elf	одиннадцать (odinnadtsat')
12 twelve	douze	doce	zwölf	двенадцать (dvenadtsat')
13 thirteen	treize	trece	dreizehn	тринадцать (trinadtsat')
14 fourteen	quatorze	catorce	vierzehn	четырнадцать (chetirnadtsat')
15 fifteen	quinze	quince	fünfzehn	пятнадцать (pyatnadtsat')

16 sixteen	seize	dieciséis	sechzehn	шестнадцать (shestnadtsat')
17 seventeen	dix-sept	diecisiete	siebzehn	семнадцать (semnadtsat')
18 eighteen	dix-huit	dieciocho	achtzehn	восемнадцать (vosemnadtsat')
19 nineteen	dix-neuf	diecinueve	neunzehn	девятнадцать (devyatnadtsat')
20 twenty	vingt	veinte	zwanzig	двадцать (dvadtsat')
21 twenty-one	vingt et un	veintiuno	einundzwanzig	двадцать один (dvadtsat' odin)
22 twenty-two	vingt-deux	veintidós	zweiundzwanzig	двадцать два (dvadtsat' dva)
23 twenty-three	vingt-trois	veinte y tres	dreiundzwanzig	двадцать три (dvadtsat' tri)
30 thirty	trente	treinta	dreissig	тридцать (tridtsat')
40 forty	quarante	cuarenta	vierzig	сорок (sorok)
50 fifty	cinquante	cincuenta	fünfzig	пятьдесят (pyat'desyat)
60 sixty	soixante	sesenta	sechzig	шестьдесят (shest'desyat)
70 seventy	soixante-dix	setenta	siebzig	семьдесят (sem'desyat)
80 eighty	quatre-vingt	ochenta	achtzig	восемьдесят (vosem'desyat)
90 ninety	quatre-vingt-dix	noventa	neunzig	девяносто (devyanosto)
100 one hundred	cent	cien	ein hundert	сто (sto)
200 two hundred	deux cents	doscientos	zweihundert	двести (dvesti)
1000 one thousand	mille	mil	ein tausend	тысяча (tisyacha)
2000 two thousand	deux mille	dos mil	zweitausend	две тысячи (dve tisyachi)
1000000 one million	un million	un millón	eine Million	миллион (million)
1/2 a half	un demi	medio	ein halb	половина (polovina)
1/3 a third	un tiers	un tercio	ein Drittel	треть (tret')
1/4 a quarter	un quart	un cuarto	ein Viertel	четверть (chetvert')
1/10 a tenth	un dixième	un décimo	ein Zehntel	десятая (desyataya)
0.5 point five	zéro virgule cinq	cero coma cinco	null Komma fünf	пять десятых (pyat' desyatih)
2.3 two point three	deux virgule trois	dos coma tres	zwei Komma drei	две целых и три десятых (dve tselih i tri desyatih)
(1-1) one all	un à un	uno por uno	eins zu eins	один один (odin odin)
(2-0) two to zero	deux à zéro	dos cero	zwei zu null	два ноль (dva nol')

1st first	premier	primero	erster	первый (perviy)
2nd second	deuxième	segundo	zweiter	второй (vtoroy)
3rd third	troisième	tercero	dritter	третий (tretiy)
4th fourth	quatrième	cuarto	vierter	четвёртый (chetvyortiy)
5th fifth	cinquième	quinto	fünfter	пятый (pyatiy)
6th sixth	sixième	sexto	sechster	шестой (shestoy)
7th seventh	septième	séptimo	siebenter	седьмой (sed'moy)
8th eighth	huitième	octavo	achter	восьмой (vos'moy)
9th ninth	neuvième	noveno	neunter	девятый (devyatiy)
10th tenth	dixième	décimo	zehnter	десятый (desyatiy)

Time	Le temps et l'heure	El tiempo	Zeit	Время
What time is it?	Quelle heure est-il?	¿Qué hora es?	Wieviel Uhr ist es?	Который час? (kotoriy chas?)
It's one o'clock	Il est une heure	Es la una	Es ist ein Uhr	Сейчас час (seychas chas)
It's five past (to) six	Il est six heures (moins) cinq	Son las seis (y cinco) (menos cinco)	Es ist fünf Minuten nach (vor) sechs Uhr	Сейчас пять минут седьмого/ без пяти шесть/ (seychas pyat' minut sed'movo/bez pyati shest'/)
It's a quarter to (past) seven	Il est sept heures moins le (et) quart	Son las siete (menos cuarto)(y cuarto)	Es ist ein Viertel vor (nach) sieben Uhr	Сейчас без пятнадцати семь/ пятнадцать минут восьмого/ (seychas bez pyatnadtsati sem'/ pyatnadtsat' minut vos'movo)
It's half past five	Il est cinq heures et demie	Son las cinco y media	Es ist halb sechs	Сейчас половина шестого (seychas polovina shestovo)
At what time?	A quelle heure?	¿A qué hora?	Um wieviel Uhr?	В котором часу? (v kotorom chasu?)
At two p.m.	A deux heures de l'après midi	A las dos	Um zwei Uhr nachmittags	В два часа дня (v dva chasa dnya)
At eight a.m.	A huit heures du matin	A las ocho de la mañana	Um acht Uhr vormittags (morgens)	В восемь часов утра (v vosem' chasov utra)

English	French	Spanish	German	Russian
From three to four	De trois à quatre heures	De tres a cuatro	Von drei bis vier Uhr	От трёх до четырёх (ot tryoh do chetiryoh)
Between nine and ten	Entre neuf et dix heures	Entre las nueve y las diez	Zwischen neun und zehn Uhr	Между девятью и десятью (mezhdu devyat'yu i desyat'yu)
In (half) an hour	Dans une (demi-) heure	Dentro de una (media) hora	In einer (halben) Stunde	Через /пол/час/а/ (cherez / pol/chas/a/)
second	seconde	segundo	Sekunde	секунда (sekunda)
minute	minute	minuto	Minute	минута (minuta)
hour	heure	hora	Stunde	час (chas)
day	jour	día	Tag	день (den')
today	aujourd'hui	hoy	heute	сегодня (sevodnya)
tomorrow	demain	mañana	morgen	завтра (zavtra)
day after tomorrow	après-demain	pasado mañana	übermorgen	послезавтра (poslezavtra)
yesterday	hier	ayer	gestern	вчера (vchera)
day before yesterday	avant-hier	anteayer	vorgestern	позавчера (pozavchera)
at noon	à midi	a mediodía	mittags	в полдень (v polden')
this (next) week	cette semaine (la semaine prochaine)	esta (la próxima) semana	diese (nächste) Woche	на этой/следующей/неделе (na etoy/sleduyushchey/nedele)
three days (weeks) ago	il y a trois jours (semaines)	hace tres días (semanas)	vor drei Tagen (Wochen)	три дня/недели/назад (tri dnya/nedeli/nazad)
Sunday	dimanche	domingo	Sonntag	воскресенье (voskresen'ye)
Monday	lundi	lunes	Montag	понедельник (ponedel'nik)
Tuesday	mardi	martes	Dienstag	вторник (vtornik)
Wednesday	mercredi	miércoles	Mittwoch	среда (sreda)
Thursday	jeudi	jueves	Donnerstag	четверг (chetverg)
Friday	vendredi	viernes	Freitag	пятница (pyatnitsa)
Saturday	samedi	sábado	Samstag (Sonnabend)	суббота (subbota)
January	janvier	enero	Januar	январь (yanvar')
February	février	febrero	Februar	февраль (fevral')
March	mars	marzo	März	март (mart)

English	French	Spanish	German	Russian
April	avril	abril	April	апрель (aprel')
May	mai	mayo	Mai	май (may)
June	juin	junio	Juni	июнь (iyun')
July	juillet	julio	Juli	июль (iyul')
August	août	agosto	August	август (avgust)
September	septembre	septiembre	September	сентябрь (sentyabr')
October	octobre	octubre	Oktober	октябрь (oktyabr')
November	novembre	noviembre	November	ноябрь (noyabr')
December	décembre	diciembre	Dezember	декабрь (dekabr')

Colors	Couleurs	Colores	Farben	Цвета
black	noir	negro	schwarz	черный (chyorniy)
blue	bleu	azul	blau	голубой (goluboy)
bright	clair	claro	hell	светлый (svetliy)
brown	brun	marrón	braun	коричневый (korichneviy)
dark	foncé	oscuro	dunkel	темный (tyomniy)
gray	gris	gris	grau	серый (seriy)
green	vert	verde	grün	зеленый (zelyoniy)
orange	orange	naranja	orange	оранжевый (oranzheviy)
pink	rose	rosa	rosa	розовый (rozoviy)
red	rouge	rojo	rot	красный (krasniy)
violet	violet	morado	violett	фиолетовый (fioletoviy)
white	blanc	blanco	weiss	белый (beliy)
yellow	jaune	amarillo	gelb	желтый (zholtiy)

Information and warnings	Renseignements et avertissements	Indicaciones y advertencias	Hinweise und Warnungen	Информация и предупреждения
Arrival	Arrivée	Llegada	Ankunft	Прибытие/Приезд (pribitiye/priyezd)
Caution!	Attention!	¡Cuidado!	Vorsicht!	Осторожно! (ostorozhno!)
Closed	Fermé	Cerrado	Geschlossen	Закрыто (zakrito)
Danger!	Danger!	¡Peligro!	Lebensgefahr!	Опасно! (opasno!)
Departure	Départ	Salida	Abfahrt	Отход (othod)
Elevator	Ascenseur	Ascensor	Aufzug	Лифт (lift)
Emergency exit	Sortie de secours	Salida de emergencia	Notausgang	Запасный выход (zapasniy vihod)
Entrance	Entrée	Entrada	Eingang	Вход/Въезд (vhod/vyezd)
Exit	Sortie	Salida	Ausgang	Выход (vihod)
For rent	A louer	Se alquila	Zu vermieten	Сдается внаем (sdayotsa vnayom)
Ground floor, First floor	Rez-de-chaussée	Planta baja	Erdgeschoss	Нижний этаж; Первый этаж (nizhniy etazh; perviy etazh)
Information	Renseignements	Información	Auskunft	Справочное бюро (spravochnoye byuro)
Ladies' washroom	Toilettes / Dames	Damas (servicio)	Damen Toilette	Женский туалет (zhenskiy tualet)
Men's washroom	Toilettes / Messieurs	Caballeros (servicio)	Herren Toilette	Мужской туалет (muzhskoy tualet)
No smoking	Défense de fumer!	Se prohibe fumar	Rauchen verboten!	Курить воспрещается (kurit' vospreshchayetsa)
Open	Ouvert	Abierto	Geöffnet	Открыто (otkrito)
Pull	Tirez!	Tire	Ziehen!	На себя (na sebya)
Push	Poussez!	¡Empuje!	Drücken!	От себя (ot sebya)
Refreshments	Rafraîchissements	Refrescos	Erfrischungen	Закуски (zakuski)
Second floor	Premier étage	Segundo piso	Zweiter Stock	Второй этаж (vtoroy etazh)

Stop	Arrêt	Parada	Haltestelle	Стоп (stop)
Telephone	Téléphone	Teléfono	Fernsprecher	Телефон (telefon)
Washroom	Toilettes	Servicios	Toilette	Туалет (tualet)
Wet Paint!	Peinture fraîche!	Recién pintado	Frisch gestrichen!	Осторожно, окрашено! (ostorozhno, okrasheno!)

Accommodation	A l'hôtel	Alojamiento	Unterkunft	Жилье
Where's the ... hotel?	Où se trouve l'hôtel..?	¿Dónde está el hotel..?	Wo ist das ... Hotel?	Где находится гостиница...? (gde nahoditsa gostinitsa...?)
Have you any vacancies?	Avez-vous des chambres libres?	¿Tienen habitaciones libres?	Haben Sie Zimmer frei?	У вас есть свободные номера? (u vas yest' svobodniye nomera?)
I'd like ...	Je voudrais ...	Quisiera ...	Ich möchte ...	Я бы хотел... (ya bi hotel...)
- a single (double) room	- une chambre pour une personne (deux personnes)	- una habitación individual (de dos camas)	- ein Einbettzimmer (Doppelzimmer)	-односпальный/двуспальный номер (-odnospal'niy/dvuspal'niy/ nomer)
- a room with a bath	- une chambre avec bain	- una habitación con baño	- ein Zimmer mit Dusche	номер с ванной (nomer s vannoy)
- a bed and breakfast	- une chambre avec petit déjeuner	- una habitación con desayuno	- ein "Bett und Frühstück" (Englisch)	комнату/номер/с завтраком (komnatu/nomer/s zavtrakom)
I booked a room	J'ai réservé une chambre	Yo había reservado una habitación	Ich habe ein Zimmer bestellt	Я забронировал номер (ya zabroniroval nomer)
How much is the room per day (a week)?	Combien coûte la chambre par jour (semaine)?	¿Cuánto cuesta la habitación por día (semana)?	Wieviel kostet das Zimmer pro Tag (Woche)?	Сколько стоит этот номер в день/в неделю/? (skol'ko stoit etot nomer v den'/v nedelyu/?)
Please do not disturb	Ne pas déranger s.v.p.	Por favor, no moleste	Bitte nicht stören	Не беспокойте, пожалуйста (ne bespokoyte, pozhalusta)
Please call me at ...	Réveillez-moi à ... heures, s'il vous plaît	Por favor, despiérteme a las ...	Wecken Sie mich bitte um ...Uhr!	Пожалуйста, звоните мне в... (pozhalusta, zvonite mne v...)
Are there any letters for me?	Y a-t-il du courrier pour moi?	¿Hay correo para mi?	Ist Post für mich da?	Есть ли письма для меня? (yest' li pisma dlya menya?)

English	French	Spanish	German	Russian
The key for room ..., please	La clé numéro ..., s'il vous plaît	La llave de la habitación ... por favor	Den Schlüssel für Zimmer ... bitte!	Дайте мне ключ от...номера, пожалуйста (dayte mne klyuch ot..nomera, pozhalusta)
I'm leaving tonight (tomorrow morning)	Je partirai ce soir (demain matin)	Saldré esta noche (mañana por la mañana)	Ich reise heute abend (morgen früh) ab	Я уезжаю сегодня вечером/завтра утром/ (ya uyezzhayu sevodnya vecherom/zavtra utrom)
Is my bill ready?	Avez-vous préparé ma note?	¿Está lista mi cuenta?	Ist meine Rechnung fertig?	Мой счет готов? (moy schyot gotov?)
Call me a taxi, please	Appelez-moi un taxi, s'il vous plaît	Por favor, llame un taxi	Rufen Sie mir bitte ein Taxi!	Вызовите мне такси, пожалуйста (vizovite mne taksi, pozhalusta)
bed	lit	cama	Bett	кровать (krovat')
bed linen	draps	ropa de cama	Bettwäsche	постельное белье (postel'noye bel'yo)
bell	sonnette	timbre	Klingel	звонок (zvonok)
boarding house	pension	pensión	Pension	пансион (pansion)
cloakroom	vestiaire	guardarropa	Garderobe	гардероб (garderob)
clothes brush	brosse à vêtements	cepillo de ropa	Kleiderbürste	платяная/одежная/щетка (platyanaya/odyozhnaya/shchotka)
clothes hanger	cintre	percha	Kleiderbügel	вешалка (veshalka)
dining room	salle à manger	comedor	Speisesaal	столовая (stolovaya)
elevator; lift	ascenseur	ascensor; elevador	Fahrstuhl	лифт (lift)
hall	hall	vestíbulo	Halle	вестибюль (vestibyul')
hotel information service	service de renseignements	oficina de información hotelera	Hotelnachweis	информационное бюро отеля (informatsionnoye byuro otelya)
key	clé	llave	Schlüssel	ключ (klyuch)
light	lumière	luz	Licht	свет (svet)

English	French	Spanish	German	Russian
locker room	vestiaire	vestuario (con casilleros)	Umkleideraum	раздевалка с индивидуальными шкафчиками (razdevalka s individual'nimi shkafchikami)
maid	femme de chambre	camarera	Zimmermädchen	горничная (gornichnaya)
manager	gérant	gerente	Geschäftsführer	начальник (nachal'nik)
porter	porteur	portero	Portier	носильщик (nosil'shchik)
room service	service d'étage (hôtel)	servicio de habitaciones	Zimmer Service	обслуживание (obsluzhivanie)
service	service	servicio	Bedienung	обслуживанье (obsluzhivanye)
single bed	lit à une personne	cama individual	Einzelbett	односпальная кровать (odnospal'naya krovat')
soap	savon	jabón	Seife	мыло (milo)
terrace	terrasse	terraza	Terrasse	терраса/веранда (terrasa/veranda)
tip	pourboire	propina	Trinkgeld	чаевые (chayeviye)
toilet paper	papier hygiénique	papel higiénico	Toilettenpapier	туалетная бумага (tualetnaya bumaga)
towel	serviette de bain	toalla	Handtuch	полотенце (polotentse)
twin bed	lit à deux personnes	camas separados	Doppelbett	двуспальная кровать (dvuspal'naya krovat')
water (cold; hot)	eau (froide; chaude)	agua (fría; caliente)	Wasser (kalt; heiss)	вода/холодная, горячая/ (voda/holodnaya, goryachaya/)

Meals	Repas	La comida	Essen	Питание
Is there a restaurant near here?	Y a-t-il un restaurant près d'ici?	¿Hay un restaurante cerca de aquí?	Ist hier in der Nähe ein Restaurant?	Есть ли здесь поблизости ресторан? (yest' li zdes' poblizosti restoran?)
When do you serve breakfast (lunch, supper)?	A quelle heure sert-on le petit déjeuner (déjeuner, dîner)?	¿A qué hora se sirve el desayuno (el almuerzo, la cena)?	Wann gibt es Frühstück (Mittagessen, Abendessen)?	Когда вы подаёте завтрак/обед, ужин/? (kogda vi podayote zavtrak/obed, uzhin/?)

English	French	Spanish	German	Russian
Is this seat taken?	Cette place est-elle libre (occupée)?	¿Está desocupado (ocupado) este asiento?	Ist dieser Platz frei (besetzt)?	Это место занято? (eto mesto zanyato?)
Waiter!	Garçon!	¡Camarero!	Ober!	Официант! (ofitsiant!)
Waitress!	Mademoiselle!	¡Señorita!	Fräulein!	Официантка! (ofitsiantka!)
Can I have the menu (list of beverages), please?	La carte (carte des boissons), s'il vous plaît!	¡la lista (el menú) por favor!	Bitte die Speisekarte (Getränkekarte)!	Могу ли я попросить меню/прейскурант/, пожалуйста? (mogu li ya poprosit' menyu/preyskurant/, pozhalusta)
ash tray	cendrier	cenicero	Aschenbecher	пепельница (pepel'nitsa)
bread (white; brown)	pain (blanc; bis)	pan (blanco; moreno)	Brot (weiss; braun)	хлеб/белый, серый/ (hleb/beliy, serij/)
butter	beurre	mantequilla	Butter	масло (maslo)
crackers	craquelins	galletas	Kracker	крекеры (krekeri)
cream	crème	nata	Sahne	сливки (slivki)
glass	verre	vaso	Glas	стакан (stakan)
honey	miel	miel	Honig	мед (myod)
jam	confiture	mermelada	Marmelade	джем (dzhem)
knife, fork and spoon	couvert	cubierto	Besteck	нож, вилка и ложка (nozh, vilka i lozhka)
mustard	moutarde	mostaza	Senf	горчица (gorchitsa)
napkin	serviette	servilleta	Serviette	салфетка (salfetka)
oil	huile	aceite	Öl	растительное масло (rastitel'noye maslo)
pepper	poivre	pimienta	Pfeffer	перец (perets)
plate	assiette	plato	Teller	тарелка (tarelka)
roll	petit pains	panecillo	Brötchen	булочки (bulochki)
salt	sel	sal	Salz	соль (sol')
sugar	sucre	azúcar	Zucker	сахар (sahar)
vinegar	vinaigre	vinagre	Essig	уксус (uksus)

wine list	carte des vins	lista de vinos	Weinkarte	прейскурант спиртного (preyskurant spirtnovo)
Hors d'oeuvres	**Hors d'oeuvres**	**Entremeses y tapas**	**Vorspeisen**	**Закуски**
antipasto	hors d'oeuvres variés	antipasta	italienische Vorspeise	соленья; маринады (solen'ya; marinadi)
caviar	caviar	caviar	Kaviar	икра (ikra)
cold meat	viande froide	fiambres	kaltes Fleisch	холодное мясо (holodnoye myaso)
oysters	huîtres	ostras	Austern	устрицы (ustritsi)
pâté	pâté	pastel (de hígado, etc.)	Pastete	паштет (pashtet)
pickled herring	harengs marinés	arenque ahumado	eingelegter Hering	маринованная селедка (marinovannaya selyodka)
shrimp cocktail	crevettes	coctel de camarones	Krevette	креветки с томатным соусом (krevetki s tomatnym sousom)
snails	escargots	caracoles	Weinbergschnecken	улитки (ulitki)
Soups	**Potages**	**Sopas**	**Suppen**	**Супы**
asparagus soup	potage aux asperges	sopa de espárragos	Spargelsuppe	суп из спаржи (sup iz sparzhi)
beef broth	consommé de boeuf	sopa de carne	Rindfleischbrühe	говяжий бульон (govyazhiy bul'yon)
chicken soup	consommé de poulet	sopa de pollo	Geflügelsuppe	куриный суп (kuriniy sup)
consommé	consommé	caldo	Gemüsesuppe	бульон (bul'yon)
French onion soup	soupe à l'oignon	sopa de cebolla	französische Zwiebelsuppe	французский луковый суп (frantsuzskiy lukoviy sup)
mushroom soup	soupe aux champignons	sopa de setas	Pilzsuppe	грибной суп (gribnoy sup)
pea soup	soupe aux pois	potaje	Erbsensuppe	гороховый суп (gorohoviy sup)
soup of the day	soupe du jour	sopa del día	Tagessuppe	дежурный суп (dezhurniy sup)

tomato soup	potage aux tomates	sopa de tomate	Tomatensuppe	томатный суп (tomatniy sup)
vegetable soup	julienne	sopa de verduras	Gemüsesuppe	овощной суп (ovoshchnoy sup)

Seafood	**Fruits de mer**	**Pescados y mariscos**	**Meeresfrüchte**	**Дары моря**
cod	morue	bacalao	Dorsch	треска (treska)
crab	crabe	cangrejo de mar	Krabben	краб (krab)
lobster	homard	langosta	Hummer	омар (omar)
mackerel	maquereau	caballa	Makrele	макрель (makrel')
pike	brochet	lucio	Hecht	щука (shchuka)
salmon	saumon	salmón	Lachs	лосось/семга (losos'/syomga)
sole	sole	lenguado	Seezunge	камбала (kambala)
trout	truite	trucha	Forelle	форель (forel')

Meat and poultry	**Viande et volaille**	**Carne y aves**	**Fleisch und Geflügelgerichte**	**Мясо и птица**
bacon	bacon	tocino (entreverado)	Schinkenspeck	бекон (bekon)
beef	boeuf	res; carne (de res)	Rindfleisch	говядина (govyadina)
chicken	poulet	pollo	Huhn	курица (kuritsa)
chop (lamb; pork)	côtelette (agneau, porc)	chuleta (de cordero; de puerco)	Kotelett (Lamm; Schweinefleisch)	отбивная котлета/из баранины, из свинины/ (otbivnaya kotleta/iz baranini, iz svinini/)
duck	canard	pato	Ente	утка (utka)
fillet steak (filet mignon)	filet mignon	filete de carne; bistec; bife	Filesteak	филе миньон (file min'yon)
fried chicken (fricassee)	fricassée (poulet)	fricasé de pollo; pollo frito	gebratenes Hähnchen	жареная курица/фрикассе/ (zharenaya kuritsa/frikasse/)

English	French	Spanish	German	Russian
fried sausage	saucisse	salchicha frita	Bratwurst	жареные сосиски (zhareniye sosiski)
goulash	goulash	gulasch	Gulasch	гуляш (gulyash)
ham	jambon	jamón	Schinken	ветчина (vetchina)
hamburger	bifteck haché	hamburguesa	Deutsches Beefsteak	рубленый шницель/котлета (rubleniy shnitsel'/kotleta)
hot dog	hot dog	perro caliente	hot dog	сосиcка с булочкой (sosiska s bulochkoy)
lamb	agneau	cordero	Lamm	баранина (baranina)
liver	foie	hígado	Leber	печень (pechen')
pork	porc	puerco	Schweinefleisch	свинина (svinina)
roast beef; roast meat	rosbif (rôti de boeuf)	carne asada; rosbif	Roastbeef	ростбиф (rostbif)
roast chicken	poulet rôti	pollo asado	Hühnchen	жаркое из курицы (zharkoye iz kuritsi)
sausages	saucisses	salchichas	Würstchen	сосиски (sosiski)
steak	bifteck	bistec	Steak	отбивная (otbivnaya)
stew	ragoût	guisado	Ragout	тушеное мясо (tushonoye myaso)
turkey	dinde	pavo	Truthanh	индейка (indeyka)
veal	veau	ternera, carne de	Kalbfleisch	телятина (telyatina)
veal cutlet	escalope de veau	chuleta de ternera	Kalbsschnitzel	телячья отбивная (telyach'ya otbivnaya)
Egg dishes	**Oeufs**	**Platos do huevos**	**Eierspeisen**	**Яичные блюда**
boiled eggs	oeufs à la coque	huevos pasados por agua	Gekochte Eier	вареные яйца (varyoniye yaytsa)
fried eggs	oeufs sur le plat	huevos fritos	Spiegeleier	глазунья (glazun'ya)
omelette	omelette	tortilla a la francesa	Omlett	яичница (yaichnitsa)
poached eggs	oeufs pochés	huevos escalfados	Pochiertes Ei	яйцо-пашот (yaytso-pashot)
scrambled eggs	oeufs brouillés	huevos revueltos	Rührreier	яичница-болтунья (yaichnitsa-boltun'ya)

215

Potatoes, rice, pasta, etc.	Pommes de terre, riz, pâtes, etc.	Papas, arroz, fideos, etc.	Kartoffel, Reis, Teigwaren, usw.	Картофель, рис, изделия из теста и т.д.
boiled potatoes	pommes à l'anglaise	papas (o: patatas) hervidas	Salzkartoffel	отварной картофель (otvarnoy kartofel')
French fries	frites	papas (o: patatas) fritas	pommes frites	жареный картофель (zhareniy kartofel')
French toast	pain perdu	torrija	paniertes Brot	французские тосты (frantsuzkiye tosti)
hash brown potatoes	hachis de pommes de terre sautées	papas picadas en trocitos y fritas hasta doradas	gebratene Kartoffel	картофель, зажаренный кубиками (kartofel', zazharenniy kubikami)
macaroni	macaronis	macarrones	Makkaroni	короткие макароны (korotkiye makaroni)
mashed potatoes	purée de pommes de terre	pureé de patatas(papas)	Kartoffelpüree	картофельное пюре (kartofel'noye pyure)
pancakes; crepes	crêpes	tortita (panqueque)	Pfannkuchen; Crêpes	оладьи/блины (olad'i/blini)
potato chips	chips	papas (patatas) fritas (a la inglesa)	Kartoffelchip	хрустящий картофель (hrustyashchiy kartofel')
potato dumplings	boulettes de pommes de terre	albóndigas de patatas, (papas)	Kartoffelklösse	картофельные клецки (kartofel'niye klyotski)
rice	riz	arroz	Reis	рис (ris)
roast potatoes	pommes de terre rôtis	patatas(papas) salteadas	Röstkartoffeln	жареная в духовке картошка (zharenaya v duhovke kartoshka)
spaghetti	spaghetti	espaguetis	Spaghetti	спагетти/длинные макароны/ (spagetti/dlinniye makaroni/)
sweet potatoes	patates (douces)	batata (boniato)	Süsskartoffel	сладкий картофель (sladkiy kartofel')

Vegetables	Légumes	Hortalizas	Gemüse	Овощи
artichokes	artichauts	alcachofas	Artischocken	артишоки (artishoki)
asparagus	asperges	espárragos	Spargel	спаржа (sparzha)
broccoli	broccoli	brócoli	Spargelkohl	брокколи (brokkoli)
Brussels sprouts	choux de Bruxelles	coles de Bruselas	Rosenkohl	брюссельская капуста (bryussel'skaya kapusta)
cabbage	chou	repollo; col	Kohl	капуста (kapusta)
carrots	carottes	zanahorias	Karotten	морковь (morkov')
cauliflower	chou-fleur	coliflor	Blumenkohl	цветная капуста (tsvetnaya kapusta)
celery	céleri	apio	Stangensellerie	сельдерей (sel'derey)
corn; maize	maïs	maíz	Mais	кукуруза (kukuruza)
cucumbers	concombres	pepinos	Gurken	огурцы (ogurtsi)
green beans	haricots verts	judías verdes	Grüne Bohnen	фасоль (fasol')
onions	oignons	cebollas	Zwiebeln	лук (luk)
peas	petits pois	guisantes	Erbsen	горох (goroh)
peppers	poivrons	pimientos	Paprikaschoten	перцы (pertsi)
red cabbage	chou rouge	berza lombarda	Rotkohl	красная капуста (krasnaya kapusta)
sauerkraut	choucroute	chucrut	Sauerkraut	кислая капуста (kislaya kapusta)
spinach	épinards	espinacas	Spinat	шпинат (shpinat)
tomatoes	tomates	tomates	Tomaten	помидоры (pomidori)
zucchini	zucchini	calabacín	Zucchini	зуккини (zukkini)

Salads	Salades	Ensaladas	Salate	Салаты
chicken salad	poulet en salade	ensalada de pollo	Geflügelsalat	салат из курицы (salat iz kuritsi)
cole slaw	salade de chou cru	ensalada de col	Krautsalat	салат из свежей капусты (salat iz svezhey kapusti)

cucumber salad	salade de concombres	ensalada de pepinos	Gurkensalat	салат из огурцов (salat iz ogurtsov)
lettuce salad	laitue	ensalada de lechuga	Kopfsalat	листья салата/салат-латук/ (list'ya salata/salat-latuk/)
mixed salad	salade variée	ensalada variada	Gemischter Salat	салат ассорти (salat assorti)
potato salad	salade de pommes de terre	ensalada de patatas	Kartoffelsalat	картофельный салат (kartofel'niy salat)
spinach salad	salade d'épinards	ensalada de espinacas	Spinatensalat	салат из шпината (salat iz shpinata)
tomato salad	salade de tomates	ensalada de tomate	Tomatensalat	салат из помидоров (salat iz pomidorov)

Sweets, cheese and desserts	Desserts	Dulces, queso y postres	Nachspeisen	Сладкое, сыр и дессерт
cake	gâteau	torta	Torte	торт (tort)
cheese	fromage	queso	Käse	сыр (sir)
cottage cheese	fromage blanc	requesones	Hüttenkäse	творог (tvorog)
fruit salad	macédoine de fruits	ensalada de frutas	Obstsalat	фруктовый салат (fruktoviy salat)
ice cream; ices	glaces	helado	Eis	мороженое (morozhenoye)
jello	gélatine aux fruits	gelatina	Wackelpeter	желе (zhele)
pastry	pâtisserie	pasteleria	Pastete	кондитерские изделия (konditerskiye izdeliya)
pie	tarte	tartas	Kuchen	пирог (pirog)
pudding	pouding	budín	Pudding	крем/пудинг (krem/puding)
sherbet	sorbet	sorbete	Fruchteis	щербет (shcherbet)
stewed fruit	fruits au sirop	compota	Kompott	компот (kompot)
yogurt	yaourt	yogur	Joghurt	йогурт (yogurt)

Fruit	Fruits	Frutas	Obst	Фрукты
apples	pommes	manzanas	Äpfel	яблоки (yabloki)
apricots	abricots	albaricoques	Aprikosen	абрикосы (abrikosi)
bananas	bananes	plátanos	Bananen	бананы (banani)
cherries	cerises	cerezas	Kirschen	вишня (vishnya)
cranberries	airelles rouges	arándanos encarnados	Preiselbeeren	клюква (klyukva)
grapefruit	pamplemousse	toronja	Grapefruit	грейпфрут (greypfrut)
grapes	raisin	uvas	Weintrauben	виноград (vinograd)
melon	melon	sandía	Melone	дыня (dinya)
oranges	oranges	naranjas	Apfelsinen	апельсины (apel'sini)
peaches	pêches	melocotones	Pfirsiche	персики (persiki)
pears	poires	peras	Birnen	груши (grushi)
pineapple	ananas	piña	Ananas	ананас (ananas)
plums	prunes	ciruelas	Pflaumen	сливы (slivi)
raspberries	framboises	frambuesas	Himbeeren	малина (malina)
strawberries	fraises	fresas	Erdbeeren	клубника (klubnika)
tangerines	mandarines	mandarinas	Mandarinen	мандарины (mandarini)

Alcoholic drinks	Boissons alcoolisées	Bebidas alcohólicas	Alkoholische Getränke	Спиртные напитки
beer	bière	cerveza	Bier	пиво (pivo)
brandy	cognac	coñac	Weinbrand	бренди (brendi)
champagne	champagne	champaña	Sekt	шампанское (shampanskoye)
gin	gin	ginebra	Gin	джин (dzhin)
liqueurs	liqueurs	Licores (vinos licorosos)	Likören	ликеры (likyori)
red wine	vin rouge	vino tinto	Rotwein	красное вино (krasnoye vino)
rosé wine	vin rosé	clarete	Roséwein	розовое вино (rozovoye vino)
Scotch whisky	whisky	whisky escocés	Scotch Whisky	шотландское виски (shotlandskoye viski)

sherry	sherry	vino de Jerez	Sherry	херес (heres)
stout	bière brune	cerveza de malta	Starkbier	портер (porter)
vermouth	vermouth	vermú	Wermut	вермут (vermut)
vodka	vodka	vodka	Vodka	водка (vodka)
whisky (bourbon, rye, Canadian)	whisky (américain; canadien)	whisky de maíz; de centeno; tipo canadiense	Whisky (Bourbon; kanadischer Whisky)	виски/бербон, ржаное, канадское/ (viski/berbon, rzhanoye, kanadskoye/)
white wine	vin blanc	vino blanco	Weisswein	белое вино (beloye vino)

Non-alcoholic drinks	Boissons non alcoolisées	Bebidas no alcohólicas	Alkoholfreie Getränke	Безалкогольные напитки
apple juice	jus de pommes	zumo de manzana	Apfelsaft	яблочный сок (yablochniy sok)
chocolate (hot)	cacao (chocolat chaud)	chocolate (caliente)	Schokolade (heiss)	какао (kakao)
coffee	café	café	Koffee	кофе (kofe)
espresso (mocha)	expresso (moka)	café exprés (moka)	Espresso (Mocha)	кофе-экспресс/кофе-мокко/ (kofe-ekspress/kofe mokko/)
grape juice	jus de raisin	zumo de uvas	Traubensaft	виноградный сок (vinogradniy sok)
grapefruit juice	jus de pamplemousse	zumo de toronja	Grapefruitsaft	сок грейпфрута (sok greypfruta)
lemonade	limonade	limonada	Limonade	лимонад (limonad)
milk	lait	leche	Milch	молоко (moloko)
milkshake	"milkshake"	batido de leche	Milchgetränk	молочный коктейль (molochniy koktel')
mineral water	eau minérale	agua mineral	Mineralwasser	минеральная вода (mineral'naya voda)
orange juice	jus d'orange	zumo de naranja	Orangensaft	апельсиновый сок (apel'sinoviy sok)
soda water	eau gazeuse	Agua de Seltz	Soda	содовая вода (sodovaya voda)
soft drinks (soda pop)	boissons pétillantes (pop)	refresos	alkoholfreie Getränke	газированные напитки (gazirovanniye napitki)

tea	thé	té	Tee	чай (chay)
tomato juice	jus de tomates	jugo de tomate	Tomatensaft	томатный сок (tomatniy sok)
water	eau	agua	Wasser	вода (voda)
Around town	**En ville**	**De paseo**	**In der Stadt**	**По городу**
How do I get to ...?	Comment puis-je aller à ...?	¿Cómo puedo llegar a ...?	Wie komme ich nach (zum) ...?	Как проехать в/на/...? (kak proyehat' v/na/...?)
Turn left (right)	A gauche (droite)	A la izquierda(derecha)	Nach links (rechts)	Поверните налево/направо/ (povernite nalevo/napravo/)
Which bus (trolley bus), subway (underground) do I have to take?	Quel bus (trolley) métro, faut-il prendre?	¿Cuál (trolebús), metro tengo que subir?	Welchen Bus (Obus, Metro) muss ich nehmen?	Каким автобусом/троллейбусом/, метро можно проехать/доехать/...? (kakim avtobusom/trolleybusom, metro mozhno proyehat/doyehat'...?)
Where is the stop?	Où se trouve l'arrêt (la station)?	¿Dónde está la parada?	Wo ist die Haltestelle (Station)?	Где остановка? (gde ostanovka?)
Where must I get off?	Où faut-il descendre?	¿Dónde tengo que bajar?	Wo muss ich aussteigen?	Где мне слезть? (gde mne slezt'?)
Where can I get a taxi?	Où peut-on trouver un taxi?	¿Dónde se consigue un taxi?	Wo kann ich ein Taxi haben?	Где можно заказать/поймать/ такси? (gde mozhno zakazat'/poymat'/taksi?)
airport	aéroport	aeropuerto	Flugplatz	аэропорт (aeroport)
avenue	avenue	avenida	Allee	проспект/бульвар (prospekt/bul'var)
botanical gardens	jardin botanique	jardin botánico	Botanischer Garten	ботанический сад (botanicheskiy sad)
bridge	pont	puente	Brücke	мост (most)
bus stop (transit zone)	arrêt (zone de transport)	parada (de ómnibus)	Bushaltestelle	автобусная остановка (avtobusnaya ostanovka)
car park	parking; stationnement	estacionamiento	Parkplatz	автопарк (avtopark)

English	French	Spanish	German	Russian
cathedral	cathédrale	catedral	Dom	кафедральный собор (kafedral'niy sobor)
church	église	iglesia	Kirche	церковь (tserkov')
city map; town plan	carte de la ville	plano de la ciudad	Stadtplan	карта города/план города (karta goroda/plan goroda)
consulate	consulat	consulado	Konsulat	консулат (konsulat)
corner	coin	esquina	Ecke	угол (ugol)
department store	grand magasin	gran almacén	Kaufhaus	универсальный магазин (universal'niy magazin)
district	quartier	barrio	Stadtteil	район (rayon)
downtown	centre-ville	centro	Innenstadt	центр города (tsentr goroda)
fountain	fontaine	fuente	Brunnen	фонтан (fontan)
freeway	voie rapide	autopista	Autobahn	шоссе (shosse)
greenhouse	serres	invernadero	Gewächshaus	оранжерея (oranzhereya)
hospital	hôpital	hospital	Krankenhaus	больница (bol'nitsa)
house	maison	casa	Haus	дом/небольшой/ (dom/nebol'shoy/)
Legislative Building	Edifice du Parlement	Capitolio	Parlament	парламент (parlament)
library	bibliothèque	biblioteca	Bücherei	библиотека (biblioteca)
main street	artère principale	calle principal	Hauptstrasse	главная улица (glavnaya ulitsa)
monument	monument	monumento	Denkmal	памятник/монумент (pamyatnik/monument)
mosque	moscuée	mezquita	Moschee	мечеть (mechet')
movie theater	cinéma	cine	Kino	кинотеатр (kinoteatr)
museum	musée	museo	Museum	музей (muzey)
night club	boîte de nuit	cabaret (club nocturno, boite)	Night Club	ночной клуб (nochnoy klub)
park	parc	parque	Park	парк (park)
planetarium	planétarium	planetario	Planetarium	планетарий (planetariy)
river	rivière	río	Fluss	река (reka)

English	French	Spanish	German	Russian
road	route	calzada	Strasse	дорога (doroga)
shop	magasin	tienda	Geschäft (Laden)	магазин (magazin)
shopping center	centre d'achats	centro comercial	Einkaufszentrum	торговый центр (torgoviy tsentr)
sightseeing tour	tour de la ville en car	vuelta por la ciudad	Stadtrundfahrt	осмотр достопримечательностей (osmotr dostoprimechatel'nostey)
square	place	plaza	Platz	площадь (ploshchad')
stadium	stade	estadio	Stadium	стадион (stadion)
station	gare	estación	Bahnhof	станция (stantsiya)
street	rue	calle	Strasse	улица (ulitsa)
supermarket	super-marché	supermercado	Supermarket	продовольственный магазин (prodovol'stvenniy magazin)
synagogue	synagogue	sinagoga	Synagoge	синагога (sinagoga)
tall building (high rise)	gratte-ciel	edificio alto	Hochhaus	многоэтажное здание (mnogoetazhnoye zdaniye)
tavern; bar	café; bar	taberna; bar	Taverne; Bar	бар (bar)
terminus	terminus	parada terminal	Endhaltestelle	конечная станция (konechnaya stantsiya)
theater	théâtre	teatro	Theater	театр (teatr)
tower; steeple	tour	torre	Turm	башня/вышка (bashnya/vishka)
town hall	hôtel de ville	ayuntamiento	Rathaus	городская ратуша (gorodskaya ratusha)
town; city	ville	ciudad	Stadt	городок/город (gorodok/gorod)
train station	gare	estación de ferrocarril	Bahnhof	вокзал (vokzal)
university	université	universidad	Universität	университет (universitet)
visitors information bureau	bureau d'information touristique	oficina de información turística	Aufkunftbüro für Besucher	справочное бюро (spravochnoye byuro)
zoo	zoo	parque zoológico	Zoo	зоопарк (zoopark)

Bank, post office	Banque, poste	Banco, correos	Bank, Post	Банк, почта
Where can I change some money?	Où peut-on changer de l'argent?	¿Dónde puedo cambiar dinero?	Wo kann ich Geld wechseln?	Где можно обменять деньги? (gde mozhno obmenyat' den'gi)
Please change this into …	Changez-moi ceci en … s'il vous plaît	Hágame el favor de cambiarme esto en …	Wechseln Sie mir dies bitte in …!	Поменяйте, пожалуйста, это на… (pomenyayte, pozhalusta, eto na…)
I want to cash this (traveller's) cheque.	Je désire encaisser ce chèque (de voyage)	Quisiera cobrar este cheque (de viajero)	Ich möchte diesen (Reise)- Scheck einlösen	Я хочу наличными этот/аккредитив/чек (ya hochu nalichnimi etot/akkreditiv/chek)
What's the postage on…?	Quel est le tarif d'affranchissement pour …?	¿Cuánto cuesta el franqueo de …?	Wie hoch ist das Porto für …?	Какой почтовый тариф на…? (kakoy pochtoviy tarif na…?)
I want to register this letter	Je voudrais envoyer cette lettre en recommandé	Quisiera certificar esta carta	Ich möchte diesen Brief eingeschrieben schicken	Я хочу отправить это письмо заказным (ya hochu otpravit' eto pis'mo zakaznim)
I would like to reverse charges on a call to …	Je voudrais une communication en P.C.V.	Quisiera pedir una conferencia pagadera por la persona llamada	Ich möchte ein R-Gespräch anmelden	Я хотел бы позвонить за счет абонента (ya hotel bi pozvonit' za schyot abonenta)
I would like to phone long distance	Je voudrais une communication interurbaine (internationale)	Quisiera hacer una conferencia interurbana	Ich möchte ein Ferngespräch haben	Я хотел бы сделать междугородный звонок (ya hotel bi sdelat' mezhdugorodniy zvonok)
address	adresse	dirección	Adresse	адрес (adres)
air mail	par avion	por avión	mit Luftpost	авиапочтай (aviapochta)
bank	banque	banco	Bank	банк (bank)
change	changer	cambio	wechseln	сдача (sdacha)
coins (change)	pièces (monnaie)	moneda	Wechselgeld	мелочь (meloch')
counter	guichet	ventanilla	Schalter	прилавок (prilavok)
credit card	carte de crédit	tarjeta de crédito	Kreditenkarte	кредитная карта (kreditnaya karta)

English	French	German	Spanish	Russian
express delivery	par exprès	mit Eilboten	por expreso	срочная доставка (srochnaya dostavka)
foreign exchange	devises	Devisen	divisas	обмен валюты (obmen valyuti)
form	formulaire	Formular	formulario	анкета (anketa)
identity card	carte d'identité	Personalausweis	documento (cédula) de identidad	удостоверение личности (udostovereniye lichnosti)
interpreter	interprète	Dolmetscher	intérprete	переводчик (perevodchik)
letter	lettre	Brief	carta	письмо (pis'mo)
local call	communication locale	Ortsgespräch	llamada urbana	местный звонок (mestniy zvonok)
long-distance call	communication interurbaine	Ferngespräch	llamada de larga distancia	междугородный/международный звонок (mezhdugorodniy/mezhdunarodniy/zvonok)
lost and found	objets trouvés	Fundbüro	depósito de objectos perdidos	бюро находок (byuro nahodok)
mailbox	boîte aux lettres	Briefkasten	buzón	почтовый ящик (pochtoviy yashchik)
money order	mandat postal	Zahlungsanweisung	giro postal	денежный перевод (denezhniy perevod)
parcel	colis	Paket	paquete	посылка (posilka)
parcel counter	réception des colis	Paketannahme	recepción de paquetes	посылочный прилавок (posilochniy prilavok)
passport	passeport	Reisepass	pasaporte	паспорт (pasport)
post office	bureau de poste	Postamt	oficina de correos	почта (pochta)
postcard	carte postale	Postkarte	tarjeta postal	почтовая открытка (pochtovaya otkritka)
poste restante	poste restante	Postlagernd	lista de correos	до востребования (do vostrebovaniya)
printed matter	imprimé	Drucksache	impresos	печатный материал (pechatniy material)
sender	expéditeur	Absender	remitente	отправитель (otpravitel')

small parcel	petit paquet	paquetito	Päckchen	бандероль (banderol')
stamps	timbres-poste	sellos	Briefmarken	марки (marki)
telephone booth	cabine téléphonique	cabina telefónica	Telefonzelle	телефонная будка (telefonnaya budka)
telephone directory	annuaire de téléphone	guía telefónica	Telefonbuch	телефонная книга (telefonnaya kniga)
telephone number	numéro de téléphone	número del teléfono	Telefonnummer	номер телефона (nomer telefona)
telex	télex	télex	Telex	телекс (teleks)
traveller's cheque	chèque de voyage	cheque de viajero	Reisescheck	аккредитив (akkreditiv)

At the police station	Au commissariat de police	En la comisaria	Auf dem Polozeirevier	В отделении полиции
I want to report ...	Je voudrais déposer une plainte	Quisiera hacer una denuncia	Ich möchte eine Anzeige erstatten	Я хочу заявить о... (ya hochu zayavit' o...)
My ... has been stolen	On m'a volé ...	Me han robado ...	Man hat mir ...gestohlen	Мой...украден (moy...ukraden)
Please notify my consulate	Prévenez le consulat de mon pays, s'il vous plaît	Tenga la bondad de informarle al cónsul de mi país	Verständigen Sie bitte mein Konsulat!	Пожалуйста, сообщите в мой консулат о... (pozhalusta, soobshchite v moy konsulat o...)
date of birth	date de naissance	fecha de nacimiento	Geburtsdatum	дата рождения (data rozhdeniya)
driver's licence	permis de conduire	permiso (carnet) de conducir; licencia de manejar	Führerschein	водительские права (voditel'skiye prava)
first name (Christian name)	prénom	nombre (de pila)	Vorname	имя (imya)
nationality	nationalité	nacionalidad	Nationalität	национальность (natsional'nost')
place of birth	lieu de naissance	lugar de nacimiento	Geburtsort	место рождения (mesto rozhdeniya)

police	police	policía	Polizei	полиция (politsiya)
profession	profession	profesión	Beruf	профессия (professiya)
residence	résidence	domicilio	Wohnort	место жительства (mesto zhitel'stva)
surname	nom	apellido(s)	Familienname	фамилия (familiya)
First aid	**Premiers soins**	**Cura de urgencia**	**Erste Hilfe**	**Первая помощь**
Can you recommend a good doctor (...specialist)?	Pouvez-vous me recommander un bon médecin (spécialiste de ...)?	¿Puede usted recomendarme un buen médico (especialista en ...)?	Können Sie mir einen guten Arzt (Spezialisten für ...) empfehlen?	Можете ли вы рекомендовать хорошего доктора/...специалиста/? (mozhete li vi rekomendovat' horoshevo doktora/...spetsialista/?)
Where is the nearest doctor (pharmacy, first-aid center, hospital)?	Où est le médecin (la pharmacie, le poste de secours, l'hôpital) le plus près d'ici?	¿Dónde se encuentra el médico (la farmacia, el centro de socorro, el hospital) más proximo (a) de aquí?	Wo ist der (die, das) nächste Arzt (Apotheke, Unfallstation Center, Krankenhaus)?	Где находится доктор/аптека, станция первой помощи, госпиталь/? (gde nahoditsa doktor/apteka, stantsiya pervoy pomoshchi, gospital'/?)
I have a pain here	J'ai mal ici	Siento dolores aquí	Ich habe hier schmerzen	У меня здесь болит (u menya zdes' bolit)
I suffer from ...	Je souffre de ...	Padezco de ...	Ich leide an ...	Я страдаю от... (ya stradayu ot...)
I need a remedy for ...	Il me faut un remède pour ...	Me falta un remedio (un tratamiento) para ...	Ich brauche ein Mittel gegen ...	Мне нужно средство от... (mne nuzhno sredstvo ot...)
I am allergic to ...	Je suis allergique à ...	Soy alérgico(a) a	Ich bin allergisch gegen ...	У меня аллергия к... (u menya allergiya k...)
I have a pain in ...	J'ai mal à ... aux ...	Me duele el (la) ...	Ich habe Schmerzen im ...	У меня болит... (u menya bolit...)

Diseases and injuries	Maladies et blessures	Enfermedades y lesiones	Krankheiten und Verletzungen	Забелевания и повреждения
abdomen	bas-ventre	abdomen	Unterleib	брюшная полость (bryushnaya polost')
abdomen; belly	ventre	vientre	Bauch	брюшная полость/живот (bryushnaya polost'/zhivot)
abscess	abcès	absceso	Geschwür	абцесс/нарыв (abtsess/nariv)
ambulance	ambulance	ambulancia	Krankenwagen	скорая помощь (skoraya pomoshch')
ankle	cheville	tobillo	Knöchel	лодыжка (lodizhka)
appendicitis	appendicite	apendicitis	Blinddarmentzündung	аппендицит (appenditsit)
appendix	appendice	apéndice	Blinddarm	аппендикс (appendiks)
arm	bras	brazo	Arm	рука (ruka)
back	dos	espalda	Rücken	спина (spina)
bandaid	pansement adhésif	esparadrapo; "curita"	Verband	лейкопластырь (leykoplastir')
bile; gall	bile	bilis	Galle	желчь (zholch')
bladder	vessie	vejiga	Blase	пузырь (puzir')
blood pressure	tension artérielle	presión arterial	Blutdruck	кровяное давление (krovyanoye davleniye)
bone	os	hueso	Knochen	кость (kost')
breast; chest	poitrine	pecho	Brust	грудь (grud')
bruise	bleu	magulladura	Bluterguss	ушиб (ushib)
burn	brûlure	quemadura	Verbrennung	ожог (ozhog)
burn ointment	pommade pour les brûlures	pomada para las quemaduras	Brandsalbe	мазь от ожога (maz' ot ozhoga)
chin	menton	barbilla	Kinn	подбородок (podborodok)
circulatory collapse	collapsus cardio-vasculaire	colapso circulatorio	Kreislaufkollaps	изнеможение/резкий упадок сил (iznemozheniye/rezkiy upadok sil)
cold	rhume	resfriado; catarro	Schnupfen	насморк (nasmork)

compress; poultice	compresse	compresa	Umschlag	компресс/припарка (kompress/priparka)
concussion of the brain	commotion cérébrale	conmoción cerebral	Gehirnerschütterung	сотрясение мозга (sotryaseniye mozga)
constipation	constipation	estreñimiento	Verstopfung	запор (zapor)
consulting hours	heures de consultation	horas de consulta	Sprechstunde	приемные часы (priyomniye chasi)
contusion	contusion	contusión	Prellung	контузия (kontuziya)
cotton	coton hydrophile	algodón hidrófilo	Watte	вата (vata)
cough	toux	tos	Husten	кашель (kashel')
cramp	crampe	calambre	Krampf	судорога/спазм (sudoroga/spasm)
crown (of tooth)	couronne (d'une dent)	corona (del diente)	Krone (Zahn)	коронка (koronka)
dentist	dentiste	dentista	Zahnarzt	зубной врач (zubnoy vrach)
diarrhea	diarrhée	diarrea	Durchfall	понос (ponos)
dislocation	luxation	dislocación	Verrenkung	вывих (vivih)
dressing	pansement	vendaje	Verband	бинт/перевязка (bint/perevyazka)
ear	oreille	oreja	Ohr	ухо (uho)
elbow	coude	codo	Ellbogen	локоть (lokot')
eye	oeil (les yeux)	ojo	Auge	глаз (glaz)
face	visage	cara	Gesicht	лицо (litso)
faint	s'évanouir	desmayarse	in Ohnmacht fallen	терять сознание (teryat' soznaniye)
fever	fièvre	fiebre	Fieber	жар/температура (zhar/temperatura)
filling; stopping	plombage	empaste	Plombe	пломба (plomba)
finger	doigt	dedo	Finger	палец руки (palets ruki)
first aid	premiers soins	cura de urgencia	Erste Hilfe	первая помощь (pervaya pomoshch')
foot	pied	pie	Fuss	нога/ступня (noga/stupnya)

English	French	German	Spanish	Russian
forehead	front	Stirn	frente	лоб (lob)
fracture	fracture	Knochenbruch	fractura	перелом (perelom)
gall bladder	vésicule biliaire	Gallenblase	vesícula biliar	желчный пузырь (zholchniy puzir')
glands	glandes	Drüsen	glándulas	гланды (glandi)
hand	main	Hand	mano	рука/кисть (ruka/kist')
head	tête	Kopf	cabeza	голова (golova)
headache	maux de tête	Kopfschmerzen	dolores de cabeza	головная боль (golovnaya bol')
heart	coeur	Herz	corazón	сердце (sertse)
heartburn	aigreurs d'estomac	Sodbrennen	ardor de estómago	изжога (izzhoga)
hemorrhage	hémorragie	Blutung	hemorragia	кровоизлияние (krovoizliyaniye)
hip	hanche	Hüfte	cadera	бедро (bedro)
infection	infection	Infektion	infección	инфекция (infektsiya)
inflammation	inflammation	Entzündung	inflamación	воспаление (vospaleniye)
influenza	grippe	Grippe	gripe	грипп (gripp)
injury	blessure	Verletzung	lesión	повреждение (povrezhdeniye)
insect bites (stings)	piqûres d'insectes	Insektenstiche	picada	укусы насекомых (ukusi nasekomih)
intestine	intestin	Darm	intestino	кишечник (kishechnik)
kidneys	reins	Nieren	riñones	почки (pochki)
knee	genou	Knie	rodilla	колено (koleno)
knuckle	articulation du doigt	Knöchel	nudillo	сустав пальца (sustav pal'tsa)
laxative	laxatif	Abführmittel	laxante	слабительное (slabitel'noye)
leg	jambe	Bein	pierna	нога (noga)
lip	lèvre	Lippe	labio	губа (guba)
liver	foie	Leber	hígado	печень (pechen')
lungs	poumon	Lunge	pulmones	легкие (lyohkiye)
medicine	médicament	Medikament	medicamento	лекарство (lekarstvo)
mouth	bouche	Mund	boca	рот (rot)

English	French	Spanish	German	Russian
nape of the neck	nuque	nuca	Genick	затылок (zatilok)
neck	cou	cuello	Gallenblase	шея (sheya)
nerve	nerf	nervio	Nerv	нерв (nerv)
nose	nez	nariz	Nase	нос (nos)
nose bleed	saignement de nez	hemorragia nasal	Nasenbluten	кровотечение из носа (krovotecheniye iz nosa)
ointment	pommade	pomada	Salbe	мазь (maz')
operation	opération	operación	Operation	операция (operatsiya)
poisoning	empoisonnement	intoxicación	Vergiftung	отравление (otravleniye)
pulse	pouls	pulso	Puls	пульс (pul's)
rheumatism	rhumatisme	reumatismo	Rheuma	ревматизм (revmatizm)
rupture of the Achilles tendon	déchirement du tendon d'Achille	desgarro del tendón de Aquiles	Achillessehnenriss	разрыв ахиллова сухожилия (razriv ahillova suhozhiliya)
shoulder	épaule	hombro	Schulter	плечо (plecho)
skin abrasion	écorchure	excoriación	Hautabschürfung	ссадина (ssadina)
sleeping pill	somnifère	somnífero	Schlaftablette	снотворное (snotvornoye)
sore throat	maux de gorge	dolores de garganta	Halsschmerzen	больное горло/ангина (bol'noye gorlo/angina)
stitch in the side	points de côté	puntos de costado	Seitenstechen	острая боль в боку (ostraya bol' v boku)
stomach	estomac	estómago	Magen	живот (zhivot)
stomach pains	maux d'estomac	dolores de estómago	Magenschmerzen	боли в животе (boli v zhivote)
strained ligament	claquage des ligaments	distensión de los ligamentos	Bänderzerrung	растяжение связки (rastyazheniye svyazki)
strained muscle	claquage musculaire	distorsión de un músculo	Muskelzerrung	растяжение мышцы (rastyazheniye mishtsi)
strained tendon	claquage d'un tendon	distensión de un tendón	Sehnenzerrung	растяжение сухожилия (rastyazheniye suhozhiliya)
sunburn	coup de soleil	quemaduras de sol	Sonnenbrand	солнечный ожог (solnechniy ozhog)
sunstroke	insolation	insolación	Sonnenstich	солнечный удар (solnechniy udar)

English	French	Spanish	German	Russian
temperature	température	temperatura	Temperatur	температура (temperatura)
temple	tempe	sien	Schläfe	висок (visok)
thermometer	thermomètre	termómetro	Thermometer	термометр/градусник (termometr / gradusnik)
thigh	cuisse	muslo	Oberschenkel	бедро (bedro)
throat	gorge	garganta	Kehle	горло (gorlo)
thumb	pouce	pulgar	Daumen	большой палец руки (bol'shoy palets ruki)
toe	orteil	dedo del pie	Zehe	палец ноги (palets nogi)
tonsils	amygdales	amígdalas	Mandeln	миндалины (mindalini)
toothache	maux de dents	dolor de muelas	Zahnschmerzen	зубная боль (zubnaya bol')
torn ligament	déchirement des ligaments	desgarro de los ligamentos	Bänderriss	разрыв связки (razriv svyazki)
torn muscle	déchirement musculaire	desgarro muscular	Muskelriss	разрыв мышцы (razriv mishtsi)
ulcers	ulcères	úlcera	Geschwür	язва (yazva)
urine	urine	orina	Urin	моча (mocha)
waiting room	salle d'attente	sala de espera	Wartezimmer	приемная (priyomnaya)
windpipe	trachée-artère	tráquea	Luftröhre	дыхательное горло (dihatel'noye gorlo)
X-ray	radiographie	radiografía	Röntgenaufnahme	рентген (rentgen)
Personal hygiene, care of clothes	**Soins du corps et des vêtements**	**Aseo y mantenimiento de vestidos**	**Körper und Kleiderpflege**	**Личная гигиена, уход за вещами**
A haircut, please	Une coupe de cheveux, s'il vous plaît!	Un corte de pelo, por favor	Haarschneiden bitte!	Постригите, пожалуйста (postrigite, pozhalusta)
A shampoo, please	Un shampooing, s'il vous plaît!	Láveme usted la cabeza por favor	Harrwaschen bitte!	Помойте мне пожалуйста голову (pomoyte mne pozhalusta golovu)

Not too short (long)	Pas trop court (long)	No muy corto (largo)	Nicht zu kurz (lang)	Не слишком коротко/длинно (ne slishkom korotko/dlinno)
I want a perm	Je désire une permanente	Quisiera una permanente	Ich möchte eine Dauerwelle	Перманент, пожалуйста (permanent, pozhalusta)
A shave, please	Faites-moi la barbe, s'il vous plaît	Un afeitado, por favor	Rasieren bitte!	Побрейте меня пожалуйста (pobreyte menya pozhalusta)
Dye (tint) my hair, please	Faites-moi une teinture (un shampooing colorant)	Teñir (matizar) el pelo	Die Haare färben (tönen) bitte!	Покрасьте/подкрасьте/мне, пожалуйста волосы (pokras'te/podkras'te/mne, pozhalusta volosi/podkras'te)
Would you please ...	Voudriez-vous, s'il vous plaît ...	Hágame el favor de ...	Wollem Sie bitte..	Можно вас попросить... (mozhno vas poprosit'...)
- brush this suit for me?	-brosser ce costume?	- cepillar este traje	- diesen Anzug ausbürsten?	-почистить этот костюм для меня (pochistit' etot kostyum dlya menya)
- press this blouse for me?	-repasser ce corsage?	- planchar esta blusa	- diese Bluse bügeln?	-погладить эту блузку для меня (pogladit' etu bluzku dlya menya)
- clean these trousers for me?	-nettoyer ce pantalon?	- limpiar estos pantalones	- diese Hose reinigen?	-почистить эти брюки для меня (pochistit' eti bryuki dlya menya)
- wash this for me?	-laver ceci	- de lavar esto	- für mich das waschen?	-постирать это для меня (postirat' eto dlya menya)
- sew this button on for me?	-recoudre ce bouton?	- coser este botón	- diesen Knopf annähen?	-пришить эту пуговицу для меня (prishit' etu pugovitsu dlya menya)
- mend this for me?	-raccommoder ceci	- de remendar esto	- bügeln?	-починить это для меня (pochinit' eto dlya menya)
after-shave lotion	lotion après rasage	loción para después de afeitar	after-shave	лосьон после бритья (los'yon posle brit'ya)
barbershop (men's)	coiffeur	barbería	Herrenfriseur	мужская парикмахерская (muzhshkaya parikmaherskaya)

English	French	Spanish	German	Russian
bath salts	sels pour le bain	sal aromática para baños	Badesalz	соли для ванны (soli dlya vanni)
brush	brosse	cepillo	Bürste	щетка (shchotka)
comb	peigne	peine	Kamm	расческа (raschyoska)
curler	rouleau	moño; rulo	Lockenwickler	бигуди (bigudi)
curls	boucles	rizos	Locken	кудри (kudri)
detergent	lessive	detergente	Waschpulver	стиральный порошок (stiral'niy poroshok)
drugstore	droguerie	farmacia	Drogerie	аптека (apteka)
dry cleaners	nettoyage à sec	tintorería	chemische Reinigung	химчистка (himchistka)
eau de Cologne	eau de Cologne	agua de Colonia	Kölnischwasser	одеколон (odekolon)
eyebrow pencil	crayon à sourcils	lápiz para las cejas	Augenbrauenstift	карандаш для бровей (karandash dlya brovey)
face cloth	gant de toilette	toallita	Waschlappen	салфетка для лица (salfetka dlya litsa)
face powder	poudre de toilette	polvo	Gesichtspuder	пудра (pudra)
hair lotion	lotion capillaire	loción capilar	Haarwasser	лосьон для волос (los'yon dlya volos)
hair style; hair-do	coiffure	peinado	Frisur	прическа (prichyoska)
hairdresser (women's)	coiffeuse	peluquería	Damenfriseur	женская парикмахерская (zhenskaya parikmaherskaya)
laundry; soiled clothing	linge à laver	ropa sucia	Wäsche; beschmutzte Wäsche	грязное белье (gryaznoye bel'yo)
lipstick	rouge à lèvres	barrita de carmín	Lippenstift	губная помада (gubnaya pomada)
makeup	maquillage	maquillaje	Make-up	подкраска (podkraska)
mascara	rimel	rimmel	Wimperntusche	тушь для ресниц (tush' dlya resnits)
mouth wash	eau dentifrice	elixir dentífrico	Mundwasser	жидкость для полоскания рта (zhidkost' dlya poloskaniya rta)

233

English	French	Spanish	German	Russian
nail clippers	ciseaux à ongles	tijeras para la uñas	Nagelschere	ножницы для ногтей (nozhnitsi dlya nogtey)
nail file	lime à ongles	lima para las uñas	Nagelfeile	пилка для ногтей (pilka dlya nogtey)
nail polish	vernis à ongles	esmalte para las uñas	Nagellack	лак для ногтей (lak dlya nogtey)
nail-polish remover	dissolvant	quitaesmaltes	Nagellackentferner	ацетон (atseton)
needle	aiguille	aguja de coser	Nähnadel	игла (igla)
perfume	parfum	perfume	Parfüm	духи (duhi)
pocket mirror	glace	espejo de bolsillo	Taschenspiegel	карманное зеркальце (karmannoye zerkal'tse)
razor	rasoir	máquina de afeitar	Rasierapparat	бритва (britva)
razor blades	lames de rasoir	hojas de afeitar	Rasierklingen	лезвия для бритвы (lezviya dlya britvi)
rubber band	élastique (serre-tête)	anilla de goma; liga	Gummibande	ластик/резинка (lastik/rezinka)
safety pins	épingles de sûreté	imperdibles	Sicherheitsnadeln	английские булавки (angliyskiye bulavki)
scissors	ciseaux	tijeras	Schere	ножницы (nozhnitsi)
shampoo	shampooing	champú	Haarwaschmittel	шампунь (shampun')
shaving brush	blaireau	brocha de afeitar	Rasierpinsel	щетка для бритья (shchotka dlya brit'ya)
shaving cream	crème à raser	crema de afeitar	Raisercreme	крем для бритья (krem dlya brit'ya)
shaving soap	savon à barbe	jabón de afeitar	Rasierseife	мыло для бритья (milo dlya brit'ya)
shoe brush	brosse à chaussures	cepillo para los zapatos	Schuhbürste	щетка для обуви (shchotka dlya obuvi)
shoe laces	lacets	cordones	Schnürsenkel	шнурки для обуви (shnurki dlya obuvi)
shoe polish	cirage	betún	Schuhcreme	вакса для обуви (vaksa dlya obuvi)
shoemaker	cordonnier	zapatero	Schuhmacher	сапожник (sapozhnik)

English	Dans le magasin	De Compras	Im Laden	Покупки
skin cream	crème de beauté	crema para el cutis	Hautcreme	крем для кожи (krem dlya kozhi)
soap	savon	jabón	Seife	мыло (milo)
stain remover	détacheur	quitamanchas	Fleckenwasser	пятновыводитель (pyatnovivoditel')
sun-tan oil	huile solaire	aceite bronceador	Sonnenöl	масло для загара (maslo dlya zagara)
sunglasses	lunettes de soleil	gafas de sol; espejuelos oscuros	Sonnenbrille	солнечные очки (solnechniye ochki)
talcum powder	talc	polvos para el cuerpo	Körperpuder	гигиеническая пудра (gigiyenicheskaya pudra)
thread	fil	hilo de coser	Zwirn	нитка (nitka)
toothbrush	brosse à dents	cepillo de dientes	Zahnbürste	зубная щетка (zubnaya shchotka)
toothpaste	dentifrice	pasta dentífrica	Zahnpasta	зубная паста (zubnaya pasta)

Shopping	**Dans le magasin**	**De Compras**	**Im Laden**	**Покупки**
Where can I buy ...?	Où puis-je acheter ...?	¿Dónde puedo comprar ...?	Wo kann ich ...kaufen?	Где можно купить...? (gde mozhno kupit'...?)
Can I try it on?	Je voudrais l'essayer	Quisiera probármelo(la)	Ich möchte ihn (sie,es) anprobieren	Могу ли я это примерить? (mogu li ya eto primerit'?)
Please develop this film	Développez ce film, s'il vous plaît	Hágame usted el favor de revelar esta película	Bitte entwickeln Sie diesen Film!	Пожалуйста, проявите эту пленку (pozhalusta, proyavite etu plyonku)
I want one print each	Je voudrais une épreuve de chaque	Quisiera una copia de cada foto	Ich möchte einen Abzug von jedem	Я хочу по одному отпечатку с каждого кадра (ya hochu po odnomu otpechatku s kazhdovo kadra)
a dozen	une douzaine	una docena	ein Dutzend	дюжина (dyuzhina)
a hundred grams	cent grammes	cien gramos	100 Gramm	сто грамм (sto gram)

English	French	Spanish	German	Russian
a kilogram	un kilo	un kilo	ein Kilogramm	килограмм (kilogramm)
a liter	un litre	un litro	ein Liter	литр (litr)
a meter	un mètre	un metro	ein Meter	метр (metr)
a pair	une paire	un par	ein Paar	пара (para)
a pound	une livre	una libra	ein Pfund	фунт (funt)
bag; sack	sachet; sac	bolsa; cartucho	Beutel; Sack	мешок (meshok)
ball point pen	stylo à bille	boligrafo	Kugelschreiber	шариковая ручка (sharikovaya ruchka)
bathing cap	bonnet de bain	gorro de baño	Badekappe	купальная шапочка (kupal'naya shapochka)
bathing trunks	slip	bañador	Badehose	плавки (plavki)
bathing-suit	maillot de bain	traje de baño	Badeanzug	купальный костюм (kupal'niy kostyum)
belt	ceinture	cinturón	Gürtel	ремень/пояс (remen'/poyas)
blouse	corsage	blusa	Bluse	блузка (bluzka)
bookshop	librairie	librería	Buchhandlung	книжный магазин (knizhniy magazin)
bottle	bouteille	botella	Flasche	бутылка (butilka)
brassiere	soutien-gorge	sostén	Büstenhalter	лифчик (lifchik)
butcher's shop	boucherie	carnicería	Metzgerei	мясной магазин (myasnoy magazin)
button	bouton	botón	Knopf	пуговица (pugovitsa)
cap	casquette	gorra, gorro	Mütze	кепка (kepka)
cigarettes	cigarettes	cigarillos	Zigaretten	сигареты (sigareti)
cigars	cigares	cigarros, puros	Zigarren	сигары (sigari)
confectionery	confiserie	confitería	Süsswaren	кондитерские изделия (konditerskiye izdeliya)
dress	robe	vestido	Kleid	платье (plat'ye)
envelopes	enveloppes	sobres	Briefumschläge	конверты (konverti)
fabrics; textiles	textiles	tejidos	Textilien	ткани (tkani)

English	French	Spanish	German	Russian
facial tissues	mouchoirs en papier	pañuelos de papel	Kleenex	бумажные салфетки для лица (bumazhniye salfetki dlya litsa)
film (color, black and white)	film (couleur; noir et blanc)	película, rollo de (color; blanco y negro)	Film (farb; schwarz und weiss)	фотопленка/цветная, черно-белая/ (fotoplyonka / tsvetnaya, chyorno-belaya)
flowers	fleurs	flores	Blumen	цветы (tsveti)
food (section)	alimentation	comestibles (departamento de)	Lebensmittel (Abteilung)	продукты питания (produkti pitaniya)
fruit and vegetables (section)	fruits et légumes (quatre saisons)	frutas y hortalizas	Obst - und Gemüse (Abteilung)	фрукты-овощи (frukti-ovoshchi)
gloves	gants	guantes	Handschuhe	перчатки (perchatki)
handkerchief	mouchoir	pañuelo	Taschentuch	носовой платок (nosovoy platok)
hat	chapeau	sombrero	Hut	шапка/шляпа (shapka/shlyapa)
jacket; windbreaker	veston; coupe-vent	saco; americano; cazadora	Jacke; Regenmantel	штормовка (shtormovka)
leather goods (section)	maroquinerie	artículos de piel; marroquinería	Lederwaren (Abteilung)	кожаные изделия (kozhaniye izdeliya)
lighter	briquet	encendedor	Feuerzeug	зажигалка (zazhigalka)
matches	allumettes	cerillas	Streichhölzer	спички (spichki)
nightdress, nightshirt	chemise de nuit	camisa de dormir	Nachthemd	ночная рубашка (nochnaya rubashka)
notebook	carnet	libreta	Notizbuch	тетрадь (tetrad')
optician	opticien	óptico	Optiker	оптик (optik)
panties	culottes	bragas	Slip	трусики женские (trusiki zhenskiye)
pantyhose	collants	medias-pantalón	Strumpfhose	колготы (kolgoti)
pencil	crayon	lápiz	Bleistift	карандаш (karardash)
playing cards	cartes à jouer	naipes	Spielkarten	игральные карты (igral'niye karti)
price	prix	precio	Preis	цена (tsena)
pull over	pull-over	jersey	Pullover	пуловер/свитер (pulover/sviter)

purse	porte-monnaie	monedero	Portemonnaie	сумка (sumka)
pyjamas	pyjama	pijama	Schlafanzug	пижама (pizhama)
sandals	sandales	sandalias	Sandalen	сандалии (sandalii)
sanitary napkins	serviettes hygiéniques	paños higiénicos; toallitas higiénicas	Damenbinde	гигиенические салфетки (gigiyencheskiye salfetki)
scarf	foulard	bufanda	Halstuch	шарф (sharf)
self-service	libre-service	autoservicio	Selbstbedienug	самообслуживание (samoobsluzhivaniye)
shirt	chemise	camisa	Hemd	рубашка (rubashka)
shoes	souliers	zapatos	Schuhe	туфли/ботинки (tufli/botinki)
shorts; briefs	short; slip	calzoncillos	Unterhose	трусы мужские (trusi muzhskiye)
skirt	jupe	falda	Rock	юбка (yubka)
slip	jupon	enaguas	Unterrock	комбинация (kombinatsiya)
socks	chaussettes	calcetines	Socken	носки (noski)
souvenir	souvenir	recuerdo	Souvenir	сувенир (suvenir)
sportcoat	blouson	chaqueta de sport	Sportjacke	спортивная куртка (sportivnaya kurtka)
stationery	papier à lettres	papel de escribir y sobres; papelería	Briefpapier	канцелярские принадлежности (kantselyarskiye prinadlezhnosti)
stationery (section)	papeterie	papelería	Papierwaren (Abteilung)	канцелярские товары (kantselyarskiye tovari)
stockings	bas	medias	Strümpfe	чулки (chulki)
suit	costume	traje	Anzug	костюм (kostyum)
tie	cravate	corbata	Krawatte	галстук (galstuk)
tights	collants	mallas	Strumpfhosen	трико (triko)
tin; roll	boîte; conserve	lata	Kanne; Büchse	банка (banka)
tobacco	tabac	tabaco	Tabak	табак (tabak)
tobacco (section)	tabacs	tabacos	Tabakwaren (Abteilung)	табачные изделия (tabachniye izdeliya)

towel	essuie-mains	toalla	Handtuch	полотенце (polotentse)
trousers; slacks	pantalon	pantalones	Hose	брюки (bryuki)
umbrella	parapluie	paraguas	Regenschirm	зонтик (zontik)
undershirt; vest	sous-vêtement; maillot	camiseta	Unterhemd	майка (mayka)
wallet	portefeuille	cartera	Brieftasche	кошелек (koshelyok)
zipper	fermeture éclair	cremallera	Reissverschluss	молния (molniya)

Media	Presse, radio, télévision	Prensa, radio, television	Presse, Rundfunk, Fernsehen	Пресса, радио, телевидение
Attention, rolling!	Attention, on tourne!	¡Silencio, se rueda!	Achtung, Aufnahme!	Внимание, съемка! (vnimaniye, syomka!)
accreditation	accréditation	con credenciales	Akkreditierung	титры (titri)
announcement	annonce	aviso	Ansage	объявление (obyavleniye)
archives; record office	archives; bureau des registres	archivos; centro de documentación	Archiv; Archivbüro	архив (arhiv)
broadcast	diffuser	emisión	Übertragung	радио-/теле-/передача (radio-/tele-/peredacha)
cable	câble	cable	Kabel	кабель (kabel')
camera	caméra	cámara	Filmkamera	телекамера/фотоаппарат (telekamera/fotoapparat)
channel	canal	canal	Kanal	канал (kanal)
close-up	gros plan	primer plano	Grossaufnahme	крупный план (krupniy plan)
color	couleur	color	Farbe	цвет (tsvet)
conference circuit	circuit de conférence	circuito de conferencia	Konferenzleitung	диспетчерская связь (dispetcherskaya svyaz')
development	développement	revelado	Entwicklung	проявление пленки (proyavleniye plyonki)
exposure	exposition	exposición	Belichtung	выдержка (viderzhka)

English	French	German	Spanish	Russian
feedback	réaction	Information zurückleiten	realimentación	обратная связь (obratnaya svyaz')
film projector	projecteur de films	Filmprojector	proyector de película	кинопроектор (kinoproyektor)
graphic artist	dessinateur	Graphiker	dibujante	художник-график (hudozhnik-grafik)
interpreter	interprète	Dolmetscher	intérprete	переводчик (perevodchik)
interval	interlude	Pause	pausa	интервал (interval)
lighting	éclairage	Belichtung	alumbrado	освещение (osveshcheniye)
lighting engineer	éclairagiste	Beleuchter	luminotécnico	инженер-осветитель (inzhenyer-osvetitel')
loss of picture	coupure d'image	Bildverlust	fallo de la imagen	потеря изображения (poterya izobrazheniya)
loss of sound	coupure de son	Tonverlust	fallo del sonido	потеря звука (poterya zvuka)
microphone	micro(phone)	Mikrofon	micrófono	микрофон (mikrofon)
mixer	pupitre de mixage	Mischpult	pupitre de mezclas	миксер (mikser)
photocopy	photocopie	Fotokopie	fotocopia	фотокопия (fotokopiya)
picture	image	Bild	imagen	изображение (izobrazheniye)
portable microphone	microphone portatif	Handmikrophon	micrófono portátil	портативный микрофон (portativniy mikrofon)
post-synchronize	postsynchroniser	nachsynchronisieren	postsincronizar	постсинхронизировать (postsinhronizirovat')
press clippings	coupures de journal	ausgeschnittene Zeitungsartikel	recortes de prensa	газетные вырезки (gazetniye virezki)
recording	enregistrement	Aufzeichnung	grabación	звуковая запись (zvukovaya zapis')
replay	reprise	zurückspielen	repetición	повторение (povtoreniye)
slide	diapositive	Dia	diapositiva	слайд (slayd)
slide projector	projecteur de diapositives	Diaprojector	proyector de diapositivas	прожектор для слайдов (prozhektor dlya slaydov)
start	démarrer	abfahren	iniciar	старт (start)
studio	studio	Studio	estudio	студия (studiya)
T.V. camera	caméra de télévision	Fernsehkamera	cámara de televisión	телекамера (telekamera)

take; shot (film)	prise	toma; rodaje	Aufnahme (Film)	снимок/кадр (snimok/kadr)
tape speed	vitesse de la bande	velocidad de la cinta	Bandgeschwindigkeit	скорость пленки (skorost' plyonki)
teleprinter	télex	télex	Fernschreiber	телекс (teleks)
television	télévision	televisión	Fernsehen	телевидение (televideniye)
VTR; video tape recording	enregistrement magnétique	grabación magnética	Magnetaufzeichnung	видеомагнитофон (videomagnitofon)

"à droite, touché!", 1565
"à gauche, touché!", 1564
à la remorque, 753
"à vos marques!", 206, 2198
abandon, 1023
abandonner, 2277, 2317, 2413
abstention, 1439
accélérer la cadence, 133
accessoires de la bicyclette, 799
accident corporel, 934
accident mécanique, 820
accompagnateurs, 494
accompagnement musical, 1907
accompagner le ballon, 2606
accorder une répétition de plongeon, 1264
accrocher un adversaire, 547
accroupir, s', 1777
achever, 2630
action de dribbler des deux mains, 455
action de s'échapper, 24
action de shooter, 378
action des bras, 2026
action des jambes, 2127
action parasite, 1204
action simultanée, 1674
adversaire, 2372
affronter, 2373
agitation mécanique de la surface de l'eau, 1308
agiter les mains pour gêner la vision, 491
agrès, 1836
aide, 383, 1737
aide-arbitre, 763
aide-entraîneur, 384
aide entre coureurs, 781
aide légère, 1903

aide-starter, 290
ailette , 1004
aire, 9
aire de chute, 152
aire d'échauffement, 369, 2018
aire d'élan, 262
alignement de corps pour l'entrée dans l'eau, 1293
"allez!", 1507, 1623
amende, 888
amorti, 2298, 2589
amorti de revers, 2235
amorti en coup droit, 2313
amplitude, 1731
amplitude des mouvements, 1732
anémomètre, 373
angle d'appel, 6
angle d'approche, 5
angle de départ, 1385
angle de lancer, 686
angle d'inclinaison de la plate-forme de départ, 2169
anneau du panier, 402
anneaux, 1946
annonce officielle du plongeon, 1154
annoncer un but, 2804
annonceur, 2025
annonceur officiel, 1314
annulation de la touche, 1411
antennes, 2519
appareil automatique de chronométrage et de classement, 2030
appareil de chronométrage de 2 minutes, 357
appareil de nivellement du sable, 267
appareil de vérification des armes, 1412

appareil électrique de signalisation des touches, 1487
appareil enregistreur, 1991
appel, 318, 1990
appel avec élan, 1356
appel des concurrents, 27
appel des coureurs, 829
appel des deux pieds, 2006
appel des tireurs, 1435
appel du pied, 1423
appel en arrière, 1172
appel en avant, 1260
appel sur place, 1376
appréciation de l'exécution; combinaison; composition; difficulté, 1804
approche, 1156
approche avant, 1255
appui, 1983
appui renversé, 1849
appui renversé (équilibre), 1266
arbitre, 657, 2489
arbitre de chaise, 2259
arbitre de terrain avant, 570
arbitre de terrain central, 752
arbitre de water-polo, 3013
arbitrer, 658
arcanson, 1949
arçons, 1931
ardoisier, 806
arène, 10
arme défectueuse, 1503
arme d'escrime, 1529
armé du bras, 65
arrêt, 704, 1681, 1976
arrêt à la manchette, 1682
arrêt de la course, 1092
arrêt du jeu, 706, 2480
arrêt marqué, 1806

arrêt prononcé, 1781
arrêter le chronomètre, 705, 2986
arrêter le jeu, 2987
arrêter un coureur, 1091
arrêter un tir, 2985
arrière, 2808
arrière centre, 2647
arrière droit, 662, 2709, 2958
arrière gauche, 573, 2633, 2892
arrières, 537, 2529
arrivée, 82, 889, 2087
arrivée en peloton, 826
arrivée serrée, 36, 341, 843, 2061
arriver dans un fondu, 1240
as, 2220, 2518
asperger, 2979
assaut, 1589
assignation des juges, 1878
assistance au plongeur
  (entraînement), 1265
assistant, 1738
assistant du chronométreur, 2806
assistant du secrétaire, 2805
Association Canadienne de Natation
  Amateur (A.C.N.A.), 2056
athlète, 346
attaquant, 602, 2526
attaquant d'aile, 2680
attaquant du centre, 2646
attaque, 67, 385, 596, 1414, 2520, 2668
attaque au fer, 1416
attaque composée, 1443
attaque de la barre, 320
attaque de la haie, 319
attaque de ligne arrière, 2530
attaque du bras, 2080
attaque d'une défense de zone, 598
attaque d'une défense individuelle, 597

attaque en flèche, 1654
attaque en force, 2696
attaque en première main, 2584
attaque maîtrisée, 450
attaque organisée, 682
attaque par derrière, 784
attaque par l'aile, 773
attaque par opposition, 1415
attaque retardée, 465
attaque simple, 1671
attaquer, 782, 2029
attaquer en tête, 783
attaques simultanées, 1675
attaques sur préparation, 1417
attendre le signal de l'arbitre, 3009
attraper le ballon, 427
attribution des couloirs, 2119
au-dessus du filet, 2380
au meilleur de trois sets, 2488
augmentation de la valeur, 2011
augmenter son avance, 132
avance, 161
avant, 2854
avant centre, 2649
avant droit, 661, 2710, 2959
avant gauche, 572, 2634, 2893
avantage, 380, 2223, 2332
avantage relanceur, 2222
avantage service, 2221
avants, 511, 2616
avertissement, 1141, 1713, 2504, 2792
avoir un tour d'avance, 163
avoir x points d'avance, 164
avoir x secondes d'avance, 165
axe, 15, 786, 1067, 1167
axe de largeur, 1858
axe de longueur, 1893, 2016
axe de manivelle, 809
axe de pédalier, 859
axe de rotation, 16

axe de roue, 1148
axe longitudinal, 1186, 1296, 1895
axe transversal, 1200

balancé, 1985
balancement intermédiaire, 1865
balancement préparatoire du disque,
  228
balancer intermédiaire, 1813
balestra, 1419
balle, 2243
balle coupée, 2492
balle de break, 2252
balle de match, 2352
balle de set, 2441
"balle facile", 2614
balle lente, 2453
balle slicée, 2450
ballon, 2534
ballon bon, 2537
ballon dans le filet, 2538
ballon de basket-ball, 404
ballon de match, 2644
ballon de set, 2735
ballon de volley-ball, 2787
ballon de water-polo, 3011
ballon dehors, 2539
ballon en jeu, 394, 2536
ballon est mort, 391
ballon est remis à, 395
ballon est vivant, 390
ballon faible, 2588
ballon franchit entièrement la ligne de
  but,
ballon gonflé, 2885
ballon hors-jeu, 396, 2812
ballon lancé dans l'eau, 2815
ballon lancé sur l'eau, 2816
ballon libre, 577
ballon mort, 458, 2540, 2570

ballon non réglementaire, 2910
ballon ricochant sur l'eau, 2814
ballon tenu, 545, 2623
ballon touchant le filet, 2542
ballon vivant, 575
banc, 411
banc de l'équipe, 720
banc des joueurs, 2692
bande horizontale du filet, 2765
barrage, 146, 1420
barre basse, 1896
barre fixe, 1859
barre haute, 1857
barre transversale du but, 2841
barre transversale du saut en hauteur,
  115
barres asymétriques, 2008
barres parallèles, 1921
barrière de rivière, 372
barrières de steeple, 298
bas d'escrime, 1525
basculer, 1882
bascules, 1883
bases de notation, 1303
basketteur, 407
bassin de compétition, 2063
bassin de plongeon, 1222
bassin d'entraînement, 2204
battement, 1422
battement de dauphin, 2073
battement de jambes, 2117
battre, 2279
bavette, 1424
bec de selle, 987
belle, 917
bicyclette, 798
bicyclette standard, 1074
bidon, 1142
bille de roulement, 790
bloc, 2543

bloc de départ, 292, 2176
bloc de service, 2728
bloc en douceur, 2745
bloc gagnant, 2799
blocage, 90, 417
bloquer, 414, 2544
bloquer un lancer, 415
bobines réceptrices, 2199
boîte d'appel, 217
bond, 1581
bond en arrière, 1418
bond en avant, 1546
bonification, 1751
bonne tenue, 1774
bonnet blanc, 3018
bonnet bleu, 2821
bonnet de bain, 2192
bonnet de compétition, 2838
bonnet de gardien de but, 2873
bonnet détaché, 2826
bonnet numéroté, 2912
bonnet rouge, 2949
bord antérieur du tremplin, 1185
bord de la piste, 1116
bord du bassin, 2849
bord du panier, 663
bord du panneau, 484
bord intérieur des lignes délimitant le
  terrain, 556
bordure, 808
borne kilométrique, 970
bouée de jambes, 2150
boulé, 2711
boulé latéral, 2741
boulon, 807
bouteille, 568
bouton, 1433, 1701
boyau, 1134
boyau de piste, 1129

boyau de route, 1035
boyau d'entraînement, 1132
braquet, 812
bras, 2028
bras armé, 17.5
bras lanceur, 332
bras libre, 316
bras non armé, 1705, 1709
brassard, 11, 780
brasse, 2040
brasse 100 m, 200 m, 2044
brasseur, 2042
"break", 2434
brevet, 1752
"briefing": stratégie, 432
bris de chaîne, 823
bris du cadre, 824, 901
brosser, 2683, 2779
brusque changement de position, 1096
bulletin des juges, 1873
bureau des calculs, 1765
but, 2863
but accordé, 2864
but de l'équipe adverse, 2916
but marqué, 2870
butoir, 306

câble de branchement, 1446
câble de filet, 2659
cadence, 26, 1434, 1651
cadence de foulée, 311
cadence irrégulière, 2049
cadre, 900
cadre de la raquette, 2402
cage de protection, 333
cale-pédale, 1055
cale-pied, 1112
caleçon de bain, 2819
calendrier des compétitions, 268

calendrier des parties, 529, 667
cambré, 1158
cambrer, 1157, 1735
caméra d'arrivée, 216
camionnette suiveuse, 897
camp, 2875
camp adverse, 2676, 2917
camp de jeu non réglementaire, 2911
capitaine, 425, 2553, 2827
capitaine d'équipe, 721, 1693, 2471
capter le rebond, 655
caravane, 831, 854
carbonate de magnésium, 1756, 1897
carpé, 1322
carpé fermé, 1189
carpé ouvert, 1317
carper, 1323
carré de service, 2433
carré de service droit, 2415
carré de service gauche, 2335
carré et un (placement défensif), 421
carte des juges, 2114
carte jaune, 2800
carte rouge, 2703
cartes d'arbitrage, 2704
casque, 919
casquette, 830
cassé, 1175
catégorie de coureurs, 832
caver le corps, 1477
centre, 428
centre-avant, 2829
centre du terrain, 539
cercle central, 429
cercle de lancer, 334
cercle de mise en jeu, 564
cérémonie de la victoire, 363
chaîne, 833
chaise d'arbitrage, 2705

chaise de l'arbitre, 2490
chambre à air, 935
chambre d'appel, 13, 187
champ de jeu, 2933
changement de balles, 2245
changement de barre, 1743
changement de camp, 2558, 2832
changement de côté, 1438
changement de direction, 434
changement de pied, 28
changement de prise, 1833
changement de roue, 1146
changement de rythme, 29, 435
changement de service, 2557
changement de vélo, 837
changement d'engagement, 1439
changement direct, 1785
changer de cadence, 838
changer de panier, 433
changer de position brusquement,
  1095
changer de vitesse, 836
changeur de vitesse, 906
changez-battez, 1437
chape, 1140
charge, 436
charger un adversaire, 437
chassé, 839
chassée, 1039
chaussette, 1061
chaussures à pointes, 278
chaussures cyclistes, 863
chaussures de gymnastique, 1834
chaussures d'escrime, 1524
"cheese board" ("maxiflex B"), 1187
chef-chronométreur, 31, 2058
chef compilateur, 1962
chef de mission, 1783, 1851
chef d'équipe, 1993

chef des officiels de soutien, 453
cheval-arçons, 1930
cheval; cheval-sautoir, 2015
cheval-sautoir en largeur (épreuves féminines), 1964
cheval-sautoir en longueur (épreuves masculines), 1894
choix des bonnets, 2834
choix du ballon, 440
choix du camp, 2835
choix du panier, 441
choix du service, 2559
chronométrage, 1109, 1110
chronométrage auxiliaire video, 2210
chronométrage électronique (poutre; exercices au sol), 1796
chronométrage manuel, 2132
chronométrage par demi-tour, 911
chronomètre, 307
chronomètre à main, 2104
chronomètre de jeu, 2861
chronomètre de 35 secondes, 2971
chronomètre des temps morts, 744
chronomètre du jeu, 528
chronomètre individuel, 1977
chronomètre manuel, 2183
chronométreur, 342, 746, 1108, 1700, 2001, 2201, 2999
chronométreur suppléant, 256
chute , 74, 882, 1065, 1814
chute accidentelle dans l'eau, 1243
chute collective, 960
cinquième faute, 502
circuit, 841
circuit routier, 1029
circulation tactique, 2763
classé, 2424
classé tête de la compétition, 2481
classement, 842, 994, 2166, 2408, 2425

classement combiné, 1761
classement des tireurs, 1441
classement général, 1249
classement individuel, 1863
classement par équipe, 1994
classer, se, 2407
clef à molette, 776
clef à pipe, 811
clef plate, 979
clinicar, 971
cloche, 794
cloche-pied, 121
club, 1190
club de plongeon, 1212
code de la piste, 1118
code de la route, 1131
code de pointage, 1759
coefficient de difficulté, 1205, 1782
coéquipier, 2472, 2768
coeur du cordage, 2466
collaborateur technique-scientifique, 1957
colle à boyau, 1135
collège des arbitres, 2643
collège des commissaires, 845
coller à la roue, 895
coller au peloton, 1057
collision, 446
combat rapproché, 1511, 1572
combinaison tactique, 2762
combinaisons, 1760
comité de course, 849
comité de jugement, 1284
comité directeur, 881
comité d'organisation de gymnastique, 1838
Comité international de plongeon (F.I.N.A.), 1278
comité technique conjoint, 1870
comité technique féminin, 2022

comité technique masculin, 1902
commencement, 2458
commencer, 2459
commissaire, 847
commissaire de course, 349, 2060
commissaire de virage, 855
commissaire du terrain, 186
commissaires du terrain, 583
commission permanente, 992, 1075
commission technique, 1103
communication entre joueurs défensifs, 717
compétiteur classé, 1051
compétition, 40, 192, 2264
compétition de plongeon, 1213
compétition individuelle, 1571, 1862
compétition par équipe, 1694
composition de l'équipe, 725
composition de l'exercice, 1768
composition monotone, 1904
compte des points, 1359
compteur de longueurs, 2124
compteur de tours, 158, 943
concours, 77
concours de haut-vol, 1326
concours de natation, 2193
concours IA; IB; II; III, 1763
concurrent classé, 1668
concurrents, 2265
conduite antisportive, 766
conférence des juges, 1874
conserver son avance, 178
constructeur de jeu, 641
construction d'attaque, 2767
consultation des juges, 1875
contact avec le terrain adverse, 2780
contact personnel, 630
contenu de l'exercice, 1773
continuation d'attaque, 1447
continuité, 448

contre, 1440, 1450
contre à deux, 2784
contre à trois, 2771
contre-attaque, 1451
contre-attaque rapide, 495
contre-coupé, 1452
contre de quarte, 1454
contre de sixte, 1458
contre défensif, 2573
contre-dégagement, 1453
contre invividuel, 2675
contre la montre, 1106
contre le filet, 2224
contre mouvement, 1775
contre offensif, 2669
contre-offensive, 1455
contre-parade, 1456
contre-riposte, 1457
contre-temps, 1459
contreur, 2547
contreur central, 2648
contreur d'aile, 2592
contrôle de dopage, 7, 871
contrôle de la pointe électrique, 1696
contrôle des arrivées, 890
contrôle des prises de relais, 2160
contrôle du ballon, 392
conventions du combat, 1448
coquille, 1554
coquille d'épée, 1497
coquille du fleuret, 1542
coquille du sabre, 1659
cordage, 2462
cordage de la raquette, 2405
cordage synthétique, 2468
corde, 47, 936
corde de boyau, 2322
corde de couloir, 2122
corde de la piste, 135
corde de liège, 2896

corde de limite, 2840
corde de prise du javelot, 43
corde de signalisation de faux départ, 2084
corder, 2461
corps à corps, 1428
costume de natation, 2190
côté du revers, 2239
côté faible, 770
côté fort, 708
cou du cheval-arçons, 1909
cou du cheval-sautoir, 1910
col (partie éloignée), 1815
coulé, 1449, 1551
coulée, 2099, 2152
couler son adversaire, 2977
couler un adversaire, 2942, 2991
couleurs, 2837
couloir, 155, 2118, 2226
couloir de lancer franc, 517
couloir intérieur, 136
coup, 2326, 2442, 2463
coup à plat, 2306
coup au sol, 2321
coup au sol en revers, 2237
coup bas, 2347
coup chopé, 2260
coup d'approche, 2230
coup d'arrêt, 1683, 1685
coup d'arrêt avec opposition, 1684, 1686
coup de coin, 2839
coup de débordement, 2311
coup de feu, 2102
coup de feu de rappel, 240
coup de pied, 2115
coup de pied de brasse, 2041
coup de pied de papillon, 2052

coup de pied rapide, 2216
coup de service, 2439
coup de taille 1464, 1569
coup de temps, 1699
coup d'estoc, 1570, 1697
coup double, 1481
coup "drive", 2296
coup droit, 1472, 1687, 2312
coup droit à deux mains, 2485
coup en angle, 2229
coup en diagonale, 2271
coup faible, 2505
coup franc, 2858
coup franc accordé, 2859
coup le long de la ligne, 2292
coup profond, 2275
coup puissant, 2393
coup sans riposte, 2494
coup trop long, 2507
coupé, 1460, 1465
couper, 456, 1203
couper à partir d'un écran, 689
couper la balle, 2451
coups à deux mains, 2487
coureur, 263, 1025
coureur de demi-fond, 198
coureur de fond, 172
coureur de haies, 126
coureur de marathon, 182
coureur de relais, 251
coureur de tête, 167, 950
coureur de virage, 21
coureur de vitesse, 281
coureur échappé, 822
coureur lâché, 876
coureur remplaçant, 314
coureur routier, 1037
coureur sur piste, 1127
courir, 1024

courir à nouveau, 1021
courroie de cale-pied, 1113
cours de juges, 1876
course, 236, 264, 1005
course contre la montre, 1107
course de demi-fond, 197
course de fond, 171
course de haies, 125
course de relais, 250
course de vitesse, 280
course d'échauffement, 370
course d'élan, 260, 1953
course en couloir, 157
course en virage, 22
course individuelle, 925
course individuelle sur route, 927
course nulle, 865
course par équipes, 326, 1101
course sur piste, 1124
course sur route par équipes, 1102
court, 2268
court central, 2256
court couvert, 2329
court extérieur, 2376
court principal, 2349
courts alternés, 2227
coussin de réception, 153
coussin d'exercice, 1712
couverture du terrain, 2566
couvrir la distance, 2066
couvrir, se, 1461, 1637
craquer, 1144
crawl, 2067
crevaison, 893, 997
critères de jugement, 1285
croisé, 1462
croisé au flanc, 1533
cronomètre de pénalité, 2926
croupe, 1778, 1908

cuissard, 1009
culotte d'escrime, 1512
cyclisme, 862
cyclisme sur piste, 1120
cyclisme sur piste couverte, 931
cyclisme sur route, 1031
cycliste, 801, 864
cylindre, 457
cylindre de pivot, 1261
cylindre de pivot réglable, 1152

danseuse, 1077
dauphin, 2072
début de jeu, 2981
début de la partie, 408, 698
début de l'exercice, 1749
début du set, 2751
décalage, 282
décarper, 1193, 1235
décathlon, 51
décathlonien, 50
décision, 2273
décision de l'arbitre, 2491
déclassement, 1019
déclivité, 130
déclivité de la piste, 348
décoller, 875
dedans, 2330
déduction de composition, 1767
déduction pour faute d'exécution; combinaison; composition; difficulté, 1779
déduction de point entier; 0.1; 0.5; etc., 1780
déduction maximum, 1900
déduction supplémentaire, 1982
déductions du juge-arbitre, 1853
déductions neutres, 1911

248

défaillance du matériel électrique, 1501
défait, 2278
défaite, 2344
défaut, 73
défense, 459, 2572
défense arrière, 2528
défense de parti-pris, 1628
défense de zone, 775
défense individuelle, 581
défense individuelle par harcèlement à partir du centre, 540
défense individuelle par harcèlement sur tout le terrain, 524
défense mixte, 447
défense mobile, 2653
défense restreinte, 695
défenseur, 460, 2574, 2844
défensif, 2280
défensive, 1468
dégagement, 1476
dégager le ballon, 2836
déjanter, 1040
délai accordé pour blessure, 741
délai d'appel, 1105
délai de lancer franc, 740
délégués aux concurrents, au jury et à la presse, 305
délimitation du champ de jeu, 2824, 2897
demande de remplacement de joueur, 2707
demande de temps mort, 745, 2774
demander un remplacement, 659
démarquer, se, 530, 2862
démarrage, 946
demi-boulé, 2621
demi-centre, 2961
demi-cercle, 681

demi-feinte, 1557
demi-finale, 2427
demi-finaliste, 2426
demi tire-bouchon arrière, 1169
demi-tour, 910
demi-volée, 2323
demi-volte, 1558
dent, 1114
dépannage, 1038, 1043
départ, 285, 1080, 1377, 1384, 2174
départ accroupi, 46
départ agrippé, 2101
départ arrêté, 1076
départ de dos, 2033
départ de la ligne de but, 2993
départ debout, 284
départ en décalage, 283
départ en groupe, 961
départ individuel, 928
départ lancé, 894
départ renversé, 1352
départ répété, 1202
départ réussi, 2128
dépassement, 1620
dépasser, 97, 210
déplacement, 1478, 2651
déplacement arrière, 2652
déplacement avant, 2654
déplacement de défense (zone), 464
déplacement latéral, 2655
déplacement sous le ballon, 2657
déplacement vers le ballon, 2656
dérailleur, 867
déraper, 1058
dernier essai, 160
dernier partant (relais), 2024
dernier tour, 159
dernier virage, 79, 120
dérobement, 1469
désarmement, 1475

descente, 868
désignation du joueur fautif, 692
détacher, se, 176
deux lancers francs, 758
"deux mètres!", 1708
deuxième mi-temps, 680, 2963
développement, 905, 1591
développer, se, 1592
différer, 2282
difficulté, 1784
dimensions du terrain, 452
directeur de course, 1006
directeur de la compétition, 41, 193, 1309, 1474
directeur de piste, 1121
directeur du concours, 1762
directeur sportif, 1070
directeur technique, 327
direction, 53
direction de la course, 853
direction du lancer, 335
directoire technique, 1473
dirigeant, 976
disposition des joueurs sur le terrain, 723
disqualification, 469, 2071
disqualifier, 2284
disque, 54
distance, 60, 1514, 1521
distance entre les coureurs, 62
distance entre les haies, 61
distancer, 207
distraire le lanceur du lancer franc, 472
doigté, 1531
donner de la force au ballon, 2754
donner des coups de pied, 2888
donner le départ, 907
donner le signal de la mise en jeu, 2974

dopage, 872
dos 100 m; 200 m, 2036
dossard, 201, 939
double, 2286, 2587
double appel, 1223
double dames, 2514
double dribble, 473
double écran, 476
double engagement, 1480
double-faute, 474, 2285
double messieurs, 2356
double mixte, 2359
double pivot, 475
doubler, 211, 986
doubler la défense, 477
drapeau; fanion, 89
drapeau jaune, 1151
drapeau rouge, 1014
drapeau vert, 908
dribble, 481
dribble à l'envers, 660
dribble des deux mains, 479
dribble en vrille, 696
dribble irrégulier, 553
dribble par derrière le dos, 409
dribbler, 478
dribbler le ballon, 2846, 2994
dribbler le ballon jusqu'au but, 2847, 2995
dribbleur, 480
droit, 1290, 1382
droits d'inscription, 1346
durée de l'assaut, 1483
durée de l'exclusion, 2929
durée de l'exercice, 1792
durée des parties de maintien, 1793
durée du jeu effectif, 2894
durée du remplacement, 742

eau chlorée, 2059

écart entre deux notes intermédiaires, 1934

échange, 2406, 2699
échappée, 821
échapper, s', 423, 819
échauffement, 368, 2791
échauffement de 30 secondes, 1998
échelle, 202
échelle de bassin, 2146
éclaboussure, 1370
éclater, 804, 827
écouteurs, 2106
écran, 632, 674, 2722
écran effectué illégalement, 554
écran effectué loin du ballon, 677
écran extérieur, 616
écran fixe, 700
écran intérieur, 557
écran mobile, 591
écran près du ballon, 678
"écraser" la planche, 1337
écrou, 975
écusson (insignes), 1199
effectuer un carpé, 1299
effectuer un groupé, 1300
effet, 2457
effet du ballon, 697
effet du ballon (anglais), 487
effet latéral, 2443
effet vers l'arrière, 2241
effet vers l'avant, 2482
effort, 552
égaler et désigner, 585
égaliser, 2301, 2478
égalité, 2283, 2476
égalité des points, 736
élan, 1734, 1954, 2467
élan arrière, 2242
élan ascendant, 2498

élan avant, 2318
élan descendant, 2293
élancer du fond du bassin, s', 2943
élancer par coup de pied à l'adversaire, s', 2889
élasticité de la planche, 1374
élément acrobatique, 1723
élément de force acrobatique, 1726
élément de liaison, 1770
élément de vol acrobatique, 1724
élément d'équilibre, 1742
éléments, 1798
éléments à partir de l'élan à l'appui renversé, 1799
éléments de base, 527
éléments de hecht, 1854
éléments de renversement, 1848
éléments de vol, 1826
éléments non caractéristiques, 2007
élever, s', 1947
éliminatoires, 229, 1334
éliminer, 2300
emballage, 328
émerger, 2078, 2188
empêcher l'accès au panier, 416, 422
empiétement, 303
empiéter, 209
emplacement des entraîneurs, 2689
emplacement des remplaçants, 2690
empoigner le bord du panier, 534
emporter le ballon, 2828
empreinte, 128, 183
"en garde!", 1607
en jeu, 2328
enduire son corps de graisse, 2874
enfermer un coureur, 23
enfermer un cycliste, 810
enfoncer le ballon sous l'eau, 2997
engagement, 879, 1490

engin, 8
enregistreur, 2156
enrouler, 1041
enrouleur, 1645
entraînement, 2394
entraînement hors piscine, 2075
entraîneur, 2263
entraîneur, 37, 445, 844, 1442, 2062, 2262, 2562
entraîneur de basket-ball, 405
entre-deux, 563
entrée, 1229, 1905
entrée courte, 1364
entrée de la ligne droite, 288
entrée douce, 1366
entrée du virage, 287, 1082
entrée longue, 1295, 1320, 1404
entrée par la tête, 1267
entrée par les pieds, 1245
entrée sans bulles, 1354
entrée sans éclaboussure, 1188
entrée (vers la gauche; vers la droite), 1184
entrée verticale, 1398
entrer, 1906
entrer en jeu, 2595
enveloppement, 1491
envol, 39, 1292
épée, 1492
épée électrique, 1484
épéiste, 1495
épreuve, 71, 851, 880, 1500
épreuve combinée, 38
épreuve de fleuret, 1539
épreuve de natation, 2194
épreuve de sabre, 1657
épreuve d'épée, 1494
épreuve éliminatoire, 878
épreuve individuelle sur piste, 929

épreuve individuelle sur route, 926
épreuve sur piste par équipes, 1128
épreuve sur route par équipes, 1034
épreuves de lancers, 336
épreuves de sauts, 148
épreuves femmes au tremplin, 1408
épreuves femmes haut-vol, 1407
épreuves hommes au tremplin, 1311
épreuves hommes haut-vol, 1310
épreuves individuelles femmes, 375, 2218
épreuves individuelles hommes, 195, 2137
épreuves par équipes hommes, 2138
épreuves par équipes femmes, 376, 2219
épreuves par équipes hommes, 196
épreuves sur piste, 347
épreuves sur route, 257
équilibre (appui renversé), 1160
équilibre de défense, 461
équilibre et chute en arrière, 1161
équilibre et passage avant, 1164
équilibre et saut périlleux; et double saut périlleux, 1165
équilibre, passage avant et plongeon renversé, 1162
équipe, 719, 1098, 1386, 1692, 1992, 2470
équipe adverse, 2374
équipe complète, 2860
équipe de réception, 2701
équipe de relais, 252
équipe de volley-ball, 2789
équipe de water-polo, 3015
équipe victorieuse, 2512
équipement de chronométrage électronique, 2077
équipement électrique, 1485

équipier de relais, 2161
erreur de jugement, 1580
erreur forcée, 2310
erreur non-forcée, 2493
e:calier de plateforme, 1380
escrime à l'épée, 1496
escrime au fleuret, 1541
escrime au sabre, 1658
escrimeur, 1510
esquive, 1482, 1499
essai, 353
essai de lancer franc, 516
essai manqué, 358
essai réussi, 315
essai supplémentaire, 3
essai valable, 360
estrade de starter, 291
établir, s', 1936
établissements, 2009
étendre, 1979
"êtes-vous prêts?", 1413
être en forme, 792
être en possession du ballon, 2820
éventail, 877
ex aequo, 340, 1388
exclure du jeu, 2919
exclusion, 2585
exécuter un coup franc, 2996
exécuter un plongeon, 1232
exécution, 1808
exécution avec virtuosité, 1807
exécution de plongeon, 1233
exécution d'un exercice, 1810
exécution parfaite, 1923
exécution technique, 1995
exemption, 2253
exercer le contrôle du ballon, 449
exercice à la barre fixe, 1860
exercice à la poutre, 1747
exercice au cheval-arçons, 1811

exercice au sol, 1828
exercice aux anneaux, 1945
exercice aux barres asymétriques, 1812
exercice d'échauffement, 769
exercices à volonté, 1913
exercices d'échauffement, 2019, 2503
exigences de l'exercice, 1942
exigences spéciales pour les engins, 1967
expiration, 2046, 2081
expiration du temps de jeu, 488
expulsion, 485, 489, 2597
extension puissante, 227
extrémité du bassin, 2825

face à la plate-forme, 1237
face à l'eau, 1239
face au tremplin, 1238
faible de la lame, 1536
faire appel, 381
faire écran, 675
faire écran et rouler, 633, 676
faire entrer, 49
faire la bordure, 958
faire le moulinet, 1066
faire le trou, 951
faire roue libre, 903
faire un amorti, 2641
faire un plat, 1298
faire une impulsion, 1969
familles des sauts (hommes), 2012
fanion, 2604, 2853
fanion blanc, 3019
fanion bleu, 2822
fanion de l'arbitre, 2952
fanion de limite de zone, 377
fanion de virage, 44
fanion du juge de but, 2866
fanion de secteur, 271

fanion indicateur du record national (olympique, mondial), 185
fanion rouge, 1015, 2950
fanion vert, 909
fanions de repère- nage de dos, 2032
fanions de steeple, 299
fausse attaque, 1502
faute, 95, 512, 1816, 2302, 2599, 2613
faute d'arbitrage, 2516
faute de disqualification, 513
faute de durée, 1999
faute de filet, 2660
faute de pied, 2308, 2607, 2637
faute de pose des mains, 1843
faute de position, 2678, 2682, 2695
faute de rotation, 2713
faute de service, 2435
faute de tenue, 1817
faute de zone, 1891
faute d'exécution, 1809
faute d'interprétation, 1818
faute disqualifiante, 471
faute d'obstruction, 418
faute flagrante, 507
faute grave, 2900
faute intentionnelle, 558
faute mineure, 2907
faute multiple, 592
faute offensive, 600
faute personnelle, 631, 2930
faute technique, 726
fautes graves, 1887
fautes moyennes, 1901
faux départ, 75, 883, 2082
Fédération Internationale d'Athlétisme Amateur (F.I.A.A.), 138

Fédération Internationale de Basket-ball Amateur (F.I.B.A.), 562
Fédération Internationale de Gymnastique (F.I.G.), 1866
Fédération Internationale de Natation Amateur (F.I.N.A.), 2086
Fédération Internationale de Volley-Ball (F.I.V.B.), 2626
Fédération Internationale d'Escrime (F.I.E.), 1574
feinte, 492, 498, 1504, 2598, 2600
feinte d'attaque, 1505
feinte de démarrage, 886
feinte de la tête, 543
feinte de lancer, 493
feinte de parade, 1506
feinte de smash, 2601
feuille de compilation, 1766
feuille de départ, 1083
feuille de marque, 672
feuille de marque officielle, 606
feuille de match, 2718
feuille de notes, 1361
feuille de pointage, 1959
feuille de poule, 1627
feuille de résultats, 1347
feuille de série, 2107
fiche d'arbitrage, 2423
fiche de marquage, 184
figure, 1254
fil d'arrivée, 87
fil de corps, 1429
filet, 594, 2360, 2658
filet de but, 2868
filin du marteau, 106
fin de set, 2594
fin de temps mort, 2596
fin d'un exercice, 1769, 1801

finale, 887, 1250, 1821
finale aux engins, 1805
finale concours multiples, 1729
finale de double, 2287
finale des plongeons, 1247
finale du simple, 2445
finales, 81
finaliste, 1820, 2416
finaliste du simple, 2446
finisseur, 312
fixer le contre, 2611
flèche, 113, 1534
flèche de la barre, 266
flèche de la lame, 1463
flèche de la trajectoire d'un sauteur, 114
fléchir, 1750, 1823
fleuret, 1537
fleurettiste, 1540
flottabilité, 2050
flotteurs, 2090
fond, 170
fond de court, 2232
fond de la piscine, 2039
fond du bassin, 1180, 2823
fondu, 1241
force de résistance de la haie, 344
force des joueurs au banc, 412
forfait, 2165, 2276, 2608
formation, 2610
formation au service, 2730
formation de départ, 699
formation de réception, 2700
formation du jeu, 2766
formation en W, 2790
forme de lancer, 687
former le bloc, 2609
fort de la lame, 1545
fossé d'eau; rivière, 371

foulée, 302, 309
fourche, 898
franchir, 32
franchir la barre, 34
franchir une haie, 304
franchir une hauteur de ..., 33
franchissement des limites, 1603
frappe du ballon, 2694
frappe en puissance, 2697
frapper, 2327
frapper le ballon avec le poing fermé, 2881, 2990
frapper un adversaire, 2880, 2989
frein, 813
freinage, 817
freiner, 814
froissement, 1549

gagnant, 2510
gagner, 2509
gagner d'un boyau, 1149
gagner d'une longueur, 2217
gagner d'une roue, 1150
gagner l'échange, 2796
gagner par forfait, 772
gain du point, 2797
gain du service, 2798
'Gainer' (saut périlleux renversé), 1262
gant cycliste, 1123
gant d'escrime, 1516
gant du lanceur de marteau, 101
garde, 1555
garder le ballon, 521
gardien de but, 2872
gaucher, 2336
gêner l'adversaire, 802
gêner un adversaire, 2879
gêner un coureur, 127

genouillère, 2631
géomètre officiel, 203
glissement, 1678
gomme laque, 1054
goulottes, 2103
grâce du plongeon, 1263
grand écart, 1968
grand écart facial, 1830
grand écart latéral, 1965
grand écart transversal, 1888
grillage de masque, 1720
gros du peloton, 177, 957
groupé, 1394
groupe de tête, 168
grouper, 1395
groupes de plongeons, 1214
groupes d'éléments, 1797
groupes des sauts (femmes), 2013
guidoline, 915
guidon, 912
gymnaste, 1835
gymnaste suppléant, 1730, 1980
gymnastique artistique, 1736

haie, 124
haie de steeple, 300
"halte!", 1559
harcèlement, 650
harcèlement en zone à partir du centre, 541
harcèlement en zone sur tout le terrain, 525
hauteur de la barre, 108
hauteur de la barre transversale, 2878
hauteur de l'engin, 1855
hauteur du filet, 2661
hauteur du plongeon, 1268
hauteur initiale, 134
hauteur minimum, 199

heptathlon, 110
heptathlonien, 109
heure d'appel, 255
homologation d'un record, 779, 1012
homologuer, 238
horaire, 2418
horaire d'entraînement, 2205
horloges digitales pour rythme d'entraînement, 2070
hors de course, 870
hors de la ligne, 2379
hors du terrain, 613
hors jeu, 2375, 2378, 2914
hors limites, 1918, 2377., 2677
hors-piste, 1616
housse de roue, 1147
hydrodynamique, 2184
hymne national, 200

imperméable de cyclisme, 1011
impulsion, 129, 1339
inclinaison de la piste, 791
inclinaison d'un virage, 866
indicateur de route, 1033
indication du saut, 1733, 1822
infériorité numérique, 2902
infraction, 818, 933
infraction aux règles, 666
inquartata, 1573
inscription, 1345
inscrire, s', 1344
inspecteur des virages, 2113
inspiration, 2045, 2112
intercepter le ballon, 559
intérieur de la piste, 1117
interrompu, 2254
interruption de jeu, 2628
intervalle de départ, 1085
intervention, 560

intervention au panier, 401
intervention sur le ballon, 533
inverser, 1943
invite, 1577

jalonner le parcours, 959
jambe d'appel, 323, 1331
jambe d'attaque, 169
jambe libre, 96, 317, 1273
jante, 1027
javelot, 139
jeu, 2319, 2385
jeu blanc, 2346
jeu de cheville, 778
jeu de filet, 2361
jeu de fond, 2247
jeu de jambes, 508, 1544
jeu de l'extérieur du terrain, 614
jeu de pivot central, 636, 647
jeu de pivot séparé, 648
jeu de possession, 645
jeu de trois points, 732
jeu d'équipe, 722
jeu d'essai, 679
jeu dur, 2960
jeu interrompu, 2627
jeu lent, 2978
jeu mobile, 2909
jeu offensif, 2367
jeu serré, 2261
jeu statique, 2984
jeu violent, 3008
jeux impairs, 2366
joindre, 1869
jouer au tennis, 2386
jouer au water-polo, 2931
joueur, 2387, 2691
joueur attaquant, 2807
joueur blessé, 2886
joueur de champ, 2851

joueur de défense, 2843
joueur de départ, 2752
joueur de double, 2290
joueur de filet, 2363
joueur de fond de court, 2233
joueur de ligne arrière, 2531
joueur de ligne avant, 2617
joueur de simple, 2448
joueur de volley-ball, 2788
joueur de water-polo, 3012
joueur démarqué, 765
joueur désigné pour la remise en jeu, 2932
joueur disqualifié, 470
joueur expulsé, 2850
joueur fautif, 2913
joueur marqué, 536
joueur-poste, 646
joueur qui mène, 2334
joueur remplaçant, 2756, 2992
joueur sortant, 2679
joueur universel, 2769
joueur victime d'une faute, 2855
juge, 1579, 1871, 1920, 2331
juge à l'arrivée, 83, 891
juge-arbitre, 243, 1342, 1850, 1981, 2157
juge-arbitre des plongeons cassés, 1176
juge-arbitre pour les concours, 244
juge-arbitre pour les courses, 245
juge-arbitre pour les épreuves, 1230
juge-arbitre pour les épreuves de marche, 246
juge au virage, 797, 1136
juge d'arrivée, 2089, 2144
juge de but, 2865
juge de concours, 78
juge de faute de pied, 2309
juge de filet, 2362

juge de ligne, 2339, 2638
juge de limites (lignes), 1892
juge de marche, 367
juge de nage, 2185
juge de terre, 1535
juge de virage, 2207
juge des difficultés, 1872
juge en chef (électronique), 2057
juges , 144
juges de plongeons, 1216
jugulaire, 840
jury, 1217, 1919
jury d'appel, 150, 940, 1288, 1583, 1881
jury de compétition, 1582
justaucorps, 1889

kilomètre contre la montre, 941

lâcher de l'engin, 52, 254
lâcher le ballon, 2848
lâcher un adversaire, 874
lame, 1426
lame cassée, 1431
lame de fleuret, 1538
lame de sabre, 1656
lame d'épée, 1493
lampe-témoin, 1664
lancement, 234, 331
lancement du disque, 57
lancement du javelot, 142
lancement du marteau, 104
lancement du poids, 276
lancer, 232, 329, 688, 2967, 2998
lancer à bras roulé, 549
lancer à deux mains, 762
lancer à deux mains par-dessus la tête, 760
lancer à la volée, 2969
lancer à une main, 610, 2915

lancer au but, 2968
lancer au panier, 500
lancer avec le poing, 2937
lancer coulé, 483, 709
lancer coulé violent, 694
lancer de disque, 55
lancer de javelot, 140
lancer de la tête, 2877
lancer de marteau, 102
lancer de pénalité, 2927
lancer de poids, 274
lancer de près, 443
lancer de revers, 2809
lancer déposé, 569
lancer déposé en force, 649
lancer droit, 2988
lancer du bout des doigts, 3000
lancer en lob, 2899
lancer en piston, 2941
lancer en raquette, 2935
lancer en suspension, 566
lancer en suspension à bras roulé, 565
lancer en vrille, 756
lancer forcé, 509
lancer franc, 515
lancer franc manqué, 589
lancer franc réussi, 519, 713
lancer ininterrompu, 2970
lancer le ballon, 684
lancer manqué, 590
lancer par-dessous, 764
lancer sur place, 683
lancer tapé, 749
lancers francs multiples, 593
lanceur, 233, 330, 685, 1001
lanceur de disque, 56
lanceur de javelot, 141
lanceur de marteau, 103
lanceur de poids, 275
lançoir, 58, 235, 337

lançoir de javelot, 143
lançoir de marteau, 105
lançoir de poids, 277
largeur de la lame, 1718
largeur de la piste, 1719
largeur du bassin, 3021
largeur du filet, 2666
latte de saut, 18
leader, 948
"let", 2337
lever, se, 1890
liaison, 1771, 1772
liaison directe, 1786
libre champ, 442
licence, 952
liement, 1425, 1587
ligne, 2338
ligne centrale, 2556
ligne d'appel, 324
ligne d'arrivée, 84, 892
ligne d'attaque, 2522
ligne d'avertissement, 1714
ligne de but, 2867
ligne de centre, 727
ligne de côté, 2743, 2972
ligne de départ, 293, 1086
ligne de fin de piste, 1642
ligne de fond, 399, 486, 2246, 2593
ligne de mensuration, 805
ligne de mise en garde, 1605
ligne de rassemblement, 12
ligne de service, 2436
ligne de touche, 690
ligne des lancers francs, 518
ligne des sprinters, 1072
ligne des stayers, 1089
ligne des 2 mètres, 3005
ligne des 200 mètres, 1138
ligne des 4 mètres, 2857

ligne droite, 308, 921
ligne droite d'arrivée, 86
ligne droite opposée, 17
ligne du milieu, 2830, 2876
ligne incurvée de départ, 48
ligne médiane, 431, 2257
ligne médiane de service, 2258
ligne opposée, 787
ligne pour le double, 2288
lignes, 1588
lignes de jeu, 2549
lignes délimitant le terrain, 420
lignes du double, 2291
lignes du simple, 2449
limite de la zone de relais, 69
limites, 225)
limites du secteur, 237
liste de départ, 286
liste des joueurs inscrits, 724
liste des plongeons choisis, 1218, 1294
lob, 2340, 2898
lob d'attaque, 2368
lob de défense, 2281
lob élevé, 2325
lob en coup droit, 2315
lob en revers, 2228
lober, 2341
"locomotive", 955
longueur, 2123, 2129
longueur de la lame, 1585
longueur de la piste, 1586
longueur du filet, 2662
lumière blanche, 1717
lumière jaune, 1721
lumière rouge, 1643, 1937
lumière verte, 1552, 1831
lunettes de nage, 2100

machine, 956

machine à bouillonner, 1181
machine à calculer (mécanique; à fiches), 1183
magnétophone à cassette, 1754
mailles du filet, 2663
maillon de chaîne, 954
maillot, 362, 938
maillot de bain (pour dames), 1178
maillot de bain (pour hommes), 1177
maillot de piste, 1122, 1130
maillot de route, 1032
maintenir la cadence, 179
maintien, 1856
maître d'armes, 1520
manche, 962, 2618
manche de la raquette, 2403
manchette, 1677, 2550
manchette à deux mains, 2781
manchette à une main, 2672
maniement du ballon, 2817
manier le ballon, 542
manière explosive, 72
manipulation du ballon, 393
manivelle, 858
manque d'amplitude; continuité; harmonie; rythme, 1884
manquer le ballon, 2650
manquer le panier, 588
marathon, 181
"marauder", 2388
marche, 366, 1410, 1547
marche arrière, 789
marche d'élan, 1402
marche et fente (développement), 1679
marche sur piste, 350
marche sur route, 258
marcher, 755, 768

marcher pendant l'appui renversé, 1757
marcheur, 365
marquage agressif, 738
marquage individuel, 2903
marquage par derrière, 535
marquage par devant, 618
marquage sur le panneau, 389
marque blanche, 3020
marque rouge, 2951
marquer, 2421
marquer l'adversaire, 2833, 2904
marquer un but, 2962
marquer un panier, 668
marques, 30
marques verticales de côté du filet, 2740
marqueur, 670, 1340, 1663, 2164, 2720
marqueur officiel, 605
marqueur principal, 1852
marteau, 100
martingale, 1593
masque d'escrime, 1519
match, 1430, 2351
match chèrement disputé, 2324
match de consolation, 2266
match de double, 2289
match du simple, 2447
match initial, 2371
match nul, 2477
match-poursuite, 999
matelas de réception, 154
matérialité de la touche, 1594
mauvaise conduite, 2810, 2908
mauvaise tenue du corps, 1861
mécanicien, 964
mécanique, 965
médaille (or; argent; bronze), 191

mener, 162, 947, 2333
mener à la marque, 166
mesurage des buts, 2905
mesurage des sauts et des lancers, 188
mesure, 1479, 1595
mesure de la piste, 963
mettre le grand braquet, 1000
mi-course, 969
mi-temps, 538
milieu de peloton, 967
milieu de piste, 968
milieu du set décisif, 2622
minutes de jeu écoulées, 587
mise en garde, 1638
mise en jeu, 653
mise en jeu d'engagement, 611
mise en jeu par l'arbitre, 2944
mise hors-course d'une équipe, 869
mode de nage, 2187
mode de virage, 2208
modifier une décision, 2803, 2831
montée, 920
montée au panier, 482
mouche du fleuret, 1543
mouliner, 1137
moulinet, 230
moyenne des deux notes intermédiaires, 1739
moyenne des points, 642
moyeu, 923
mur, 2212
mur d'entraînement, 2231
mur des arrivées, 2088
mur d'extrémité, 2079
mur latéral, 2168
musette de ravitaillement, 972
musique orchestrée, 1914

nage de compétition, 2065
nage de demi-fond, 2140

nage de fond, 2131
nage de vitesse, 2173
nage libre, 2095
nage libre 100 m; 200 m; 400 m; 800 m; 1500 m, 2098
nage papillon, 2053
nage sur le côté, 2973
nage sur le dos, 2031
nager, 2189
nager debout, 3003
nageur, 2191
nageur de compétition, 2064
nageur de crawl, 2068
nageur de demi-fond, 2139
nageur de dos, 2034
nageur de grand fond, 2130
nageur de papillon, 2054
nageur de quatre nages, 2135
nageur de relais, 2159
nageur de style libre, 2097
nageur de vitesse, 2172
niveau de l'eau, 1405, 2213
nom du plongeon, 1312
non-classé, 2495
normes du saut en hauteur, 117
notation, 1283, 1302
note, 1301
note de départ, 1744
note la plus basse, 1297
note la plus haute, 1270
notes barrées, 1304
notes retenues, 1305
numéro de plongeon, 1210
numéro du couloir, 2121
numérotage des joueurs, 637

observer une autre équipe, 673
octave, 1601
offensive, 1604
officiel de soutien, 714

officiel supplémentaire, 2023
officiels, 607, 2142
officiels de direction, 180
officiels de la compétition, 42, 194
officiels de la réunion, 205
officiels de soutien, 1984
officiels des compétitions, 1007
officiels techniques, 1996
opérateur de l'appareil des trente secondes, 729
opposer, 2353
opposition, 1613
ordinateur, 1198
ordonner à un joueur de sortir de l'eau, 2918
ordre d'arrivée, 980
ordre de départ, 1087
ordre de départ des concurrents, 1378
ordre de passage, 1764, 1915
ordre de rotation des joueurs, 2714
ordre de servir, 2437
ordre pour recevoir, 2411
organisation de réception, 2759
originalité de l'exercice, 1917
ouverture, 1192, 1226, 1318, 1612, 2794
ouvrir, 1316

palier, 793
panier, 400, 424, 532, 550
panier adverse, 612
panier annulé, 468
panier de la raquette, 2401
panier de support, 2818
panier réussi, 693, 712
panier réussi du terrain de jeu, 499
panneau, 388
panneau d'affichage des performances, 214
panneau d'attaque, 599

panneau de touche, 2203
papier d'émeri, 1800
papillon, 2051, 2091
papillon 100 m; 200 m, 2055
"par terre!", 1608
parade, 1618
parade composée, 1444
parade diagonale, 1470
parade directe, 1471
parade d'opposition, 1427, 1614
parade en cédant, 1436
parade semi-circulaire, 1669
parade simple, 1672
parcours, 856
"paré!", 1617
partenaire, 2381
partie A, 1722
partie B, 1740
partie C, 1753
partie C exécutée en plus, 1727
partie de basket-ball; match, 406
partie de force, 1978
partie de l'exercice, 1922
partie d'élan, 1986
partie perdue par forfait, 510
partie peu profonde (du bassin), 2966
partie profonde du bassin, 2842
parties de valeur, 2010
partout, 2225
pas chassé, 1758, 1975
pas croisé, 45, 1776
"pas de touche!", 1599
passage, 35
passage de la ligne centrale, 2568
passage de la main au-dessus du filet, 2686
passage du ballon derrière la ligne de but, 2811
passage du plan du filet, 2569
passata di sotto, 1619

passe, 623, 2684, 2923
passe à bras roulé, 548
passe à deux mains, 761, 2783
passe à deux mains par bond du ballon, 759
passe à travers le terrain, 454
passe à une main, 398, 609, 2674
passe arrière, 2533
passe au joueur de tête, 571
passe au niveau de la poitrine, 439
passe avant, 2612
passe avec rebond, 419
passe aveugle, 413
passe courte, 2738
passe d'attaque, 2737
passe directe, 467
passe en cloche, 576
passe en manchette, 2551
passe en suspension, 2629
passe et va, 531
passe haute, 2624
passe par derrière le dos, 410
passe par-dessus la tête, 619
passe tendue, 2602
passer, 2685, 2734
passer le ballon, 496, 624, 2924
passer le ballon au joueur de tête, 544
passeur, 625, 2736
passing-shot, 2382
patin de frein, 815
paume de la main, 2922
pause, 561, 2687
pause entre sets, 2772
pédale, 988
pédaler, 989
pédaler en danseuse, 922, 990
pédalier, 835
peloton, 25, 99, 825
peloton de tête, 949

peloton groupé, 848
pénalité, 627, 991, 1048, 2383, 2925
pénétrant, 2532
pénétration, 2688
pentathlon, 213
percer la défense, 628
perche, 221
perdant, 2343
perdre, 2342
perdre le ballon, 578
perdre le contrôle du ballon, 526
perdre l'échange, 2639
perdre volontairement du temps, 2890, 3010
périlleux au vol, 1253
période, 2928
période de jeu, 629
période de sept minutes, 2965
permutation, 715, 2757
personnel de la piscine, 2147
personnel de la table de marque, 1362
perte de terrain, 1590
perte du ballon (sanction), 579
perte du service, 2640
petit matériel de réparation, 1060
petites fautes, 1966
phase aérienne, 2, 92
photo-d'arrivée, 215, 993
phrase d'armes, 1522
pianiste, 1925
piano, 1925
pied arrière, 351, 1706
pied avant, 523, 1584
pied d'appel, 322, 716
pied de pivot, 635
pied libre, 514, 595
pieds pointés en extension, 1329
pignon, 1073
piquer de la perche, 218

pirouetter, 1927
piscine, 2145, 2195
piscine extérieure, 2143
piscine intérieure, 2111
piscine rapide, 2085
pistard, 1125
piste, 345, 1115
piste couverte, 857, 930
piste de plein air, 981
piste de 3000 m steeple, 301
piste d'élan, 265
piste d'escrime, 1526, 1622
piste métallique, 1597
pistolet de départ, 2179
pistolet de starter, 294, 1088
pivot, 634
pivot bas, 580
pivot haut, 546
pivoter, 1924
placement de départ, 2982
placement du bout des doigts, 2775
placer la balle, 2384
placer le ballon, 2583, 2590, 2776
placer le ballon dans le trou, 2778
placer le ballon derrière le contre, 2777
plan, 1324
plan d'attaque, 601
plan horizontal, 1272
plan vertical, 1399
planche, 1179
planche d'appel, 321
planche de plasticine, 220
planche d'entraînement, 2116
planche dure, 1381
planche lente, 1365
planche rapide, 1244
planche (suspension horizontale), 1928

plaque de cadre, 902
plaques pour les pieds (sur les blocs de départ), 91
plaquette du marqueur, 582
plasticine, 219
plastron métallique, 1598
plat, 1252
plate-forme, 1325
plate-forme (plate-forme de 10 m, 1269
plateau, 834
plongeoir, 1215
plongeon, 1207, 2586
plongeon à partir d'un appui renversé, 1163
plongeon arrière, 1168
plongeon au tremplin, 1373
plongeon avant; avec demi tire-bouchon; avec tire-bouchon, 1257
plongeon avec bulles, 1182
plongeon avec élan, 1355
plongeon de départ, 2177
plongeon de haut-vol, 1328, 1392
plongeon d'échauffement, 1403
plongeon en arrière, 1174
plongeon en avant, 2615
plongeon latéral, 2739
plongeon manqué, 1242
plongeon renversé, 1348
plongeon renversé avec demi tire-bouchon; avec tire-bouchon, 1349
plongeon renversé périlleux avec demi tire-bouchon; avec tire-bouchon; avec 1 1/2 tire-bouchon; avec 2 1/2 tire-bouchons, 1350

plongeon renversé périlleux; et demi; 2 sauts renversés périlleux; double et demi... 1351
plongeon retourné, 1279
plongeon retourné avec demi ou 1 tire-bouchon, 1280
plongeon retourné périlleux et demi avec tire-bouchon; avec double tire-bouchon, 1282
plongeon retourné périlleux; 1 et demi sauts périlleux; 2 sauts périlleux; 2 et demi sauts périlleux..., 1281
plongeons au choix avec limite, 1400
plongeons au choix; libres, 1319
plongeons au choix sans limite, 1401
plongeons avec tire-bouchons, 1397
plongeons imposés; imposés, 1197
plongeons préliminaires, 1335
plonger, 1208
plongeur, 1211
plongeur au tremplin, 1372
plongeur de haut-vol, 1327
podium, 1929
podium de départ, 2180
podium des vainqueurs, 364
poids, 273
poids de contrôle, 1695
poids du ballon, 3016
poignée, 1553, 1561
poignée de départ, 2178
poignée de frein, 816
poignée du guidon, 914
poignée française, 1548
poignée italienne, 1578
poignée orthopédique, 1615
point, 2389
point de contact, 2390
point décisif, 2511
point d'impulsion, 1332

point d'ouverture, 1195
pointage, 1958
pointage final, 1819
pointage ouvert, 1912
pointe d'arrêt électrique, 1486
pointe de la lame, 1624
pointes, 279
points, 643
pommeau, 1625
pompe, 996
pont, 2069
porte-bidon, 1143
porter le ballon, 426, 2554
pose des mains, 1842
pose des mains sur la croupe, 1844
pose des mains sur le cou, 1845
position, 1330, 2391
position accroupie, 1970
position d'attaque, 604
position d'attente, 2409
position de défense, 463, 2575
position de départ, 295, 1379, 1974, 2181, 2753
position de garde, 1606
position de la main, 1560
position de retour, 2412
position des bras, 1159
position des jambes, 1291
position d'escrime, 1523
position en croix, 1201
position fondamentale, 1421, 1550, 1745
position légale de défense, 574
position libre, 1256
position mi-renversée, 1841
position pour la volée, 2502
possession, 644
possession du ballon, 397
poste de contrôle, 852
poste de ravitaillement, 885

postes de ravitaillement, 76, 247
poteau de but, 2869
poteau de filet, 2364
poteau de saut, 226, 359
poteaux d'arrivée, 85
poteaux de filet, 2664
poteaux du saut à la perche, 225
potence, 913, 1090
poule, 1626
poule finale, 1530
pourcentage de lancers francs, 520
pourcentage panier, 501
poursuite, 998
poursuite individuelle, 924
poursuite par équipes, 1100
poussée, 2938
poussée de la pointe des pieds, 1389
poussée du bras, 2151
poutre, 1746
poutre d'équilibre, 1741
pratiquer, 2395
pré-appel, 1277
précipiter vers le filet, se, 2417
prélèvement, 1047
premier arbitre, 2603
premier essai, 88
premier partant du relais, 2126
premier secrétaire, 1251
première balle de service, 2305
première intention, 1532
première mi-temps, 505, 2852
prende position sur le plongeoir, 1166
prendre le ballon en mains, 2535
prendre le départ, 1081
prendre le service adverse, 2251
prendre l'engagement, 1489
prendre pied sur le fond du bassin, 2980
prendre son élan, 261
prendre un virage à la corde, 123

préparation d'attaque, 1629
préposé à la cloche, 795
préposé à l'anémomètre, 374
préposé à l'appareil électrique, 1689
présentation, 1276
président du comité de gymnastique, 1837
président du jury, 1631, 1932
président d'un match, 1630
presser un adversaire, 651
pression, 1632
"prêts!", 272
prévu, 2419
prime, 1633
priorité, 1634, 1652
prise, 98, 1832, 1846, 2320
prise continentale, 2267
prise de fer, 1635, 1691
prise de revers, 2236
prise du ballon par en dessous, 2884
prise du coup droit, 2314
prise eastern, 2299
prise solide, 2303
prise western, 2506
procédé subsidiaire pour classement d'équipe, 737
procès-verbal général, 1315
profondeur de l'eau, 1206
profondeur minimum de l'eau, 2906
programme de la compétition, 1196, 1231
progresser avec le ballon, 652
progression avec le ballon, 379
prolongation, 490, 621
prolongation du jeu, 2920
pronation, 1636
propre ligne de but, 2921
propre panier, 622
protégé, 1099
protège-mains, 1847

protester, 2396
pyramide de marquage des couloirs, 156
pyramide de marquage des distances, 64

qualification, 1002, 2153
qualifier, se, 2397
quart de finaliste, 2398
quarte, 1639
quartier des coureurs, 850, 1026
quarts de finale, 2399
quatre nages, 2136
quatre nages 200 m; 400 m, 2110
quinte, 1640
quitter l'eau, 1236, 2891

rail de T.V., 2197
ramasseur de balles, 2244
ramasseur de ballons, 2541
rampe de signalisation des distances, 63
raquette, 2400
rassemblement, 1641
rater, 2358
rater le service, 2729
rattraper; doubler, 982
rattraper ou dépasser par l'intérieur, 983
rattraper ou doubler à l'extérieur, 984
ravitaillement, 884
rayon, 1069
réaction de la planche, 1387
rebond, 654, 2248
rebond d'attaque, 603
rebond de défense, 462
rebondir, 2249, 2946
rebondir sur le poteau, 2947
réception, 1885, 2702

réception au sol, 151
réception de ballon, 2948
réception en manchette, 2552
réclamation, 231, 995, 1338, 1933, 2148
record, 1013
record homologué, 204
récupération à deux mains, 2782
récupération à une main, 2673
récupération difficile, 2580
récupération du ballon, 2523, 2582
récupérer le ballon, 656
récupérer le service, 2591, 2795
redoublement, 1644
refuser d'exécuter un plongeon, 1343
réglage de l'engin, 1728
réglage des blocs de départ, 4
règle de l'avantage, 2802
règle de trois pour deux, 731
règle des trois secondes, 734
règle des 10 secondes, 728
règle des 30 secondes, 730
règle des 5 secondes, 506
règle du jeu, 2934
règlement, 1017
règlement de water-polo, 3014
règlement technique, 1997
réglementaire, 1016
règlements, 1938
règles, 1042, 1952
relais, 248, 1018, 2158
relais de nage libre, 2096
relais nage libre 4 x 100 m; 4 x 200 m, 2092
relais quatre nages, 2134
relais quatre nages 4 x 100 m, 2093
relanceur, 2410
relayé, 131
relayeur, 208

remettre le ballon en jeu, 2945
remis, 2392
remise, 1646
remise en jeu, 735
remise en jeu après un but, 2954
remise en jeu de la ligne de touche, 691
remise en jeu par l'arbitre, 2955
remise en jeu par le gardien de but, 2871
remplaçant, 710, 2755
remplacement, 711
remplacement de joueur, 638, 2706
remplir les couloirs, 503
rencontre, 966, 1596, 1704, 2354, 2642
rencontre internationale, 1867
rencontrer, 2355
renversement, 2496
renversement du jeu, 757
renverser, 2497
renverser la barre, 59
renvoi croisé, 2270
renvoi profond, 2274
renvoyer, 2414
repêchage, 1020
répertoire des plongeons, 1220
répétition d'un élément, 1940
repos, 2708
repos entre les périodes, 2887
repousser de l'adversaire, se, 2939
repousser du mur du bassin, se, 2940
reprendre le jeu, 2956
reprise, 1647
reprise d'attaque, 1648
reprise de l'exercice, 1941
reprise du temps de jeu, 739
résistance de l'eau, 2214
respecter ses marques, 118

respiration à deux temps, 2074
respiration à quatre temps, 2094
respiration bilatérale, 2038
respiration unilatérale, 2209
responsable de la gymnastique, 1840
rester accroché au tremplin, 1353
résultat, 1022
résultat final, 504, 1248
résultats, 2162
résultats préliminaires, 1336
retarder intentionnellement le jeu, 2579
retarder le jeu, 466
retenir un adversaire, 2882
retirer du concours,se, 2021
retour de service, 2438
retour du ballon en arrière, 617
retour du bras, 2027
retrait, 2513
retraite, 1650, 1680
réussir le coup, 2350
revenir au jeu, 2957
revers, 2234
revers à deux mains, 2486
revers croisé, 2269
revêtement anti-dérapant de la plate-forme, 1313
révocation d'un juge, 1939
riposte, 1653
riposte à temps perdu, 1432
riposte composée, 1445
riposte simple, 1673
risque, 1948
rompre, 1649
rondes; tours, 259
rotation, 1369, 2712
rotation dans le sens des aiguilles d'une montre, 2561
rotation des épreuves, 1950

rotation des équipes, 1951
roue, 1145
roue arrière, 788
roue avant, 904
roue de rechange, 1063
rouler vers le ballon, 664
rouler vers le panier, 665
route, 1028
ruban-cassette, 1755
ruban de mesure, 190
rythme, 1944
rythme de foulée, 310
rythme respiratoire, 2047, 2155

sabre, 1655
sabreur, 1660
saisir le ballon, 2555
salle d'armes, 1517
salle d'entraînement, 2003
salto, 1956
salut, 1661
saut, 145, 1286
saut à la perche, 222
saut au centre, 430
saut d'appel, 1274
saut d'essai, 1227
saut en hauteur, 111
saut en longueur, 173
saut "Fosbury", 93
saut périlleux, 1367
saut périlleux arrière avec 1/2
  tire-bouchon; avec tire-bouchon;
  avec 1 1/2 tire-bouchon; avec
  double tire-bouchon; avec 2 1/2
  tire-bouchon, 1171
saut périlleux arrière groupé, 1170
saut périlleux avant avec demi
  tire-bouchon; avec tire-bouchon;
  avec 2 tire-bouchons, 1258

saut périlleux avant; un et demi
  avant; double saut périlleux avant;
  double et demi avant..., 1259
saut périlleux et demi arrière; 2 sauts
  périlleux arrière; 2 1/2 sauts
  périlleux arrière, 1173
sauter, 1880
sauter sur ses pieds, 1287
sauteur, 147, 567
sauteur à la perche, 223
sauteur de triple saut, 355
sauteur en hauteur, 112
sauteur en longueur, 175
sautoir, 149
sautoir à la perche, 224
sautoir de triple saut, 356
sautoir en hauteur, 116
sautoir en longueur, 174
sauts d'essai, 1333
sauver des genoux fléchis, 1289
sauver un plongeon, 1357
sauver un plongeon jambes pliées, aux
  genoux, 1358
sauver un saut périlleux, 1368
schème tactique, 2764
score, 2420
score (pointage), 2717
séance, 1963
second arbitre, 2723
second secrétaire, 1363
seconde, 1667
seconde intention, 1665
secouer le peloton, 1068
secrétaire, 1050, 2964
secrétaire de la réunion, 269
secrétaire du jury, 242
secrétaire pour aider les marqueurs,
  1341
secrétaires, 1219

secteur, 270
secteur de lancement, 339
selle, 1044, 1955
sensibilité du panneau de touche,
  2167
septième, 1670
série, 1052
série acrobatique, 1725
série de gymnastique, 1839
série initiale, 2304
série qualificative, 1003
séries, 107, 2108
séries interrompues, 1868
serrer, 1104
serveur, 2430, 2726
service, 2428, 2431, 2725
service à effet coupé, 2452
service à effet toppé, 2483
service à plat, 2307
service au-dessus de l'épaule, 2681
service balancier, 2715
service bas latéral, 2742
service-canon, 2255
service correct, 2635
service coupé, 2625, 2744
service de filet, 2665
service flottant, 2605
service par en dessous, 2785
service puissant, 2698
service tennis, 2770
service-volée, 2432
servir, 2429, 2724
set, 2440, 2733
set décisif, 2475, 2571
set gagné, 2620
set perdu, 2619
sets consécutifs, 2460
shooteur éclair, 707
shooteur favori, 444
sifflet, 771, 3017

signal, 551
signal d'arrêt de jeu, 2975
signal de départ, 296, 2983
signal sonore (durée), 2000
signaler avec le fanion, 2976
signaux d'arbitre, 608
signaux électroniques, 1795
signaux manuels, 1898
sillage, 1059
simple, 2444
simple dames, 2515
simple messieurs, 2357
situations de surnombre, 615
sixte, 1676
smash, 2454, 2747
smash balancier, 2716
smash contré, 2546
smasher, 2455, 2748
smasher dans le contre pour faire
  sortir le ballon, 2749
smasheur, 2750
socquette, 777
soigneur, 1062
sol, 1827
sonnerie, 2105
sortie, 1787
sortie de virage, 68, 70
sortir, 1788
sortir du terrain, 2632
soulever le ballon, 2636, 2895
souplesse, 1824
soutien d'attaque, 2521
soutien de réception, 2567
spécialiste, 2746
spécialiste de la défense, 2576, 2581
spécialiste de l'attaque, 2524
spécialiste du contre, 2545
spécialiste du service, 2731
sprint, 1071
sprint final, 80

stabilité, 1971
stabilité à la réception, 1972
starter, 289, 1084, 2175
starter de rappel, 241
station, 1973
statisticien, 701
statistiques, 702
steeple (course d'obstacles), 297
style, 313, 2186
style "Fosbury", 94
subtiliser le ballon, 703
suiveur autorisé, 785
supériorité numérique, 2901
supination, 1690
support des paniers, 403
supports-signalisation de faux départs, 2083
sur la ligne, 2369
sur place, 1078, 1375
surcharge, 620
surface, 2464
surface de l'eau, 1383, 2215
surface de service, 2727
surface du jeu, 2693
surface non valable, 1576
surface synthétique, 2469
surface valable, 1711
surnoter, 1321
suspendre, 1093
suspendu, 2465
suspension, 1094
système, 2758
système d'attaque, 2670
système de défense, 2577
système de pointage, 1961
système de taxation, 1879
système d'évaluation, 1802
système électronique d'affichage, 1794

table de marque, 2721
table des officiels mineurs, 586
table du marqueur, 671
tableau, 932, 1275
tableau d'affichage, 974
tableau de difficultés, 1988
tableau de marque, 669
tableau de marques, 2163
tableau des fautes, 1989
tableau des plongeons, 1209
tableau des résultats, 1360, 1662
tableau indicateur, 2719
tableau indicateur des résultats, 2422
tableau R.O.V., 1987
tactique, 2760, 2761
tactique de contre, 2548
tactique de deuxième intention, 1666
tactique de service, 2732
tactique défensive, 2578
tactique offensive, 2671
taper, 718, 747
taper le ballon dans le panier, 748
tapis, 1899
tapis de chute, 1886
tapis pour exercices au sol, 1829
tassage, 803
taxation, 1377, 1960
taxation pour les finales, 1803
technique, 328
technique de départ, 2182
technique de nage, 2196
technique de plongeon, 1221
technique de respiration, 2048
témoin, 19, 249
température de l'eau, 1406, 2200
temps automatique, 2076
temps de jarret, 1225
temps de jeu, 640
temps de jeu effectif, 2801

temps de passage, 2125, 2171
temps de qualification, 2154
temps de réaction, 239
temps défavorable, 1153
temps d'escrime, 1527
temps intermédiaire, 137
temps mort, 743, 2773
temps mort accordé, 438
temps officiel, 2141
tendre après la position groupée, se, 1194
tendre après le plongeon, se, 1234
tenir immobile, se (position de départ), 2037
tenir la corde, 122
tenir le ballon sous l'eau, 2883
tennis-elbow, 2473
tension du cordage, 2474
tentative, 14
tentative de sur place, 1079
tenue de l'arme, 1556
tenue de l'engin, 119
tenue d'échauffement, 2020
tenue du joueur, 2786
terrain, 451, 2565
terrain de jeu, 639
tête de fourche, 899
tête de la raquette, 2404
tête de série, 918
tie-break, 2479
tierce, 1698
tige de selle, 1045
tirage au sort, 873, 1224, 2295, 2563, 2845
tirage au sort des couloirs, 66
tirage au sort des paniers, 750
tirage au sort pour finale, 1789
tirage au sort pour les rotations, 1791

tirage au sort pour répartition des juges, 1790
tire-bouchon, 1396
tirer, 1508
tirer à soi son adversaire, 2936
tirer au sort, 2294
tirer en barrage, 1509
tireur, 1513
titulaire, 1111
toise, 189, 2645
topomètre, 343
touche, 1562, 1702, 2202
touche de ballon, 497, 2564
touche de pénalisation, 1621
touche donnée, 1566
touche non valable, 1567, 1575, 1600, 1602
touche reçue, 1568
touche valable, 1710
toucher, 1563, 1688, 1703
toucher la ligne de lancer franc, 751
toucher le ballon, 3001
toucher le ballon des deux mains en même temps, 3002
toucher le filet, 2484
toucher le fond du bassin, 1390
toucher le tremplin, 1271
toucher l'engin, 2002
tour, 942, 1391
tour d'avance, 944
tour de neutralisation, 973
tour de piste, 945
tour éliminatoire, 1488
tourner, 2005
tournoi "open", 2370
toute position, 1155
toutes positions, 1191
traction du bras, 2149
trajectoire, 1393

trajectoire du ballon, 382, 754
trajectoire d'un engin, 352
trajet effectué par un joueur, 626
tranchant de la lame, 1466
transmission du témoin, 20
transport latéral, 2004
travail sous l'eau, 3006
tremplin, 1371, 1748
tremplin "duraflex", 1228
tremplin en fibre de verre, 1246
tremplin "maxiflex", 1307
tremplin "maxiflex-B", 1306
treuil du filet, 2667
tribune d'arbitre, 2953
triple saut, 354
tromper une parade, 1467, 1498
trou, 2793
tube , 1133

"un mètre!", 1609
une-deux, 1610
une-deux-trois, 1611

Union Cycliste Internationale (U.C.I.), 937
usage illégal des mains, 555

valeur des sauts, 2014
valeur d'originalité, 1916
valeur exceptionnelle, 1935
validité d'un but, 3007
valve, 1139
vélo de course, 1008
vélo de piste, 1119, 1126
vélo de route, 1030, 1036
vélocité, 985
vélodrome, 800, 861
vent arrière, 1097
vent de face, 916
vent latéral, 1056
vérification, 361
vérification des armes, 1716
vérification des engins, 1864
vérification des licences, 953
veste d'escrime, 1518
vestiaire de couloir, 2120

victoire, 2499, 2508
violation, 767
violation en zone arrière, 387
virage, 796, 860, 2206
virage-culbute, 2170
virage de brasse, 2043
virage de dos, 2035
virage en quatre nages individuel, 2109
virtuosité, 2017
vis, 1049
viscosité, 2211
vitesse, 1064, 2456
voiture-balai, 1046
voiture de service, 1053
voiture des commissaires, 846, 978
voiture officielle, 977
voiture-radio, 1010
voiture suiveuse, 896
vol, 1825
volée, 2500
volée-amortie, 2297
volée basse, 2348

volée croisée, 2272
volée de revers, 2240
volée du coup droit, 2316
volée en angle, 2228
volleyer, 2501
volte, 338, 1707

zéro, 2345, 2517
zone , 774
zone arrière, 386, 2527
zone avant, 522
zone d'attaque, 2525
zone de désignation, 584
zone de passage du témoin, 325
zone de passage du témoin d'arrivée, 212
zone de rassemblement, 2133
zone de relais, 253
zone d'élan, 1
zone des trois secondes, 733
zone des 2 mètres, 3004
zone des 4 mètres, 2856
zone libre, 2560
zone neutre, 2365

"¡a sus puestos!", 206, 2198
abalanzarse hacia la red, 2417
abandonar, 2277, 2317
abandono, 510, 1023, 2276, 2513
abanico, 877
abertura, 1612
abstención, 1409
accelerar el ritmo, 133
accesorios de la bicicleta, 799
accidente mecánico, 820
acción de las piernas, 2127
acción del brazo para el lanzamiento, 65
acción simultánea, 1674
acertar el salto mortal, 1368
acertar el tiro, 2350
acertar en las marcas, 118
acierto, 749
acompañamiento musical, 1907
acta de arbitraje, 606
acta de series, 2107
acta del partido, 672
actuación monótona, 1904
adelantamiento, 1620
adelantar, 982, 986
adelantar; rebasar, 210
"¡adelante!", 1507, 1623
adversario, 2372
advertencia, 1141, 1713, 2504
agarradero de salida, 2178
agarrarse del aro, 534
agarro, 2320
agarro al revés, 2236
agarro continental, 2267
agarro derecho, 2314
agarro firme, 2303
agarro occidental, 2506
agarro oriental, 2299
agilidad, 1824

agitación mecánica de la superficie del agua, 1308
agrupado; en bola, 1394
agrupar, 1395
agua con cloro, 2059
ahuecada, 1158
ahuecar la espalda, 1157
"¡al suelo!", 1608
ala, 2680
ala izquierdo, 572
alcanzar (o: ir hacia adelante) al lado exterior, 984
alcanzar (o: ir hacia adelante) al lado interior, 983
alero derecho, 661
aleros delanteros, 511
alineamiento del cuerpo para la entrada en el agua, 1293
alojamiento de los competidores, 850
"¡alto!", 1559
altura de la red, 2661
altura del aparato, 1855
altura del listón, 108
aitura del salto, 1268
altura del travesaño, 2878
altura inicial, 134
altura mínima, 199
amagar hacia el defensa girando hacia la cesta, 633
amagar un tiro, 493
amago, 492
amago de alejarse del balón seguido del impulso hacia el balón, 664
amonestación, 2792
amortiguar, 2641
amplitud, 1731
amplitud de los movimientos, 1732
anchura de la hoja, 1718
anchura de la pista, 1719

anchura de la red, 2666
andarín, 365
anemómetro, 373
angular el cuerpo, 1477
ángulo de acercamiento, 5
ángulo de inclinación del partidero, 2169
ángulo de salida, 1385
ángulo del bote, 6
ángulo del tiro, 686
anillas, 1946
anotación, 693, 1301
anotación anulada, 468
anotación de base, 1744
anotador, 670, 806, 2164, 2720
anotar, 668
antenas, 2519
anticipo de pase por la defensa, 618
anulación del toque, 1411
anunciador oficial, 1314
anunciar un gol, 2804
anuncio oficial del salto, 1154
aparato, 8
aparato de comprobación de las armas, 1412
aparato de gimnasia, 1836
aparato eléctrico de señalización, 1487
apelar, 381
apertura, 2794
aplazado, 2254
apoyarse en el fondo de la piscina, 2943, 2980
apoyo, 1983
apoyo (asistencia de entrenamiento), 1265
apoyo de la recepción, 2567
apoyo en el ataque, 2521

apreciación de la ejecución; combinación; composición; dificultad, 1804
apretar, 1104
aproximación, 1156
apuntador, 1340
arbitrar, 658
árbitro, 2489
árbitro auxiliar, 763
árbitro de brazada, 2185
árbitro de la línea de fondo, 570
árbitro de polo acuático, 3013
árbitro de pruebas, 1230
árbitro de rompimiento de impulso, 1176
árbitro del centro del campo, 752
árbitro principal, 657
arcos, 1931
área, 9
área de agrupamiento, 2133
área de caída, 152
área de los 4 metros, 2856
área de precalentamiento, 369, 2018
área de servicio, 2433
arma de esgrima, 1529
arma defectuosa, 1503
aro, 402, 550, 663
arqueamiento del listón, 266
arquearse, 1735
arrancada, 946
arrancar, 1081
arranque, 72, 285
arrebatar el balón, 703
arreglos mientras el ciclista anda, 1043
arremeter al adversario, 437
arremeter con el puño, 2937
arresto, 1681
as, 2220, 2518

asalto, 1589
ascenso, 920
asignación de calles, 2119
asistente, 1738
Asociación Canadiense de Natación Amateur (A.C.N.A.), 2056
atacador, 2526
atacante, 602
atacar, 782, 2029
ataque, 385, 596, 1414, 2520, 2668
ataque al hierro, 1416
ataque al primer pase, 2584
ataque atrasado, 465
ataque central, 2646
ataque compuesto, 1443
ataque contra la zona de defensa, 598
ataque contra una defensa personal, 597
ataque controlado, 450
ataque de fondo, 2530
ataque delantero, 783
ataque desde atrás, 784
ataque en flecha, 1654
ataque en fuerza, 2696
ataque planeado, 682
ataque por el ala, 773
ataque por oposición, 1415
ataque simple, 1671
ataque triple de pivote con dos, 648
ataques simultáneos, 1675
ataques sobre la preparación, 1417
atleta, 346
atuación magnífica, 1807
aumentar la ventaja, 132
auriculares, 2106
autoridades, 2142
autorizar una repetición del salto, 1264
auxiliar de salida, 1001
auxiliar del juez de salida, 290

avance, 1410
avanzar con el balón, 379, 652, 2846, 2994
avanzar y retroceder, 617
aventajar a, 2333
avituallamiento, 884
ayuda, 383, 1737
ayuda entre corredores, 781
ayuda menor, 1903
ayudante del cronometrador, 2806
ayudante del secretario, 2805

bajada, 868
bajarse, 1788
balanceo, 1985, 2711
balanceo al revés, 1775
balanceo intermedio, 1813, 1865
balanceo lateral, 2741
balanceo preparatorio para el lanzamiento del disco, 228
balestra, 1419
balón, 2534
balón a favor de, 395
balón antirreglamentario, 2910
balón bueno, 2537
balón de baloncesto, 404
balón de polo acuático, 3011
balón de voleibol, 2787
balón detenido, 2623
balón en juego, 394, 2536
balón está muerto, 391
balón está vivo, 390
balón fácil, 2614
balón fuera, 2539
balón fuera de banda, 396
balón fuera de juego, 2812
balón inflado, 2885
balón lanzado al agua, 2815
balón lanzado al ras del agua, 2816
balón muerto, 458, 2540, 2570

balón no bloqueado a propósito, 2588
balón perdido, 526
balón que franqueó por completo la línea del gol, 2813
balón que toca la red, 2542
balón rebotando sobre el agua, 2814
balón retenido, 545
balón sobre la red, 2538
balón suelto, 577
balón vivo, 575
banco, 411
banco de los jugadores, 2692
banco del equipo, 720
banda, 2226
banda horizontal de la red, 2765
bandas laterales de la red, 2740
bandera amarilla, 1151
bandera: banderín, 89
bandera roja, 1014
bandera verde, 908
banderín, 2604, 2853, 3019
banderín azul, 2822
banderín de límite de zona, 377
banderín de sector, 271
banderín de viraje, 44
banderín del árbitro, 2952
banderín del juez de gol, 2866
banderín indicador del récord nacional (olímpico, mundial), 185
banderín marcador de la tirada, 184
banderín rojo, 1015, 2950
banderín verde, 909
banderines de la carrera de obstáculos, 299
banderines indicadores de las vueltas para estilo espalda, 2032
barra, 1746
barra baja, 1896
barra de equilibrio, 1741
barra fija, 1857, 1859

bascular, 1882
básculas, 1883
batido de piernas, 2117
batimiento, 1422
bicicleta, 798
bicicleta de carreras, 1008
bicicleta de carretera, 1030
bicicleta de pista, 1119, 1126
bicicleta de ruta, 1036
bicicleta standard, 1074
biela, 858
bloqueador, 2547
bloqueador central, 2648
bloqueador del ala, 2592
bloquear, 414, 2544
bloquear un disparo, 415
bloquear y girar hacia la cesta, 676
bloqueo, 417, 2543
bloqueo a dos, 2784
bloqueo al saque, 2728
bloqueo de tres, 2771
bloqueo defensivo, 2573
bloqueo en movimiento, 591
bloqueo exterior, 616
bloqueo fuerte hacia abajo que anota, 2754
bloqueo indirecto, 677
bloqueo individual, 2675
bloqueo ofensivo, 2669
bloqueo suave, 2745
bocina, 551
bola, 790
bolsa de avituallamiento, 972
bomba de aire, 996
bonificación, 1751
borde anterior del trampolín, 1185
borde de la pista, 1116
borde del tablero, 484
borde interior de la pista, 936

borde interno de las líneas de demarcación del terreno de juego, 556
bordillo, 47, 808
bordillo de la pista, 135
botar, 2249
bote, 318, 1990, 2248
botella de bebida, 1142
botón, 1433
botón del florete, 1543
braceo, 2026
braza de espalda, 2031
braza de mariposa, 2053
braza de pecho, 2040
brazalete, 11, 780
brazo armado, 1715
brazo de impulso, 332
brazo desarmado, 1705
brazo libre, 316
brazo no armado, 1709
brazos, 2028
brinco, 121

caballo de través (mujeres), 1964
caballo para saltos (hombres), 1894
cabeza de horquilla, 899
cabeza de la raqueta, 2404
cable de conexión, 1446
cable de la red, 2659
cable del martillo, 106
cadena, 833
cadena rota, 823
cadencia, 26, 1434, 1651
caer de pleno, 1298
caída, 74, 882, 1065, 1226, 1814
caída accidental al agua, 1243
caída al suelo, 151
caída colectiva, 960
cajetín, 217

calapié, 1112
calcetín, 1061
calcetines, 777
calculadora (mecánica; de cartolina), 1183
calendario de los partidos, 529
calendario de partidos, 667
calificación, 1002
calificación por equipos, 1994
calificar, 2397
calzada, 1039
calle, 155, 2118
cámara de aire, 935
cámara de llamadas, 187
cámara para los finales de carrera, 216
cambiar de ritmo, 838
cambiar de velocidad, 836
cambio, 711
cambio al rebote, 455
cambio de balón, 2699
cambio de barra, 1743
cambio de bicicleta, 837
cambio de campo, 433, 2558, 2832
cambio de dirección, 434
cambio de jugador, 638, 2706
cambio de lado, 1438
cambio de ligamento, 1439
cambio de pelotas, 2245
cambio de pie, 28
cambio de posesión, 757
cambio de puño, 1833
cambio de ritmo, 29, 435
cambio de rueda, 1146
cambio de saque, 2557
cambio de servicio, 2434
cambio directo, 1785
cambio tipo derailleur, 867

camino hacia el extremo de la plataforma, 1402
camiseta, 362
camiseta de carretera, 1032
campana, 794
campanillas, 2105
campo, 10, 2875
campo contrario, 2676
campo de juego, 2933
campo de juego antirreglamentario, 2911
campo opuesto, 2917
canasta anotada, 712
cancha, 2268, 2565
cancha central, 2256, 2349
cancha del fondo, 2232
cancha exterior, 2376
cancha interior, 2329
canchas alternativas, 2227
capitán, 425, 2553, 2827
capitán del equipo, 721, 1693, 2471
captura del balón, 2555
cara (de frente) a la plataforma, 1237
cara (de frente) al agua, 1239
cara (de frente) al trampolín, 1238
cara de la raqueta, 2401
caravana, 831, 854
carbonato de magnesio, 1756, 1897
careta de esgrima, 1519
carga, 436
carpa abierta, 1317
carpa cerrada, 1189
carpa; en escuadra, 1322
carrera, 236, 264, 1005
carrera a medio terminar, 969
carrera contra el reloj, 1107
carrera de calificación, 1003
carrera de fondo, 171
carrera de impulso, 260, 1953

carrera de media distancia, 197
carrera de obstáculos, 297
carrera de precalentamiento, 370
carrera de relevos, 250
carrera de vallas, 125
carrera de velocidad, 280
carrera eliminatoria, 878
carrera en curva, 22
carrera en pista, 1124
carrera individual, 925
carrera por equipos, 326, 1101
carrera por pasillo, 157
carrete, 1645
carretera, 1028
carretes receptores, 2199
casco protector, 919
casetas para la ropa del nadador, 2120
categoría de corredores, 832
cazoleta, 1554
cazoleta de espada, 1497
cazoleta de florete, 1542
cazoleta de sable, 1659
centro de control de atletas, 13
centro de pista, 968
centro del pelotón, 967
centro delantero, 428, 2829
ceremonia de palmarés, 363
cero, 2345, 2517
cerrar a un corredor, 23, 810
cerrar el paso, 49
certamen de natación, 2194
cesta, 400, 424
cesta; canasta, 532
cesta del adversario, 612
cesta propia, 622
ciclismo, 862
ciclismo en pista, 1120
ciclismo en ruta, 1031
ciclismo en velódromo cubierto, 931

ciclista, 801, 864
cilindro, 457
cinta de llegada, 87
cinta de manillar, 915
cinta magnética, 1755
circuito, 841
circuito de carretera, 1029
circulación táctica, 2763
círculo central, 429, 564
círculo de lanzamiento, 334
clasificación, 842, 994, 2153, 2408, 2425
clasificación combinada, 1761
clasificación de los tiradores, 1441
clasificación general, 1249
clasificación individual, 1863
clasificación por tiempo, 2166
clasificado, 1051, 1668, 2424
clasificar, 2407
clavado; salto, 1207
clavados preliminares, 1335
clínica ambulante, 971
club, 1190
club de saltos ornamentales, 1212
cobertura del terreno, 2566
coche escoba, 1046
coche oficial, 977
código de carretera, 1131
código de la pista, 1118
código de puntuación, 1759
codo de tenis, 2473
coeficiente de dificultad, 1205, 1782
coger el balón, 427
coger el rebote, 655
cojinete de bolas, 793
colaborador técnico-científico, 1957
colchoneta, 153, 154, 1899
colchoneta de salida, 1886
colegio de árbitros, 2643
colegio de comisarios, 845

colocación de las manos, 1842
colocación de las manos sobre el cuello, 1845
colocación de las manos sobre la grupa, 1844
colocación de los jugadores en la pista, 723
colocar el balón con la yema de los dedos, 2583
colocar la pelota, 2384
colores, 2837
combate, 1430
combate cuerpo a cuerpo, 1511, 1572
combinación táctica, 2762
combinaciones, 1760
combinaciones de zancadas, 310
combinado (estilos), 200 m, 400 m, 2110
comienzo, 2458
comienzo de la salida, 1277
comienzo del ejercicio, 1749
comienzo del juego, 2751, 2981
comienzo del partido, 408, 698
comisario de pista, 186
comisario del encuentro, 2060
comisión permanente, 992, 1075
comisión técnica, 1103
comité de competición, 849
comité de evaluación, 1284
comité directivo, 881
Comité Internacional de Saltos Ornamentales (F.I.N.A.), 1278
comité organizador de gimnasia, 1838
comité técnico conjunto, 1870
comité técnico femenino, 2022
comité técnico masculino, 1902
compañero, 2381, 2472, 2768
compensación de curvas a la salida, 282
competición, 40, 2264

competición de saltos, 1213
competición de saltos de plataforma, 1326
competición IA; IB; II; III, 1763
competición individual, 1571, 1862
competición por equipos, 1694
competidores, 2265
composición del ejercicio, 1768
composición del equipo, 725
comprobación de las armas, 1716
comprobación de licencias, 953
computadora, 1198
comunicación entre la defensa, 717
conceptos fundamentales, 527
conducta antideportiva, 766
conferencia de jueces, 1874
congelar el balón, 521
construcción del ataque, 2767
consulta de jueces, 1875
contacto con el terreno adversario, 2780
contacto personal, 630
contador de vueltas, 158, 2124
contenido del ejercicio, 1773
continuación, 448
continuación del ataque, 1447
contra, 1440, 1450
contra-batimiento, 1437
contra-coupé, 1452
contra de cuarta, 1454
contra de sexta, 1458
contra la red, 2224
contra ofensiva, 1455
contra parada, 1456
contra-respuesta, 1457
contra-tiempo, 1459
contraataque, 1451
contraataque rápido, 495
contrapase, 1453
control antidoping, 871

control de la punta eléctrica, 1696
control de las tomas de relevos, 2160
control de llegada, 890
control del balón, 392
control electrónico (barra de equilibrio; gimnasia a manos libres), 1796
controlar el balón, 449
convenciones, 1448
corazón de la raqueta, 2466
corchera, 2896
corchera de demarcación, 2840
cordaje de la raqueta, 2405
cordaje de tripas, 2322
cordaje sintético, 2468
correa de calapié, 1113
correa del casco, 840
corredor, 263, 1025
corredor de carretera, 1037
corredor de fondo, 172
corredor de maratón, 182
corredor de medio fondo, 198
corredor de pista, 1125, 1127
corredor de relevos, 251
corredor de vallas, 126
corredor delantero, 950
corredor escapado, 822
corredor especialista en curva, 21
corredor suplente, 314
correr, 1024
correr en abanico, 958
correr pegado al bordillo, 122
correspondencia en la defensa, 584
corriente, 2099
cortado, 2492
cortar, 456
cortar después de una pantalla de pivote alto, 689
coupé, 1460

crawl, 2067
criterios de juicio, 1285
crolista, 2068
cronometrado suplente, 256
cronometrador, 342, 746, 1108. 1700, 2001, 2201, 2999
cronometrador-jefe, 31, 2058
cronometrador manual, 2104
cronometraje, 1109, 1110
cronometraje cada media vuelta, 911
cronometraje manual, 2132, 2183
cronómetro, 307
cronómetro de juego, 528
cronómetro de los tiempos muertos, 744
cronómetro de los 35 minutos, 2971
cronómetro del juego, 2861
cronómetro individual, 1977
cruzada, 1452
cuadro, 900
cuadro de dificultades, 1988
cuadro de resultados, 2422
cuadro derecho de saque, 2415
cuadro izquierda de saque, 2335
cuadro roto, 824
cuadro R.O.V., 1987
cualquier posición, 1155
cuarta, 1629
cuartel de corredores, 1026
cuartos de finales, 2399
cubierta, 2069
cubo de la rueda, 923
cubrirse, 1461, 1637
cuello del caballo de arcos, 1909
cuello del caballo de saltos, 1910
cuerda de la calle, 2122
cuerda de salida falsa, 2084
cuerdas, 2462
cuerpo a cuerpo, 1428

cuidador, 1062
cursos de jueces, 1876
curva, 860
curvatura de la hoja, 1463

chapa, 1140
chaquetilla de esgrima, 1518
chaquetilla metálica, 1598
"cheese board" (trampolín "Maxiflex B"), 1187
choque, 446

dar efecto lateral, 2451
dar efecto liftado, 2683, 2779
dar la salida, 907
dar la vuelta, 2005
dar patadas, 2888
de fondo, 170
decatlón, 51
decatloniano, 50
decisión, 2273
decisión del árbitro, 2491
dedeo, 1531
deducción de composición, 1767
deducción de 1.0 punto; 0.1; 0.5; etc., 1780
deducción máximo, 1900
deducción por ejecución; combinación; composición; dificultad, 1779
deducción suplementaria, 1982
deducciones del juez árbitro, 1853
deducciones neutrales, 1911
defensa, 459, 2572, 2808, 2843
defensa central, 2647
defensa de atrás, 2528
defensa de la cesta, 533
defensa de zona, 775
defensa de zona de cuatro y un volante, 421

defensa derecho, 662
defensa floja, 695
defensa individual presionante en medio campo, 540
defensa individual presionante en todo el campo, 524
defensa izquierdo, 573, 2392, 2958
defensa mixta, 447
defensa móvil, 2653
defensa personal, 581
defensa preparada, 1628
defensa zonal de presión en todo el campo, 525
defensa zonal de presón desde el centro del terreno, 541
defensas, 537
defensiva, 1468
defensivo, 2280
defensivo deslizante (zona), 464
defensor, 460, 2574, 2844
dejada, 2298
dejada de derecho, 2313
dejada de revés, 2235
dejada de volea, 2297
dejar atrás, 207
dejar un hueco, 951
delantero, 2807, 2854
delantero centro, 2649
delantero derecho, 2710. 2959
delantero izquierdo, 2634, 2893
delanteros, 2616
delegados para atender a los participantes, jurado y prensa, 305
delfín, 2072
delimitación del campo de juego, 2824, 2897
demorar, 2282
demorar el juego, 466
derecho, 1382

derecho; en la posición extendida, 1290
derechos de inscripción, 1346
derrota, 2278, 2344
derrotar, 2279
desacierto con el rebote del trampolín, 1241
desalojar el listón, 59
desarme, 1475
descalificación, 469, 2071
descalificación de un equipo, 869
descalificado, 870
descalificar, 2284
descanso, 538, 561, 2480, 2687, 2708, 2887
desempatar, 1509
desempate, 1420
desempate de puestos, 737
desempate (en saltos), 146
desencarpar, 1193, 1235
deslizamiento, 1678
desmarcarse, 530, 2862
despegarse, 176
despegarse de un adversario, 874
despegue a dos pies, 2006
despejar el balón, 2836
despeje, 442
despistarse, 1058
desplazamiento, 1478, 2651
desplazamiento debajo del balón, 2657
desplazamiento hacia adelante, 2654
desplazamiento hacia atrás, 2652
desplazamiento hacia el balón, 2656
desplazamiento lateral, 2004, 2655
desplomarse, 1240
destitución de un juez, 1939
desviar, 1095
desvío, 1096
devolución al fondo, 2274

devolución buena, 2330
devolución con una mano, 2673
devolución cruzada, 2270
devolución de puños, 2552
devolución de servicio, 2438
devolución del revés, 2234
devolver, 2414
diente, 1114
diferencia entre dos marcas medianas, 1934
dificultad, 1784
dirección de la carrera, 853
dirección del lanzamiento, 335
directo, 2312
directo a dos manos, 2485
director de carrera, 1006
director de equipo, 1993
director de la competencia, 193
director de la competición, 1474, 1762
director de pista, 1121
director deportivo, 1070
director técnico, 327
directorio técnico, 1473
dirigente, 976
disco, 54
disparo, 2102
disparo de salida nula, 240
disparo del instrumento de lanzar, 52, 254
distancia, 60, 1479, 1514, 1521, 1595
distancia entre las vallas, 61
distancia entre los corredores, 62
distraer al lanzador de tiros libres, 472
doblar, 1750, 1823
doble, 2587
doble defensa, 477
doble dribleo, 473
doble falta, 2285
doble ligamiento, 1480

doble salida, 1223
dobles, 2286
dobles femenino, 2514
dobles masculino, 2356
dobles mixtos, 2359
doblista, 2290
doping, 872
dorsal (número), 939
dos de tres sets, 2488
"¡dos metros!", 1708
dos tiros libres, 758
driblador, 480
driblar con el balón hasta la meta, 2995
driblar con el balón hasta la portería, 2847
driblar; regatear, 478
dribleo con efecto, 696
drive, 2296
drive plano, 2306
"drop", 2589
duración de cada vuelta, 2125
duración de las posturas, 1793
duración del asalto, 1483
duración del ejercicio, 1792
duración del juego efectivo, 2894

efecto, 2457
efecto al balón, 697
efecto hacia atrás, 2241
efecto inglés, 487
efecto lateral, 2443, 2450
eje, 15, 786, 1067, 1167
eje de anchura, 1858
eje de la manivela, 809
eje de rotación, 16
eje de rueda, 1148
eje longitudinal, 1186, 1296, 1893, 1895, 2016
eje "pedalier", 859

eje transversal, 1200
ejecución, 1808
ejecución de un ejercicio, 1810
ejecución del salto, 1233
ejecución perfecta, 1923
ejecutar un salto, 1232
ejercicio a manos libres, 1828
ejercicio con el caballo de arzón, 1811
ejercicio de anillas, 1945
ejercicio de barras asimétricas, 1812
ejercicio en la barra, 1747
ejercicio en la barra fija, 1860
ejercicios de precalentamiento, 769, 2019

ejercicios facultativos, 1913
ejercicios para entrar en forma, 2503
elasticidad del trampolín, 1374
elección de balón, 440
elección de campo, 441, 2835
elección del gorro, 2834
elemento acrobático, 1723
elemento de conexión, 1770
elemento de equilibrio, 1742
elemento de fuerza acrobática, 1726
elemento de vuelo acrobático, 1724
elementos, 1798
elementos de hecht, 1854
elementos de impulso a pino vertical, 1799
elementos de salto de paloma, 1848
elementos de vuelo, 1826
elementos no característicos, 2007
elevaciones, 2009
elevarse, 1890, 1947
eliminar, 2300
eliminar una prueba, 2165
eliminatorias, 107, 1334
eliminatorias; series, 229
emerger, 2188
emparejar, 2353

empatar, 2301
empatar la puntuación, 2478
empate, 340, 865, 1388, 2476
empuje del brazo, 2151
empujón, 2938
empujón de empeines, 1389
empuñadura, 1553
empuñadura de freno, 816
empuñadura del manillar, 914
empuñadura francesa, 1548
empuñadura italiana, 1578
empuñadura ortopédica, 1615
en el proceso de tirar, 378
"¡en guardia!", 1607
en juego, 2328
encargado de la campana, 795
encargado de la competición, 41, 1309
encargado de oficiales, 453
encargado del aparato eléctrico, 1689
encargados de la competición, 180
enceste brusco, 709
enceste forzoso, 483
enceste muy brusco, 694
encordadura de la jabalina, 43
encordar, 2461
encuentro, 192, 966, 1596, 1704, 2354
encuentro de natación, 2193
encuentro de persecución, 999
encuentro internacional, 1867
enderezarse después de la posición agrupada, 1194
enderezarse después de saltar, 1234
enfrentar, 2373
enfrentarse con, 2355
engrasar el cuerpo, 2874
enlace, 1771, 1772
enlace directo, 1786
entorpecer a un contrario, 2879
entrada, 1229

entrada a, 1905
entrada al agua, 2080
entrada corta, 1364
entrada de cabeza, 1267
entrada de pie, 1245
entrada en el viraje, 1082
entrada en la curva, 287
entrada nítida, 1354
entrada pasada, 1295, 1320, 1404
entrada plana, 1252
entrada poco salpicada, 1366
entrada salpicada, 1182
entrada sin salpicar, 1188
entrada vertical, 1398
entrar a, 1936
entrar desplomado (hacia la izquierda; hacia la derecha), 1184
entrar en juego, 2595
entrega por detrás de la espalda, 410
entrenador, 37, 445, 844, 1442, 2062, 2262, 2562
entrenador auxiliar, 384
entrenador de baloncesto, 405
entrenamiento en seco, 2075
entrenar, 2263
enviar el balón después del primer toque, 2590
enviar el balón detrás del bloqueo, 2777
envolvimiento, 1491
equilibrio de defensa, 461
equilibrio y caída hacia atrás, 1161
equipo, 719, 1098, 1386, 1692, 1992, 2470
equipo automático de control secundario de tipo vídeo-tape, 2210
equipo completo, 2860

equipo de cronometraje electrónico, 2077
equipo de polo acuático, 3015
equipo de relevos, 252
equipo de voleibol, 2789
equipo eléctrico, 1485
equipo receptor, 2701
equivocar una parada, 1467
error de juicio, 1580
error forzado, 2310
error no forzado, 2493
escalera de la piscina, 2146
escalera de la torre, 1380
escapada, 24, 821
escaparse, 819
esfuerzo dinámico, 227
esgrima de espada, 1496
esgrima de florete, 1541
esgrima de sable, 1658
esgrimidor, 1510
eslabón de cadena, 954
espada, 1492
espada eléctrica, 1484
espadista, 1495
espalda, 100 m; 200 m, 2036
espaldista, 2034
especialista, 2746
especialista de ataque, 2524
especialista de defensa, 2576
especialista del bloqueo, 2545
especialista del saque, 2731
esperar la señal del árbitro, 3009
espiración, 2046, 2081
esquema táctica, 2764
esquiva, 1482, 1499
esquivar una parada, 1498
estabilidad, 1971
estabilidad en la llegada, 1972
establecerse, 1936

estadística, 702
estadístico, 701
estar en posesión del balón, 2820
estar preparado, 792
estatutos, 1952
estela, 1059
esterilla antideslizante de la plataforma, 1313
estilo , 313, 2186
estilo "Fosbury", 94
estilo marinero, 2973
estilos de natación, 2187
estirarse, 1316
estocada, 1570
estocada (acción), 1591, 1697
estrado del juez de salida, 291
estrategia de bloqueo frente a la cesta, 416
estuche de reparación, 1060
etapa del recorrido, 962
evaluación, 1877, 1960
evaluación para los finales, 1803
evaluar dificultades, 1872
exclusión de un jugador, 2919
exención, 2253
exigencias del ejercicio, 1942
expiración del tiempo de juego, 488
expulsar del agua, 2918
expulsión, 485, 489, 2585, 2597
extenderse, 1979
extensión, 1192, 1318
extremo de abordaje, 1908
extremo final, 1815
fallo en la colocación de las manos, 1843
falso ataque, 1502
falta, 95, 512, 1816, 2302, 2599, 2613

falta de amplitud; continuación; armonía; ritmo, 1884
falta de ataque, 600
falta de ejecución, 1809
fa.lta de interpretación, 1818
falta de línea, 1891
falta de pie, 2308, 2607, 2637
falta de posición, 2695
falta de red, 2660
falta de rotación, 2713
falta de saque, 2435
falta de secuencia en la rotación, 2682
falta de tiempo, 1999
falta descalificante, 471
falta doble, 474
falta en la posición del cuerpo, 1817
falta en la zona de defensa, 387
falta grave, 2900
falta intencionada, 558
falta menor, 2907
falta múltiple, 592
falta personal, 631, 2930
falta técnica, 726
faltas graves, 1887
faltas medianas, 1901
faltas menores, 1966
fallar, 2358
fallar al balón, 2650
fallar al cesto, 588
fallar el saque, 2729
fallo, 73
fallo del equipo eléctrico, 1501
fase aérea, 2, 92
faul de bloqueo, 418
faul fuera, 513
favorito, 1099
Federación Internacional de Atletismo Aficionado (F.I.A.A.), 138

Federación Internacional de Baloncesto Amateur (F.I.B.A.), 562
Federación Internacional de Balonvolea (F.I.V.B.), 2626
Federación Internacional de Esgrima (F.I.E.), 1574
Federación Internacional de Gimnasia (F.I.G.), 1866
Federación Internacional de Natación Amateur (F.I.N.A.), 2086
ficha de tanteo, 2423
figura, 1254
filo, 1449, 1551
filo de la hoja, 1466
fin de un ejercicio, 1769, 1801
final, 887, 1821
final de concursos múltiples, 1729
final de dobles, 2287
final de individuales, 2445
final de tiempo muerto, 2596
final del set, 2594
finales, 81, 1250
finales en los aparatos, 1805
finalista, 1820
finalista de cuartos, 2398
finalista de individuales, 2446
finta, 498, 1504, 2598, 2600
finta de ataque, 1505
finta de cabeza, 543
finta de parada, 1506
finta de remate, 2601
flanconada, 1533
flecha, 1534
florete, 1537
floretista, 1540
flotabilidad, 2050
flotador, 2116
flotadores, 2090
fogueo, 679

fondo de la piscina, 1180, 2039, 2823
forma de empuñar el arma, 1556
forma de lanzamiento, 687
formación, 2610
formación de juego, 2766
formación de salida, 699
formación en W, 2790
formación para el saque, 2730
formación para recibir el saque, 2700
formar el bloqueo, 2609
formar un bloqueo, 2611
foso de agua, 371
fotografía de llegada, 215, 993
franqueamiento, 35
franquear, 32
franquear el listón, 34
franquear una valla, 304
frase de esgrima, 1522
frenaje, 817
frenar, 814
freno, 813
fuera, 2375, 2677
fuera de juego, 1918, 2378, 2914
fuera de la línea, 2379
fuera de la pista, 1603, 1616
fuera de los límites, 2377
fuera del orden, 2678
fuera del terreno de juego, 613
fuerte de la hoja, 1545
fulcro, 1261
funda de rueda, 1147

gafas de natación, 2100
"Gainer" (salto inverso con los pies por delante), 1262
ganador de serie, 918
ganancia del punto, 2797
ganancia del saque, 2798
ganar, 2509
ganar el cambio, 2796

ganar por ausencia del equipo contrario, 772
ganar por un largo, 2217
ganar por un neumático, 1149
ganar por una rueda, 1150
gimnasia artística, 1736
gimnasta, 1835
gimnasta suplente, 1730, 1980
girar, 1924
girar hacia la cesta, 665
giro, 1369
globo, 2340
globo de revés, 2238
globo defensivo, 2281
globo directo, 2315
globo elevado, 2325
globo ofensivo, 2368
gol anotado, 2870
gol concedido, 2864
gol del equipo contrario, 2916
golpe, 2326, 2463
golpe a dos manos, 2487
golpe al rebote, 2321
golpe bajo, 2347
golpe de arresto, 1683, 1685
golpe de arresto al guante, 1682
golpe de arresto con oposición, 1684, 1686
golpe de ataque, 2230
golpe de filo, 1464, 1569
golpe de puños, 2550
golpe de servicio, 2439
golpe de tiempo, 1699
golpe derecho, 1472
golpe doble, 1481
golpe franco concedido, 2859
golpe por debajo, 2672
golpe que obliga, 2311
golpe recto, 1687
golpear, 2327

golpear a un contrario, 2880, 2989
golpear con dos manos, 2781
golpear con potencia, 2697
golpear el balón, 2694
golpear el balón con el puño, 2881, 2990
golpear el balón con los dedos, 2776
golpecito, 2775
goma laca, 1054
gorra, 830
gorro azul, 2821
gorro blanco, 3018
gorro de baño, 2192, 2838
gorro del portero, 2873
gorro desabrochado, 2826
gorro numerado, 2912
gorro rojo, 2949
gracia en el salto, 1263
gran spagat facial, 1830
grueso del pelotón, 177, 957
grupa, 1778
grupo de fugados, 949
grupo de tiradores, 1626
grupo delantero, 168
grupo final de tiradores, 1530
grupos de elementos, 1797
grupos de saltos, 1214
guante de ciclista, 1123
guante de esgrima, 1516
guante del lanzador de martillo, 101
guantes, 1847
guardameta, 2872

hacer piruetas, 1927
hacer rueda libre, 903
hacer un aclarado, una escapada, 423
hacer un agrupado, 1300
hacer un bote, 1969
hacer una carpa, 1299, 1323

heptatlón, 110
heptatloniano, 109
hidrodinámico, 2184
himno nacional, 200
hincha, 494
hoja, 1426
hoja de anotación, 2718
hoja de compilación, 1766
hoja de espada, 1493
hoja de florete, 1538
hoja de poule, 1627
hoja de puntuación, 1361, 1959
hoja de resultados, 1347
hoja de sable, 1656
hoja de salida, 1083
hoja rota, 1431
homologación de un récord, 779, 1012
homologar, 238
hora de presentación, 255
horquilla, 898
hueco, 2560, 2793
huella, 128, 183
hundir al adversario, 2942, 2977, 2991
hundir el balón, 2883, 2997
hundir la tabla, 1337

iguales, 2225, 2283
impermeable de ciclismo, 1011
impulsado hacia abajo con la raqueta, 2293
impulsarse al rebotar el trampolín, 1353
impulsarse sobre el contrario, 2889
impulso, 129, 1339, 1734, 1954
impulso del pie, 1423

impulso hacia afuera con los pies, 2216
inclinación, 130
inclinación de la pista, 348, 791
inclinación en el viraje, 866
incremento al valor de la ejecución, 2011
incuartata, 1573
indicación de salto, 1733, 1822
indicación del infractor, 692
indicador de carretera, 1033
indicador de distancia, 63
indicador de las marcas, 214
individuales femenino, 2515
individuales masculino, 2357
inferioridad numérica, 2902
infracción, 767, 818, 933
infracción contra la regla de pasos, 768

infracción de las reglas, 666
iniciar, 2459
inscribirse, 1344
inscripción, 879, 1345
insignia, 1199
insistencia, 1646
inspiración, 2045, 2112
instalación de lanzamientos, 235, 337
instalación de lanzamientos de disco, 58
instalación de lanzamientos de jabalina, 143
instalación de lanzamientos de martillo, 105
instalación de lanzamientos de peso, 116
instalación de salto de altura, 277
instalaciones para saltos, 1215
integrante del equipo de relevo, 2161
intento, 353

intento de mejora, 3
intento de tiro de campo, 500
intento de tiro libre, 516
intento fallido, 358
intento válido, 315, 360
intercambio, 2406
interceptar el balón, 559
interferencia, 560
interferencia sobre la cesta, 401
interior de la pista, 1117
interrupción del juego, 2628
intervalo de salida, 1085
intervalos entre sets, 2772
invadir, 2388
invasión, 2568
invertir, 1943
invitación, 1577
ir adelante, 162

jabalina, 139
jaula de protección, 333
jefe compilador, 1962
jefe de delegación, 1783, 1851
jefes del terreno, 583
jersey, 938
jersey de pista, 1122
jueces, 144
jueces de lugares, 2144
jueces de saltos, 1216
juego, 2618
juego de equipo, 722
juego de fondo, 2247
juego de piernas, 508, 1544
juego de pivote central, 636
juego de posesión, 645
juego del pivote central, 647
juego en la red, 2361
juego estático, 2978
juego ganado, 2620

juego interrumpido, 2627
juego movido, 2909
juego nulo, 2346
juego ofensivo, 2367
juego; pase, 2733
juego perdido, 2619
juego poco movido, 2984
juego rudo, 3008
juego sucio, 2960
juegos impares, 2366
juez, 1579, 1871, 2157, 2331
juez árbitro, 243, 1342, 1850, 1981
juez árbitro para las carreras, 245
juez árbitro para las pruebas de marcha, 246
juez colegial, 1920
juez de carrera, 349, 847
juez de curva, 855
juez de faltas de pie, 2309
juez de gol, 2865
juez de las pruebas de pista, 244
juez de las vueltas, 943
juez de límites, 1892
juez de línea, 2339, 2638
juez de llamada de salida, 241
juez de llegada, 83, 891, 2089
juez de marcha, 367
juez de pista, 78
juez de red, 2362
juez de salida, 289, 1084, 2175
juez de silla, 2259
juez de toques al suelo, 1535
juez de virajes, 2113, 2207
juez de vuelta, 797, 1136
juez en jefe por cronometraje eléctrico, 2057
jugada, 2385
jugada de tres puntos, 732
jugada del puesto en juego, 614
jugador, 2387, 2691

jugador base, 641
jugador de baloncesto, 407
jugador de campo, 2851
jugador de fondo, 2233
jugador de individuales, 2448
jugador de la línea delantera, 2617
jugador de la línea trasera, 2531
jugador de pivote, 646
jugador de polo acuático, 3012
jugador de red, 2363
jugador de voleibol, 2788
jugador descalificado, 470
jugador designado para la reanudación, 2932
jugador desmarcado, 765
jugador en falta, 2913
jugador expulsado, 2850
jugador lesionado, 2886
jugador marcado, 536
jugador que saca, 2752
jugador saliente, 2679
jugador suplente, 2992
jugador sustituto, 2756
jugador universal, 2769
jugador víctima de una falta, 2855
jugadores de fondo, 2529
jugar al polo acuático, 2931
jugar al tenis, 2386
juntar (las piernas), 1869
jurado, 1919
jurado de apelación , 150, 940, 1288, 1583, 1881
jurado de la competición, 42, 1582
jurado de saltos, 1217

kilómetro contra reloj, 941

labor de actuar como juez, 1878
lado, 539
lado del revés, 2239

lado flojo, 770
lado fuerte, 708
lado opuesto, 2079
lámpara testigo, 1664
lanzador, 330, 685
lanzador de disco, 56, 233
lanzador de jabalina, 141
lanzador de martillo, 103
lanzador de peso, 275
lanzamiento, 331
lanzamiento al aire, 563
lanzamiento de disco, 57
lanzamiento de jabalina, 142
lanzamiento de la jabalina, 140
lanzamiento de martillo, 104
lanzamiento de peso, 232, 276
lanzamiento del disco, 55
lanzamiento del martillo, 102
lanzamiento del peso, 234, 274
lanzamiento en firme, 683
lanzamiento seguido, 2970
lanzar, 2967, 2998
lanzar a la portería, 2968
lanzar apoyándose en la pared de la piscina, 2940
lanzar; lanzamiento, 329
lanzar un tiro franco, 2996
largo, 2129
leotardo, 1889
lesión, 934
levantar el balón, 2636, 2895
levantar globos, 2341, 2899
libramiento; acción de librar la hoja, 1469
libre; libres, 2095
libres, 100 m; 400 m; 800 m; 1500 m, 2098
libreta de los árbitros, 2114
licencia, 952
líder, 2334

liftado, 2482
ligamento, 1425, 1490, 1587
ligar, 1489
límite de la piscina, 2825
límite de la zona de relevo, 69
límites, 2250
límites del sector, 237
línea, 2338
línea central, 431, 727, 2556, 2876
línea curva de partida, 48
línea de advertencia, 1714
línea de agrupamiento, 12
línea de ataque, 2522
línea de base, 399
línea de contrameta, 787
línea de división de servicio, 2258
línea de dobles, 2288
línea de final de pista, 1642
línea de fondo, 486, 2246, 2593
línea de gol, 2867
línea de los sprinters, 1072
línea de los 4 metros, 2857
línea de llegada, 84
línea de medición, 805
línea de medio campo, 2830
línea de meta de la defensa, 2921
línea de salida, 293, 1086
línea de saque, 2436
línea de "stayers", 1089
línea de tiro libre, 518
línea de toque, 690
línea de 2 metros, 3005
línea de 200 metros, 1138
línea lateral, 2743, 2972
línea mediana, 2257
líneas, 1588
líneas de demarcación, 420
líneas de juego, 2549
líneas laterales para dobles, 2291
líneas laterales para sencillos, 2449

lista de los jugadores inscriptos, 724
lista de salida, 286
lista de saltos escogidos, 1218, 1294
listón, 18, 115
"¡listos!", 272, 1413
local de entrenamiento, 2003
"locomotoras", 955
locutor, 2025
longitud de la hoja, 1585
longitud de la pista, 1586
longitud de la red, 2662
luz amarilla, 1721
luz blanca, 1717
luz roja, 1643, 1937
luz verde, 1552, 1831

llamada a los corredores, 829
llamada a los participantes, 27
llamada a los tiradores, 1435
llamada errónea, 2516
llanta, 1027
llave de pipa, 811
llave fija, 979
llave inglesa, 776
llegada, 82, 889, 2087
llegada a la recta final, 288
llegada al suelo, 1787, 1885
llegada cerrada, 2061
llegada en pelotón, 826
llegada reñida, 36, 341, 843
llevar, 947
llevar el balón, 2554, 2828
llevar la pelota, 426
llevar una vuelta de ventaja, 163
llevar x puntos de ventaja, 164
llevar x segundos de ventaja, 165

madera de contención, 306
maestro de armas, 1520

magnetofón, 1991
magnetófono para cassette, 1754
maillot de pista, 1130
mala conducta, 2810, 2908
mallas de la red, 2663
manejar el balón, 542
manejo del balón, 393, 497, 2535
manga, 1677
mango de la raqueta, 2403
manillar, 912
maniquí, 1712
mantener la cadencia, 179
mantener la ventaja, 178
mantenerse a flote, 3003
mantenerse inmóvil (posición de salida), 2037
máquina, 956
máquina burbujadora, 1181
maratón, 181
marca blanca, 3020
marca más alta concedida, 1270
marcador, 669, 1663, 2163
marcador de calle, 156
marcador de clavados, 1209, 1275
marcador de dos minutos, 357
marcador electrónico, 1794
marcador electrónico de cronometraje y clasificación, 2030
marcador oficial, 605
marcador rojo, 2951
marcaje del tablero, 389
marcaje hombre a hombre, 585
marcaje hombre a hombre severo, 738
marcaje individual, 2903
marcar, 2421
marcar al adversario, 2833
marcar al contrario, 2904
marcar por detrás, 535
marcar un gol, 2962

marcas, 30
marco de la raqueta, 2402
marcha, 366, 1255
marcha atrás, 789
marcha con fondo, 1679
marcha en pista, 350
marcha en ruta, 258
marchar, 755
marchar durante el equilibrio (apoyo invertido), 1757
mariposa, 2051, 2091
mariposa, 100 m; 200 m, 2055
mariposista, 2054
martillo, 100, 2747
martingala, 1593
match point, 2352
materialidad del tocado, 1594
mecánico, 964, 965
medalla (presea de oro; plata; bronce), 191
media volea, 2323
media vuelta, 910
medias de esgrima, 1525
medición de las porterías, 2905
medición de los saltos y de los lanzamientos, 188
medida de la pista, 963
medidas contra el uso de las drogas, 7
medidas del campo, 452
medidor oficial, 203
medio balanceo, 2621
medio centro, 2961
mérito de originalidad, 1916
mérito excepcional, 1935
mesa de los anotadores, 586
mesa de marcador, 2721
mesa del anotador, 671
meta, 892
meter el balón en el hueco, 2778

métrica, 190
mitad del juego decisivo, 2622
modificar una decisión, 2803, 2831
mojón kilométrico, 970
molestar al adversario, 802
molestar la visión del contrario con las manos, 491
molinete, 230
movimiento de piernas estilo delfin, 2073
multa, 888
música instrumental, 1914

nadador, 2191
nadador de competición. 2064
nadador de estilo libre, 2097
nadador de estilos, 2135
nadador de larga distancia, 2130
nadador de media distancia, 2139
nadador de relevos, 2159
nadador de velocidad , 2172
nadar, 2189
natación de competición, 2065
natación de estilos, 2136
natación de larga distancia, 2131
natación de media distancia, 2140
natación de velocidad, 2173
neumático de carretera, 1035
neumático de entrenamiento, 1132
neumático de pista, 1129
neutral, 2944
nivel del agua, 1405, 2213
nivelador de arena, 267
"¡no hay tocado!", 1599
no presentado, 2608
nombre del salto, 1312
normas del salto de altura, 117
numeración de los jugadores, 637
número de cuadro, 902

número de la calle, 2121
número del salto, 1210
número dorsal, 201

observación de otro equipo, 673
obstaculizar a un corredor, 127
obstáculos, 298
obstrucción, 803
octava, 1601
ocupar los carriles, 503
ofensiva, 1604
oficial auxiliar, 714, 2023
oficiales, 607
oficiales auxiliares, 1984
oficiales de competición, 1007
oficiales de la mesa de puntuación, 1362
oficiales de la reunión, 205
oficiales del encuentro, 194
oficiales técnicos, 1996
oficina de cálculos, 1765
operador del anemómetro, 374
operador del marcador de 30 segundos, 729
oposición, 1613
orden de actuación, 1764
orden de llegada, 980
orden de paso a la ejecución, 1915
orden de recibir, 2411
orden de salida, 1087
orden de salida de los participantes, 1378
orden de saque, 2437
organización de la recepción, 2759
originalidad del ejercicio, 1917

palanca de cambio, 906
palma de la mano, 2922
palmear, 747
palmear la pelota, 718

palomilla, 1004
pantalón corto, 1009
pantalón de esgrima, 1512
pantalla, 674, 2722
pantalla; bloqueo, 632
pantalla cerca del balón, 678
pantalla doble, 476
pantalla fija, 700
pantalla interior, 557
pantalla no reglamentaria, 554
papel de lija, 1800
parada, 1618, 1976
parada compuesta, 1444
parada de cesión, 1436
parada de manos al frente, 1164
parada de manos con una vuelta; con dos vueltas, 1165
parada de manos; equilibrio, 1160
parada de manos inverso, 1162
parada de oposición, 1427, 1614
parada diagonal, 1470
parada directa, 1471
parada limpia, 1806
parada pronunciada, 1781
parada semicircular, 1669
parada simple, 1672
parado, 1078, 1375, 1617
paralela a la línea, 2292
paralelas, 1921
paralelas asimétricas, 2008
parar a un corredor, 1091
parar el cronómetro, 705, 2986
parar el juego, 2987
parar un tiro, 2985
pared, 2212
pared de llegadas, 2088
pared lateral, 2168
pareja adversaria, 2374
pareja vencedora, 2512
paro de la carrera, 1092

parón, 704
parte A, 1722
parte B, 1740
parte C, 1753
parte C adicional, 1727
parte de balanceo, 1986
parte de fuerza, 1978
parte débil de la hoja, 1536
parte del ejercicio, 1922
parte honda de la piscina, 2842
parte llana, 2966
partes de valor, 2010
partido, 2319, 2351, 2642
partido de baloncesto, 406
partido de consolación, 2266
partido de dobles, 2289
partido de individuales, 2447
partido empatado, 2477
partido inicial, 2371
partido reñido, 2261, 2324
pasa y va, 531
pasador, 625, 2736
pasante, 1429
pasar, 211, 2685
pasar el balón, 496, 624, 2924
pasar el balón al jugador más avanzado, 544
pasar el balón sobre la línea de meta, 2811
pasar por fuera, 97
pase, 623, 1476, 2684, 2923
pase a través de la cancha, 454
pase adelantado, 571
pase adelante, 2612
pase al nivel del pecho, 439
pase alto, 2624
pase bombeado, 576, 2898
pase ciego, 413
pase con dos manos, 761
pase con una mano, 609

pase corto, 2738
pase de ataque, 2737
pase de dos manos, 2783
pase de gancho, 548
pase de puños, 2551
pase de rebote, 419
pase de rebote con dos manos, 759
pase de una mano, 2674
pase del testigo, 20
pase directo, 467
pase en suspensión, 2629
pase hacia atrás, 2533
pase por encima de la cabeza, 619
pase veloz, 2602
pasillo de tiro libre, 517
pasillo interior, 136
pasillo para la cámara de televisión, 2197
paso, 302
paso cruzado, 1776
paso cruzado; tijera, 45
paso chassé, 1758
passata di sotto, 1619
passing-shot, 2382
patada, 2115
patada de braza, 2041
patada de mariposa, 2052
patente, 1752
pechista, 2042
pecho, 100 m; 200 m, 2044
pedal, 988
pedalear, 778, 989, 1066, 1137
pedalear de pie, 1077
pedalear parado, 922, 990

pedalista rezagado, 876
pedir una sustitución, 659
pegamento para neumático, 1135
pegarse a la rueda, 895
pegarse al pelotón, 1057
pelota, 2243
pelota lenta, 2453
pelotón , 25, 99, 825
pelotón compacto, 848
penal, 2925
penalización, 991, 2383
penalty, 627
penetración, 2688
penetrador, 2532
penetrar la defensa, 628
pentatlón, 213
perdedor, 2343
perder, 2342
perder el balón, 578
perder el cambio, 2639
perder tiempo adrede, 2890, 3010
pérdida de balón (penalty), 579
pérdida de terreno, 1590
pérdida del saque, 2640
período de juego, 629
período de 7 minutos, 2965
permutación, 715, 2757
perno, 807
persecución, 839, 998
persecución individual, 924
persecución por equipos, 1100
pértiga; garrocha, 221
peso; bala, 273
peso de control, 1695
peso del balón, 3016
peto, 1424
pianista, 1925
piano, 1926
picar la pértiga, 218

pico del sillín, 987
pie adelantado, 523
pie adelante, 1584
pie atrás, 1706
pie de apoyo, 635
pie de impulso, 322
pie libre, 514, 595
pie posterior, 351
pierna de apoyo, 1331
pierna de ataque, 96, 169, 317
pierna de impulso, 323, 716
pierna libre 1273
pies en punta, 1329
pinchazo, 893, 997
pino vertical; parada de manos, 1266, 1849
piñón, 1073
pirámide de marcaje de las distancias, 64
pisar la línea de tiros libres, 751
pisar la raya, 209
piscina, 2145, 2195
piscina al aire libre, 2143
piscina cubierta, 2111
piscina de competición, 2063
piscina de entrenamiento, 2204
piscina para carreras, 2085
piscina para saltos, 1222
pista, 345, 451, 1115
pista al aire libre, 981
pista cubierta, 857, 930
pista de esgrima, 1526, 1622
pista de impulso, 265
pista de obstáculos de 3000 m, 301
pista metálica, 1597
pistola de juez de salida, 1088
pistola de salida, 294, 2179
pito, 3017
pivote, 634

pivote alto, 546
pivote bajo, 580
pivote doble, 475
pizarra, 932
placas de toque, 2203
plan de juegos de ataque, 601
plancha, 2586
plancha de muelles, 1748
plancha hacia adelante, 2615
plancha lateral, 2739
plancha (suspensión horizontal), 1928
plano, 1324
plano horizontal, 1272
plano vertical, 1399
plaqueta del marcador, 582
plastilina, 219
plataforma, 1325
plataforma alta (de 10 metros), 1269
plataforma de salida, 2176, 2180
plato, 834
plazo de la exclusión, 2929
plazo de reclamación, 1105
plazo para el tiro libre, 740
plazo para sustitución, 742
podio, 1929
podio de palmarés, 364
pomo, 1625
poner el balón en juego, 2945
poner gran desarrollo, 1000
ponerse en cuclillas , 1777
porcentaje de tiros de campo, 501
porcentaje de tiros libres acertados, 520
portador, 131
portarrecipiente, 1143
porte correcto, 1774
posesión, 644
posesión de la pelota, 397
posición, 1330, 2391

posición de ataque, 604
posición de defensa, 2575
posición de defensa reglamentaria, 574
posición de esgrima, 1523
posición de espera, 2409
posición de guardia, 1555, 1606
posición de la mano, 1560
posición de las piernas, 1291
posición de los brazos, 1159
posición de los jugadores, 2714
posición de recepción, 2412
posición de salida, 295, 1379, 1974, 2181
posición defensiva, 463
posición defensiva frente a la cesta, 422
posición en cruz, 1201
posición en cuclillas, 1970
posición en firmes, 1973
posición fundamental, 1421, 1550, 1745
posición incorrecta del cuerpo, 1861
posición inicial, 2753, 2982
posición libre, 1256
posición mantenida, 1856
posición para la volea, 2502
posición para pasar la valla, 319
posición seminvertida, 1841
posiciones combinadas, 1191
poste, 403
poste de la red, 2364, 2664
poste de portería, 2869
poste de salto, 226, 359
postes de llegada, 85
postes de salto de pértiga, 225
potro, 2015
potro con arzón, 1930
práctica, 2394

practicar, 2395
precalentamiento, 368, 2791
precalentamiento de los 30 segundos, 1998
preparación de ataque, 1629
preparar la jugada, 2734
presa, 1832, 1846
presentación, 1276
presidente de un match, 1630
presidente del comité de gimnasia, 1837
presidente del jurado, 1631, 1932
presión, 552, 650, 1632
presión al salir del trampolín, 1225
presión hacia la cesta, 482
presionar a un contrario, 651
primer árbitro, 2603
primer clasificado, 2481
primer intento, 88
primer relevista, 2126
primer secretario, 1251
primer servicio, 2305
primer tiempo, 505, 2852
primera, 1633
primera fase de la trayectoria, 67
primera intención, 1532
prioridad, 1634, 1652
profundidad del agua, 1206
profundidad mínima del agua, 2906
programa, 268, 2418
programa de entrenamiento, 2205
programa de la competencia, 1231
programa de la competición, 1196
programado, 2419
prolongación, 621
promedio de puntos, 642
promedio entre dos notas intermedias, 1739
pronación, 1636
prórroga, 490, 2920

protestar, 2396
prueba, 14, 71, 851, 880, 1500
prueba al florete, 1539
prueba combinada, 38
prueba contra reloj, 1106
prueba de espada, 1494
prueba de plataforma—hombres, 1310
prueba de plataforma—mujeres, 1407
prueba de sable, 1657
prueba en carretera por equipos, 1102
prueba femenina de trampolín, 1408
prueba individual en carretera, 927
prueba individual sobre carretera, 926
prueba individual sobre pista, 929
prueba masculina de trampolín, 1311
prueba por equipos en carretera, 1034
prueba sobre pista por equipos, 1128
pruebas de lanzamientos, 336
pruebas de pista, 77
pruebas de saltos, 148
pruebas en carretera, 257
pruebas en pista, 347
pruebas individuales de mujeres, 375
pruebas individuales hombres, 195, 2137
pruebas individuales mujeres, 2218
pruebas por equipos femeninos, 2219
pruebas por equipos hombres, 196
pruebas por equipos masculinos, 2138
pruebas por equipos mujeres, 376
puesta en guardia, 1638
puesta en juego, 653, 735
puesto de alimentos, 885
puesto de control, 852
puesto de refresco, 247
puestos de alimentos, 76
puestos de refresco, 247
puño, 1561
punta, 1701
punta de la hoja, 1624

punta eléctrica de arresto, **1486**
puntear, 166
puntero, 167, 948
puntero (a), 1852
punto, 2389
punto de apoyo graduable, 1152
punto de contacto, 2390
punto de extensión, 1195
punto de impulso, 1332
punto de rompimiento, 2252
punto decisivo, 2511
puntos, 643
puntos eliminados, 1304
puntos válidos, 1305
puntuación, 1283, 1359, 1958, 2420, 2717
puntuación abierta, 1912
puntuación más baja dada, 1297

quedarse atrás, 875
quinta, 1640
quinta falta, 502
quitar el neumático, 1040

radio, 1069
raqueta, 2400
raya de posición de guardia, 1605
raya de salida, 324
reacción del trampolín, 1387
realización técnica, 1995
realizar un bloqueo, 675
reanudación, 1647
reanudación del juego, 739
reanudación del juego por el árbitro, 2955
reanudación del partido después de un gol, 2954
reanudarse el juego, 2956
rebosadero de la piscina, 2849
rebosaderos, 2103

rebotar, 2946
rebotar en el poste, 2947
rebote, 654
rebote defensivo, 462
rebote ofensivo, 603
rebote seco, 1227
recepción del balón, 2948
receptor, 2410
receptor del testigo, 208
recibo, 2702
reclamación, 231, 995, 1338, 1933, 2148
recobro del brazo, 2027
recogepelotas, 2244, 2541
récord, 1013
récord homologado, 204
recorrer la distancia, 2066
recorrido, 856
recta contraria, 17
recta de la pista, 308
recta de llegada, 86, 921
recuperación con dos manos, 2782
recuperación del balón, 2523
recuperación del balón; salvar, 2582
recuperación difícil, 2580
recuperador, 2581
recuperar el balón, 656
recuperar el saque, 2591, 2795
rechazo, 2260
red, 594, 2360, 2658, 2868
redoble, 1644
regate antirreglamentario, 553
regate con dos manos, 479
regate de pronación, 660
regate por detrás de la espalda, 409
regateo, 481
registrador, 2156
regla de los tres segundos, 734
regla de los 10 segundos, 728
regla de los 30 segundos, 730

regla de los 5 segundos, 506
regla de tres por dos, 731
regla de ventaja, 2802
regla del juego, 2934
reglamentario, 1016
reglamento, 1017, 1042
reglamento de polo acuático, 3014
reglamento técnico, 1997
reglamentos, 1938
reglas de puntuación, 1303
regulación de los bloques de salida, 4
regulación del aparato, 1728
rehusar saltar, 1343
rejilla de la careta, 1720
relegación, 1019
relevista de cierre, 2024
relevo, 248, 1018
relevo combinado, 400 m, 2093
relevo de estilos individual; relevo combinado, 2134
relevo libre, 2096
relevo libre, 400 m; 800 m, 2092
relevos, 2158
reloj de exclusión, 2926
relojes digitales para controlar el ritmo del paso, 2070
rematador, 2750
rematar, 2455, 2630, 2748
remate, 2454
remate bloqueado, 2546
remate contra el bloqueo para hacer salir el balón, 2799
remate contra el bloqueo para sacar el balón, 2749
remate rotativo, 2716
reparaciones en el camino, 1038
repertorio de los saltos, 1220
repesca, 1020
repetición de un elemento, 1940

repetición del ataque, 1648
repetición del ejercicio, 1941
requisitos especiales del aparato, 1967
resbalamiento, 1549
resina, 1949
resistencia de la valla, 344
resistencia del agua, 2214
respiración a doble brazada, 2074
respiración bilateral, 2038
respiración cada cuatro brazadas, 2094
respiración unilateral, 2209
responsables de la piscina, 2147
respuesta, 1653
respuesta a tiempo perdido, 1432
respuesta compuesta, 1445
respuesta simple, 1673
resultado, 1022
resultado final, 1248
resultado final del juego, 504
resultados, 2162
resultados oficiales de la competición, 1315
resultados preliminares, 1336
retardar intencionadamente el juego, 2579
retener al adversario, 2936
retener al contrario, 2882
retirada de cuerpo, 1650
retirada de pie, 1641
retirado de cuerpo, 1680
retirarse de, 2413
retirarse de la competición, 2021
reventar, 304, 827, 1144
revés, 2242
revés a dos manos, 2486
revés al rebote, 2237
revés cruzado, 2269
riesgo, 1948

ritmo, 1944
ritmo de respiración, 2047, 2155
ritmo de zancada, 311
ritmo irregular, 2049
rodando, 1041
rodillera, 2631
romper, 1649, 2251
romper el impulso, 1175
romper el pelotón, 1068
ronda inicial, 2304
rotación, 2712
rotación de equipos, 1951
rotación de pruebas, 1950
rotación hacia la derecha, 2561
rotura del cuadro, 901
rueda, 1145
rueda delantera, 904
rueda repuesto, 1063
rueda trasera, 788

sable, 1655
sablista, 1660
sacador, 2726
sacar, 2429, 2724
sala de esgrima, 1517
salida, 1080, 1377, 1384, 2174
salida agachada, 46
salida brusca, 1204
salida con compensación, 283
salida con impulso, 1356, 2152
salida correcta, 2128
salida de agarre, 2101
salida de espalda, 2033
salida de la curva, 68, 70
salida de pie, 284
salida desde la línea de gol, 2993
salida en grupo, 961
salida falsa, 75, 883, 2082
salida hacia adelante, 1260

salida hacia atrás, 1172
salida individual, 928
salida inversa, 1352
salida lanzada, 894
salida levantado, 1076
salida sin impulso, 1376
salir del agua, 1236, 2078, 2891
salir del terreno, 2632
salpicadura, 1370
salpicar el agua, 2979
saltadero, 149
saltadero de pértiga, 224
saltadero de triple salto, 356
saltadero para el salto de longitud, 174
saltador, 147, 567, 1211
saltador de altura, 112
saltador de longitud, 175
saltador de palanca, 1327
saltador de pértiga, 223
saltador de trampolín, 1372
saltador de triple salto, 355
saltar, 1208, 1880
saltar con las rodillas dobladas, 1289
saltar empinado, 1287
saltar una altura de ..., 33
salto, 145, 1286, 1581. 1956
salto adentro, 1203, 1279
salto adentro con medio o con un giro, 1280
salto al frente con medio giro; con un giro, 1257
salto atrás, 1168, 1418
salto atrás con bola, 1170
salto atrás con medio giro, 1169
salto con impulso, 1355
salto con pértiga, 222
salto de altura, 111
salto de la plataforma, 1392

salto de longitud, 173
salto de palanca, 1328
salto de precalentamiento, 1403
salto de salida, 2177
salto de trampolín, 1373
salto en el círculo, 430
salto en equilibrio, 1163
salto "Fosbury", 93
salto fracasado, 1242
salto hacia adelante, 1546
salto hacia atrás, 1174
salto inverso, 1348
salto inverso con medio giro; con un giro, 1349
salto mortal al vuelo, 1253
salto mortal; vuelta, 1367
saltos con tirabuzones; con giros, 1397
saltos de ensayo, 1333
saltos libres con límite, 1400
saltos libres sin límite, 1401
saltos obligatorios; obligatorios, 1197
saltos optativos; optativos, 1319
saludo, 1661
salvar un clavado con las piernas recogidas y los pies arqueados, 1358
salvar un salto, 1357
sanción, 1048
saque, 2428, 2725
saque a la red, 2665
saque cortado, 2744
saque de abajo, 2785
saque de banda, 691
saque de espaldas, 2681
saque de esquina, 2839
saque de tenis, 2770
saque del portero, 2871
saque en potencia, 2698
saque flotante, 2605
saque gancho, 2625

saque lateral, 2742
saque reglamentario, 2635
saque repetido, 2337
saque rotativo, 2715
secretario, 1050, 2964
secretario de la reunión, 269
secretario del jurado, 242
secretario del marcador, 1341
secretarios, 1219
sector, 270
sector de lanzamiento, 339
seguidor autorizado, 785
seguir el balón, 2606
segunda, 1667
segunda intención, 1665
segundo árbitro, 2723
segundo impulso, 1202
segundo secretario, 1363
segundo tiempo, 680, 2963
semicírculo, 681
semifinales, 2427
semifinalista, 2426
semifinta, 1557
semivuelta, 1558
señal acústica, 2000
señal de partida, 2983
señal de salida, 296
señal para parar el juego, 2975
señalar con el banderín, 2976
señalar el comienzo del juego, 2974
señales de salida falsa, 2083
señales del árbitro, 608
señales electrónicas, 1795
señales manuales, 1898
sencillos, 2444
sensibilidad de la placa de toque, 2167
sentido, 53
separarse de un adversario por empujón, 2939

séptima, 1670
serie, 1052
serie eliminatoria; buena, 917
series, 259, 2108
series acrobáticas, 1725
series de gimnasia, 1839
series de saltos (hombres), 2012
series de saltos (mujeres), 2013
series interrumpidas, 1868
servicio, 2431
servicio cortado, 2452
servicio fuerte, 2255
servicio liftado, 2483
servicio plano, 2307
servicio y volea, 2432
servidor, 2430
sesión, 1963
sesión de estrategia, 432
set, 2440
set decisivo, 2475, 2571
set-point, 2441
sets consecutivos, 2460
sexta, 1676
silbato, 771
silla, 1955
silla del árbitro, 2490, 2705
sillín, 1044
simular un arranque, 886
sin clasificar, 2495
sistema, 2758
sistema de ataque, 2670
sistema de defensa, 2577
sistema de evaluación, 1802, 1879
sistema de propulsión, 812, 835
sistema de puntuación, 1961
sitio de los suplentes, 2690
sitio para entrenadores, 2689
sobre la línea, 2369
sobre la red, 2380
sobrecarga, 620

sobreestimar, 1321
sobrepaso, 303
solicitud de cambio de jugadores, 2707
solicitud de tiempo muerto, 745, 2774
soltar el balón, 2848
soporte para el balón, 2818
sortear, 2294
sorteo, 611, 873, 2295, 2563, 2845
sorteo de calles, 66
sorteo de finales, 1789
sorteo de jueces, 1790
sorteo de las cestas, 750
sorteo de participantes, 1224
sorteo de rotaciones, 1791
sorteo del saque, 2559
sostener el balón con la palma de la mano, 2884
spagat, 1968
spagat lateral, 1965
spagat transversal, 1888
sprint, 828, 1071
sprint final, 80
subcampeón, 2416
"sueco", 2935
"sueco" (con los dedos), 3000
suelo, 1827
sujetar al adversario, 547
sujetar el instrumento, 119
superficie, 2464
superficie de juego, 639, 2693
superficie del agua, 1383, 2215
superficie no válida, 1576, 1711
superficie sintética, 2469
superioridad numérica, 2901
supervisor de gimnasia, 1840
supinación, 1690
suplente, 710
suspender, 1093
suspendido, 2392, 2465

suspensión, 1094
sustituir, 2755

tabla de faltas, 1989
tabla de fibra de cristal, 1246
tabla de impulso, 321
tabla flotadora para los pies, 2150
tablero de avisos, 974
tablero de meta, 388
tablero de resultados, 1662
tablero indicador, 2719
tablero ofensivo, 599
tablero posterior, 2231
tablón de plastilina, 220
taco, 1055
taco de salida, 90, 292
tacos, 279
táctica, 2760
táctica de bloqueo, 2548
táctica de saque, 2732
táctica de segunda intención, 1666
táctica defensiva, 2578
táctica ofensiva, 2671
táctico, 2761
tallo del sillín, 1045
tanteador, 1360
tanteo, 1302
tanteo empatado, 736
tanteo final, 1819
tanto; portería, 2863
tarima para ejercicios a manos libres,
    1829
tarjeta amarilla, 2800
tarjeta roja, 2703
tarjetas del árbitro, 2704
técnica, 328
técnica de natación, 2196
técnica de respiración, 2048
técnica de salida, 2182

técnica de salto, 1221
técnica de viraje, 2208
técnica del manejo del balón, 2817
temperatura del agua, 1406, 2200
tensión del cordaje, 2474
tentativa de pararse, 1079
tercera, 1693
testigo, 19, 249
tie-breaker, 2479
tiempo, 2928
tiempo concedido por lesiones, 741
tiempo corrido, 587
tiempo de clasificación, 2154
tiempo (de esgrima), 1527
tiempo de juego, 640
tiempo de juego efectivo, 2801
tiempo de reacción, 239
tiempo desfavorable, 1153
tiempo electrónico, 2076
tiempo intermedio, 137
tiempo muerto, 706, 743, 2773
tiempo muerto cargado, 438
tiempo oficial, 2141
tiempos parciales, 2171
tierra de nadie, 2365
tija de la horquilla, 913
tija del sillín, 1050
tirabuzón; giro, 1396
tirador, 1513
tirador controlado, 444
tirador relámpago, 707
tirar, 1508
tirar el balón, 684
tirar la pelota en la cesta, 748
tirarse a fondo, 1592
tiro, 688, 2442
tiro a media vuelta con salto, 756
tiro al fondo, 2275
tiro angulado, 2229

tiro con la cabeza; cabecear, 2877
tiro con las dos manos, 762
tiro con una mano, 398, 610, 2915
tiro cruzado, 2271
tiro de campo acertado, 499
tiro de cerca, 443
tiro de gancho, 549
tiro de gancho en suspensión, 565
tiro de penal, 2927
tiro de presión, 2941
tiro de revés, 2809
tiro de volea, 2969
tiro débil, 2505
tiro derecho, 2988
tiro en carrera, 569
tiro en suspensión, 566
tiro fallado, 590
tiro forzado, 509
tiro forzado en carrera, 649
tiro fuera, 2507
tiro imparable, 2494
tiro libre, 515, 2858
tiro libre acertado, 519
tiro libre convertido, 713
tiro libre fallado, 589
tiro por abajo, 764
tiro por encima de la cabeza con dos
    manos, 760
tiro violento, 2393
tiros libres múltiples, 593
titular, 1111
tocado, 1562, 1702
"¡tocado a la derecha!", 1565
"¡tocado a la izquierda!", 1564
tocado concedido, 1566
tocado de penalización, 1621
tocado no válido, 1567, 1575, 1600,
    1602
tocado recibido, 1568

tocado válido, 1710
tocar, 1563, 1688, 1703
tocar el aparato, 2002
tocar el balón, 3001
tocar el balón con las dos manos al
    mismo tiempo, 3002
tocar el fondo del foso de saltos, 1390
tocar el trampolín, 1271
tocar la red, 2484
toma, 98
toma de hierro, 1635, 1691
toma de impulso y acercamiento al
    listón, 320
toma de muestras, 1047
tomar impulso, 261
tomar la curva muy cerrada, 123
tomar la posición de salida, 1166
topómetro, 343
toque, 2202
toque de balón, 2564
torneo abierto, 2370
tornillo, 1049
torno de mano de la red, 2667
torre (de saltos), 1391
trabajo bajo el agua, 3006
tracción del brazo, 2149
traje de baño, 2190, 2819
traje de baño (hombres), 1177
traje de baño (mujeres), 1178
traje de esgrima, 1515, 1528
trampolín, 1179, 1371
trampolín "duraflex", 1228
trampolín duro, 1381
trampolín lento, 1365
trampolín "maxiflex", 1307
trampolín "maxiflex B", 1306
trampolín rápido, 1244
travesaño, 2841
trayectoria, 1393

trayectoria de un instrumento, 352
trayectoria del balón, 382, 754
trayectoria del jugador, 626
trazar el recorrido, 959
tribuna de los jueces, 202
tribuna del árbitro, 2953
triple salto, 354
triunfo, 2508
tubo, 1133
tubular, 1134
tuerca, 975

última vuelta, 79, 159
últimas series de clavados, 1247
último intento, 160
último punto decisivo del juego, 2735
último punto del juego, 2644
último viraje, 120
un-dos, 1610
un-dos-tres, 1611
"¡un metro!", 1609
una y media vueltas adentro con un giro; con dos giros, 1282
una y media vueltas atrás; dos vueltas atrás; dos y media vueltas atrás, 1173
uniforme, 2786
Unión Ciclista Internacional (U.C.I.), 937
uso no reglamentario de los brazos, 555

validez de un gol, 3007
valor de los saltos, 2014

valorización de los suplentes, 412
válvula, 1139
valla, 124
valla de la carrera de obstáculos, 300
valla del foso de agua, 372
vara de medir, 189, 2645
vehículo acompañante, 896
vehículo de comisarios, 846, 978
vehículo de servicio, 1053
vehículo radio, 1010
vehículo seguidor, 897
velocidad, 985, 1064, 2456
velocidades, 905
velocista, 281
velocista en el remate, 312
velódromo, 800, 861
vencedor, 2510
vencer inesperadamente, 2497
ventaja, 161, 380, 2223, 2332
ventaja al receptor, 2222
ventaja al saque, 2221
ventaja numérica, 615
verificación, 361
verificación de los aparatos, 1864
vértice, 113
vértice de la trayectoria de la tirada, 114
vestuario de precalentamiento, 2020
victoria, 2499
victoria inesperada, 2496
viento de espalda, 1097
viento en contra, 916
viento lateral, 1056
violación flagrante, 507

viraje, 796, 2206
viraje de braza, 2043
viraje de espalda, 2035
viraje de voltereta, 2170
viraje en estilos individual, 2109
virtuosidad, 2017
viscosidad, 2211
volante, 1465
volea, 2500
volea angulada, 2228
volea baja, 2348
volea cruzada, 2272
volea de revés, 2240
volea directa, 2316
volear, 2501
voleo, 2467
volver a correr, 1021
volver al juego, 2957
votación de los jueces, 1873
vuelo, 39, 1292, 1825
vuelo hacia adelante, 2318
vuelta, 942, 1707, 2123
vuelta a la pista, 945
vuelta adentro; una y media, dos, dos y media vueltas adentro, 1281
vuelta al frente con medio giro; con un giro; con dos giros, 1258
vuelta al frente; una vuelta al frente; una y media, dos, dos y media vueltas al frente, 1259
vuelta atrás con medio giro; con un giro; con uno y medio giros; con dos giros; con dos y medio giros, 1171

vuelta de impulso, 338
vuelta de neutralización, 973
vuelta de ventaja, 944
vuelta eliminatoria, 1488
vuelta inversa con medio giro; con un giro; con una y media, dos, dos y medio giros, 1350
vuelta inversa; una y media, dos, dos y media vueltas inversas, 1351

zaguero, 753
zaguero derecho, 2709
zaguero izquierdo, 2633
zancada, 309
zapata de freno, 815
zapatillas de ciclista, 863
zapatillas de esgrima, 1524
zapatillas de gimnasia, 1834
zapatillas de tacos, 278
zócalos del taco de salida, 91
zona, 568, 774
zona de ataque, 522, 2525
zona de defensa, 386, 2527
zona de impulso, 1, 262
zona de los tres segundos, 733
zona de relevo, 253
zona de saque, 2727
zona de transmisión del batón, 212
zona de transmisión del testigo, 325
zona de 2 metros, 3004
zurdo, 2336

A-Teil, 1722
Abblende (den Impuls des Sprunges verlieren), 1241
abblenden (den Impuls des Sprunges verlieren), 1240
Abbruch des Rennens, 1092
Abdruck der Füsse. 2006
Abflug, 39
Abgang, 1377, 1787
abgeblockter Schmetterball, 2546
abknicken, 1175
abprallen, 2946
Abrollen, 2711
abrupte Bewegung, 1204
Abrutscher, 1678
abschneiden, 456
Absetzung eines Kampfrichters, 1939
absichtlicher Angriff, 450
absichtlichas Foul, 558
abspielen und freilaufen, 531
Absprung, 318, 1384
Absprung aus dem Anlauf, 1356
Absprung rückwärts, 1172
Absprung vorwärts, 1260
Absprungl nie, 324
Absprungmoment, 1332
Absprungphase, 67
eine Absprungwiederholung zugestehen, 1264
Absprungwinkel, 6, 1385
Abstand zwischen Hürden, 61
Abstand zwischen Läufern, 62
Abstandlinie, 805
Abstimmung der Kampfrichter, 1873
Abstopper, 704
Abstoss, 2938
Abstossphase, 2152
Abwehr im Hinterfeld, 2528
Abwehrbereich; Freiraum, 2560

Abwehrblock, 2573
Abwehrspezialist, 2576, 2581
Abwehrspieler, 2574
Abwehrstellung, 2575
abwerfende Verteidigung, 695
Abwurf; Abstoss, 52, 254
Abzug eines ganzen Punktes; 1.0; 0.1; 0.5; etc., 1780
Abzug in der Bewertung der Ausführung; Kombination; Komposition; Schwierigkeit, 1779
Abzug in der Bewertung der Kombination, 1767
Abzüge des Oberkampfrichters, 1853
Achse, 15, 786, 1067, 1167
Achse der Kurbel, 809
aggressive Manndeckung, 738
akrobatische Serie, 1725
akrobatisches Element, 1723
akrobatisches Flugelement, 1724
akrobatisches Kraftelement, 1726
allgemeiner Fehler, 1901
als Erster gesetzt, 2481
als Rekord anerkannt, 204
alternierende Plätze, 2227
am Pfosten abprallen, 2947
am Rad kleben, 895
Amplitude, 1731
an der Spitze angreifen, 783
das andere Ende, 1815
anderthalb Auerbachsalto; 2 Auerbachsalto; 2 1/2 Auerbachsalto, 1173
anderthalb Delphinsalto mit Schraube; mit 2 Schrauben, 1282
anerkanntes Tor, 2864
anerkennen, 238
Anerkennung eines Tores, 3007
Anfang, 2458

angedeuteter Halt, 1806
Angehen der Hürde, 319
angreifen, 782
Angreifer, 602, 2807
Angreiferfoul, 600
Angriff, 385, 596, 1414, 2520, 2668
Angriff aus der ersten Ballberührung, 2696
Angriff aus der Manndeckung, 597
Angriff aus der Zonendeckung, 598
Angriff gegen Angriffsvorbereitung, 1417
Angriff über den ersten Pass, 2584
Angriff von hinten, 784
Angriffsabpraller, 603
Angriffsblock, 2669
Angriffsbrett, 599
Angriffsdeckung, 2521
Angriffslinie, 2522
Angriffspieler, 2526
Angriffsposition, 604
Angriffsschema, 601
Angriffsschlag, 2601
Angriffsspezialist, 2524
Angriffssystem, 2670
Angriffstaktik, 2671, 2767
Angriffsvorbereitung, 1629
Angriffswiederholung, 1644, 1648
Angriffszone, 2525
Anhebestoss, 1465
Anhebestoss ins Tempo. 1452
Ankündigung des Sprunges, 1154
Anlauf, 260, 1156, 1255, 1402, 1734, 1953, 1954
Anlauf nehmen, 261
Anlaufbahn, 262, 265
Anlauffläche, 1
Anlaufwinkel, 5
Anlehnung, 1632

Anmeldung, 1345
Anmeldungskosten, 1346
Anmut des Sprunges, 1263
Annahme, 2702
annehmende Mannschaft, 2701
annehmende Unterstützung, 2567
Ansager, 1314, 2025
Anschlagmatte, 2203
Anschlusskabel, 1446
Anschreibebogen, 529, 672, 724
Anschreiber, 670, 2720
Anschweben, 1292
Anschwung, 1985
Anschwung des Diskus, 228
Anschwung des Hammers, 230
Anspiel, 611
Antennen, 2519
Antidopingkontrolle, 871
Antrag auf Auszeit, 2774
Antrag auf Spielerwechsel, 2707
antreten, 946
Antreten in Fechtstellung, 1638
ein Antreten vortäuschen, 886
Anwurf nach Torerfolg, 2954
Anzeige des Foulspielers, 692
Anzeige des Spielbretts, 389
Anzeigelampe, 1664
Anzeigen des Sprunges, 1733, 1822
Anzeigetafel, 214, 669, 974, 1662, 2163, 2422, 2719
Anzeigetafel der Sprünge, 1209
anziehen, 1104
Arena, 10
Armarbeit, 2026
Armbinde, 11, 780
Ärme, 2028
Armhaltung, 1159
Armvorhieb, 1682
Arztwagen, 971
As, 2220, 2518

Atemrhythmus, 2047
Atemtechnik, 2048
Atmungrhythmus, 2155
attakieren, 2029
Auerbachabsprung, 1352
Auerbachsalto mit halber Schraube;
    mit Schraube; mit 1 1/2
    Schraube; mit 2 1/2 Schrauben,
    1350
Auerbachsalto mit halber Schraube;
    mit 1 Schraube; mit 1 1/2
    Schraube; mit 2 Schrauben; mit 2
    1/2 Schrauben, 1171
Auerbachsalto; 1 1/2 Salto; 2
    doppelter Salto; 2 1/2 Salto, 1351
Auerbachsprung, 1348
Auerbachsprung mit halber Schraube;
    mit Schraube, 1349
auf dem Beckengrund stehen, 2980
auf dem Wasser aufsetzen, 2814
auf der Aussenbahn überholen, 984
auf der Innenbahn laufen, 122
auf der Innenbahn überholen, 983
auf der Linie, 2369
"auf die Plätze!", 206, 2198
auf festem Boden trainieren, 2075
auf Zeit spielen, 521
aufeinanderfolgende Sätze, 2460
Aufgabe, 1023, 2276, 2725
eine Aufgabe erhalten, 2798
eine Aufgabe gewinnen, 2591, 2795
Aufgabe von unten, 2785
Aufgabeblock, 2728
Aufgabefehler, 2729
Aufgabenwechsel, 2557
Aufgaberaum, 2727
Aufgabespezialist, 2731
Aufgabetaktik, 2732
Aufgabeverlust, 2640
Aufgang, 1905

aufgeben, 2277, 2317, 2413, 2724
Aufgeber, 2726
aufgehoben, 2465
aufgepumpter Ball, 2885
Aufhaltstoss, 1683, 1685
Aufhaltstoss mit Opposition, 1684
Aufkommen eines Treffers, 1594
Aufprall, 2248
aufrollen, 1041
Aufruf, 1990
Aufruf der Fechter, 1435
Aufruf der Wettkämpfer, 27
aufs Tor werfen, 2968
Aufsatzsprung, 1274
Aufschlag, 2428, 2431
Aufschlag - Flugball, 2432
Aufschlagdurchbruch, 2434
aufschlagen, 2429
Aufschläger, 2430
Aufschlaglinie, 2436
Aufschlagsbewegungsablauf, 2439
Aufschlagsdurchbruch, 2251
Aufschlagsfehler, 2435
Aufschlagsfeld, 2433
Aufschlagsmittellinie, 2258
Aufschlagsreihenfolge, 2437
Aufsetzen der Hände, 1842
Aufsetzen der Hände am Hals, 1845
Aufsetzen der Hände am Kreuz, 1844
Aufsetzen des Fusses, 1423
aufspringen, 2249
Aufstellung, 2610
Aufstellung bei der Ballannahme,
    2700
Aufstellung bei Spielbeginn, 699
Aufstellung der Spieler, 2714, 2753
Aufstellung im Augenblick der
    Aufgabe, 2730
Aufstellungsfehler, 2695, 2713
auftauchen, 2078, 2188

Aufwärmen, 368, 2791
Aufwärmhalle, 2018
Aufwärmraum, 369
Aufwärmsanzug, 2020
Aufwärmübung, 769
Aufwärmübungen, 2503
Aufwärtsschwung, 2498
Aufwärtsschwünge, 2009
Aufwickelspulen, 2199
aus dem Rennen disqualifiziert, 870
aus; "out", 2375
Ausatmung, 2046, 2081
Ausball, 396, 2539
ausdrücken, 422
Ausfall, 1591
einen Ausfall machen, 1592
Ausführung, 1808
Ausführung des Sprunges, 1233
Ausführung einer Übung, 1810
Ausgang der Kurve, 68, 70
Ausgangshöhe, 134
Ausgangsstellung, 1379, 1974
Ausgangsstellung einnehmen, 1166
die Ausgangsstellung aufnehmen, 1276
ausgeführter Freiwurf, 519
ausgeprägter Halt, 1781
ausgleichen, 2301, 2478
Ausholschwung, 2242
auslosen, 2294, 2563, 2845
Auslosung, 2295
ausreissen, 423, 819
Ausreisser, 822
Ausreissversuch, 24, 821
ausrutschen, 1058
ausscheiden, 2300
Ausscheidungsrennen, 878
Ausscheidungsrunde, 1488
Ausscheidungswettkämpfe, 229
ausschliessen, 1093
Ausschluss, 1094

Aussenplatz, 2376
ausser Bewegung sein, 2678, 2682
ausser Spiel, 2378
äusserer Angriffsspieler, 2680
äusserer Schirm, 616
äusserer Spieler bei Dreierblock, 2592
ausserhalb der Bahn, 1616
ausserhalb der Grenzen, 2377
ausserhalb der Linie, 2379
ausserhalb des Spielfeldes, 613
Auswechseln, 638
Auswechselspieler, 710, 2755, 2756
Ausweichen, 1482, 1499
Ausweichstoss, 1469
auswerfen, 485
Auszeit, 743, 2773
die Auszeit verlangen, 745
Auszeituhr, 744
automatische Zeitmessanlage und Resultatanzeige, 2030
automatische Zeitnahme, 2076

B-Teil, 1740
Badeanzug, 2190
Badeanzug (Damen), 1178
Badehose (Herren), 1177
Bademütze, 2192
Bahn, 155, 1115, 2118
Bahnblöcke, 2120
Bahneinfassung, 135
Bahnfahrer, 1125, 1127
Bahngehen, 350
Bahnlänge, 963, 1586, 2123, 2129
Bahnleine, 2122
Bahnneigung, 348
Bahnnummer, 2121
Bahnrennen, 1124
Bahnrennen auf überdachten Bahnen, 931

Bahnrennrad, 1119, 1126
Bahnrennsport, 1120
Bahnrichter, 349
Bahntrikot, 1122, 1130
Bahnverteilung, 2119
Bahnverteilung auslosen, 66
Balestra, 1419
Balken des Wassergrabens, 372
Ball, 2243, 2534
den Ball abfangen, 559
den Ball atnehmen, 427
den Ball auf das Wasser werfen, 2816
den Ball berühren, 3001
der Ball berührt das Netz, 2542
den Ball bis ins Tor dribbeln, 2847
den Ball dem leitenden Spieler geben, 544
den Ball dribbeln, 2846, 2994
der Ball entspricht nicht den Regeln, 2910
den Ball fangen, 2555
dem Ball folgen, 2606
den Ball freispielen, 2836
den Ball führen, 2554, 2828
Ball gehalten, 2623
der Ball geht hinter der Torlinie, 2811
der Ball hat mit dem gesamten Umfang die Torlinie überschritten, 2813
den Ball haben, 2636, 2895
Ball im Aus, 2812
Ball im Spiel, 394, 2536
den Ball ins Spiel bringen, 653
den Ball ins Tor dribbeln, 2995
den Ball ins Wasser werfen, 2815
der Ball ist gut, 2537
der Ball ist zugesprochen, 395
den Ball lobben, 2583, 2776

den Ball mit beiden Händen gleichzeitig berühren, 3002
den Ball mit dem Kopf spielen, 2877
den ball mit der Faust schlagen, 2937
den Ball mit der geballten Faust schlagen, 2881, 2990
den Ball passen, 624
den Ball plazieren, 2384
den Ball rückspielen, 617
den Ball tragen, 426
der Ball überquert das Feld, 454
den Ball unter Kontrole bringen, 2523, 2582
den Ball untertauchen, 2883, 2997
den Ball verfehlen, 2650
den Ball verlieren, 578, 2848
den Ball wegschnappen, 703
den Ball werfen, 684
den Ball wieder ins Spiel bringen, 2945
der Ball wird lebend, 390
der Ball wird tot, 391
den Ball zuführen, 495
den Ball zuspielen, 2924
Ballannahme, 2759, 2948
Ballannahme in Baggerstellung, 2552
Ballbehandlung, 393, 542, 2817
Ballberührung, 497, 2564, 2694
Ballbesitz, 397
Balldrehung, 697
Ballgewicht, 3016
Balljunge, 2244, 2541
Ballkontrolle, 392
die Ballkontrolle haben, 449
Ballkorb, 2818
Ballstörung, 533
Ballverlust (Strafe), 579
Ballwahl, 440
Ballwechsel, 2245, 2406, 2699

einen Ballwechsel gewinnen, 2796
einen Ballwechsel verlieren, 2639
Bank, 411
Bank für die Auswechselspieler, 2690
Barren, 1921
Barrenübung, 1860
Barrenwechsel, 1743
Baseballpass, 398
Basisnote, 1744
Basketball, 404
Basketballspiel, 406
Basketballspieler, 407
Basketballtrainer, 405
Beckenbegrenzung, 2825
Beckenboden, 1180, 2823
den Beckenboden berühren, 1390
Beckenpersonal, 2147
Beckenrand, 2849
Bediener des Windmessers, 374
Befragung der Kampfrichter, 1875
begegnen, 2373
Begegnung, 1596, 1704
Beginn der Übung, 1749
beginnen, 2459
Begleiter, 785
Begleitfahrzeug, 896, 897
Begrenzung des Wechselraums, 69
Begrenzungsflagge, 377
Begrenzungslinien, 2549
Behinderung, 803
beide, 2225
beidhändig baggern, 2781
beidhändiger Bodenpass, 759
beidhändiger Pass, 761
beidhändiger Überkopfwurf, 760
beidhändiges Dribbeln, 479
Beidhandwurf, 762
Beinarbeit, 508, 2117, 2127

Beinarbeit beim Brustschwimmen, 2041
Beinarbeit beim Delphin, 2073
Beinbewegung, 1544
Beinhaltung, 1291
Beinschlag, 2115
Beinschlagbrett, 2116
Berechnungskarte, 1766
Berechnungsstelle, 1765
Bereitschaftsstellung, 2409
Berichterstatter, 1340
Berichtssekretär, 1341
Berichtungszeit, 255
Berufungsgericht, 940, 1881
Berufungsstelle, 1583
Berührung, 2202
Berührung des Balles, 2535
Beseitigung, 35
Besitz, 644
Besitzspiel, 645
besondere Erfordernisse der Geräte, 1967
bespannen, 2461
Bespannungshärte, 2474
Bespannungszentrum, 2466
Betreuer, 1062
Betreuer für Wettkämpfer, Offizielle und Presse, 305
beugen, 1750, 1823
beweglicher Schirm, 591
Bewegung, 2651
Bewegung des Armes beim Abwurf bzw.   Abstoss, 65
Bewegungsamplitude, 1732
Bewertung, 1283, 1302
Bewertung der Ausführung; Kombination; Komposition; Schwierigkeit, 1804
Bewertungsgrundlagen, 1303

binden, 1489
Bindung, 1490, 1587, 1635
Bindung mit Transport, 1425
Birne, 568
bis zum Ring rollen, 665
blaue Flagge, 2822
blaue Kappe, 2821
Blinderpass, 413
Blitzkorbwerfer, 707
Block, 417, 2543
einen Block bilden, 2609, 2611
den Block überlobben, 2777
blocken, 2544
blockendes Foul, 418
blockieren, 414
Blockierung, 416
Blockspezialist, 2545
Blockspieler, 2547
Blocktaktik, 2548
Boden, 1827
Boden des Schwimmbeckens, 2039
Bodenrichter, 1535
"Bodentreffer!", 1608
Bodenturnfläche, 1899
Bodenübung, 1828
Bodenverlust, 1590
Bogen des Balles, 382
Bogenpass, 576
Bogenwurf, 2899
Bolzen, 807
"break"-Punkt, 2252
Breite der Fechtbahn, 1719
Breite der Klinge, 1718
Breite des Netzes, 2666
Breitenachse, 1858
Bremsbelag, 815
Bremse, 813
bremsen, 814, 817
Bremsgriff, 816
Bremshandschuh, 1123

Brett, 1179
Brett aus Duraflex, 1228
das Brett berühren, 1271
den Brettimpuls total ausnützen, 1353
Brettspringer, 1373
Brettspringen, 1372
Brettwiederstand, 1387
Brevet, 1752
Brustschwimmen, 2040
Brustschwimmen; ein 100-m; 200-m, 2044
Brustschwimmer, 2042
Brustwende, 2043

C-Teil, 1753
Center, 428
"center court", 2256
Center-Pivotspiel, 636, 647
Centersprung, 430
"chalk talk", 432
Chassée (Seitschritt), 1758
"Cheese Board" ("Maxiflex B"), 1187
Chopschlag, 2260
Computer, 1198
Contra-Quart, 1454
Contra-Sixt, 1458
Contrariposte, 1457
Contratempo, 1459
Coupé, 1460
Croisé, 1462
"Cross"-Flugball, 2272
"Cross-Schlag", 2271
"Cutaway"; Delphinkopfsprung, 1203

"D"-Sprung, 1155
Damen-Doppel, 2514
Damen-Einzel, 2515
Dauer der effektiven Spielzeit, 2894
Dauer der Halteteile, 1793
Dauer der Herausstellung, 2929

Dauer der Übung, 1792
Dauer des Assaut, 1483
Dauer des Spielerwechsels, 742
Deck, 2069
defekte Waffe, 1503
Defensive, 1468
Defensivtaktik, 2578
Degen, 1492
Degenfechten, 1496
Degenfechter, 1495
Degenglocke, 1497
Degenklinge, 1493
Degenwettbewerb, 1494
Deklassierung, 1019
Delphin, 2072
Delphinbeinschlag, 2052
Delphinkopfsprung, 1279
Delphinkopfsprung mit halber oder 1 Schraube, 1280
Delphinsalto; 1 1/2 Delphinsalto; 2; 2 1/2..., 1281
"Deuce"; Einstand, 2283
Diagonalparade, 1470
Digitalstoppuhren für Rhytmus beim Training, 2070
direkte Parade, 1471
direkte Verbindung, 1786
direkter Wechsel, 1785
Direktpass, 467
Direktwurf, 2988
Diskus, 54
Diskuswerfen, 57
Diskuswerfer, 56
Diskuswurf, 55
Diskuswurfanlage, 58
Disqualifikation, 469, 2071
Disqualifikation einer Mannschaft, 869
disqualifizieren, 2284
disqualifizierendes Foul, 471

disqualifizierter Spieler, 470
Doping, 872
Dopingkontrolle, 7
Doppel, 2286
Doppel-Center, 475
Doppelblock, 476
Doppeldribbling, 473
Doppelfehler, 2285
Doppelfinal, 2287
Doppelfinte, 1611
Doppelfoul, 474
Doppellinie, 2288
Doppellinien, 2291
Doppelmannschaft, 477
doppeln, 2969
Doppelschlag, 2587
Doppelspieler, 2290
doppelte Übertragung, 1491
doppeltes Abspringen, 1223
Doppeltreffer, 1481
Doppelwettkampf, 2289
Doppelzugatmung, 2074
Dornen, 279
Dornschuhe, 278
Drall, 2457
Drehachse, 16
Drehdribbling, 696
drehen, 2005
Drehschuss, 756
Drehung, 338, 1369
drei-für-zwei-Regel, 731
drei-Punkten-Spiel, 732
drei-Sekunden-Regel, 734
drei-Sekunden-Zone, 733
Dreierblock, 2771
Dreierzugatmung, 2038
Dreispringer, 355
Dreisprung, 354
Dreisprunganlage, 356

dreissig-Sekunden Aufwärmen, 1998
dribbeln, 478, 481
Dribbler, 480
Dribbling hinter dem Rücken, 409
Drive; Schlag, 2296
Drop, 2585
Drop spielen, 2641
Druckpass, 439
Druckphase der Armarbeit, 2151
Druckwurf, 2941
Durchhang der Sprunglatte, 266
dynamische Abwehr, 2653

"Eastern-Griff", 2299
Ebene, 1324
Eckwurf, 2839
effektive Spielzeit, 2801
eigene Torlinie, 2921
eigener Korb, 622
Eimer, 424
ein-km Zeitfahren, 941
"ein Meter!", 1609
Einatmung, 2045, 2112
Eindringen, 2688
Eindruck; Abdruck, 128, 183
Einerblock, 2675
einfache Riposte, 1673
einfacher Angriff, 1671
Einfachfinte, 1610
Eingang der Kurve, 287
Eingang der Ziegeraden, 288
einhändig baggern, 2672
einhändiger Pass, 609
Einhandwurf, 610
Einladung, 1577
Einlauf, 82
Einlaufen, 370
einseitige Zugatmung, 2209
Einspruch, 1338, 1933, 2148

Einspruch erheben, 381
Einstand, 2476
Einstellen des Geräts, 1728
Einstellung der Startblöcke, 4
Einstich des Sprungstabes, 218
Einstichkasten, 217
Eintauchen, 1229
Eintauchen ins Wasser, 2080
Eintauchen mit Sprudeln, 1182
eintauchen (nach links; nach rechts),
    1184
Eintauchen von mehr als 90°, 1404
eintönige Darstellung, 1904
Einwurf, 735
Einwurf von der Seitenlinie, 691
Einwurfspiel, 614
Einzel, 2444
Einzelfahren, 925
Einzelfahren auf der Bahn, 929
Einzelfinal, 2445
Einzelfinalist, 2446
Einzelkampf, 1571, 1862
Einzellinien, 2449
Einzelmatch, 2447
Einzelspieler, 2448
Einzelstart, 928
Einzelstrassenfahren, 926
Einzelverfolgungsrennen, 924
Einzelwertung, 1863
Einzelwettbewerbe, Frauen, 375, 2218
Einzelwettbewerbe, Männer, 195,
    2137
eklatantes Foul, 507
Elastizität des Brettes, 1374
elektrische Ausrüstung , 1485
elektrische Spitzenkrone, 1486
elektrische Trefferanzeigetafel, 1487
elektrischer Degen, 1484
elektronische Anzeigetafel, 1794

elektronische Zeichen, 1795
elektronische Zeitnahme (Schwebe-
    balken; Bodenübung), 1796
elektronische Zeitnehmerausrüstung,
    2077
Elemente, 1798
Elemente vom Schwung bis zum
    Handstand, 1799
Elementgruppen, 1797
Empfindlichkeitsgrad der
    Anschlagmatte, 2167
Ende der Auszeit, 2596
Ende der Spielzeit, 488
Ende einer Übung, 1769, 1801
Endergebnis, 504, 1819
Endkämpfe, 1821
Endlinie, 486, 1642
Endrunde, 1530
Endspiele, 81, 1805
die Endspiele entscheiden, 1789
Endsprünge, 1247
Endspurt, 80
Endstand, 1248
enge Hechte, 1189
Englisch (Dreh), 487
Entfernung, 60
Entfernung zwischen zwei
    Durchschnittsspielständen, 1934
Enthaltung, 1409
Entscheid, 2273
entscheidender Block, 2754
eine Entscheidung ändern, 2803, 2831
Entscheidungen treffen, 658
Entscheidungsrennen, 917
Entscheidungssatz, 2475, 2571
Entwaffnung, 1475
erfolgreicher Freiwurf, 713
erfolgreicher Korb, 712
Erfordernisse der Übung, 1942

Ergebnislisten, 1347
erhaltener Treffer, 1568
Erhöhung des Werts, 2011
Erkundung, 673
E-öffnung, 1612
Eröffnungsmatch, 2371
Ersatzdecke, 1147
Ersatzläufer, 314
Ersatzpieler, 2992
Ersatzrad, 1063
Ersatzturner, 1730, 1980
Ersatzzeitnehmer, 256
erste Absicht, 1532
erste Halbzeit, 505
erste Serie, 2304
erster Aufschlag, 2305
erster Schiedsrichter, 657, 2603
erster Spielabschnitt, 2852
erster Versuch, 88
erzwungener Fehler, 2310

Fahne, 89
Fahrbeobachter, 806
fahren, 1024
Fahrer, 1025
Fahrer an der Spitze, 950
einen Fahrer anhalten, 1091
einen Fahrer in die Zange nehmen, 810
Fahrerlager, 850, 1026
Fahrradnummertafel, 902
falscher Angriff, 1502
falscher Ausruf, 2516
Farben, 2837
Farbwahl der Kappen, 2834
Faustlage, 1560
Faustlage mit Handrücken oben, 1636
Faustlage mit Handrücken unten, 1690
Fechtabstand, 1514, 1521, 1595

Fechtanzug, 1515, 1528
Fechtbahn, 1526, 1622
fechten, 1508
Fechter, 1510, 1513
Fechtergruss, 1661
Fechtgang, 1522
Fechthandschuh, 1516
Fechthose, 1512
Fechtjacke, 1518
Fechtmaske, 1519
Fechtmeister, 1520
Fechtsaal, 1517
Fechtschuhe, 1524
Fechtstellung, 1523, 1555, 1606
Fechtstrümpfe, 1525
Fechttempo, 1527
Fechtwaffe, 1529
fehlende Amplitude; Bewegungsab-
lauf; Harmonie; Rhytmus, 1884
Fehler, 1816, 2302, 2599, 2613
Fehler im E-Material, 1501
Fehler im Handaufsatzes, 1843
Fehler in der Ausführung, 1809
Fehler in der Entscheidung, 1580
Fehler in der Haltung, 1817
Fehler in der Interpretation, 1818
Fehlertabelle, 1989
Fehlstart, 75, 883, 2082
Fehlstartpfosten, 2083
Fehlversuch, 73, 358
Fehlwurf, 590
Fehlstartleine, 2084
Feld, 25, 99, 825
das Feld sprengen, 1068
Feldspieler, 2851
Feldverweis, 2585, 2597
Felge, 1027
Fernsehkamerabahn, 2197
"fertig!", 272, 1413
fester Griff, 2303

Figur, 1254
Finalbewertung, 1803
Finale, 887, 1250
Finalist, 1820, 2416
Fintangriff, 1505
Finte, 1504
Fintparade, 1506
Fläche, 2464
flacher Aufschlag, 2307
flacher Beckenteil, 2966
flacher Schlag, 2306
flaches Eintauchen, 1252
Flachschlüssel, 979
Flagge, 2604, 2853
Flagge des Torlinienrichters, 2866
Flagge, die den Landesrekord
(Olympischen Rekord,
Weltrekord) anzeigt, 185
Flanconnade, 1533
Flaschenhalter, 1143
Flatteraufgabe, 2605
fliegender Salto, 1253
fliegender Start, 894
Florett, 1537
Florettfechten, 1541
Florettfechter, 1540
Florettglocke, 1542
Florettklinge, 1538
Florettknopf, 1543
Florettwettbewerb, 1539
Flug, 1825
Flugbahn des Balls, 754
Flugball, 2500
Flugball spielen, 2501
Flügelangriff, 773
Flügelelemente, 1826
Flügelschraube, 1004
Flugkurve, 1393

Flugkurve des Stoss bzw.
Wurfgeräts; Flugbahn des Stoss
bzw. Wurfgeräts, 352
Flugphase, 2, 92
Flugschlagstellung, 2502
Flugstoppball, 2297
Fortbewegung mit dem Ball, 379
Fortsetzung des Angriffs, 1447
"Fosbury Flop", 93
"Fosbury-Technik", 94
Foul, 95, 512
Französischer Griff, 1548
Freibad, 2143
freier Arm, 1705
freier Ball, 577
Freigefecht, 1589
Freilos, 2253
freistehender Spieler, 765
Freistellung, 1256
Freistilschwimmen, 2095
Freistilschwimmer, 2097
Freistilstaffel, 2096
den Freiwerfer stören, 472
Freiwurf, 515, 2858
einen Freiwurf ausführen, 2996
einen Freiwurf zuerkennen, 2859
Freiwurfgasse, 517
Freiwurflinie, 518
die Freiwurflinie berühren, 751
Freiwurfprozentsatz, 520
Freiwurfversuch, 516
führen, 162, 947, 2333
der Führende, 2334
der Führende Fahrer, 948
führender Läufer, 167
führender Pass, 571
Führung des laufenden Ergebnisses,
667
Führungsgruppe, 168

fünf-Sekunden-Regel, 506
Fünfkampf, 213
fünftes Foul, 502, 513
fünfunddreissigSekundenuhr, 2971
Funkwagen, 1010
Fussfehler, 2308, 2607
Fussfehlerrichter, 2309
Fussplatten (an den Startblöcken), 91
Fusswechsel, 28

Gabel, 898
Gabelkopf, 899
"Gainer" (Auerbachsalto), 1262
Gangschaltung, 906
gechlortes Wasser, 2059
gedeckter Spieler, 536
Gedränge, 679
Gefälle, 868
Gefecht, 1500
Gefecht; Trainingsgefecht, 1430
gegebener Treffer, 1566
gegen das Netz, 2224
Gegenangriff, 1451, 1455
Gegendruckparade, 1427, 1614
Gegengerade, 17, 787
Gegenwind, 916
Gegner, 2372
einen Gegner abhängen, 874
den Gegner an sich ziehen, 2936
den Gegner behindern, 802, 2879
den Gegner decken, 651, 2833, 2904
einen Gegner festhalten, 2882
den Gegner halten, 547
den Gegner rempeln, 437
einen Gegner schlagen, 2880, 2989
den Gegner unter dem Wasser
  festhalten, 2977
einen Gegner untertauchen, 2942,
  2991

gegnerische Hälfte, 2917
gegnerische Mannschaft, 2374
gegnerische Spielfeldhälfte, 2676
gegnerisches Tor, 2916
Gehen, 366
"Gehen" im Handstand, 1757
Geher, 365
gehockt, 1570
Gehrichter, 367
gekrümmte Startlinie, 48
gelbe Fahne, 1151
gelbe Karte, 2800
gelbe Lampe, 1721
gelüfteter Aufschlag, 2483
gemeinsame technische Kommission,
  1870
gemischte Verteidigung, 447
gemischtes Doppel, 2359
Gerade, 308
gerader Stoss, 1472, 1687
Gerät, 8
das Gerät berühren, 2002
gerechnete Auszeit, 438
Gesamtergebnis, 1249
geschlossenes Feld, 848
Geschmeidigkeit, 1824
geschnitterer Aufschlag, 2452
geschnitterer Ball, 2450
Geschwindigkeit, 1064, 2456
gesetzliche Deckungsstellung, 574
gesetzt, 2424
Gesicht zum Brett, 1238
gestaffelte Formation, 877
eine Gestaffelte Formation machen,
  958
gestreckt, 1290, 1382
gestrichene Wertungen, 1304
gewinkelter Flugball, 2228
gewinkelter Schlag, 2229

gewinnen, 2509
Gewinnschlag, 2494
gewonnener Satz, 2620
gezwungener Wurf, 509
glattes Eintauchen, 1366
Gleichgewichtsteil, 1742
Gleichstand, 340, 736, 1388
gleichzeitige Aktion, 1674
gleichzeitige Angriffe, 1675
Gleitbindung, 1549
Gleitphase, 2099
Gleitstoss, 1449, 1551
Glocke, 794, 1554
Glöckner, 795
Grab-Start, 2101
Grenzen, 2250
Griff, 98, 1553, 1561, 1832, 1846,
  2320
Griffwechsel, 1833
Griffwerfer, 444
grosser Fehler, 1887
Grundangriff, 2530
Grundlage, 527
Grundlinie, 399, 2246, 2593
Grundlinien Rückhand, 2237
Grundlinienspiel, 2232, 2247
Grundlinienspieler, 2233
Grundschlag, 2321
Grundspieler, 2529, 2531
Grundstellung, 1421, 1550, 1745
grüne Anzeigelampe, 1552
grüne Fahne, 908, 909
grüne Lampe, 1831
Gruppenführer, 918
gültige Aufgabe, 2635
gültige Trefffläche, 1711
gültiger Korbwurf, 499
gültiger Start, 2128
gültiger Treffer, 1710

gültiger Versuch, 315, 360
gute Haltung, 1774
Gutpunkte, 1751
Gutpunktfaktor (R.O.V.), 1987
Gymnastikschuhe, 1834

Hakenaufgabe, 2625, 2744
Hakenpass, 548
Hakenschlag, 2716
Hakenwurf, 549
halb abrollen, 2621
halbe Finte, 1557
halbe Runde, 910
halbe Volte, 1558
halbes Rennen, 969
Halbfinale, 2427
Halbfinalist, 2426
Halbflugball, 2323
Halbkreis, 681
Halbkreisparade, 1669
Halbzeit, 538
Hälfte des Spielfelds, 2875
Hallenbad, 2111
Hallenplatz, 2329
Hals, 1909, 1910
"halt!", 1559
Halte, 1856
Halteball, 545
Haltegriff, 2178
Halten des Geräts, 119
Hammer, 100
Hammerverbindungsdraht, 106
Hammerwerfen, 104
Hammerwerfer, 103
Hammerwurf, 102
Hammerwurfanlage, 105
Hammerwurfhandschuh, 101
Handfläche, 2922
Handgriff, 914

Handleder, 1847
Handstand, 1160, 1266, 1849
Handstand, Durchschub und Auerbachsprung, 1162
Handstand mit Durchschub, 1164
Handstand mit Rückwärtsabfallen, 1161
Handstand, Salto; mit Doppelsalto, 1165
Handstandsprünge, 1163
Handzeichen, 1898
Handzeitnahme, 2104, 2132
hart umkämpfter Match, 2324
hart umkämpftes Spiel, 2261
hartes Brett, 1381
hartes Spiel, 2960
Harz, 1949
Hauptangriffsspieler, 2750
Hauptanschreiber, 1852
Hauptfeld, 177, 957
Hauptplatz, 2349
heben, 1890
Hechtbagger, 2586
Hechtbagger nach vorn, 2615, 2739
Hechte, 1322
Hechtelemente, 1854
hechten, 1323
Helfer, 1738
Heptathlet, 109
heraufschalten, 1000
herausgestellter Spieler, 2850
Herrendoppel, 2356
Herreneinzel, 2357
hervorragende Ausführung, 1807
Hieb unter der Vorderschneide, 1464, 1569
Hilfe, 383
Hilfe unter den Fahrern, 781
Hilfestellung, 1265
Hilfsfunktionär, 714

Hilfsschiedsrichter, 1984
Hilfstrainer, 384
Hindernislauf, 297
Hindernislauf auf einer Strecke von 3000 m, 301
Hindernislaufflaggen, 299
Hindernislaufsperren, 298
hinten links, 2633
hinterer Zahnkranz, 1073
hinteres Bein, 1706
Hinterrad, 788
Hinterspieler, 537
Hinweis für den Herausgestellten, 2932
hochspringen, 1287
Hochspringer, 112
Hochsprung, 111
Hochsprunganlage, 116
Hochsprunglatte, 115
Hochsprungsnormen, 117
Hochstart, 284
höchste Wertung, 1270
Hocke, 1394
hocken, 1395, 1777
Hoffnungslauf, 1020
Höhe der Torlatte, 2878
Höhe des Geräts, 1855
eine Höhe von ...überspringen, 33
hoher Holm, 1857
hoher Lob, 2325
hoher Pass, 2624
hoher Pivot, 546
Hohlkreuz, 1158
ein Hohlkreuz machen, 1157
Hop, 121
Hupe, 551
Hürde, 124
Hürde für Hindernislauf, 300
die Hürde überlaufen, 304
Hürdenlauf, 125

Hürdenläufer, 126
Hürdenwiederstand, 344
Hydrodynamik, 2184

im Abseits, 2914
im Aus, 1918, 2677
im Feld bleiben, 1057
im Spiel, 2328
im Spielplan vorgesehen, 2419
im Vorteil sein, 380
im Wiegetritt fahren, 990
Impuls, 129, 1339
Impuls vom Brett, 1225
in Ballbesitz sein, 2820
in das Spiel eintreten, 2595
in den Block schmettern, 2749
in den Korb tippen, 748
in der Innenkurve laufen, 123
in die Lücke lobben, 2778
in die Streckung gehen, 1936
in Form sein, 792
in Startstellung verharren, 2037
in Wiegetritt fahren, 922
Inhalt der Übung, 1773
inkorrekte Körperhaltung, 1861
Innenraum, 1117
innere Bahneinfassung, 47, 136
innere Seitenlinienbegrenzung, 556
innerer Rand der Bahn, 936
innerer Schirm, 557
innerhalb, 2330
Inquartata, 1573
Internationale Radfahrer-Union (I.R.U.), 937
Internationaler Basketballverband (F.I.B.A.), 562
Internationaler Fechtverband (F.I.E.), 1574
Internationaler Leichtathletikverband (I.A.A.F.), 138

Internationaler Schwimmverband (F.I.N.A.), 2086
Internationaler Turnverband (F.I.G.), 1866
internationaler Turnwettkampf, 1867
Internationaler Volley-ballverband (I.V.V.), 2626
Internationales Komitee für Wasserspringen (F.I.N.A.), 1278
Italienischer Griff, 1578

Jagd, 839
Juror, 1920

Kabelrolle, 1645
Kadenz, 26
Kampfgericht, 1217, 1919, 2643
Kampfleiter, 1474, 1630
Kampfrichter, 144, 1579, 1871
die Kampfrichter entscheiden, 1790
Kampfrichter für Sprung-, Wurf-und Stosswettbewerbe, 78
Kampfrichter (Schwierigkeit), 1872
Kampfrichterkollegium, 845
Kampfrichterkonferenz, 1874
Kampfrichterlehrgänge, 1876
Kampfrichterobmann, 1850
Kampfrichtertisch, 586, 671
Kampfrichtertischbelegschaft, 1362
Kanadischer Amateurschwimmverband (C.A.S.A.), 2056
Kanonenball-Aufschlag, 2255
Kapitän, 425, 2553, 2827
Karten des Kampfgerichts, 2114
Kassettenrecorder, 1754
Kavation nach Kreisbindung oder Wechselbindung, 1453
Kette, 833
Kettenblatt, 834
Kettenbruch, 823

Kettenglied, 954
Kettenrad, 812
Kettenschaltung, 867
Kilometerstein, 970
kippen, 1882
Klassement, 994
Klasseneinteilung, 832, 1441
Klassierung, 2408
Klavier, 1926
Klavierspieler, 1925
kleine Fehler, 1966
kleine Reparaturwerkzeuge, 1060
kleiner Fehler, 2907
Klinge, 1426
Klingenangriff, 1416
Klingenbiegung, 1463
Klingenbindung, 1691
Klingenbruch, 1431
Klingenführung mit den Fingern,
    1531
Klingenlänge, 1585
Klingenschlag; Battuta, 1422
Klingenschneide, 1466
Klingenschwäche, 1536
Klingenspitze, 1624
Klingenstärke, 1545
knapper Einlauf, 36, 341
knapper Zieleinlauf, 843
Knauf, 1625
ein Kniebeuge ausgleichen, 1289
Knieschützer, 2631
Knopf, 1433, 1701
Kombinationen, 1760
kombinierte Sprünge, 1191
kombinierte Wertung, 1761
"Kontinental-Griff"; Einheitsgriff,
    2267
Kontinuität, 448
Kontraktion, 1699

Kontraparade, 1456
Kontrolle der elektrischen Spitze,
    1696
Kontrollgewicht, 1695
Kontrollpfosten, 852
Kontrollzentrum für Athleten, 13
Konventicum, 1448
Konvoi, 831, 854
Koordinator des Berechnungsaus-
    schusses, 1962
Kopfhörer, 2106
Kopfsprung, 1207
einen Kopfsprung gutmachen, 1357
Kopftäuschung, 543
Koppelbindung, 1480
Korb, 400, 532
Korb des Gegners, 612
einen Korb erzielen, 668, 693
den Korb verfehlen, 588
die Körbe wechseln, 433
Korbfassung, 402
Korbleger, 569
Korbspielzerteilung, 648
Korbstörung, 401
Korbstützung, 403
Korbwahl, 441
die Korbwahl auslosen, 750
Korbwerfer, 685
Korbwurfprozentsatz, 501
Korbwurfversuch, 500
Kordelgriff (am Speer), 43
Korkleine. 2840, 2896
Körper an Körper, 1428
den Körper strecken zum Eintauchen
    in das Wasser, 1293
Körperberührung, 630
Körperkabel, 1429
Korridor, 2226
kräftiger Korbleger, 649

kraftloser Ball, 2588
Kraftteil, 1978
kraftvoller Schlag, 2393
Kraul, 2067
Kraulschwimmer, 2068
Kreisdeckung, 1440, 1450
Kreuz, 1778
Kreuzschritt, 45, 1776
kreuzweise Stellung, 1201
Kugel; Schuss, 273
Kugellager, 793
Kugelstoss, 276
Kugelstossanlage, 277
Kugelstossen, 274
Kugelstosser, 233, 275
Kulminationspunkt, 113
Kulminationspunkt der Flugkurve
    eines Springers, 114
Kunstspringwettbewerbe (Damen),
    1408
Kunstspringwettbewerbe, Herren,
    1311
Kunstturnen, 1736
Kurbel, 858
Kurbellager, 835
Kürsprünge, 1319
Kürsprünge mit Limit, 1400
Kürsprünge ohne Limit, 1401
Kürübungen, 1913
Kurve, 860
Kurvenbeobachter, 855
Kurveneingang, 1082
Kurvenflagge, 44
Kurvenlauf, 22
Kurvenläufer, 21
Kurvenneigung, 866
Kurvenvorgabe, 282
kurze Schlange, 1364
kurzer Pass, 2738

Kurzstreckbecken, 2085
Kurzstreckenlauf, 280
Kurzstreckenläufer, 281
Kurzstreckenschwimm, 2173
Kurzstreckenschwimmer, 2172

Läfer, 263
Lagenschwimmen, 2136
Lagenschwimmer, 2135
Lagenstaffel, 2134
Landung, 74, 151, 1885
Länge des Netzes, 2662
langer Rückschlag, 2274
langer Schlag, 2275
langes Eintauchen, 1295
Langpferd (Männer), 1894
längs der Linie, 2292
Längsachse, 1186, 1296, 1893, 1895,
    2016
langsamer Ball, 2453
langsames Spiel, 2978
Längsseite, 2168
Langstrecken, 170
Langstreckenlauf, 171
Langstreckenläufer, 172
Langstreckenschwimmen, 2131
Langstreckenschwimmer, 2130
die Latte berühren, 59
die Latte überspringen, 34
Lattenhöhe, 108
Lauf, 236
Lauf in Bahnen, 157
Laufberichtsbogen, 2107
Läufe, 107, 2108
Läufer, 2532
einen Läufer behindern, 127
einen Läufer einschliessen, 23
Laufwettbewerbe, 347
lebender Ball, 575

Leichtathlet, 346
leichte Hilfe, 1903
"leichter Ball", 2614
Leiter (am Beckenrand), 2146
Lenker, 912
Lenkerband, 915
Leotard, 1889
letzte Runde, 159
letzter Versuch, 160
Linie, 2338
Linien, 1588
die Linien besetzen, 503
Linienrichter, 2339, 2638
linker Hinterspieler, 573
linker Verteidiger, 2892
linker Vorderspieler, 572, 2893
linkes Aufschlagsfeld, 2335
"links, getroffen!", 1564
Linkshänder, 2336
Lizenz, 952
"Lob", 2340, 2775, 2898
"loben", 2341
Loge und eine Verteidigung, 421
"Lokomotive", 955
"los!", 1507, 1623
Losen, 873
Losentscheid, 1224
Lücke, 2793, 2794
eine Lücke machen, 951

Magnesium, 1756, 1897
Mahnung, 2504
Manndeckung, 581, 2903
Manndeckung durch Pressdeckung ab
  Spielfeldmitte, 540
Manndeckung durch Pressdeckung
  über das ganze Spielfeld, 524
Mannschaft, 719, 1098, 1386, 1692,
  1992, 2470
Mannschaftsanhänger, 494

Mannschaftsaufstellung, 725
Mannschaftsbank, 720
Mannschaftsfahren, 1101
Mannschaftsfahren auf der Bahn,
  1128
Mannschaftsführer, 453, 721, 1693,
  1783, 1851, 1993
Mannschaftskampf, 1694
Mannschaftskapitän, 2471
Mannschaftslauf, 326
Mannschaftsresultaten, 1994
Mannschaftsspiel, 722
Mannschaftsstrassenfahren, 1034
Mannschaftsverfolgungsrennen, 1100
Mannschaftswettbewerbe, Frauen,
  376
Mannschaftswettbewerbe, Männer,
  196

Marathon, 181
Marathonläufer, 182
Markierungen, 30
Maschen, 2663
Maschine, 956
Maskengitter, 1720
Maskenlatz, 1424
Massband, 190
Massenankunft, 826, 2061
Massenstart, 961
Massensturz, 960
match-up Zone, 584
Matchausgleich, 2477
Matchball, 2352, 2644
Matte, 1829
Maxiflex-B-Brett, 1306
Maxiflexbrett, 1307
Mechaniker, 964
mechanisch, 965
mechanischer Defekt, 820
mechanisches Aufwühlen der
  Oberfläche des Wassers, 1308

Medal (Gold; Silber; Bronze), 191
mehr als gestrecktes Eintauchen,
  1320
mehrere Freiwürfe, 593
Mehrfachfoul, 592
Mehrkampf, 1729
Mehrkampf, 38
Meldestelle, 187
Meldung, 879
Mensur; Abstand, 1479
Messen bei Sprung, Stoss und Wurf,
  188
Messgerät, 2645
Messlatte, 189
Messlatte bei Weit und Dreisprung,
  63
Metallmatte, 1597
Metallweste, 1598
Mindestwassertiefe, 2906
Minimalhöhe, 199
Minuten gespielt, 587
missglückter Sprung, 1242
mit dem Kopf eintauchen, 1267
mit den Füssen eintauchen, 1245
mit den Füssen treten, 2888
mit den Händen die Sicht verwehren,
  491
mit der Fahne anzeigen, 2976
mit einer Hand abwehren, 2673
mit einer Hand werfen, 2915
mit einer Länge gewinnen, 2217
mit einer Nummer versehene Kappe,
  2912
mit einer Radlänge gewinnen, 1150
mit einer Reifenbreite gewinnen, 1149
mit zwei Händen abwehren, 2782
Mitarbeiter des Kampfgerichts, 2023
Mitarbeiter in der Auswertung, 2060
Mitspieler, 2768
Mitte des Feldes, 967

Mittelbahn, 968
Mittelkreis, 429, 564
Mittellinie, 431, 727, 2257, 2556,
  2830, 2876
Mittelstreckenlauf, 197
Mittelstreckenläufer, 198
Mittelstreckenschwimmen, 2140
Mittelstreckenschwimmer, 2139
Mittelstürmer, 2829
Mittelwert der beiden mittleren
  Noten, 1739
mittlerer Angriffsspieler, 2646
mittlerer Blocker, 2648
mittlerer Grundspieler, 2647
Moment der Streckung, 1195
Musikbegleitung, 1907
Mutter, 975
Mütze, 830

Nabe, 923
nach Ball ins Aus schmettern, 2799
nach der Fassung greifen, 534
nach Punkten führen, 166
Nachgebeparade, 1436
nachkommender Spieler, 753
nachkommendes Bein, 351
Nachzügler, 876
das nähere Ende, 1908
Nahkampf, 1511, 1572
Nahschuss, 443
Natursaiten, 2322
Nazionalhymne, 200
Neigung, 130
Neigung der Piste, 791
Neigung der Standfläche des
  Startblocks, 2169
Netz, 594, 2360, 2658, 2868
das Netz berühren, 2484
Netzaufgabe, 2665
Netzball, 2337, 2538

Netzfehler, 2660
Netzhöhe, 2661
Netzoberkante, 2765
Netzpfosten, 2364, 2664
Netzrichter, 2362
Netzspanner, 2667
Netzspiel, 2361
Netzspieler, 2363, 2616, 2617
neutrale Abzüge, 1911
neutrale Zone, 2365
Neutralisationsrunde, 973
nicht am Wettkampf teilnehmen, 2021
nicht den Regeln entsprechendes Spielfeld, 2911
nicht erzwungener Fehler, 2493
nicht gesetzt, 2495
"nicht getroffen!", 1599
nicht-rutschender Belag der Plattform, 1313
Niederlage, 2278, 2344
niedriger Flugball, 2348
niedriger Holm, 1896
niedriger Schlag, 2347
niedrigste Wertung, 1297
Null, 2345, 2517
Nullspiel, 2346

Oberarmkipplage, 1841
Obmann der Platzaufsicht, 186
Obmann des Wettkampfgerichts, 1631
offene Bahn, 981
offene Hechte, 1317
offene Wertung, 1912
offenes Turnier, 2370
Offensive, 1604
offensiver Lob, 2368
Offensivspiel, 2367

offiz. Leitung, 180
Offizielle, 42, 194, 2142
Offizielle des Rennens, 1007
Offizielle des Treffens, 205
offizielle Zeit, 2141
Offizieller, 976
offizieller Anschreiber, 605
offizieller Spielberichtsbogen, 606
Öffnung, 1226, 1318
ohne Verzögerung werfen, 2970
Oktav, 1601
opponieren, 2353
Opposition, 1613
orchestrierte Musik, 1914
Originalität der Übung, 1917
Originalitätswert, 1916
orthopädischer Griff, 1615

Parade, 1618, 1672
eine Parade umgehen, 1467, 1498
"pariert!", 1617
Partner, 2381, 2472
Pass, 623, 2684, 2923
Pass hinter dem Rücken, 410
Pass mit beiden Händen, 2783
Pass mit e ner Hand, 2674
Pass nach vorn, 2612
Passata di sotto, 1619
passen, 2685
Passen im Flug, 2629
Passierschlag, 2382
pauschen, 1931
Pauschenpferd, 1930
Pause, 2687, 2708
Pause zwischen Sätze, 2772
Pedal, 988
Pedalachse, 859
Pedalarbei, 778
Pedalriemen, 1113

persönlicher Fehler, 2930
persönliches Foul, 631
Pfeifen, 771
Pfeilangriff, 1534, 1654
Pfiff, 3017
Pflichtsprünge, 1197
Pflock, 184
Piste, 345
Pisteneinfassung, 808
Pistenordnung, 1118
Pistenrand, 1116
Pistenreifen, 1129
Pivot, 634
Pivot-Fuss, 635
Pivot-Spieler, 646
Plastikbrett, 1246
Plastilin, 219
Plastilinstreifen, 220
Plattform, 1325
Platz, 2268
den Platz freimachen, 442
platzen, 804, 827
Platzen (Reifen), 893, 997
Platzwärter, 583
Platzwechsel, 1438, 1478
plazierter Fahrer, 1051
plazierter Fechter, 1668
Podium, 1929
Positionen; Zonen, 2566
Positionsangriff, 682
Präsident der Wettkampfleitung, 1932
Pressdeckung, 650
Prim, 1633
Probesprung, 1403
Profil, 1140
Protest, 231
protestieren, 2396
Protokollführer, 1219, 1251, 2156

Proviantbeutel, 972
Pull-buoys, 2150
Pumpe, 996
Punkt, 2389
einen Punkt erzielen, 2797
Punkte, 643
Punkte erzielen, 2421
Punktendurchschnitt, 642
Punkthöchstabzug, 1900
Punktstand, 2717
Punktwert, 1301
Pyramide zum Anzeigen der Weiten, 64
Pyramide zur Bahnbezeichnung, 156

Qualifikation, 1002
Qualifikationsrennen, 1003
Qualifikationszeit, 2154
qualifizierend, 2153
Quart, 1639
Querachse, 1200
Querspagat, 1830
Quint, 1640

Rad, 1145
Radachse, 1148
Radfahrer, 864
Radlager, 790
Radrennbahn, 800, 861
Radrennschuhe, 863
Radschlüssel, 776
Radsport, 862
Radwechsel, 1146
Radzubehör, 799
Rahmen, 900
Rahmenbruch, 824, 901
Rand des Spielbretts, 484
rauhes Spiel, 3008
Raum, 9

Reboundpass, 419
Rechner (mechanisch; Pappe), 1183
Rechter hinten rechts, 2709
rechter Hinterspieler, 662
rechter Verteidiger, 2958
rechter Vorderspieler, 661, 2959
Rechter vorne rechts, 2710
rechtes Aufschlagsfeld, 2415
"rechts, getroffen!", 1565
Reck, 1859
regelgemäss, 1016
Regeln, 1017, 1042, 1952
Regelübertretung, 666
Regelverletzung, 767, 818, 933
Regelverletzung im Rückfeld, 387
regelwidrige Benutzung der Hände, 555
regelwidriges Dribbling, 553
regelwidriges Sperren, 554
Regenmantel, 1011
den Reifen von der Felge nehmen, 1040
Reihenfolge der Teilnehmer, 1378
Reihenfolge der Turner, 1764
die Reihenfolge der Turner entscheiden, 1791
Reihenfolge des Zieleinlaufs, 980
Reinigungsfahrzeug, 1046
reissen, 1144
Reklamation, 995
Rekord, 1013
einen Rekord homologisieren, 779, 1012
rempeln, 436
Rennen, 264, 962, 1005
Rennfahrer, 801
Rennhose, 1009
Rennleiter, 1006, 1121
Rennleitung, 853
Rennleitungswagen, 846, 978

Rennrad, 798, 1008
Rennradwechsel, 837
Rennstrecke, 1029
Reparatur, 1038
Reparatur unterwegs, 1043
Reprise, 1647
Resultat, 1022
Resultaten, 2162
Resultatsblatt, 1361, 1959
Resultatstafel, 1360
reverses Dribbling, 660
Rhythmus, 1434, 1651
Rhythmuswechsel, 435
Richter, 2331
Richtung, 53
Richtungsanzeiger, 1033
Richtungswechsel, 434
Riemen der Sturzkappe, 840
Rimesse, 1646
Ring, 550
Ringe, 1946
Ringrand, 663
Riposte, 1653
Riposte mit Zeitfinte, 1432
Risiko, 1948
rollen lassen, 903
Rotation, 2712
Rotation im Uhrzeigersinn, 2561
rote Anzeigelampe, 1643
rote Fahne, 1014, 1015
rote Flagge, 2950
rote Kappe, 2949
rote Karte, 2703
rote Lampe, 1937
rote Markierung, 2951
Rückenfahnen, 2032
Rückenschwimmen, 2031
Rückenschwimmen, 100-m; 200-m, 2036
Rückenschwimmer, 2034

Rückenstart, 2033
Rückenwende, 2035
Rückenwind, 1097
Rückfeld, 386
Rückhand, 2234
Rückhand-Cross, 2269
Rückhandflugball, 2240
Rückhandgriff, 2236
Rückhandlob, 2238
Rückhandseite, 2239
Rückhandstoppball, 2235
Rückhandwurf, 2809
Rückholphase der Arme, 2027
rücklings, 1237
Rückpass, 2533
Rückschlag, 2438
Rückschlag-Cross, 2270
Rückschläger, 2410
Rückschlagsreihenfolge, 2411
Rückschlagstellung, 2412
Rückschwünge, 1775
Rückstarter, 241
Rückwärtsbewegung, 2652
Rückwärtsdrall, 2241
Rückwärtsgang, 789
Rückwärtssprung, 1168, 1174
Rückwärtssprung mit halber Schraube, 1169
Rückzug, 2513
Runde, 942, 945, 1626
eine Runde Vorsprung haben, 163
Runden, 259
Rundentabelle, 1627
Rundenzähler, 158, 943
Rythmus, 1944

Säbel, 1655
Säbelfechten, 1658
Säbelfechter, 1660
Säbelglocke, 1659

Säbelklinge, 1656
Säbelwettbewerb, 1657
Saiten-Bespannung, 2462
Salto, 1367, 1956
einen Salto gutmachen, 1368
Salto rückwärts mit Hocke, 1170
Salto vorwärts mit halber Schraube; 1 Schraube; 2 Schrauben, 1258
Salto vorwärts; 1 1/2 Salto vorwärts; 2; 2 1/2..., 1259
Sammellinie, 12
Sandplaniergerät, 267
Sattel, 1044, 1955
Sattelspitze, 987
Sattelstange, 1045
Satz, 2440, 2618, 2733
Satzball, 2735
Satzbeginn, 2751
Satzende, 2594
Satzpunkt, 2441
Satzung, 1938
Schaltung, 905
Scharf geschlagene Aufgabe, 2698
Schellen, 2105
Schiedsgericht, 150, 1288
Schiedsrichter, 243, 1230, 1342, 1981, 2157, 2489
Schiedsrichter (Abknicken), 1176
Schiedsrichter für Gehwettbewerbe, 246
Schiedsrichter für Laufwettbewerbe, 245
Schiedsrichter für Sprung-, Wurf-und Stosswettbewerbe, 244
Schiedsrichter im Mittelfeld, 752
Schiedsrichter im Vorderfeld, 570
Schiedsrichterball, 2955
Schiedsrichterblatt, 2423
Schiedsrichtereinwurf, 2944
Schiedsrichterentscheid, 2491

Schiedsrichterflagge, 2952
Schiedsrichterkarten, 2704
Schiedsrichterobmann (elektronisch), 2057
Schiedsrichterplatz, 2953
Schiedsrichterstuhl, 2490, 2705
das Schiedsrichterzeichen abwarten, 3009
Schild zum Anzeigen der Anzahl der Fouls, 582
Schirm, 632, 674
Schlag, 2326, 2442, 2463
den Schlag gewinnen, 2350
Schlag im Vorlaufen, 2230
schlagen, 2279, 2327
Schläger, 2400
Schlägerbespannung, 2405
Schlägerfläche, 2401
Schlägergriff, 2403
Schlägerkopf, 2404
Schlägerrahmen, 2402
Schlauch, 935, 1133, 1134
Schlauchkleber, 1135
schliessen (Beine), 1869
Schlingband, 1593
Schlussschwimmer, 2024
Schmetterball, 2454, 2747
Schmetterling, 2091
Schmetterlingsschwimmen, 2051, 2053
Schmetterlingsschwimmen, 100-m; 200-m, 2055
Schmetterlingsschwimmer, 2054
Schmettern, 2455, 2697, 2748
Schmirgelpapier, 1800
schneiden, 2451
schnell wechseln, 1095
schneller Beinschlag, 2216
schneller Gegenangriff, 495
schnelles Brett, 1244

schnelles Dribbeln zum Korb, 482
schnelles Spiel, 2909
schnelles Treten, 1066
schnellgezogener Pass, 2602
Schnellwechseln, 1096
Schöpfgriff, 2884
Schraube, 1049, 1396
eine Schraube ausführen, 1924, 1927
Schraubensprünge, 1397
Schreiber 1663, 2164
Schriftführer, 242, 269
Schritt rückwärts. 1680
einen Schritt rückwärts machen, 1649
Schritt vorwärts und Ausfall, 1679
Schritte; Seitschritte, 1975
Schrittfehler, 755, 768
Schrittfolge, 311
die Schrittfolge beibehalten, 179
die Schrittfolge erhöhen, 133
eine Schrittlänge, 302, 309
Schrittrhythmus, 310
Schuhplatte, 1055
einen Schuss halten, 2985
Schutzgitter, 333
Schützling, 1099
schwache Seite, 770
schwacher Schlag, 2505
Schwebebalken, 1741, 1746
schwerer Fehler, 2900
schwierige Abwehr, 2580
Schwierigkeit, 1784
Schwierigkeitsgrad, 1205
Schwierigkeitsgrad der Sprünge, 2014
Schwierigkeitsgradtabelle, 1988
Schwierigkeitskoeffizient, 1782
Schwimmbad, 2145, 2195
Schwimmbrille, 2100
schwimmen, 2189
Schwimmer, 2191

Schwimmfähigkeit, 2050
Schwimmhose, 2819
Schwimmkörper, 2090
Schwimmrichter, 2144, 2185
Schwimmstil, 2187
Schwimmtechnik, 2196
Schwimmwettbewerb, 2194
Schwimmwettkampf, 2193
Schwingbein, 96
Schwung, 2467
Schwung nach unten, 2293
Schwungarm, 316
Schwungbein, 169, 317, 1273
Schwünge, 1883
Schwungholen, 1277
Schwungteil, 1986
einen "scoop" gutmachen, 1358
Seitendrall, 2443
Seitenlinie, 420, 690, 2743, 2972
Seitenspagat, 1965
Seitenstreifen des Netzes, 2740
Seitenwahl, 2835
Seitenwechsel, 2558
Seitenwechsel während des Entscheidungssatzes, 2622
Seitenwind, 1056
seitlich abrollen, 2741
seitliche Aufgabe, 2715, 2742
seitlicher Spagat, 1888
Seitpferd (Frauen), 1964
Seitschwimmen, 2973
Seitwärtsbewegung, 2655
Sekond, 1667
Sekretär, 1050, 2964
Sekretär des Schiedsrichters, 2805
Sektor, 270
Sektorenfahne, 271
Sektorgrenzen, 237
Selbstdoppler, 2935

Seltenheitswert, 1935
senkrechte Eben, 1399
Sensation, 2496
Septime, 1670
Servicefahrzeug, 1053
Setzen, 2166, 2425
Shellack, 1054
sich anbieten, 2862
sich anmelden, 1344
sich aufrichten, 1947
sich aus dem Sprung strecken, 1234
sich aus der Hechtlage strecken, 1193, 1235
sich aus der Hocke strecken, 1194
sich beeilen, 552
sich decken, 1461, 1637
sich den Körper mit Fett einschmieren, 2874
sich eindrängen, 49
sich freispielen, 530
sich ins Hohlkreuz strecken, 1735
sich klassieren, 2407
sich lösen, 176, 875
sich mit dem Ball vorwärts bewegen, 652
sich mit dem Fuss vom Gegner abstossen, 2889
sich öffnen, 1316
sich qualifizieren, 2397
sich unter den Ball stellen, 2657
sich vom Beckenrand abstossen, 2940
sich vom Gegner abstossen, 2939
sich wieder im Ballbesitz bringen, 656
sich zum Ball stellen, 2656
Sichtblock, 2722
Siebenkampf, 110
Sieg, 2499, 2508
Sieger, 2510
Siegerpodest, 364

Siegesprotokoll, 363
Siegespunkt, 2511
siegreiche Mannschaft, 2512
Sitzung, 1963
Sixt, 1676
"Slice", 2492
Söckchen, 777
Socke, 1061
Spagat, 1968
Speer, 139
Speerwerfen, 142
Speerwerfer, 141
Speerwurf, 140
Speerwurfanlage, 143
Speiche, 1069
sperren, 675
Sperren im Stand, 700
Sperren in der Nähe des Balls, 678
sperren und rollen, 633, 676
Sperren weit vom Ball, 677
Sperrstoss, 1415
Spezialist, 2746
Spiel, 2319, 2351, 2385
das Spiel abpfeifen, 2975
das Spiel anpfeifen, 2974
das Spiel nach Strafpunkten gewinnen, 772
das Spiel unterbrechen, 2987
das Spiel verzögern, 466
das Spiel wiederaufnehmen, 2956
Spielanfang von der Torlinie, 2993
Spielaufstellung, 2766
Spielausschluss, 489
Spielbeginn, 408, 698, 2981
Spielbein, 514, 595
Spielberichtsbogen, 2718
Spielbrett, 388
Spieler, 2387, 2691
Spieler, an dem ein Foul begangen wurde, 2855

Spieler, der einen Fehler begeht, 2913
einen Spieler herausstellen, 2918
Spieleraufstellung, 723
Spielerbank, 2692
Spielerkleidung, 2786
Spielernumerierung, 637
Spielerstellung beim Anspiel und Wiederbeginn, 2982
Spielerwechsel, 2706
Spielerweg, 626
Spielfeld, 451, 639, 2565, 2693, 2933
das Spielfeld verlassen, 2632
das Spielfeld verlassender Spieler, 2679
Spielfeldabmessungen, 452
Spielfeldgrenze, 2824, 2897
Spielfeldhälfte, 539
Spielmacher, 641
Spielpause, 561
Spielperiode, 629
Spielplan, 2418
Spielregel, 2934
Spielrichter, 607
Spielstand, 2420
Spieluhr, 528, 2861
Spielunterbrechung, 706, 2628
Spielunterbruch, 2480
Spielverlängerung, 2920
Spielverzögerung, 2579
Spielzeit, 640
Spielzeit von 7 Minuten, 2965
Spitzengruppe, 949
Sportleiter, 1070
springen, 1208, 1880, 1969
Springer, 147, 567, 1211
Sprint, 1071
Sprintlinie, 1072
Spritzen, 1370, 2979
spritzloses Eintauchen, 1188, 1354
Sprudelmaschine, 1181

Sprung, 145, 1286, 1581
Sprung aus dem Stand, 1376
einen Sprung ausführen, 1232
einen Sprung gehechtet ausführen, 1299
einen Sprung gehockt ausführen, 1300
Sprung mit Anlauf, 1355
Sprung rückwärts, 1418
einen Sprung verweigern, 1343
Sprung vorwärts, 1546
Sprunganlage, 149, 1215
Sprungbalken, 321
Sprungball, 563
Sprungbecken, 1222
Sprungbein, 323, 716, 1331
Sprungbezeichnung, 1312
Sprungbrett, 1371, 1748
das Sprungbrett niederdrücken, 1337
Sprungergebnis, 1359
Sprungfamilien (Herren), 2012
Sprungfuss, 322
Sprunggruppen, 1214
Sprunggruppen (Damen), 2013
Sprunghakenwurf, 565
Sprunghöhe, 1268
Sprungkraft, 72, 227
Sprunglatte, 18
Sprungliste, 1218, 1294
Sprungmatten, 153, 154
Sprungnummer, 1210
Sprungpferd, 2015
Sprungphase, 320
Sprungstab, 221
Sprungständer, 226, 359
Sprungständer für Stabhochsprung, 225
Sprungtabelle, 1220
Sprungtechnik, 1221
Sprungturm (10 m-Turm), 1269
Sprungverein, 1212

Sprungwettbewerbe, 148
Sprungwurf, 566
Spurt, 828
Stab, 19
stababgebender Läufer, 131
stababnehmender Läufer, 208
Stabhochspringer, 223
Stabhochsprung, 222
Stabhochsprunganlage, 224
Stabilität, 1971
Stabilität in der Landung, 1972
Staffel, 248, 1018, 2158
Staffellauf, 250
Staffelläufer, 251
Staffelmannschaft, 252
Staffelschwimmer, 2159, 2161
Staffelstab, 249
Staffelübergabe, 20
Staffelwettbewerbe, Frauen, 2219
Staffelwettbewerbe, Männer, 2138
Stahlseil zum Spannen des Netzes, 2659
Stammspieler, 2752
Stand, 1375, 1958, 1973
Stand für Starter, 291
Standardrad, 1074
Ständige Kommission, 992, 1075
Stärke der Ersatzspieler, 412
starke Seite, 708
starker Endspurtläufer, 312
Start, 285, 1080, 2174
Startabstand, 1085
Startaufruf, 829
Startblock, 292, 2176
Starten, 1081
Starter, 289, 1084, 2175
Startfolge, 1087
Starthelfer, 1001
Startlinie, 293, 1086, 1605
Startliste, 286, 1083

Startnummer, 201, 939
Startordner, 290
Startpistole, 294, 1088, 2179
Startpodium, 2180
Startschuss, 2102
Startschwimmer, 2126
Startsignal, 2983
Startsprung, 2177
Startstellung, 295, 2181
Starttechnik, 2182
Startzeichen, 296
das Startzeichen geben, 907
Statistik, 702
Statistiker, 701
Steckschlüssel, 811
Steckwurf, 709
stehender Start, 1076
Steherlinie, 1089
Stehversuch, 1079
Steigung, 920
stellen, 2734
Stellspiel, 2737
Stellspieler, 2736
Stellung, 1330, 1607, 2391
Stellwalze, 1261
Stichkampf, 146, 1420
einen Stichkampf austragen, 1509
Stil, 313, 2186
Stillstand, 1078
Stirnwände, 2079
Stoppball, 2298
Stoppuhr, 307, 1977, 2183
Stören, 560
Stoss, 234, 1570, 1697
Stoss nach unten, 483, 694
Stossanlage, 235
Stossbalken, 306
stossen, 232
Stosskissen, 1712

Stosskreis; Wurfkreis, 334
Strafe, 627, 991, 1048, 2383, 2925
Strafpunkt, 888
Strafpistole, 1621
Strafuhr, 2926
Strafwurf, 2927
Strasse, 1028, 1039
Strasseneinzelfahren, 927
Strassenfahrer, 1037
Strassengehen, 258
Strassenrannschaftsrennen, 1102
Strassenordnung, 1131
Strassenreifen, 1035
Strassenrennrad, 1030, 1036
Strassenrennsport, 1031
Strassentrikot; Strassenweste, 1032
Strecke, 841, 856
die Strecke markieren, 959
eine Strecke zurücklegen, 2066
strecken, 1979
Streckung, 1192
streichen, 2165
Stufenbarren, 2008
Stuhlrichter, 2259
Stulpe, 1677
Stürmer, 2854
Sturz, 882, 1065, 1814
Sturzkappe, 919
Stütz, 1983
Stützwaage, 1928
Switch, 2757
synthetische Fläche, 2469
synthetische Saiten, 2468
System, 2758

tadellose Ausführung, 1923
Tafel, 932
Taktik, 2760

Taktik des Angriffs in zweiter Absicht, 1666
taktisch, 2761
taktische Kombination, 2762
taktisches Aufstellen, 2763
taktisches Schema, 2764
täuschen, 2598
Täuschung, 492, 498, 2600
Taxation, 1877, 1960
Taxationssystem, 1879
Taxationsübertragung, 1878
Technik, 328
technische Ausführung, 1995
technische Kommission, 1103
technische Kommission für Frauenwettbewerbe, 2022
technische Kommission für Männerwettbewerbe, 1902
technische Leitung, 1473
technische Schiedsrichter, 1996
technischer Leiter, 327
technischer Mitarbeiter, 1957
technisches Foul, 726
technisches Reglement, 1997
Tempo, 985
Tempowechsel, 836, 838
Tennis spielen, 2386
Tennisaufgabe, 2681, 2770
Tennisellbogen, 2473
Terz, 1698
"Tiebreak"; Entscheidung, 2479
"Tiebreaker" für Mannschaftsresultate, 737
tiefer Beckenteil, 2842
tiefer Pivot, 580
Tiefstart, 46
tippen, 747
Tisch des Anschreibers, 2721
Titelverteidiger, 1111

Tonband, 1755, 1991
Tonzeichen, 2000
Topometer; Entfernungsmesser, 343
Topspin, 2683, 2779
Tor, 2863
ein Tor anzeigen, 2804
ein Tor erzielen, 2962
Tor erzielt, 2870
Torabwurf, 2871
Torausmasse, 2905
Torhüterkappe, 2873
Torlatte, 2841
Torlinie, 2867
Torlinienrichter, 2865
Torpfosten, 2869
Torwart, 2872
toten, 2630
toter Ball, 458, 2540, 2570
totes Rennen, 865
Trainer, 37, 445, 844, 1442, 2062, 2262, 2562
Trainerbank, 2689
trainieren, 2263, 2395
Training, 2394
Trainingbecken, 2204
Trainingslager, 2003
Trainingsprogramm, 2205
Trainingsreifen, 1132
Trainingswand, 2231
Treffen, 966, 1563, 1688, 1703, 2354, 2355
Treffer, 1562, 1702
den Treffer für ungültig erklären, 1411
Treffpunkt, 2390
Treffvorrecht, 1634, 1652
Treppen des Sprungturms, 1380
treten, 989, 1137
Trikot, 362, 938

Trinkflasche, 1142
Trostspiel, 2266
Turm (Plattform), 1391
Turmspringen, 1326, 1328, 1392
Turmspringen (Damen), 1407
Turmspringen (Herren), 1310
Turmspringer, 1327
Turner, 1835
Turngeräte, 1836
Turnleiter, 1840
Turnorganisationskomitee, 1838
Turnserie, 1839
Turnvorsitzende, 1837

über das Netz, 2380
über das Netz reichen, 2686
über dem Kopf passen, 619
über zwei Gewinnsätze, 2488
Überbelastung, 620
überdachte Bahn, 857, 930
überholen, 210, 211, 982, 986
Überlaufrinne, 2103
Überprüfung, 361
Überprüfung der Geräte, 1864
Überprüfung der Lizenzen, 953
überqueren, 32, 209
Überrumpelungsschlag, 2311
Überschlagelemente, 1848
Überschlagwende, 2170
Überschreiten, 1620
Überschreiten der Bahnbegrenzung, 1603
Überschreiten der Linie, 2637
Überschreiten der Mittellinie, 2568, 2569, 2780
Übersetzen, 90
überspielen, 618
übertreten, 97, 303
Überwachung der Staffelablösung, 2160

überwerten, 1321
Überzahlverhältnis, 615
Übung am Schwebebalken, 1747
Übung am Seitpferd, 1811
Übung am Stufenbarren, 1812
Übung an den Ringen, 1945
die Übung beginnen, 1906
eine Übung gegengleich ausführen, 1943
Übungen zum Aufwärmen, 2019
Übungsbewertung, 1802
Übungsteil, 1922
Übungszusammenstellung, 1768
die Uhr anhalten, 2986
die Uhr stoppen, 705
Umgehung, 1476
umstellen, 2497
unbeabsichtigter Fall in das Wasser, 1243
unbefestigte Kappe, 2826
unbewaffneter Arm, 1709
unerwartete Rückkehr nach dem ersten Pass, 2590
ungerade Spiele, 2366
ungültige Treffläche, 1576
ungültiger Korberfolg, 468
ungültiger Treffer, 1567, 1575, 1600, 1602
ungünstiges Wetter, 1153
Universalspieler, 2769
unregelmässiger Beinschlag, 2049
unsauber eintauchen, 1298
unsportliches Verhalten, 766, 2810, 2908
Unterbrechung, 1681, 1976
Unterbrechung einer Begegnung, 2627
unterbrochen, 2254
unterbrochene Serie, 1868
unteres Zuspiel, 2550, 2551

Unterstützung, 1737
Unterwasserarbeit, 3006
untypische Elemente, 2007

Ventil, 1139
Verantwortlicher für die E-Anlage, 1689
Verbinder, 2961
Verbindung, 1772
Verbindung von Übungselementen, 1771
Verbindungsteil, 1770
verbleibende Wertungen, 1305
Verein, 1190
verfehlen, 2358
verfehlter Freiwurf, 589
Verfolgung, 998
Verfolgungsrennen, 999
Verkehrung nach Pivotschirm, 689
Verlängerung, 490, 621
Verlaufsfolge, 1915
verletzter Spieler, 2886
Verletzung, 934
verlieren, 2342
Verlierer, 2343
verlorener Satz, 2619
Verlust der Spielberechtigung, 510
Verlust des Spiels, 2608
Vermessungstechniker, 203
Verpflegung, 884
Verpflegungsstationen, 76, 247
Verpflegungsstelle, 885
verschoben, 2392
versetzter Start, 283
verstellbare Gummiwalze, 1152
Versuch, 14, 353
verteidigend, 2280
Verteidiger, 460, 2808, 2843, 2844
Verteidigung, 459, 2572
die Verteidigung durchbrechen, 628

Verteidigungsabpraller, 462
Verteidigungsgespräch zwischen den Spielern, 717
Verteidigungslob, 2281
Verteidigungsposition, 463
Verteidigungsrutsche (Zone), 464
Verteidigungssystem, 2577
Verteidigungszone, 2527
Verteidigungsgleichgewicht, 461
vertikales Eintauchen, 1398
verunsichert sein, 526
Verwarnung, 1141, 1713
Verweis, 2792
verzögern, 2282, 2890, 3010
verzögerter Angriff, 465
Videobandzeitnahme, 2210
vier-m-Linie, 2857
vier-m-Raum, 2856
vier x 100-m Freistilschwimmen; vier x 200-m, 2092
vier x 100 m Lagenschwimmen, 2093
Viererzugatmung, 2094
Viertel, 2928
Viertelfinale, 2399
Viertelfinalist, 2398
Viertelpause, 2887
Virtuosität, 2017
Viskosität, 2211
Volleyball, 2787
Volleyballmannschaft, 2789
Volleyballspieler, 2788
vollzählige Mannschaft, 2860
Volte, 1707
vom Beckengrund hochspringen, 2943
vom Gerät gehen, 1788
vom Spiel ausschliessen, 2919
von hinten decken, 535
Vorbau des Remlenkers, 913, 1090
vorbereiteter Korbwurf, 683
vorderer Fuss, 523

vorderes Bein, 1584
vorderes Ende des Sprungbretts, 1185
Vorderrad, 904
Vorderspieler, 511
Vorfeld, 522
Vorgabe, 1047
Vorgaberunde, 944
Vorhand, 2312
Vorhandflugball, 2316
Vorhandgriff, 2314
Vorhandlob, 2315
Vorhandstoppball, 2313
vorherbestimmte Verteidigung, 1628
Vorkämpfe, 1334, 1335
Vorkampfergebnisse, 1336
vorlings, 1239
vorne links, 2634
vorne Mitte, 2649
Vorrennen, 1052
vorschriftsmässig wechseln, 118
Vorsprung, 161
den Vorsprung ausbauen, 132, 207
den Vorsprung halten, 178
Vorteil, 2223, 2332
Vorteil Aufschläger, 2221
Vorteil Rückschläger, 2222
Vorteilregel, 2802
Vorwärtsbewegung, 1410, 1547, 2654
Vorwärtsdrall, 2482
Vorwärtsschwung, 2318
Vorwärtssprung; mit halber Schraube; mit Schraube, 1257

W-Formation, 2790
waagerechte Ebene, 1272
waffenführender Arm, 1715
Waffenhaltung, 1556
Waffenkontrolle, 1716
Waffenprüfgerät, 1412

Wagen der Wettkampfleitung, 977
Wahl der Aufgabe, 2559
Wand, 2212
Wanderkreisen, 2004
Wappen; Insignien, 1199
Warnlinie, 1714
das Wasser treten, 3003
das Wasser verlassen, 1236. 2891
Wasserball, 3011
Wasserball spielen, 2931
Wasserballmannschaft, 3015
Wasserballregel, 3014
Wasserballschiedsrichter, 3013
Wasserballspieler, 3012
Wassergraben, 371
Wasserhöhe, 2213
Wasseroberfläche, 1383, 1405, 2215
Wassertemperatur, 1406, 2200
Wassertiefe, 1206
Wasserwiderstand, 2214
Wechsel, 711, 715
Wechsel der Bindung, 1439
Wechsel der Geräte, 1950
Wechsel der Mannschaften, 1951
Wechsel der Spielfeldseiten, 2832
Wechsel im Schrittrhythmus, 29
einen Wechsel verlangen, 659
Wechselklingenschlag, 1437
wechselndes Dribbling, 455
Wechselraum, 212, 253, 325
Weichboden, 1886
weicher Block, 2745
weiches Brett, 1365
weisse Anzeigelampe, 1717
weisse Flagge, 3019
weisse Kappe, 3018
weisse Markierung, 3020
Weitspringer, 175
Weitsprung, 173

Weitsprunganlage, 174
Wende, 796, 2206
Wende im Spielverlauf, 757
Wenden beim Lagenschwimmen, 2109
Wendepunktbeobachtungszone, 2133
Wendepunktrichter, 797, 1136
Wenderichter, 2113, 2124, 2207
Wendetechnik, 2208
wenig bewegendes Spiel, 2984
das Werfen, 378, 2967, 2998
Werfen; Stossen, 329
Werfer; Stosser, 330
Werteile, 2010
Wertung, 842
Wertungsfaktoren, 1285
Wertungsrichter, 1216, 1284
Wertungstafeln, 1275
Wertungsvorschrift, 1961
Wertungsvorschriften, 1759
"Westerngriff", 2506
Wettbewerb, 851, 880
Wettbewerbe, 77
Wettbewerbe auf der Strasse, 257
Wettbewerbe im Kopfsprung, 1213
Wettbewerbmütze, 2838
Wettbewerbsleiter, 1309
Wettfahrausschuss, 849
Wettkampf, 40, 71, 192, 2264, 2642
Wettkampf IA; IB; II; III, 1763
Wettkampfbecken, 2063
Wettkämpfer, 2265
Wettkampfgericht, 1582
Wettkampfleiter, 41, 193, 1762
Wettkampfleitung, 881
Wettkampfprogramm, 268, 1196, 1231
Wettkampfprotokoll, 1315
Wettkampfrichter, 847

Wettkampfschwimmen, 2065
Wettkampfschwimmer, 2064
wieder ins Spiel gehen, 2957
Wiederaufnahme der Grundstellung, 1641
Wiederaufnahme der Spielzeit, 739
wiederholen, 1021
Wiederholschuss bei einem Fehlstart, 240
wiederholter Versuch, 3
Wiederholung einer Übung, 1941
Wiederholung eines Elementes, 1940
Wiegetritt, 1077
"wildern", 2388
Windmesser, 373
Windschatten, 1059
einen Winkelstoss durchführen, 1477
Wippen auf dem Brett, 1227, 1333
Wurf, 688
Wurf- und Stossdisziplinen, 336
einen Wurf blocken, 415
Wurf mit Fingerspitzen, 3000
Wurf; Stoss, 331
Wurf von unten, 764
Wurfanlage ; Stossanlage, 337
Wurfarm; Stossarm, 332
Wurfart, 687
Wurfrichtung; Stossrichtung, 335
Wurfsektor, 339
Wurfsektor; Stosssektor; Sprunggrube, 152
Wurftäuschung, 493
Wurfwinkel, 686

x Punkte Vorsprung haben, 164
x Sekunden Vorsprung haben, 165

zahlenmässige Überlegenheit, 2901
zahlenmässige Unterlegenheit, 2902

Zahn, 1114
Zehedruck, 1389
Zehen gestreckt, 1329
Zeheplatte, 1112
Zehnkampf, 51
Zehnkämpfer, 50
Zeichen der Schiedsrichter, 608
Zeit für Freiwurf, 740
Zeitfahren, 1106, 1107
Zeitfehler, 1999
Zeitnehmen, 1109, 1110
Zeitnehmer, 342, 746, 1108, 1700, 2001, 2201, 2999
Zeitnehmerassistent, 2806
Zeitnehmerobmann, 31, 2058
Zeitnehmertreppe, 202
Zeitreagierung, 239
Zeitvorgabe für Reklamation, 1105
Zeitzuschuss wegen Verletzung, 741
Ziel, 889, 2087
Zielanschlag, 2088

Zielband, 87
Zielfoto, 215, 993
Zielgerade, 86, 921
Zielkamera, 216
Zielkontrolle, 890
Zielkurve, 79, 120
Ziellinie, 84, 892
Zielpfosten, 85
Zielrichter, 83, 891, 2089
Zone, 774
Zonenfehler, 1891
Zonenpressdeckung, 525
Zonenpressdeckung ab Spielfeldmitte, 541
Zonenrichter, 1892
Zonenverteidigung, 775
zu langer Schlag, 2507
Zugphase, 2149
zum Ball zurückrollen, 664
zum Netz stürzen, 2417
Zurückprallen, 654, 655

zurückschlagen, 2414
zurückweichen, 1650
zusammengesetzte Parade, 1444
zusammengesetzte Riposte, 1445
zusammengesetzter Angriff, 1443
Zusammenpassung, 585
Zusammenstoss, 446
zusätzlicher Abzug, 1982
zusätzlicher Anschwung, 1813, 1865
zusätzlicher C, 1727
Zuspieler, 625
zutippen, 718, 749
Zwei Freiwürfe, 758
zwei-m-Linie, 3005
zwei-m-Raum, 3004
"zwei Meter!", 1708
Zwei-Minuten-Uhr, 357
Zweierblock, 2784
zweifaches Wippen, 1202
zweihändige Rückhand, 2486
Zweihandschläge, 2487

Zweihandvorhand, 2485
zweihundert-m-Linie, 1138
zweite Absicht, 1665
zweite Spielhälfte, 680
zweite Spielzeit, 2963
zweiter Protokollführer, 1363
zweiter Schiedsrichter, 763, 2723
Zwischenstoss mit Opposition, 1686
Zwischenzeit, 137, 2125, 2171
Zwischenzeit nach halber Bahnlänge, 911
Zylinder, 457
10-Sekunden-Regel, 728
100-m-Freistilschwimmen; 200-m; 400-m; 800-m; 1500-m, 2098
200-m Lagenschwimmen; 400-m, 2110
30-Sekunden-Regel, 730
30-Sekunden-Zeitnehmer, 729

абсолютное первенство, 1729
автоматическая потеря игры, 510
автоматическое устройство для определения времени и места, 2030
автомобиль с ремонтной мастерской, 1053
автомобиль судейской коллегии, 846, 978
акробатический силовой элемент, 1726
акробатический элемент, 1723
"Але!" "Начинайте!", 1507
амплитуда, 1731
амплитуда движения, 1732
анемометр, 373
аннулирование укола, 1411
антенны, 2519
антидопинговая проба, 1047
антидопинговый контроль, 7, 871
апелляционное жюри, 150, 940, 1583, 1881
арена, 10
атака, 385, 1414, 1604, 2520
атака барьера, 319
атака бегом, 1654
атака из головной группы, 783
атака на оружие, 1416
атака на подготовку, 1417
атака планки, 320
атака по краю , 773
атака с задней линии, 2530
атака с захватом: захват, 1635
атака с оппозицией, 1415
атака с первой передачи, 2584
атака сзади, 784
атака стрелой, 1534
атаковать, 482, 782, 2029
атакующая игра, 2367

атакующий, 2526
атакующий игрок, 2807
атакующий удар, 2747

балка для седла или руля, 1090
балка, держащая седло, 1045
балка, поддерживающая руль, 913
барьер, 124
барьер для бега с препятствиями, 300
барьерист, 126
барьерный бег, 125
барьеры для стипль-чеза, 298
баскетболист, 407
баскетбольная игра, 406
баскетбольный мяч, 404
баскетбольный тренер, 405
бассейн, 2145, 2195
бассейн для прыжков в воду, 1222
бассейн для соревнования, 2063
батман, 1422
батман ногой, 1423
баттерфляй, 2051, 2091
бег, 236, 264, 1954
бег для разминки, 370
бег на дальнюю дистанцию, 171
бег на средние дистанции, 197
бег по дорожке, 157
бегун, 263
бегун в эстафете, 251
бегун на дальние дистанции, 172
бегун на средние дистанции, 198
бегун, передающий эстафету, 131
бегун, принимающий палочку, 208
безупречное выполнение, 1923
белая разметка, 3020
белая шапочка, 3018
белый свет, 1717
белый флажок, 3019

бить по блоку, 2749
бить по мячу, 2748
ближний бой, 1572
ближняя часть, 1908
близкая игра, 2261
близкий бросок, 443
близкий финиш, 36, 341, 843, 2061
блок, 2543
блок подачи, 2728
блок с отведенными назад кистями, 2745
блок, забивающий очко, 2754
блокированный удар, 2546
блокировать, 414, 2544
блокировать бросок, 415
блокировать противника от корзины, 416, 422
блокирующий, 2547
бой, 1430
боковая линия, 2743, 2972
боковая линия поля, 690
боковая подача, 2742
боковая стенка, 2168
боковое кручение, 2443
боковой ветер, 1056
боковые границы сектора, 237
боковые линии для одиночного разряда, 2449
боковые линии для парного разряда, 2291
болельщики , 494
болт, 807
больше у подающего, 2221
борт бассейна, 2069, 2849
брасс, 2040
брасс, 100 м.; 200 м., 2044
брассист, 2042
бревно, 1741, 1746
бровка, 47

бросание, 378
бросающий игрок , 685
бросить, 2998
бросить без промедления, 2970
бросить мяч по воротам, 2967
бросить мяч по корзине , 684
бросить с паса, 2969
бросок, 329, 688
бросок в прыжке , 566
бросок в прыжке с поворотом , 756
бросок двумя руками, 762
бросок двумя руками из-за головы, 760
бросок крюком , 549
бросок крюком в прыжке , 565
бросок назад, 2809
бросок одной рукой , 610, 2915
бросок одной рукой в прыжке , 569
бросок от ворот, 2871
бросок с игры, 500
бросок сверху , 709
бросок сверху из-под кольца, 483
бросок снизу , 764
бросок, кручёный по-английски, 487
брусок для отталкивания, 321
брусья, 1921
брусья разной высоты, 2008
буёк для поддержки ног, 2150
быстро действовать, 552
быстро крутить педали, 1066
быстро крутить педалями , 1137
"быстрый" бассейн, 2085
быстрый отрыв, 495
быть в форме, 792
быть свободным от игры, 2253
бьющий игрок, 2750

в игре, 2328

"в пол!", 1608
в сетку, 2224
вбрасывание , 735
введение мяча в игру , 653
введение мяча из-за боковой линии , 691
введённый в игру судьей, 2944
ввести мяч в игру, 2945
вдыхание, 2045, 2112
вдыхание в двухкратном такте, 2074
вдыхание в четырёхкратном такте, 2094
ведение клинка пальцами, 1531
ведение мяча, 481
ведение мяча за спиной, 409
ведение мяча с повотором , 660
ведение мяча со сменой рук, 455
ведущая группа, 949
ведущий запись, 2156
ведущий игру, 2334
ведущий мяч, 480
велодром, 861
велоперчатки, 1123
велорубашка, 1130
велосипед, 798, 956
велосипедист, 801
велосипедист; велогонщик, 864
велосипедные туфли, 863
велосипедный спорт, 862
велотрек, 800
велошапочка, 830
вентиль, 1139
верёвка фальстарта, 2084
верёвочная ручка копья, 43
вернуться к игре, 2957
вертикальная ось, 2016
вертикальная плоскость, 1399
вертикальный вход, 1398
верхнее вращение, 2683

верхний боковой удар, 2716
верхний конец вилки, 899
верхний край сетки, 2765
верхняя боковая подача, 2715
верхняя жердь, 1857
верхняя подача, 2681
верхняя прямая подача, 2770
вес мяча, 3016
вес, провоцирующий гибкость клинка, 1695
вести в очках, 166
вести игру, 2333
вести мяч, 478
вести мяч со сменой рук, 479
вести перебой, 1509
ветер в спину, 1097
взаимопомощь велосипедистов, 781
взмах вверх, 2498
взять мяч под воду, 2997
вид плавания, 2194
вид соревнования, 71, 880, 1500
виды метания, 336
виды прыжков, 148
виды соревнований, 1196, 1231
вилка, 898
винт, 1049, 1396
вираж, 796, 860
виражист, 21
виражный бег, 22
виртуозность, 2017
владение мячом, 392, 393, 644, 2535
владеть мячом , 542, 2820
вмешательство , 560
вне дорожки, 1616
вне игры, 2378
"внимание!", 272
вновь завладеть мячом , 656
внутренний заслон , 557

внутренний край ограничительных линий , 556
внутренняя бровка дорожки, 135, 936
внутренняя дорожка, 136
внутри, 2330
возвратиться к мячу, 664
возвращение подачи, 2438
возвышение стартера, 291
воздерживание, 1409
возобновление, 1644
возобновление игры , 739
возобновление игры после гола, 2954
возобновление игры судьей, 2955
возражение, 1338
войти в игру, 2595
волейболист, 2788
волейбольная команда, 2789
волейбольный мяч, 2787
вольное упражнение, 1828
вольный стиль, 2095
вольный стиль, 100 м.; 200 м.; 400 м.; 800 м.; 1500 м., 2098
вооружённая рука, 1715
ворота противника , 2916
восточный захват ракетки, 2299
восьмая позиция, 1601
вратарь, 2872
вращение, 1369
вращение при метании, 338
вращение, не доходящее до девяноста градусов, 1364
время игры, 640
время на отрезке дистанции, 2125, 2171
время по ручному секундомеру, 2104
время реакции на стартовый сигнал, 239

время фехтовального движения, 1527
время явки на соревнование, 255
время, выделенное для штрафного броска , 740
время, данное на замену , 742
время, данное на травму, 741
все партии, выигранные подряд, 2460
всплеск, 1370
всплыть, 2078
вспомогательный штат, 583
встретиться, 2355
встреча, 966, 1596, 2354
встречный ветер, 916
втискивать бегуна, 23
вторая неправильная подача, 2285
вторая нога, проходящая над барьером, 351
вторая позиция, 1667
вторая половина игры , 680
второе намерение, 1665
второй секретарь, 1363
второй судья, 2723
второй тайм, 2963
втыкание шеста, 218
вход, 1229
вход без всплеска, 1354
вход в воду головой вниз, 1267
вход в воду ногами вниз, 1245
вход в поворот, 287
вход в соревнование, 879
вход с пузырьками, 1182
выбор корзины, 441
выбор мяча, 440
выбор подачи, 2559
выбор сторон, 2835
выбор шапочек, 2834
выбывать, 2413

выбывать из состязания, 2300
выгодная ситуация, 380
выделенное "мёртвое" время, 438
выдержка, 1856
выдыхание, 2046, 2081
вызов, 1577
вызов соревнующихся, 1435
вызов участников, 27
выигранная игра, 2620
выиграть, 2509
выиграть из-за неявки противника 772
выиграть на одну длину колеса, 1150
выиграть на одну ширину шины, 1149
выиграть обмен, 2796
выиграть обмен от блока, 2799
выиграть подачу, 2591, 2795
выиграть с подачи соперника, 2251
выигрыш , 2508
выигрыш очка, 2797
выигрыш подачи, 2798
выигрыш принимающего, 2434
выйти за..., 97
выйти из воды, 2891
выйти из своего поля защиты и в него вернуться , 617
выйти из соревнования, 2277
выйти на поверхность, 2188
вынос руки, 2027
вынуждать противника, 651
вынужденная ошибка, 2310
вынужденный бросок, 509
выпад, 1591
выполнение , 1808
выполнение прыжка, 1233
выполнение упражнения, 1810
выполнить прыжок, 1232

выполнить прыжок в группировке, 1300
выполнить прыжок согнувшись, 1299
выпрямиться, 1192, 1316
выпрямиться из прыжка в группировке, 1194
выпрямиться из прыжка согнувшись, 1193
выпрямиться из прыжка согнувшись или в группировке, 1235
выпрямление, 1318
выпрямление из прыжка, 1234
выпрямление тела у входа в воду, 1293
вырваться вперёд, 24
высокая передача, 2624
высокая свеча, 2325
высокий старт, 284
высота планки, 108
высота поперечной перекладины, 2878
высота прыжка, 1268
высота сетки, 2661
высота снаряда, 1855
выталкивание снаряда, 52
вытягивать, 1979
вытянутые пальцы ног, 1329
вытянутый, 1290
выход из воды, 1236
выход из гонки, 1023
выход из состязания, 2513
выход с задней линии, 2688
выходящий игрок, 2679
вычислитель/механический; картонный/, 1183
вышка, 1325, 1391
вышка судьи, 2490, 2953

вязкость, 2211

гаечный ключ, 811
гайка, 975
гарда, 1554
гарда рапиры, 1542
гарда сабли, 1659
гарда шпаги, 1497
гасить, 2455, 2630
гибкость, 1824
гимнаст, 1835
гимнастические туфли, 1834
гимнастический мостик, 1748
гимнастический организационный комитет, 1838
гимнастический снаряд, 1836
глава делегации, 1783
главная группа, 957
главный корт, 2349
главный секретарь, 1852
главный секундометрист, 2058
главный судья, 1850. 1920, 2057
главный судья-секундометрист, 31
гладилка, 267
глубина воды, 1206
глубокая сторона, 2842
глубокий ответный удар, 2274
глубокий удар, 2275
гол, 2863
гол забит, 2870
голова ракетки, 2404
головка эфеса, 1625
голубая линия, 805
голубая шапочка, 2821
голубой флажок, 2822
гонка, 1005
гонка на время, 1106, 1107
гонка на треке, 1124
гоночные трусы, 1009

гоночный велосипед, 1008
гонщик, 1025
гонщик на треке, 806, 1127
гонщик-трековик, 1125
гонщик-шоссейник, 1037
горизонтальная ось, 1858
горизонтальная плоскость, 1272
горизонтальный упор, 1928
горизонтальный шпагат, 1888
государственный гимн, 200
"Готовы?", 1413
граница бассейна, 2825
граница поля игры, 2824
граница трека, 1116
грациозность прыжка, 1263
гребок в баттерфляе, 2053
грубая игра, 2960, 3008
грубая ошибка, 2900
грубые ошибки, 1887
группа, 25, 99, 825
группа С, 1753
группа судей, 1919
группироваться, 1395
группировка, 1394
групповое падение, 960
групповой старт, 961
групповой финиш, 826
группы прыжков/женчины/, 2013
группы элементов, 1797

давать сигнал флажком, 2976
давать толчок, 1969
давление, 1632
дальняя дистанция, 170
дальняя часть, 1815
дальняя часть коня для прыжков, 1910
дальняя часть коня с ручками, 1909
дать знак на старт, 907
дать пас на удар, 2734

дать сигнал начала игры, 2974
"два метра!", 1708
два штрафных броска, 758
две из трех партий, 2488
двенадцатиметровая линия, 1138
движение, 2651
движение в сторону, 2655
движение вперед, 1410, 2654
движение к мячу, 2656
движение назад, 2652
движение ног, 2115
движение ног при плавании брассом, 2041
движение под мяч, 2657
движение соединения, 1770
двойная опека, 477
двойное ведение, 473
двойное соединение, 1480
двойной блок, 2784
двойной заслон, 476
двойной отскок, 1223
двойной укол, 2587
двойной укол, 1481
двойной фол, 474
двустороннее дыхание, 2038
двусторонний обход центрового, 648
двухметровая зона, 3004
двухметровая линия, 3005
двухминутные часы, 357
действие в воздухе, 2
действие рук, 2026
действительность гола, 3007
действительный укол, 1710
дельфин, 2072
держаться бровки, 122
держаться бровки при повороте, 123
десятиборец, 50
десятиборье, 51

десятиметровая вышка, 1269
дефектное оружие, 1503
диагональная защита, 1470
диагональные поля подачи, 2227
диктор, 2025
диктор соревнований, 1314
дирижер, 641
диск, 54
дисквалификация , 469, 2071, 2585
дисквалификация команды, 869
дисквалифицированный, 870
дисквалифицированный игрок, 470
дисквалифицировать, 2284
дисквалифицирующий фол, 471
дискобол, 56
дистанция, 60, 1479
дистанция между барьерами, 61
длина, 2129
длина дорожки, 1586
длина клинка, 1585
длина разбега, 1
длина сетки, 2662
дно бассейна, 1180, 2039, 2823
добавочная попытка, 3
добавочная сбавка, 1982
добивание, 749
добить , 747
добить мяч в корзину , 748
добиться участия, 2397
догнать, 210, 982
догнать изнутри, 983
догнать снаружи, 984
допинг, 872
дополнительное время, 2920
дополнительный бросок, 621
дополнительный мах, 1813
дополнительный период, 490
дополнительный судья, 2023
дополнительный элемент группы С, 1727

дорога, 1028
дорожка, 155, 345, 1622, 2118
дорожка для разбега, 265
дорожная майка, 1032
дорожная линия, 1035
дорожное кольцо, 1029
дорожный разметочный столб, 1033
доска, 1179
доска "максифлекс В", 1187
доска из стекловолокна, 1246
доска объявлений, 932, 974
доставание трудного низкого мяча, 2580
дотронуться до мяча, 3001
дотронуться до мяча двумя руками одновременно, 3002
дриблинг, 2846
дуга, 1157
дыхательный ритм, 2155

езда на велосипеде по закрытому треку, 931
езда назад, 789
езда по треку, 1120
езда по шоссе, 1031
ехать, 1024
ехать на доске, 1353

ждать сигнала судьи, 3009
желтая карточка, 2800
желтый свет, 1721
желтый флажок, 1151
женская техническая комиссия, 2022
женские командные виды соревнований, 376, 2219
женские одиночные виды соревнований, 375
женский одиночный разряд, 2515

женский парный разряд, 2514
женское соревнование по прыжкам с вышки, 1407
женское соревнование по прыжкам с трамплина, 1408
жеребьевка, 873, 1224, 2295, 2563
жеребьевка на дорожки, 66
жеребьевка на корзины , 750
жеребьевка на порядок выступления, 1791
жеребьевка на распределение судей, 1790
жеребьевка на финал, 1789
жесты судьи , 608
"живой" мяч , 575
жюри, 1582
жюри по прыжкам в воду, 1217
жюри по рассмотру протестов , 1288

за границами, 1918, 2677
за границами поля/аут , 613
за линией, 2379
за пределами площадки, 2377
за!, 2375
забеги, 107
забить гол, 2962
забить очко, 2421
забросить мяч , 668
заведующий вычислением результатов, 1962
заведующий оборудованием, 327
заведующий сбором спортсменов, 186
заведующий соревнованием, 41
завысить очки, 1321
завязывание, 1425, 1587, 1691
загородить путь соперника, 802
заграждение пути, 803

задержанный мяч, 2623
задержать противника , 547
задерживать игру, 2579
задерживать мяч, 521
заднее колесо, 788
задняя граница дорожки, 1642
задняя линия, 2246
задняя нога, 1706
задняя стойка, 1238
задняя часть корта, 2232
заезд, 962
заезд преследования, 999
заезд; гит, 917
закрыть велосипедиста, 810
закончить дистанцию, 2066
закрепить, 1104
закрытый бассейн, 2111
закрытый игрок , 536
закрытый корт, 2329
закрытый трек; 857, 930
закрыться, 1461
замах, 2467
замах вниз, 2293
замах вперед, 2318
замах назад, 2242
замедленное нападение, 465
замедлить игру, 466
замена , 711, 2706
замена брусьев, 1743
замена велосипеда, 837
замена игрока, 638
замена колеса, 1146
заменяющий игрок, 2755
занос, 1058
занявший второе место , 2416
западный захват ракетки, 2506
запасное измерение времени при помощи телекамеры, 2210
запасное колесо. 1063

запасной бегун, 314
запасной гимнаст, 1730, 1980
запасной игрок , 710, 2756, 2992
запасной хронометрист, 256
зарегистрироваться, 1344
заслон, 632, 674, 2722
заслон глаз соперника рукой, 491
заслон и поворот , 633, 676
заслонить , 675
заступ, 303
заступить, 209
засчитанная попытка, 360
затормозить, 814
затягивать, 2282
затягивать время, 3010
затяжной прыжок; переворот, 1320
захват, 2080
захват ракетки, 2320
захват ракетки для удара слева, 2236
захват ракетки для удара справа, 2314
зашаг, 2308, 2607
защита, 459, 2572
защита "игрок в игрока", 581
защита задней линии, 2528
защита корзины от мяча, 401, 533
защититься, 1637
защитная позиция, 1638
защитная расстановка, 2575
защитная свеча, 2281
защитная тактика, 2578
защитник, 460, 2574, 2808, 2843
защитники , 537
защитное положение, 1555
защитные очки, 2100
защитные очки, 1468, 2280
защитный блок, 2573
заявить протест, 2396

звено цепи, 954
звонок , 551
зеленый вымпел, 909
зеленый свет, 1552
зеленый сигнал, 1831
зеленый флажок, 908
зона, 774
зона защиты, 2527
зона нападения, 2525
зона передачи палочки, 212
зона передачи эстафетной палочки, 325
зона передачи эстафеты, 253
зона подбора опеки , 584
зона приземления, 152
зона разбега, 262
зонная защита , 775
зонная защита/квадрат с одним лично опекающим игроком, 421
зонный прессинг на своей половине поля , 541
зонный прессинг по всему полю, 525
зуб, 1114

игра, 2319, 2385, 2618
игра для разминки , 679
игра из-за границ , 614
игра с контролированием мяча , 645
игра у задней линии, 2247
игра у сетки, 2361
играть в водное поло, 2931
играть в теннис, 2386
играть на свободное место, 2384
игровая площадка , 639, 2693
игрок, 2387, 2691
игрок водного поло, 3012
игрок задней линии, 2531

игрок защиты, 2844
игрок линии нападения, 2617
игрок на задней части площадки, 2233
игрок одиночного разряда, 2448
игрок парного разряда, 2290
игрок стартового состава, 2752
игрок у сетки, 2363
игрок, назначенный для возобновления игры, 2932
игрок, пострадавший от нарушения правил, 2855
игрок, преследующий мяч, 753
игроки задней линии, 2529
игроки передней линии, 2616
из задней стойки вперед, 1203
изгиб клинка, 1463
изменение батмана, 1437
изменить решение, 2803
измерение ворот, 2905
измерение времени на половине круга, 911
измерение прыжков и метаний, 188
измерительная лента, 190
измерительная планка, 2645
изогнутый, выгнутый, 1158
изоляция на руле, 915
индивидуальная гонка, 925
индивидуальная шоссейная гонка, 927
индивидуальное преследование, 924
индивидуальное соревнование на треке, 929
индивидуальное шоссейное соревнование, 926
инспектор соревнований по гимнастике, 1840

инструменты и запчасти велосипеда, 799
интервал между партиями , 2772
интервал между периодами, 2887
Интернациональная федерация любительского плавания/ ФИНА/, 2086
Интернациональный комитет по прыжкам в воду, 1278
исключить из соревнования, 2165
исправить неправильный прыжок, 1357
исправление прыжка согнув ноги при входе, 1358
исправление сальто, 1368
исходная оценка, 1744
итальянская рукоятка, 1578

"к бою!", 1607
каденс, 1434
камера, 1133
камера шины, 935
Канадская любительская ассоциация плавания/КАСА/, 2056
канат, 2659
канифоль, 1949
капитан, 2553, 2827
капитан команды, 425, 721, 1693, 2471
каретка, 835
карточки судьи, 2704
касание, 2202
касание линии штрафного броска , 751
касание мяча, 2564
касание поля игры противника, 2780
касание сетки, 2660

кассета, 1755
катапультирующий конец трамплина, 1185
категория велосипедистов, 832
катиться, 1041
катиться свободно, 903
катушка, 1645
катушки, 2199
квалификационный заезд, 1003
квалификация, 1002
квалифицирование, 2153
квалифицирующее время, 2154
километровая отметка, 970
километровый заезд, 941
классификация, 842
классификация соревнующихся, 1441
классифицированный участник соревнования, 1051
классифицированный участник соревнования, 1668
классы прыжков в воду, 1214
клей для однотрубки, 1135
клей; шеллак, 1054
клинок, 1426
клинок рапиры, 1538
клинок сабли, 1656
клинок шпаги, 1493
клуб, 1190
клуб прыжков в воду, 1212
ключевой игрок, 444
колесо, 1145
количество и качество игроков на скамье, 412
количество набранных очков, 1305
колокол, 794
колышек для разметки дорожки, 156
кольца, 1946
кольцо , 550, 841

кольцо корзины, 402
команда, 719, 1098, 1386, 1692, 1992, 2470
команда в большинстве, 2901
команда в меньшинстве, 2902
команда водного поло, 3015
команда противника, 2374
команда-победительница, 2512
командная гонка, 1101
командная гонка на треке, 1128
командная гонка на шоссе, 1102
командная гонка по шоссе, 1034
командная гонка преследования, 1100
командная игра , 722
командное соревнование, 1694
командные результаты, 1994
командный бег, 326
комбинации, 1760
комбинация центрового, 647
комбинированная защита, 447
комбинированная эстафета, 2134
комбинированное плавание , 2136
комбинированные положения, 1191
комбинированные результаты, 1761
комитет соревнования, 849
комплексное плавание, 200 м.; 400 м., 2110
комплект маленьких инструментов, 1060
композиция упражнения, 1768
компютор, ЭВМ, 1198
конец виража, 68
конец времени игры, 488
конец зоны передачи эстафеты, 69
конец партии, 2594
конец поворота, 70
конец упражнения, 1769, 1801
конечная стенка, 2079

конструкция, поддерживающая корзину, 403
консультация судей, 1875
континентальный захват ракетки, 2267
контратака, 1451, 1683
контратака по перчатке, 1682
контратака с оппозицией, 1684
контрнападение, 1455
контролер соревнования, 2060
контролирование мяча, 397
контролированное нападение, 450
контролировать мяч, 449
контроль финиша, 890
контрольный пункт, 852
контрперенос; контрпереход, 1452
контррипост, 1457
контртемп, 1459
контртьерце, 1454
контршесть, 1458
кончик, 1701
кончик рапиры, 1543
конь для женских опорных прыжков, 1964
конь для мужских опорных прыжков, 1894
конь для прыжков, 2015
конь с ручками, 1930
копье, 139
корзина, 400, 424
корзина для мячей, 2818
корзина противника , 612
коридор, 2226
короткая передача, 2738
корт, 2268
коснуться дна бассейна, 1390
коснуться сетки, 2484
коснуться снаряда, 2002
косой отбой, 2270

косой удар, 2229, 2271
косой удар с лета, 2228, 2272
косой удар слева, 2269
костюм для разминки, 2020
коэффициент трудности, 1782
край щита, 484
крайний атакующий, 2680
крайний блокирующий, 2592
красная карточка, 2703
красная разметка, 2951
красная шапочка, 2949
красный вымпел, 1015
красный свет, 1643
красный сигнал, 1937
красный флажок, 1014, 2950
крепкий захват ракетки, 2303
кривая стартовая линия, 48
кроль, 2067
круг, 942
круг для метания, 334
круг для грыжков , 564
круг спереди, 944
круг трека, 945
круговая защита, 1440, 1450, 1456
круговая система с выбыванием, 1488
круговое завязывание, 1491
круп, 1778
крутить педали стоя, 922, 990
кручение, 2457
кручение мяча, 697
крученое ведение мяча, 696
крученый удар назад, 2241
крыло, 1147
купальная шапочка, 2192
купальный костюм, 1178

ладонь руки, 2922
лампочка, 1664

лебедка для сетки, 2667
левая сторона , 2239
левое поле подачи, 2335
левша, 2336
левый защитник , 573, 2892
левый игрок задней линии, 2633
левый игрок передней линии, 2634
левый нападающий , 572, 2893
легко коснуться, 1549
легкоатлет, 346
лезвие, 1466
лестница бассейна, 2146
лидер, 167, 948
лидирование, 161
лидировать, 162, 947
лидировать на один круг, 163
лидировать на...очков, 164
лидировать на...секунд, 165
лидирующая группа, 168
лидирующий гонщик, 950
линии, 1588
линии, ограничивающие
   площадку, 420, 2250
линии, ограничивающие поле
   игры, 2897
линия, 2338
линия в гонках за мотоциклами, 1089
линия ворот, 2867
линия для парного разряда, 2288
линия для спринтеров, 1072
линия нападения, 2522
линия подачи, 2436
линия предупреждения, 1714
линия с буйками, 2896
линия сбора бегунов перед стартовой линией, 12
линия финиша, 84
линия штрафного броска, 518

лист с результатами. 1347
лицевая линия, 399, 486, 2593
лицензия, 952
лицом к вышке, 1237
личное соревнование, 1571
личные мужские соревнования, 195
личные результаты, 1863
личные соревнования, 1862
ложная атака, 886, 1502
"локомотив", 955
локоть теннисиста, 2473
любая позиция , 1155
любимец команды, 1099

магнезия, 1756, 1897
магнитофон, 1754, 1991
майка, 362, 938
максимальная высота, 113
максимальная высота полета, 114
максимальная сбавка, 1900
маленькие ошибки, 1966
марафон, 181
марафонец, 182
маршрут, 856
массажист, 1062
мастер по фехтованию, 1520
мат, 1899
мат для вольных упражнений, 1829
мат для приземления, 154, 1886
матч, 2351, 2642
матч одиночного разряда, 2447
матч парного разряда, 2289
матч с напряженной борьбой, 2324
матч с равным счетом, 2477
матчбол, 2352
мах, 1985
махи вверх, 2009
маховая нога, 169, 317
маховая рука, 316

маховая часть, 1986
машина для выбывших из гонки велосипедистов, 1046
машина с радиопередатчиком, 1010
медаль/золотая; серебряная; бронзовая/, 191
медленная игра, 2978
медленно летящий мяч, 2453
международная встреча, 1867
международная любительская федерация баскетбола/ФИБА/, 562
Международная любительская федерация легкой атлетики /ИААФ/, 138
Международная федерация велосипедистов/УСИ/, 937
Международная федерация волейбола/ИВБФ/, 2626
Международная федерация гимнастики/ФИЖ/, 1866
Международная федерация фехтования/ФИЭ/, 1574
мелкая сторона, 2966
меньше у подающего, 2222
менять корзины, 433
"мертвый" мяч/мяч вне игры, 458
место для разминки, 2018
место занятое, 994
место опоры шатуна, 812
место сбора, 187
место сбора перед соревнованием, 2133
место сбора спортсменов, 13
место тренировки, 2003
метание, 331
метание диска, 55, 57
метание копья, 140, 142
метание молота, 102, 104

метатель, 330
метатель копья, 141
метатель молота, 103
метающая рука, 332
механик, 964
механический, 965
механическое колебание водной поверхности, 1308
мешать игроку, пробивающему штрафной бросок, 472
минимальная высота, 199
минимальная глубина воды, 2906
минутный перерыв, 743
мишень для уколов, 1712
многоборье, 38
многократные штрафные броски, 593
многократный фол, 592
молот, 100
момент выпрямления, 1195
мощный удар, 2393
мужская техническая комиссия, 1902
мужские командные виды соревнований, 2138
мужские командные соревнования, 196
мужские соревнование по прыжкам с вышки, 1310
мужское соревнование по прыжкам с трамплина, 1311
музыкальное сопровождение, 1907
мягкий вход в воду, 1366
мяч, 2243, 2534
мяч в игре, 394, 2536
мяч в пределах площадки, 2537
мяч в сетку, 2538
мяч в сторону, 2507
мяч вне игры, 2540, 2570, 2812
мяч выходит из игры, 391

мяч для водного поло, 3011
мяч за границами площадки, 396
мяч за линию ворот, 2811
мяч за пределами площадки, 2539
мяч засчитан, 2864
мяч коснувшийся сетки, 2542
мяч присужден, 395
мяч совсем переходит линию ворот, 2813
мяч становится "живым", 390
мяч, брошенный в воду, 2815
мяч, брошенный по воде, 2816
мяч, не отвечающий правилам, 2910
мяч, отскакивающий от воды, 2814

на линии, 2369
на спине, 100 м.; 200 м., 2036
"на старт!", 206, 2198
наблюдение за командой противника, 673
навесная передача, 576
навесной бросок, 2899
нагрудник, 1424
надутый мяч, 2885
нажать на доску, 1337
наждачная бумага, 1800
нажим пальцами его, 1389
название прыжка, 1312
назначенный на..., 2419
наклон, 130
наклон дорожки, 348
наклон стартовой площадки, 2169
наклониться, 1750
наклонения, 2631
наконечник клинка, 1624
накрывание, 417
намазать свое тело, 2874
нападающие, 511
нападающий, 602, 2854

нападающий блок, 2669
нападение, 596, 2668
нападение на игрока, 436
нападение против зонной защиты, 598
нападение против личной защиты, 597
напасть на игрока, 437
направить мяч, 718, 2583, 2776
направить мяч в незащищенную зону, 2778
направить мяч за блок, 2777
направление, 53, 2775
направление метания, 335
напряжение струн, 2474
нарочно тратить время, 2890
наружный заслон, 616
наручавная нашивка, 11, 780
нарушение, 767, 933
нарушение в тыловой зоне, 387
нарушение правил, 818
нарушение правила, 666
наскок, 1274, 1905
наскочить, 1906
насос, 996
нательная электропроводящая проволока, 1429
натягивать струны, 2461
научный технический сотрудник, 1957
наушники для связи, 2106
находиться в группе, 1057
начало, 2458
начало виража, 1082
начало игры, 408, 698, 2981
начало партии, 2751
начало полета, 39, 67
начало толчка, 1277
начало упражнения, 1749
начало финишной прямой, 288

начальная высота, 134
начальник соревнования , 1309
начальник состязания, 193
начальный матч, 2371
начальный спорный мяч , 611
начать, 2459
"начинайте!", 1623
нашивка, 1199
"не был!", 1599
не давать противнику поймать мяч , 618
не отобранный, 2495
не по порядку, 2678, 2682
неадекватная поражаемая поверхность, 1576
неблагоприятная погода, 1153
небольшая страховка, 1903
невозвращаемый удар, 2494
невооруженная рука, 1705, 1709
недействительный укол, 1575, 1600
незавершенное движение , 1175
незасчитанный мяч, 468
незащищенное место, 2793
неисправность электрофиксирующего оборудования, 1501
нейтральная зона, 2365
нейтральный круг, 973
неожиданная победа, 2496
неожиданно выиграть, 2497
неопекаемый игрок , 765
неопорная нога , 595
неоправданная ошибка, 2493
неподвижная игра, 2984
неподвижность/стартовая позиция/, 2037
неподвижный заслон, 700
непостоянно попадающий игрок , 707

неправильная подача, 2435
неправильно поданный мяч, 2302
неправильное ведение мяча , 553
неправильное использование рук , 555
неправильное положение тела, 1861
неправильное решение судьи, 2516
неправильный заслон, 554
непрерывность, 448
нескользящая поверхность вышки, 1313
несомненная остановка, 1781
неспортивное поведение, 766
нести мяч, 426, 2554, 2828
нетипичные элементы, 2007
неточное следование действию доски, 1241
неудавшийся прыжок, 1242
неудавшийся штрафной бросок , 589
неудача, 73
неудачная попытка, 358
нечетные игры, 2366
неявка, 2276, 2608
нижняя жердь, 1896
нижняя подача, 2785
низкая передача, 2551
низкий старт, 46
низкий удар, 2347
низкий удар с лета, 2348
ничья, 1388
нога отскока , 716, 1331
нога спереди, 523
ноль, 2345, 2517
номер дорожки, 2121
номер на майке, 939
номер на раме, 902
номер прыжка, 1210

номер участника, 201
номера игроков , 637
носок, 777, 1061
нулевой заезд, 865
нырок игрока в сторону, 2739

обвести защиту, 1467
обводящий удар, 2382
обезоруживание, 1475
обжаловать, 381
обладающий сильным финишем, 312
область штрафного броска, 517, 568
обман атаки, 1505
обманная атака, 2601
обманное движение, 2598
обманный отбив, 1506
обмен ударами, 2406, 2699
обод, 1027
обод корзины , 663
обод ракетки, 2402
обозначить трассу, 959
обойти, 207
оборудование для электронного хронометража, 2077
обратные махи, 1775
обтекаемый, 2184
общие сбавки, 1911
объединенная техническая комиссия, 1870
объявить гол, 2804
объявление прыжка, 1154, 1733
обязательные прыжки, 1197
ограничение времени апелляции, 1105
ограничительные ленты сетки, 2740
ограничительные линии, 2549

один два, 1610
один два три, 1611
"один метр!", 1609
одиночные виды плавания для женщин, 2218
одиночные виды плавания для мужчин, 2137
одиночный блок, 2675
одиночный мужской разряд, 2357
одиночный разряд, 2444
одновременное действие, 1674
одновременность атаки, 1675
одновременность в выступлении, 1904
одностороннее дыхание , 2209
однотрубка, 1134
оказание помощи прыгуну, 1265
окончание перерыва, 2596
окончательные результаты состязания, 1249
окончательный результат, 1248
окончательный счет, 504
опека один на один, 2903
опекать противника, 2833
опекать своего противника, 2904
опекать соперника сзади , 535
опередить, 211
опорная нога, 635
оппозиция, 1613
опустить мяч, 2589, 2641
организатор соревнования, 1762
оригинальность упражнения, 1917
оркестрованная музыка, 1914
ортопедическая рукоятка, 1615
освобождение места для броска, 442
осмотр оружия, 1716
осмотр снаряда, 1864
основная группа, 177
основная стойка, 1745

основы, 527
оставить позади соперника, 874
оставить пробел, 951
останавливающий удар, 1699
останавливающий укол, 1685
останавливающий укол с оппозицией, 1686
остановить гонщика, 1091
остановить игру, 2987
остановить секундомер , 705, 2986
остановка , 704, 1681, 1976
остановка удар, 2985
остановка гонки, 1092
остановка игры , 706, 2628
остановленная игра, 2627
ось, 15, 786, 1067, 1167
ось вращения, 16
ось колеса, 1148
ось шатуна, 809, 859
отбив, 1618
отбив с оппозицией, 1427, 1614
отбить мяч, 2836
отбор, 2425
отбор общих критерий судьями, 1876
ответный удар: рипост, 1653, 1673
ответственный за электрофиксирующее устройство, 1689
отвод руки, 65
отдача доски, 1387
отделиться от...., 176
отдых, 2708
отказаться от участия в соревновании, 2021
откатить/шину/, 1040
открытое место, 1612

открытое присуждение оценок, 1912
открытый бассейн, 2143
открытый корт, 2376
открытый прыжок согнувшись, 1317
открытый трек, 981
открытый турнир, 2370
открыться, 530
отличное выполнение, 1807
отложен, 2465
отменено, 2254, 2392
отметка, 184
отметки, 30
отобранные участники, 2424
отобранный первым, 2481
отобрать мяч , 703
оторвавшийся велосипедист, 822
оторваться, 819
оторваться от соперника, 423
отплыть от линии ворот, 2993
отрезок дистанции, 2123
отрыв, 821
отскок , 654, 2248
отскочить, 2249, 2946
отскочить от стойки ворот, 2947
отставший гонщик, 876
отстать, 875
отступить, 1649
отступление, 1650
отсутствие амплитуды; слитности; гармоничности; ритмичности, 1884
отталкивание, 1339, 1990, 2152, 2938
отталкивание от доски, 1225
отталкивания от дна, 2943
оттиск, 128
оттолкнуться от бортика, 2940

оттолкнуться от противника, 2939
оттолкнуться от противника ногами, 2889
официально утвержденный рекорд, 204
официальное время, 2141
официальное лицо, 976
официальные лица , 607
официальные лица встречи, 205
официальные лица гонки, 1007
официальные лица матча, 2643
официальные лица состязания, 194
официальные результаты соревнования, 1315
официальный автомобиль, 977
официальный протокол игры , 606
официальный счетчик , 605
офсайд/вне игры, 2914
оценка, 1958
оценка исполнения; комбинации; композиции; трудности упражнения, 1804
оценка оригинальности, 1916
оценки, 1283
оценки в финалах, 1803
оценочная система, 1961
оценочные элементы, 2010
очень грубый фол, 507
очередность подачи, 2437
очертание в воздухе, 1254
очки, 643
очко, 2389
ошибка, 95, 1816, 2599, 2613
ошибка в интерпретации, 1818
ошибка в положении рук, 1843
ошибка в положении тела, 1817
ошибка в расстановке, 2695
ошибка во времени, 1999
ошибка на линии, 1891, 2637
ошибка при выполнении, 1809

ошибка при переходе, 2713
ошибка при подаче, 2729
ощутимость укола, 1594
падение, 74, 882, 1065, 1226, 1814
падение вперед, 2615
падение игрока за мячом, 2586
падение перекатом, 2711
падение перекатом на бедро, 2741
падение полуперекатом, 2621
панель для прикосновения, 2203
парный мужской разряд, 2356
парный разряд, 2286
партия, 2440
партнер, 2381, 2768
пас , 623, 2923
пас и атаковать, 531
пас на удар, 2733
пас одной рукой, 398
пасовать, 496, 2685
пасовать мяч , 624
пасовка на гол, 383
пассивная защита , 695
пасующий , 625
пасующий игрок задней линии, 2532
педалировать, 989
педаль, 988
пенальти, 2383, 2925
пенопластовая доска, 2116
первая подача, 2305
первая позиция, 1633
первая половина игры, 505
первая попытка, 88
первое намерение, 1532
первоначальное представление, 1276
первый круг, 2304
первый секретарь, 1251
первый судья, 2603

первый тайм, 2852
перебой, 1420
перевод, 1476
перевод в темп, 1469
перевод в четвертую позицию, 1573
переворот, 1295, 1404
перегрузка , 620
передать мяч, 2924
передать мяч передовому игроку , 544
передать мяч через сетку, 2629
передача, 2684
передача в прыжке, 2612
передача вперед, 2612
передача вслепую, 413
передача двумя руками , 761, 2783
передача двумя руками отскоком, 759
передача из-за спины, 410
передача крюком , 548
передача на удар, 2737
передача назад, 2533
передача одной рукой , 609, 2674
передача от груди , 439
передача отскоком, 419
передача палочки, 20
передача передовому игроку , 571
передача сверху , 619
передача через игровую площадку, 454
передающий игрок, 2736
передвижной пункт медицинской помощи, 971
переднее колесо, 904
передняя нога, 1584
передняя стойка, 1239
передняя часть седла, 987
передняя шестерня, 834

передовая зона, 522
переиграть игру, 2956
перекладина, 1859
переключатель передач, 867
переключить передачу, 836
перемена мячей, 2245
перемена направления, 434
перемена ноги, 28
перемена опекаемых , 715
перемена положения руки во время упора прогнувшись, 1757
перемена ритма, 29
перемена соединения, 1439
перемена сторон, 1438
перемена хвата, 1833
переменить дорожки, 49
переменить решение, 2831
переменить ритм, 838
перемещение, 2757
перемещение защитной зоны, 464
перенос, 1460
перенос руки через сетку, 2686
перепрыжка, 146
перерыв , 561, 2480, 2687, 2773
пересечение границ, 1603
перехватить мяч , 559
переход, 1465, 2004
переход игроков, 2712
переход линии сетки, 2569
переход по часовой стрелке, 2561
переход подачи, 2557
переход средней линии, 2568
перешагнуть барьер, 304
период, 2928
период удаления, 2929
персональная ошибка, 2930
персональное столкновение , 630
персональный фол, 631
перчатка для метания молота, 101

перчатки, предохраняющие руки, 1847
петли сетки, 2663
петля, 1593
пианист, 1925
питание, 884
питательные пункты, 247
плавание на боку, 2973
плавание на дальние дистанции, 2131
плавание на спине, 2031
плавание на среднюю дистанцию, 2140
плавать, 2189
плавающие линии поля, 2840
плавки, 1177, 2190, 2819
плавучесть, 2050
планирующая подача, 2605
планка, 18
планка для прыжков в высоту, 115
пластилин , 219
пластилиновый валик, 220
плащ, 1011
плескаться, 2979
плитки для ног/на стартовых колодках/, 91
пловец, 2191
пловец баттерфляем, 2054
пловец в комбинированном плавании, 2135
пловец вольным стилем, 2097
пловец на дальние дистанции, 2130
пловец на спине, 2034
пловец на среднюю дистанцию, 2139
пловец начинающий первым, 2126
пловец стилем кроль, 2068
пловец эстафеты, 2159
плоская подача, 2307

плоский вход в воду, 1252
плоский ключ, 979
плоско войти в воду, 1298
плоскость, 1324
плотная группа, 848
плотная защита "игрок в игрока" , 738
плохо управляемый мяч, 577
плохое поведение, 2810, 2908
площадка, 451, 2565
площадка для разминки, 369
площадь, 9
плыть с мячом, 2994
по правилам, 1016
победа, 2499
победитель, 2510
победитель в заезде, 918
победить, 2279
победить на одну длину тела, 2217
повернуться к корзине, 665
поверхность, 2464
поверхность воды, 1383, 2215
поворачиваться, 2005
поворот , 634, 1707, 2206
поворот в плавании брассом, 2043
поворот в плавании на спине, 2035
поворот полусальто, 2170
поворот при комплексном плавании, 2109
повторение атаки, 1648
повторение упражнения, 1941
повторение элемента, 1940
повторить заезд, 1021
повторная атака, 1647
повторный выстрел, 240
повторный укол, 1646
повышение ценности, 2011
подать, 2724
подать мяч, 2429

подать свечу, 2341
подача, 2428, 2431, 2725
подача в сетку, 2665
подача и удар с лета, 2432
подача крюком, 2625
подающий, 2430, 2726
подбирать, 655
подбирать противника, 2353
подбор опеки, 585
подбор у своего щита, 462
подбор у щита соперника, 603
подвижная доска, 1244
подвижная защита, 2653
подвижная игра, 2909
подвижный заслон, 591
подбивание коленей к животу во время входа в воду, 1289
подготовительный удар, 2230
подготовка атаки, 1629
подготовленный бросок, 683
поддерживать лидирование, 178
поддерживать ритм бега, 179
поднять мяч, 2636, 2895
подняться, 1947
подняться силой, 1882
поднять/ся/, 1890
подплыть с мячом прямо к воротам, 2995
подпрыгивание перед прыжком в воду, 1227
подпрыгнуть, 1287
подрезанный удар, 2492
подрезка, 2260
подталкивающий помощник, 1001
подтягивание противника, 2936
подушка для приземления, 153
подхватывать мяч, 2884
подход, 1156
подход; разбег, 1734
подшипник, 793

подъем, 1292
подъемы силой, 1883
позиционное нападение, 682
позиция, 2391
позиция в стойке, 1550
позиция готовности, 2409
позиция для принятия, 2412
поймать мяч, 427, 2555
покинуть площадку, 2632
пол, 1827
поле игры, 2933
поле игры, не отвечающее правилам, 2911
поле подачи, 2433, 2727
поле противника, 2676
полевой игрок, 2851
полет, 1825
полная команда, 2860
половина времени игры, 538
половина гонки, 969
половина круга, 910
половина поля, 539, 2875
половина решающей партии, 2622
положение, 1330
положение "кор-а-кор", 1428
положение в линии, 1605
положение для удара с лета, 2502
положение к бою, 1606
положение ног, 1291
положение ноги перед отталкиванием, 90
положение рук, 1159, 1842
положение рук на крупе, 1844
положение рук на шее, 1845
положение руки, 1560
положение согнувшись, 1189, 1841
поломка, 820
поломка рамы, 901
полузащитник, 2961
полукруг , 681

полукруговая защита, 1669
полуоборот, 1558
полуфиналист, 2426
полуфинала, 2427
полуфинт, 1557
полученный укол, 1568
получить мяч, 2948
поменяться сторонами, 2832
помещение для гонщиков, 1026
помост, 1929
помощник секретаря, 2805
помощник секундометриста, 2806
помощник стартера, 290
помощник судей , 714
помощник тренера, 384
помощники судей, 1984
попадание, 532, 712
попасть в контрольные отметки, 118
поперечная ось, 1200
поперечная перекладина ворот, 2841
поперечное положение, 1201
поплавки, 2090
попытка, 14, 353
попытка сделать остановку, 1079
попытка сделать штрафной бросок, 516
поражаемая поверхность, 1711
поражение, 2278
порыв , 946
порядок выступления гимнастов, 1764, 1915
порядок выступления команд, 1951
порядок перехода, 2714
порядок прибытия, 980
порядок приема, 2411
порядок старта, 1087, 1378
порядок упражнений, 1950
последний вираж, 79, 120

последний круг, 159
последний пловец/эстафета/, 2024
последний спринт, 80
последняя попытка, 160
последовательность шагов, 310
поставить большую передачу, 1000
постоянная комиссия, 992
постоянный комитет, 1075
потеря дорожки, 1590
потеря мяча , 757
потеря мяча /наказание/, 579
потеря подачи, 2640
потерянные очки, 1304
потерять мяч , 578
починка велосипеда у краев дороги, 1038
починка на ходу, 1043
правила, 1017, 1042, 1938, 1952
правила движения, 1131
правила езды по треку, 1118
правило водного поло, 3014
правило десяти секунд , 728
правило игры, 2934
правило преимущества, 2802
правило пяти секунд, 506
правило трех секунд , 734
правило три на два , 731
правило тридцати секунд , 730
правильная опекающая позиция , 574
правильная подача, 2635
правильное положение тела , 1774
правое поле подачи, 2415
правый защитник, 662, 2958
правый игрок задней линии, 2709
правый игрок передней линии, 2710
правый нападающий , 661, 2959
практика движения ног, 2117

предварительное раскачивание диска, 228
предварительные забеги, 229, 259
предварительные заплывы, 2108
предварительные махи молотом, 230
предварительные прыжки , 1335
предварительные результаты, 1336
предварительные соревнования, 1334
предварительный заезд, 878
предмеренная защита, 1628
предохранительная сетка, 333
предохраняющие покрышки на тормозных рычагах, 816
председатель жюри, 1932
предупредительные звонки, 2105
предупреждение, 1141, 1713, 2504, 2792
преимущество, 1634, 1652, 2223, 2332
преодоление, 35
преодолеть, 32
преодолеть высоту планки, 34
преодолеть высоту.... 33
препятствовать бегуну, 127
препятствовать противнику, 2879
прерванный ряд движений, 1868
прерванный темп, 2049
преследование, 839, 998
преследовать , 650
прессинг в личной защите на одной половине поля , 540
прессинг по всему полю в личной защите, 524
прибавка, 1751
привести мяч прямо к воротам, 2847
приветствие, 1661

прием, 2702
прием мяча двумя руками, 2781
прием мяча одной рукой, 2672
прием низкого мяча, 2582
прием снизу одной рукой снизу, 2673
прием снизу, 2550, 2552
прием удара, 2523
прием удара двумя руками снизу, 2782
приземление, 151, 1885
приказать выйти из игры, 2919
приказать игроку выйти из воды, 2918
прикрытие от ветра, 1059
принимающая команда, 2701
принимающий, 2410
приносящий мяч, 2541
приносящий мяч, 2244
принять положение, 1936
принять стартовую позицию, 1166
присед, 1970
присесть, 1777
приставить ноги, 1869
присуждение оценок, 1960
присужденная оценка, 1301
пробежка , 755, 768
пробные отскоки, 1333
проверка, 361
проверка лицензии, 953
проверка электрофиксирующего наконечника, 1696
провинившийся игрок, 2913
провисание планки, 266
проволока молота, 106
прогибаться, 1735
продвигаться вперед с мячом, 379
продвигаться по линиям нападения , 503
продвигаться с мячом , 652

продолжение атаки, 1447
продолжительность боя, 1483
продолжительность положения, 1793
продолжительность упражнения, 1792
продолжительность чистого времени, 2894
продольная ось, 1186, 1296, 1893, 1895
проехать мимо, 986
проигравший, 2343
проигранная игра, 2619
проиграть, 2342
проиграть ввиду неявки, 2317
проиграть обмен, 2639
проигрыш, 2344
производитель пузырьков, 1181
произвольные прыжки, 1319
произвольные прыжки без ограничения, 1401
произвольные прыжки с ограничением, 1400
произвольные упражнения, 1913
прокол, 997
проколоться/о шине/, 827
промах, 590
промахнуться, 2358
промахнуться по корзине , 588
промахнуться по мячу, 2650
промежуточное время, 137
промежуточный мах, 1865
пронация, 1636
прорвать защиту, 628
прорвать оборону от заслона , 689
просить замену, 659
простая атака, 1671
простая защита, 1672
простая ошибка, 2907

прострельная передача, 2602
просьба о замене, 2707
просьба о минутном перерыве , 745
просьба о перерыве . 2774
протест, 231, 995, 1933, 2148
противоположная прямая, 17, 787
протокол, 1959
протокол игры , 672, 2718
протокол пульки, 1627
проход мимо, 1620
процент бросков с игры, 501
процент штрафных бросков, 520
прошедшие минуты игры , 587
прыгать, 1208
прыгнуть, 1880
прыгун, 147, 567
прыгун в воду, 1211
прыгун в воду с вышки, 1327
прыгун в воду с трамплина, 1372
прыгун в высоту, 112
прыгун в длину, 175
прыгун с шестом, 223
прыгун тройным прыжком, 355
прыжки в воду с трамплина, 1373
прыжки с винтом, 1397
прыжки с вышки, 1328, 1392
прыжок, 145, 1207, 1286
прыжок в высоту, 111
прыжок в длину, 173
прыжок вперед; с полувинтом; с винтом, 1257
прыжок из задней стойки вперед, 1279
прыжок из задней стойки вперед с полувинтом или винтом, 1280
прыжок из передней стойки назад, 1348

прыжок из передней стойки назад с полувинтом, 1349
прыжок из стойки на руках, 1163
прыжок из стойки на руках вперед, 1164
прыжок назад, 1168, 1174
прыжок с полувинтом назад, 1169
прыжок с разбега, 1355
прыжок с шестом, 222
прыжок фосбюри-флоп, 93
прыжок через яму с водой, 371
прыжок, номер которого уже показан, 1822
прыжок/сальто/из передней стойки на руках назад, 1162
прямая, 308
прямая передача, 467
прямая связка, 1786
прямо, 1382
прямое изменение, 1785
прямой бросок, 2988
прямой отбив; прямая защита, 1471
прямой укол, 1472, 1687
пуговка, 1433
пулька, 1626
пункт питания, 885
пункты питания, 76
путь игрока , 626
пушечная подача, 2255
пьедестал почета, 364
пятая позиция, 1640
пятиборье, 213
пятый фол, 502

работа ног, 508, 1544, 2127
работа ног в баттерфляе, 2052
работа ног в брассе, 2216
работа ног в дельфине, 2073

работа педалями , 778
работа под водой, 3006
равновесие в защите, 461
равный результат, 340
равный счет , 736, 2476
разбег, 260, 1255, 1953
разбегаться, 261
разводной ключ, 776
разговор на защите , 717
разделительная веревка, 2122
разделить группу, 1068
раздельный старт, 928
размер трека, 963
размеры площадки, 452
разметки на щите, 389
разминка, 368, 2503, 2791
разминочные упражнения , 769, 2019
разминочный прыжок, 1403
разрешить повторный прыжок, 1264
разрыв, 828
ракетка, 2400
рама, 900
рапира, 1537
рапирист, 1540
расписание, 2418
расписание игр, 529, 667
расписание соревнований, 268
расписание тренировок, 2205
расположение защиты, 463
распределение дорожек, 2119
распределение нападающих , 604
распределение судей, 1878
рассеивание, 2166, 2408
рассеивать, 2407
расстановка, 2610
расстановка бегунов на разные стартовые линии, 282
расстановка для блока, 2611

расстановка игроков , 723
расстановка игроков на площадке, 2566
расстановка игроков при подаче, 2730
расстановка игроков уступами, 2790
расстановка команды, 2766
расстановка при приеме, 2700
расстояние между двумя бегунами, 62
расстояние между двумя средними оценками, 1934
регистрация, 1345
регулируемая точка опоры, 1152
редкая оценка, 1935
резаная подача, 2452, 2744
резаный удар, 2450
резкая перестройка, 1096
резко изменить направление, 456
резко перестроиться, 1095
результат, 1022
результаты, 2162
рейка для измерения высоты планки, 189
рекорд, 1013
рельсы для телекамеры, 2197
ремень туклипса, 1113
ремешок шлема, 840
решающая игра, 2479
решающая партия, 2475, 2571
решающее очко, 2511
решающее очко матча, 2644
решающее очко партии, 2441, 2735
решение, 2273
решение судьи, 2491
ринуться к сетке, 2417
рипост, отнимающий больше одного отрезка фехтовального времени, 1432
риск, 1948

ритм, 26, 1651
ритм дыхания, 2047
ритмичность, 1944
ровно, 2225, 2283
рукав, 1677
руки, 2028
руководители, 180
руководители гонки, 853
руководитель вспомогательного штата, 453
руководитель гонки, 1006
руководитель делегации, 1851
руководитель команды, 1993
руководитель соревнований по гимнастике, 1837
руководитель соревнования, 1474
руководитель трека, 1121
руководящий комитет, 881
рукоятка, 1561
руль, 912
ручка ракетки, 2403
ручка руля, 914
ручки коня, 1931
ручной хронометраж, 2132
ручные сигналы, 1898
рычаг на колесе, 1004
рычаг переключения передач, 906
ряд акробатических движений, 1725
ряд гимнастических движений, 1839

саблист, 1660
сабля, 1655
сальто, 1367, 1956
сальто в воздухе, 1253
сальто вперед с полувинтом; с винтом; с двумя винтами, 1258

сальто вперед; в полтора оборота; в два оборота; в два с половиной оборота.... 1259

сальто из задней стойки вперед в полтора оборота с винтом; с двумя винтами, 1282

сальто из задней стойки вперед; в полтора оборота; в два оборота; в два с половиной оборота...., 1281

сальто из передней стойки назад, 1262

сальто из передней стойки назад с полувинтом; с винтом; с полутора винтами; с двумя с половиной винтами, 1350

сальто из стойки на руках; двойное сальто.... 1165

сальто назад в группировке , 1170

сальто назад в полтора; в два; в два с половиной оборота, 1173

сальто назад с полувинтом; с винтом; с полутора винтами; с двумя винтами; с двумя с половиной винтами, 1171

сальто / в полтора оборота; в два оборота; в два с половиной оборота...; из передней стойки назад, 1351

самая высокая оценка, 1270

самая низкая оценка, 1297

сбавка за композицию, 1767

сбавка за ошибки в исполнении; комбинации, композиции; трудности, 1779

сбавка на 1.0 балл; 0.1; 0.5; и т.д., 1780

сбить планку, 59

сбор велосипедистов, 829

сборный пункт участников, 850

сбрасывание метательного снаряда, 254

сверх кручёная подача, 2483

свеча, 2340, 2898

свеча при нападении, 2368

свеча слева, 2238

свеча справа, 2315

свидетельство интернациональной известности, 1752

свисток . 771, 3017

свободная нога, 96, 514

свободная нога при наскоке, 1273

свободное место, 2560, 2794

свободное положение, 1256

свободный бросок, 2858

свободный бросок назначен, 2859

своя корзина, 622

своя линия ворот, 2921

связка, 1772

сгибание при отталкивании, 1204

сдвоенный центр, 475

сделать выпад, 1592

сделать заслон вблизи от мяча , 678

сделать заслон далеко от мяча 677

сделать обманный бросок, 493

сделать обратное движение, 1943

сделать пируэт, 1927

сделать полный оборот, 1924

сделать свободный бросок, 2996

сделать удачный удар, 2350

сегмент, 306

седло, 1044, 1955

седьмая лозиция, 1670

секретарь по прыжкам в воду, 1219

секретарь, 242, 269, 1050, 1340, 1341, 2720, 2964

сектор, 270

сектор для метания, 337, 339

сектор для метания молота, 105

сектор для прыжков в высоту, 116

сектор для прыжков с шестом, 224

сектор для тройных прыжков, 356

сектор метания диска, 58

сектор метания копья, 143

сектор прыжков, 149

сектор прыжков в длину, 174

сектор толкания ядра, 235, 277

секундомер, 307, 1977, 2183

секундомер минутного перерыва , 744

секундометрист , 746, 2999

секундометрист тридцатисекундного времени , 729

семиборец, 109

семиборье, 110

семиминутный период, 2965

середина группы, 967

середина трека, 968

серия, 1052

серия фехтовальных движений , 1522

сессия, 1963

"сетка", 2337, 2360, 2658

сетка ворот, 2868

сетка корзины , 594

сетка маски, 1720

сигнал времени, 2000

сигнал остановить игру, 2975

сигнал старта, 2983

сигнал, обозначающий фол, 692

сидеть на колесе у...., 895

сила движения, 129

сила, сбивающая барьер, 344

силовая атака, 2696

силовая подача, 2698

силовая часть, 1978

силовой бросок одной рукой в прыжке, 649

силовой удар, 2697

сильная сторона , 708

сильная часть клинка, 1545

сильное выпрямление при отталкивании, 227

сильный бросок в корзину сверху , 694

сильный удар, 2296

сильный удар без вращения, 2306

синтетическая поверхность, 2469

синтетические струны, 2468

система, 2758

система защиты, 2577

система игры в нападении, 2767

система нападения, 2670

система оценок, 1302, 1802

система приема, 2759

ситуации численного превосходства , 615

скамейка запасных, 2690

скамейка игроков, 2692

скамейка тренеров, 2689

скамья, 411

скамья для команды , 720

скачок, 1581

скачок вперед, 1419, 1546

скачок назад, 1418

скачок/в тройном прыжке/, 121

скольжение, 1678, 2099

скользящий укол, 1449, 1551

скользящий укол в бок, 1533

скорость , 905, 1064, 2456

скрестный шаг, 45, 1776

слабая сторона , 770
слабая часть клинка, 1536
слабый мяч, 2588, 2614
слабый удар, 2505
след, 183
следить за мячом, 2606
сложная атака, 1443
сложная защита, 1444
сложный рипост, 1445
сломанная рама, 824
сломанная цепь, 823
сломанный клинок, 1431
служащие бассейна, 2147
случайное падение в воду, 1243
смена ритма, 435
сменить стороны, 2558
смертельная подача, 2220, 2518
смешанная разряд, 2359
смэш, 2454
снаряд, 8
снижение оценок главным судей, 1853
снос/налево; направо/, 1184
совещание судей, 1874
согнувшись, 1322
согнуться, 1323, 1823
содержание упражнения, 1773
соединение, 1490
соединительная электропроводящая проволока, 1446
соединить, 1489
сооружения для прыжков в воду, 1215
соперник, 2372
соперничать, 2373
сопровождающая машина, 896
сопровождающие, 831

сопровождающие и гиды для спортсменов, официальных лиц и прессы, 305
сопровождающий автобус, 897
сопровождение, 854
сопротивление воды, 2214
соревнование, 40, 2264
соревнование на рапирах, 1539
соревнование на саблях, 1657
соревнование на шпагах, 1494
соревнование по плаванию, 2065
соревнование по прыжкам в воду, 1213
соревнование по прыжкам с вышки, 1326
соревнование 1А; 1Б; 11; 111, 1763
соревнования вне стадиона, 257
соревнования для финалистов, 1805
соревнования по бегу, 347
соревнования по прыжкам и метанию, 77
соревнующиеся, 2265
соревнующийся пловец, 2064
соскок, 1787
соскочить, 1788
состав команды , 725
составить блок, 2609
состязание, 192, 851
состязание по плаванию, 2193
спад назад из стойки на руках, 1161
специалист, 2746
специалист по атаке, 2524
специалист по блокированию, 2545
специалист по защите, 2576
специалист по низким мячам, 2581
специалист по подачам, 2731

специальные требования для работы на снаряде, 1967
список гимнастов и видов соревнований, 1766
список команды , 724
список предварительных заплывов, 2107
список прыжков, 1294
список прыжков в воду, 1218
спица, 1069
спорный матч для команд с равным счетом , 737
спорный мяч , 563
спортивная ходьба, 258, 366
спортивный руководитель, 1070
спортсмен со званием, 1111
способ держания метательного снаряда, 119
способ держать оружие, 1556
способность отталкиваться, 72
спринт, 280, 1071, 2173
спринтер, 281, 2172
спуск, 868
спуститься/о шине/, 804
спущенная шина, 893
сравнять счет, 2301, 2478
среднее количество очков , 642
средние ошибки, 1901
средний блокирующий игрок, 2648
средний игрок задней линии, 2647
средний игрок передней линии, 2649
средний нападающий, 2646
средняя линия, 2556
срезать, 2451
стандартный велосипед, 1074
стандарты прыжков в высоту, 117
старт, 285, 1080, 1377, 2174
старт на спине, 2033

старт с места, 1076
старт с разных стартовых линий, 283
старт с ходу, 894
старт со стартовым пистолетом, 2102
старт схвативших, 2101
стартер, 289, 1084, 2175
стартер, возвращающий бегунов, 241
стартовать, 1081
стартовая колодка, 292
стартовая линия, 293, 1086
стартовая площадка, 2180
стартовая позиция, 295, 1379, 1974, 2181, 2982
стартовая расстановка, 2753
стартовая техника, 2182
стартовая тумба, 2176
стартовый захват, 2178
стартовый интервал, 1085
стартовый пистолет, 294, 1088, 2179
стартовый протокол, 1083
стартовый прыжок, 2177
стартовый сигнал, 296
стартовый состав, 699
стартовый список, 286
старший судья, 1630, 1631, 1981
статистик , 701
статистика , 702
стенка, 2212
стенка для практики, 2231
стенка финиша, 2088
стенка шины, 1140
степень трудности, 1205
стилем баттерфляй, 100 м.; 200 м., 2055
стиль, 313, 2186
стиль в воздухе, 92

стиль плавания, 2187
стиль фосбюри, 94
стиль-чез, 297
стоимость регистрации, 1346
стойка, 226, 1421, 1973
стойка ворот, 2869
стойка для планки в прыжках в высоту, 359
стойка на руках, 1160, 1266, 1849
стойки для прыжков с шестом, 225
стойки сетки, 2664
"стойте!", 1559
стол для вспомогательного штата , 586
стол секретаря соревнования , 671
стол судьи-секретаря, 2721
столб сетки, 2364
столбики фальстарта, 2083
столбики финиша, 85
столкновение, 446
сторона противника, 2917
сточные канавки, 2103
стоять на дне бассейна, 2980
стоять неподвижно, 1375
страховка, 1737
страховка нападающих, 2521
страховка принимающего, 2567
страхующий, 1738
струнная часть ракетки, 2401
струны из сухожилий, 2322
струны ракетки, 2405, 2462
ступеньки вышки, 1380
ступица, 923
судейская вышка, 2705
судейская карта, 2114
судейская коллегия, 845, 2142
судейская ошибка, 1580
судейская система, 1879
судейские критерии, 1285

судейский комитет, 1284
судейский протокол, 2423
судейский протокол соревнования, 1361
судейский список оценки, 1873
судейство, 1877
судейство отталкивания на эстафете, 2160
судить, 658
судьи, 144
судьи по прыжкам в воду, 1216
судьи соревнования, 42
судьи-секретари, 1362
судья, 243, 657, 763, 847, 1342, 1579, 1871, 2157, 2331, 2489
судья в водном поло, 3013
судья на вираже, 855
судья на вираже/повороте, 797
судья на вышке, 2259
судья на дистанции, 349
судья на линии, 1892, 2339, 2638
судья на повороте, 1136, 2113, 2207
судья на финише, 83, 891, 2089
судья переднего поля , 570
судья по бегу, 245
судья по видам прыжков и метаний, 78
судья по видам соревнований, 1230
судья по видам спортивной ходьбы, 367
судья по гребкам, 2185
судья по зашагам, 2309
судья по метаниям и прыжкам, 244
судья по незавершенным движениям, 1176
судья по спортивной ходьбе , 246
судья по трудностям, 1872
судья у колокола, 795
судья у линии ворот, 2865

судья у сетки, 2362
судья центрального поля идущий сзади , 752
судья-измеритель, 203
судья-секретарь , 670, 1663, 2164
судья-секундометрист, 342, 2201
судья-счетчик кругов, 158
судья, определяющий финиш, 2144
судья, фиксирующий удары в пол, 1535
сумка с питанием, 972
супинация, 1690
сухая игра, 2346
сформировать эшелон, 958
схема нападения , 601
счет, 2420, 2717
счет меньше на подачу соперника, 2252
счет очков, 1359
счетчик кругов, 943
счетчик отрезков дистанции, 2124
сыграть по мячу на половине корта партнера, 2388
сюрпляс, 1078

таблица оценок, 1303
таблица ошибок, 1989
таблица прибавок за POB. 1987
таблица трудности, 1759, 1988
таблицы прыжков в воду, 1220
табло, 1275, 1662
табло игры, 528
табло очков, 2163, 2422
табло прыжков, 1209
табло результатов, 214
табло с указателем дистанции, 63
табло счета , 669, 1360, 2719
тайм, 629
тактика, 2760

тактика блокирования, 2548
тактика второго намерения, 1666
тактика нападения, 2671
тактика перемещения, 2763
тактика подачи, 2732
тактическая комбинация, 2762
тактический, 2761
тактический план, 2764
танцовщица, 1077
темп, 985
темп шагов, 311
температура воды, 1406, 2200
терять мах прыжка, 1240
техника, 328
техника броска , 687
техника владения мячом, 2817
техника дыхания, 2048
техника плавания, 2196
техника поворотов, 2208
техника прыжков в воду, 1221
техническая комиссия , 1103
технические официальные лица, 1996
технический директорат, 1473
технический регламент, 1997
технический фол , 726
техническое выполнение, 1995
типы прыжков/мужчины/, 2012
толкание ядра, 234, 274, 276
толкатель ядра, 233, 275
толкать, 232
толчковая линия, 324
толчковая нога, 322, 323
толчок, 318, 1384, 2151
толчок в прыжке вперед, 1260
толчок двумя ногами, 2006
толчок из передней стойки назад, 1352
толчок мяча, 2941

толчок назад , 1172
толчок с места, 1376
толчок с подбрасыванием, 2935, 3000
толчок с разбега, 1356
топить мяч, 2883
топить противника, 2942, 2991
топить своего противника, 2977
топометр, 343
топслин, 2482, 2779
торможение, 817
торможенный удар с лета, 2297
торможенный удар слева, 2235
торможенный удар справа, 2313
тормоз, 813
тормозная колодка, 815
точка опоры, 1261
точка отскока, 1332
точка соприкосновения, 2390
травма, 934
травмированный игрок, 2886
траектория, 1393
траектория полета мяча, 382, 754
траектория полета снаряда, 352
трамплин, 1371
трамплин "дюрафлекс", 1228
трамплин "максифлекс", 1307
трамплин "максифлекс-В", 1306
требования упражнения, 1942
трек, 1115
трековая майка , 1122
трековая однотрубка, 1129
трековый велосипед , 1119, 1126
тренер, 37, 445, 844, 1442, 2062, 2262, 2562
тренировать, 2263
тренироваться, 2395
тренировка, 2394
тренировка на суше, 2075
тренировочная однотрубка, 1132

тренировочный бассейн, 2204
тренировочный бой, 1589
третья позиция, 1698
трехсекундная зона , 733
три тысячи-метровая дорожка для бега с препятствиями, 301
трибуна для официальных лиц, 202
тридцатисекундная разминка, 1998
трико, 1889
тридцатипятисекундный секундомер, 2971
тройной блок, 2771
тройной прыжок, 354
трудность, 1784
тугая, неэластичная доска, 1381
туклипс, 1112
тумбочки для вещей пловцов, 2120
турнир, 1704
тыловая зона, 386
тяга руками, 2149
тянуть жребий, 2294
тянуть жребий, 2845

увеличить опережение, 132
увеличить ход, 133
угловой бросок, 2839
угловой флажок, 44
угол броска, 686
угол наклона виража, 866
угол наклона трека, 791
угол отскока, 6
угол приближения, 5
угол толчка, 1385
удавшийся старт, 2128
удаление, 1094, 2597
удаление игрока с поля игры, 489
удаление с площадки, 485
удаленный игрок, 2850
удалить, 1093

удар, 2326, 2442, 2463
удар двумя руками слева, 2414, 2486
удар двумя руками справа, 2485
удар по линии, 2292
удар по подаче, 2694
удар при подаче, 2439
удар с лета, 2500
удар с лета слева, 2240
удар с лета справа, 2316
удар с отскока, 2321
удар с полулета, 2323
удар слева, 2234
удар слева с отскока, 2237
удар справа, 2312
ударить, 1688, 2327
ударить кулаком, 2937
ударить лезвием, 1464
ударить мяч головой, 2877
ударить мяч сжатым кулаком, 2881
ударить ногой, 2888
ударить по мячу сжатым кулаком, 2990
ударить по трамплину, 1271
ударить противника, 2880, 2989
ударить с лета, 2501
удары двумя руками, 2487
удвоение, 1202
удержанный мяч , 545
удерживать противника, 2882
уйти от соперника, 2862
указания тренера команде, 432
указатель дистанции, 64
указка фолов , 582
уклонение, 1478, 1499
уклонение ноги, 1641
уклонение от удара, 1482
уклониться, 1477
уклониться от отбива, 1498
укол, 1562, 1702

укол вниз, 1619
укол засчитывается, 1566
укол лезвием клинка, 1569
укол нажимом, 1462
укол наконечником, 1570, 1697
"укол налево", 1564
"укол направо", 1565
укол не засчитывается, 1567
укол не по цели, 1602
"укол отбит!", 1617
уколоть, 1563, 1703
уколоть с удвоенным переводом, 1453
укороченный удар, 2298
укрепление для флияги, 1143
умышленный фол , 558
универсальный игрок, 2769
уполномоченный сопровождающий , 785
упор, 1983
управляющий анемометром, 374
упражнение на бревне, 1747
упражнение на коне для махов, 1811
упражнение на брусьях разной высоты, 1812
упражнения на перекладине, 1860
упругая доска, 1365
уровень воды, 1405, 2213
уронить мяч, 526, 2848
условия, 1448
успешная попытка, 315
успешный бросок , 693
успешный бросок с игры, 499
успешный штрафной бросок, 519, 713
усредненная из двух средних оценок, 1739
установка снаряда, 1728

установка стартовых колодок, 4
устать, 1144
устойчивость, 1971
устойчивость при приземлении, 1972
устройство для проверки оружия, 1412
уступающая защита, 1436
утвердить, 238
утверждение рекорда , 779, 1012
утешительный заезд, 1020
утешительный матч, 2266
ухватиться за кольцо , 534
участник командной эстафеты, 2161
участник соревнования по фехтованию, 1513

фальстарт, 75, 883, 2082
фехтовальная дистанция, 1514, 1521, 1595
фехтовальная дорожка, 1526
фехтовальная маска, 1519
фехтовальная одежда, 1515
фехтовальная перчатка, 1516
фехтовальная позиция, 1523
фехтовальная форма, 1528
фехтовальное оружие, 1529
фехтовальные брюки, 1512
фехтовальные туфли, 1524
фехтовальные чулки, 1525
фехтовальный зал, 1517
фехтовальщик, 1510
фехтование на близком расстоянии, 1511
фехтование на рапирах, 1541
фехтование на саблях, 1658
фехтование на шпагах, 1496
фехтовать, 1508

финал, 887
финал одиночного разряда, 2445
финалист, 1820
финалист одиночного разряда, 2446
финалы, 31, 1250, 1821
финалы гарного разряда, 2287
финальная оценка, 1819
финальная пулька, 1530
финальные прыжки, 1247
финиш, 82, 889, 2087
финишная ленточка, 87
финишная линия, 892
финишная прямая, 86, 921
финт, 492, 498, 2600
финт головой , 543
финт; обман, 1504
флажки для заплыва на спине, 2032
флажки для стипль-чеза, 299
флажок, 89, 2604, 2853
флажок на границе зоны, 377
флажок с обозначением национального/олимпийского, мирового/рекорда, 185
флажок сектора, 271
флажок судьи, 2952
флажок судьи у ворот , 2866
фляга, 1142
фол, 512
фол в нападении , 600
фол при блокировке, 418
фол с удалением, 513
форма игроков, 2786
форсирующий удар, 2311
фортепьяно, 1926
фотофиниш, 215, 993
фотофинишный аппарат, 216
французская рукоятка, 1548

хват, 98, 1553, 1832, 1846
хлорированная вода, 2059
ходок, 365
ходьба в воде, 3003
ходьба по дорожке, 350
холм, 920
хронометр игры , 2861
хронометраж, 1109, 1110
хронометрист, 1108, 1700, 2001
художественная гимнастика, 1736

цвета, 2837
ценность прыжков, 2014
центр вычисления результатов, 1765
центр струн ракетки, 2466
центр трека, 1117
центральная линия, 431, 727, 2257, 2830, 2876
центральная линия подачи, 2258
центральная площадка, 2256
центральный круг, 429
центральный нападающий, 2829
центровая комбинация , 636
центровой, 428, 646
центровой в области штрафного броска , 546
центровой под щитом , 580
центровой прыжок, 430
цепь, 833
церемония награждения, 363
цилиндр, 457
цифровое табло для измерения темпа, 2070

часть упражнения, 1922
через сетку, 2380
четвертая позиция, 1639
четверть финал, 2399

четверть финалист, 2398
четыре на 100 м. комбинированная эстафета, 2093
четырехметровая зона, 2856
четырехметровая линия, 2857
чистое время игры, 2801
чистый вход, 1188
член той же команды, 2472
чувствительность панели, 2167
чувство мяча, 497

шаг, 302, 309, 1402
шаг вперед, 1547
шаг назад, 1680
шаг-выпад, 1679
шаги шассе, 1758
шаги; шаги шассе, 1975
шапочка, 2838
шапочка вратаря, 2873
шапочка с номером, 2912
шапочка, не завязанная под подбородком, 2826
шарикоподшипники, 790
шатун, 858
шест, 221
шестая позиция, 1676
шестерня, 1073
шип, 1055
шиповки, 278
шипы, 279
ширина дорожки, 1719
ширина клинка, 1718
ширина сетки, 2666
шлем, 919
шоссе, 1039
шоссейный велосипед, 1030, 1036
шпага, 1492
шпагат, 1968
шпагат вперед, 1830

шпагат продольно, 1965
шпажист, 1495
штраф , 627, 888, 991, 1048
штрафное передвижение в конец группы, 1019
штрафной бросок, 515, 2927
штрафной бросок после успешного броска , 732
штрафной секундомер, 2926
штрафной укол, 1621

щит, 388
щит соперника , 599

эластичность доски, 1374

электронное время, 2076
электронное вычисление времени/ бревно; вольные упражнения/, 1796
электронное табло, 1794
электронные сигналы, 1795
электропроводящая дорожка, 1597
электропроводящая куртка, 1518
электропроводящий жилет, 1598
электрофиксирующая аппаратура, 1487
электрофиксирующая шпага, 1484
электрофиксирующее оборудование, 1485
электрофиксирующий наконечник, 1486

элемент акробатического полета, 1724
элемент группы А, 1722
элемент или соединение группы В, 1740
элемент на равновесие, 1742
элемент связки, 1771
элементы, 1798
элементы от маха до стойки на руках, 1799
элементы переворота , 1848
элементы полета, 1826, 1854
эстафета, 248, 1018, 2158
эстафета вольным стилем, 2096
эстафета вольным стилем, 4 x 100 м.; 4 x 200 м., 2092

эстафетная команда , 252
эстафетная палочка, 19, 249
эстафетный бег, 250
эшелон, 808, 877

явная остановка, 1806
ядро, 273
яма с водой, 372
ящик для упора шеста, 217